"The first volume of Niehaus's  mon grace covenants of the what he offers his readers is a cu... and study. This work must be taken into accou... ing about the important theme of covenant. All students of and theology will benefit from Niehaus's insights that build on and advance previous research on the topic."

—Tremper Longman III, Robert H. Gundry,
Professor of Biblical Studies, Westmont College, CA

"This first volume of Niehaus's Old Testament theology is a fresh and refreshing study of covenantal theology, which engages ancient near eastern parallels informatively and corroboratively. His interpretive work with the text hardly leaves a stone unturned, and he does theology with an awareness that this testament is only one of two. The reader will be challenged to re-think earlier paradigms as the covenants unfold with new insights into God's master plan of grace."

—C. Hassell Bullock, Franklin S. Dyrness,
Professor of Biblical Studies Emeritus, Wheaton College;
Pastor, Warren Park Presbyterian Church, Cicero, IL

"Niehaus brings to culmination his lifelong study of ancient near eastern covenants and their importance for understanding biblical covenant as the foundation to biblical theology. He contends that Scripture in its entirety and God's relationship with human life from creation are covenantal in nature. By showing a pattern in God's covenantal designs, he demonstrates the cohesive message of the Bible. Every scholar and pastor will benefit from this refreshingly new and lively written approach."

—Kenneth Matthews, Professor of Divinity, Old Testament,
Beeson Divinity School, Samford University, AL

BIBLICAL THEOLOGY

VOLUME 1

THE COMMON GRACE COVENANTS

JEFFREY J. NIEHAUS

WEAVER BOOK
COMPANY
WOOSTER, OHIO

Biblical Theology, Volume 1: The Common Grace Covenants
© 2014 by Jeffrey J. Niehaus

Published by
Weaver Book Company
1190 Summerset Dr.
Wooster, OH 44691
weaverbookcompany.com

All rights reserved. No part of this book may be reproduced, stored in a retrieval system, or transmitted in any form or by any means—electronic, mechanical, photocopy, recording, or otherwise—without written permission of the publisher, except for brief quotations in printed reviews.

Unless otherwise noted, Scripture quotations are from THE HOLY BIBLE, NEW INTERNATIONAL VERSION®, NIV®. Copyright © 1973, 1978, 1984, 2011 by Biblica, Inc.™ Used by permission. All rights reserved worldwide.

Copyedited by Scribe Inc.
Designed by Scribe Inc.

ISBN (13): 978-0-9891671-5-4

Library of Congress Cataloging-in-Publication Data

Niehaus, Jeffrey Jay.
    Biblical theology / Jeffrey J. Niehaus.
        volumes cm
    Contents: Volume 1. the common grace covenants.
    ISBN 978-0-9891671-5-4
    1. Covenants—Biblical teaching. I. Title.

    BS680.C67N54 2014
    231.7—dc23   2014000589

Printed in the United States of America

14 15 16 17 18/ 5 4 3 2 1

Dem lieben Gott

CONTENTS

PREFACE

I have called the work that follows a biblical theology. It follows in the tradition of Geerhardus Vos and Meredith Kline and those giants upon whose shoulders—to borrow Newton's phrase—they stood. I have always thought Kline had a touch of the poet about him. I had the privilege of studying under him, of learning from him notwithstanding the nigh indecipherable notes he scribbled on the overhead projector he used. And of course, I have learned from others, as we all do. Those who employ the phrase, "Those who can't do, teach," might do well to reflect on how much they owe teachers who set them on the path of doing.

I have undertaken the following work as a teacher, as a person with some theological understanding, and perhaps most importantly, for me, as a poet. The sabbatical year in which I composed the draft of the following chapters also saw the composition of the first draft of *Preludes: An Autobiography in Verse*, a work published in January 2013, after nearly seven years of revision.[1] That narrative poem—some three hundred lines longer than *Paradise Lost*—also stands in a tradition, and anyone who reads it will see its kinship, in some small way perhaps to Milton, but even more to another admirer of Milton, Wordsworth.

---

1. Jeffrey Jay Niehaus, *Preludes: An Autobiography in Verse* (Eugene, OR: Wipf & Stock, 2013).

Though a person stands in one tradition or another—though I stand in a certain tradition of biblical theology and in a certain poetical tradition—one is after all a separate person. I stand in the tradition of Vos and Kline, yet I disagree with them on some points. I stand in the tradition of Milton and Wordsworth, yet my long narrative poem tells its own story (and in its own way), a story neither of them could tell.

One seeks to honor the tradition in which one stands. In both cases mentioned above, I have had one and the same goal: to be in step with the Spirit in the composition of the work. If I have been, the result most likely should be clarity, and, closely akin to it, beauty and goodness—and all of those articulating some portion of the truth.

I have reached a point in my own life at which I feel the call to poetry much more strongly than I feel the call to biblical theology. Nonetheless, I am aware that I am called to compose both.

Faced with such callings, I have chosen to compose a biblical theology that—as I hope, possessing clarity, beauty, truth, and goodness—will be accessible to anyone with a college education. In an earlier day I could perhaps have written, "anyone with a high school education," but, *mutatis mutandis*, things are what they are in the United States of the early twenty-first century.

One may read the pages that follow, then, as the reflections of a poet who has written some biblical theology. In that spirit, and for simplicity's sake, I have chosen not to encumber the work with numerous footnotes or extensive technical discussions of the sort that, in my opinion, really belong in commentaries. Some discussions of that kind can be found in books and articles of my own that are referenced along with other such works. Readers aware of the issues discussed in one passage or another and interested in pursuing them further can find ample resources in the bibliography provided at the end of this book.

The present volume is subtitled *The Common Grace Covenants* (i.e., the Adamic and Noahic covenants), and the second and concluding volume will be subtitled *The Special Grace Covenants* (i.e., the Abrahamic, Mosaic, Davidic, and New covenants). Those acquainted with the tradition of covenant theology will quickly see that this division of the matter is at variance with what they have been taught. I hope that such a difference will not be off-putting. The perspective offered here is I believe—if I may borrow from the German—*sachgemäß*.

Danvers, December 2013

ACKNOWLEDGMENTS

Donne once said no man is an island, and in that spirit I would like to express gratitude for the many sorts of help given me that facilitated the production of this work. First, I thank my wife, Maggi, for reading the chapters and giving valuable thoughts and raising sensible questions. Next, I am thankful for the work of my research assistant, Fiona Paisley, who also read the chapters and gave valuable feedback, and who prepared the Scripture Index. I am grateful also for the provision of sabbatical time by the Trustees of Gordon-Conwell Theological Seminary. More broadly, I am a grateful recipient of the work of others, both literary and theological, both teachers and writers, who in one way or another have contributed to whatever literary and theological acumen the following pages may have. Finally, and most importantly, I am thankful for the work of the Holy Spirit, without whom this work, though it cannot claim to be God-breathed, would nonetheless lack even what merit I hope it possesses and others may find in it.

ABBREVIATIONS

AfO	*Archiv für Orientforschung*
AION	*Annali dell'Instituto Orientale di Napoli*
AJBI	*Annual of the Japanese Biblical Institute*
AMIF	*Association des Medécins Israélites de France*
AnBib	*Analecta Biblica*
AnSt	*Anatolian Studies*
AOAT	*Alter Orient und Altes Testament*
ATANT	*Abhandlungen zur Theologie des Alten und Neuen Testaments*
AusBR	*Australian Biblical Review*
AUSS	*Andrews University Seminary Studies*
AYBD	*Anchor Yale Bible Dictionary*
BA	*Biblical Archaeologist*
BAR	*Biblical Archaeology Review*
BASOR	*Bulletin of the American Schools of Oriental Research*
BCPE	*Bulletin du Centre Protestant d'Etudes*
BDB	*Hebrew and English Lexicon of the Old Testament*
BeO	*Biblia e Oriente*
Bib	*Biblica*
BibRes	*Biblical Research*
Bijd	*Bijdragen: Tijdschrift voor Filosofie en Theologie*
BMik	*Beth Mikra*
BN	*Biblische Notizen*
BSac	*Bibliotheca Sacra*
BT	*The Bible Translator*
BTB	*Biblical Theology Bulletin*

BWANT	*Beiträge zur Wissenschaft vom Alten und Neuen Testament*
BZ	*Biblische Zeitschrift*
BZAW	*Beihefte zur Zeitschrift für die alttestamentliche Wissenschaft*
CBQ	*Catholic Biblical Quarterly*
CBQMS	*Catholic Biblical Quarterly Monograph Series*
CRAIBL	*Comptes rendus de l'Acadamie des Inscriptions et Belles-lettres*
CT	*Christianity Today*
CTJ	*Calvin Theological Journal*
CTM	*Concordia Theological Monthly*
CurTM	*Currents in Theology and Mission*
DBAT	*Dielheimer Blätter zum Alten Testament und seiner Rezeption in der Atlen Kirche*
EI	*Eretz-Israel*
ETL	*Ephemerides theologicae Iovanienses*
ETR	*Etudes Théologiques et Religieuses*
EvQ	*Evangelical Quarterly*
EvT	*Evangelische Theologie*
ExpTim	*Expository Times*
GTJ	*Grace Theological Journal*
GTT	*Gereformeerd theologisch tijdschrift*
HAR	*Hebrew Annual Review*
Hen	*Henoch*
HTR	*Harvard Theological Review*
HUCA	*Hebrew Union College Annual*
IDB	*The Interpreter's Dictionary of the Bible*
IDBSup	*Interpreter's Dictionary of the Bible: Supplementary Volume*
IEJ	*Israel Exploration Journal*
Int	*Interpretation*
IrBS	*Irish Biblical Studies*
ITQ	*Irish Theological Quarterly*
JAAR	*Journal of the American Academy of Religion*
JANESCU	*Journal of the Ancient Near Eastern Society of Columbia University*

JAOS	*Journal of the American Oriental Society*
JATS	*Journal of the Adventist Theological Society*
JBL	*Journal of Biblical Literature*
JCS	*Journal of Cuneiform Studies*
JETS	*Journal of the Evangelical Theological Society*
JJS	*Journal of Jewish Studies*
JNES	*Journal of Near Eastern Studies*
JNSL	*Journal of Northwest Semitic Languages*
JQR	*Jewish Quarterly Review*
JRT	*Journal of Religious Thought*
JSJ	*Journal for the Study of Judaism in the Persian, Hellenistic, and Roman Periods*
JSOT	*Journal for the Study of the Old Testament*
JSOTSS	*Journal for the Study of the Old Testament: Supplement Series*
JTS	*Journal of Theological Studies*
KD	*Kerygma und Dogma*
LingBib	*Linguistica Biblica*
LTQ	*Lexington Theological Quarterly*
MDOG	*Mitteilungen der Deutschen Orient-Gesellschaft*
MTZ	*Münchener theologische Zeitschrift*
NICOT	New International Commentary on the Old Testament
NRT	*La Nouvelle Revue Théologique*
NSBT	New Studies in Biblical Theology
OBO	*Orbis Biblicus et Orientalis*
Or	*Orientalia*
OTS	*Old Testament Studies*
PWCJS	*Published Material from the Cambridge Genizah Collection*
RA	*Revue d'assyriologie et d'archeologie orientale*
RB	*Revue Biblique*
Rel	*Religion*
ResQ	*Restoration Quarterly*
RevThom	*Revue Thomiste*
RHPR	*Revue d'Histoire et de Philosophie Religieuses*
RivB	*Rivista Biblica Italiana*

RSR	Recherches de Science Religieuse
RTL	Revue Théologique de Louvain
SBLMS	Society of Biblical Literature Monograph Series
SBS	Stuttgarter Bibelstudien
ScEs	Science et Esprit
SEA	Studia ephemeridis Augustinianum
Sem	Semitica
SJLA	Studies in Judaism in Late Antiquity
SJT	Scottish Journal of Theology
SR	Studies in Religion
ST	Studia Theologica
TA	Tel Aviv
TB	Tyndale Bulletin
TBT	The Bible Today
TD	Theology Digest
TGI	Textbuch zur Geschichte Israels
TGUOS	Transactions of the Glasgow University Oriental Society
TJ	Trinity Journal
TLZ	Theologische Literaturzeitung
TQ	Theologische Quartalschrift
TR	Theologische Rundschau
TRev	Theologische Revue
TS	Theological Studies
TTZ	Trierer theologische Zeitschrift
TZ	Theologische Zeitschrift
UF	Ugarit-Forschungen
VR	Vox Reformata
VT	Vetus Testamentum
VTSup	Vetus Testamentum Supplements
WO	Die Welt des Orients
WTJ	Westminster Theological Journal
ZA	Zeitschrift für Assyriologie
ZAW	Zeitschrift für die alttestamentliche Wissenschaft
ZTK	Zeitschrift für Theologie und Kirche

PROLEGOMENA
AMEN ET ALIA

"Alles Vergängliche
ist nur ein Gleichnis."
—Goethe[1]

Some years ago, I suggested that a hierarchical structure of ideas offers a conceptual background for theophanies in the Old Testament. The hierarchy of ideas was (and is) God as king, God's kingdom, God's covenant(s), and God's covenant administration.[2] The proposal assembles ideas that are fairly familiar: God is a great king (suzerain), has a kingdom, and appears not randomly but in order to initiate or administer major covenants.[3] Put another way, God's royal character and kingdom purposes form a background for his theophanic appearances in *suzerain–vassal* (covenant) relationships, and those theophanies take place when God establishes a form

---

1. Johann Wolfgang von Goethe, *Faust der Tragödie zweiter Teil* (Oxford: Basil Blackwell, 1943), 225 (Part 2, Act V, lines 12104–5; cf. 12104–11). The translation is "All that is transitory is but a likeness."
2. Jeffrey J. Niehaus, *God at Sinai: Covenant and Theophany in the Bible and Ancient Near East* (Grand Rapids: Zondervan, 1995), 83–84.
3. Ibid., 108–41.

of his kingdom among people by way of covenant through a covenant mediator prophet, or when he appears in order to administer or advance the work of a form of his kingdom so established. The hierarchy of ideas thus offers a theological foundation or rationale for biblical theophanies. Broadly speaking, the same structure of ideas may also be said to be foundational to the whole Bible, which from the outset has to do with God as king and all that flows from his suzerainty, including his forms of kingdom establishment and advance. The claim is not unjust—if we consider that structure of ideas exactly as a structure of *ideas.*

But I would propose another paradigm that is not so much a structure of ideas as more explicitly a structure or paradigm of *behavior,* and in particular a dynamic illustration of God's consistent and reliable behavior toward his *vassals* (humans). I have called that illustration the *Major Paradigm.* It incorporates the structure of ideas just considered, and I explain it below.[4]

God's behavior, according to the Bible, is always covenantal— that is, God has always chosen to relate to humanity through various covenants he has ordained.[5] And although God's covenants and God's covenant administration are a subset of the hierarchy of ideas articulated earlier, it is also true that the whole Bible is a product of the covenantal relationships God has instituted among humans. Since that is the case, the whole Bible may be called covenantal literature. But what does such a claim mean?

We know that some portions of the Bible not only report God's covenants but also partake of a second millennium BC international

---

4. I have presented the paradigm already in a preliminary way, although with far less discussion, in *Ancient Near Eastern Themes in Biblical Theology* (Grand Rapids: Kregel, 2008), hereafter *ANETBT,* 30–32, 172–76.

5. As we consider in chapter 1, God relates in a way that we call covenantal because God's very nature in relationship with other, created beings has certain aspects or components. Those relational components were, later in human history, construed by humans into formal, legal treaties or covenants. Humans are made in God's image and thus inevitably in some ways followed (and follow) a pattern of supernal realities of which many people were (and are) not even aware. Covenant is thus *primordially* an expression of God's nature in relationship, and since God has a perfect idea of all that, I have also called covenant an idea in the mind of God. Cf. Jeffrey J. Niehaus, "Covenant: An Idea in the Mind of God," *JETS* 52, no. 2 (June 2009): 225–46.

treaty form, as Mendenhall, Kline, and Kitchen demonstrated decades ago.[6] We also know that the prophetical corpus moves largely in the domain of covenant lawsuit. Consequently, the Bible's covenant narratives and the prophetical books may be called covenantal literature. But other genres also aptly fall under the covenantal aegis. For example, any history that purports to show the outworkings of a covenantal relationship may also be termed *covenantal*. Hittite annals, for instance, mainly show the progress of the Hittite suzerain against rebellious vassals. The covenant gods bless the valiant effort of Hatti, the Hittite emperor sends covenant lawsuit messages to the rebels, and the storm god confounds the insubordinate. Assyrian literature (annals and even poetry) display the same governing principles.[7] Even a cursory examination shows that Egyptian annals are composed of comparable material (i.e., they illustrate relationships between pharaohs and the conquered—relationships that are in effect covenantal and involve fealty, tax, tribute, and so on, even though we have no recorded Egyptian suzerain–vassal treaties). Historiography in the ancient Near East was in fact largely covenantal. Such a phenomenon should not surprise us. For the ancients, history had mostly to do with kings, especially suzerains, and their doings.[8] Human nature being what it is, vassals would rebel, and their recapture by the suzerains formed much of the stuff of royal annals—that is, historiography.[9]

---

6. Cf. G. E. Mendenhall, "Covenant Forms in Israelite Tradition," *BA* 17 (1954): 49–76; Meredith G. Kline, *Treaty of the Great King* (Grand Rapids: Eerdmans, 1963); Kenneth A. Kitchen, *Ancient Orient and Old Testament* (Chicago: InterVarsity Press, 1973); Kitchen, *The Bible in Its World* (Downers Grove, IL: InterVarsity Press, 1978).

7. Cf. Niehaus, *God at Sinai*, 128–30. For a discussion of Hittite and Assyrian covenant lawsuits and their parallelism with biblical covenant lawsuits, cf. Jeffrey J. Niehaus, "Amos," in *The Minor Prophets: An Exegetical and Expository Commentary*, ed. T. E. McComiskey, vol. 1 (Grand Rapids: Baker, 1992), 318–20. The annals also display Assyrian conquest and subordination of vanquished foes to a state of vassaldom, epitomized by the claim "I made them swear the oath of the great gods." Cf. Niehaus, *God at Sinai*, 105.

8. Cf. H. Gunkel, *The Legends of Genesis* (New York: Schocken, 1964), 1–2, "Such history has for its subjects great public events, the deeds of popular leaders and kings, and especially wars." Gunkel's comments form part of a very different argument, however.

9. For the argument that ancient near eastern historiography is fundamentally covenantal, see Jeffrey J. Niehaus, "The Warrior and His God: The Covenant Foundation of History and Historiography," in *Faith, Tradition and History—Old Testament Historiography in Its Near Eastern Context*, ed. A. R. Millard et al. (Winona Lake, IN:

A history that shows the establishment or the outworkings of a covenantal relationship may be called *covenantal literature*. Such was the nature of historiography in the ancient Near East, including that greatest written product of the ancient world, the Bible. Biblical history shows the establishment and outworkings of the Lord's covenantal relationships with humans, be it on the personal or national level. In that sense, then, biblical historiography, like that of the ancient Near East, is covenantal in nature. More specifically, because of Israel's chronic covenant breaking, her history was composed from a covenant lawsuit perspective. Since covenant lawsuit is the province of those prophets who were covenant lawsuit messengers, the Jewish tradition that calls Joshua through 2 Kings "The Former Prophets" shows sensitivity to this covenant lawsuit tone of OT historiography. If we look beyond the historical books and the prophets, we can see that even the Psalms (as expressions of the covenant community or of its earthly king or other individuals in that community) and the wisdom literature (as life applications of God's *torah* for a vassal of Yahweh) are flowers of the covenantal soil.

EXCURSUS: A NOTE ON BIBLICAL HISTORIOGRAPHY

Historiography in the ancient Near East appears for the most part in two forms: the historical prologue portions of second millennium BC international treaties, and the historical records found in royal annals. The covenant prologues document the relationship that existed between the suzerain-to-be and the vassal-to-be before they entered into a new, covenantal relationship. The royal annals document the history of the suzerain in relation to his vassals, including

Eisenbrauns, 1994), 299–312. Cf. further Jeffrey J. Niehaus, "Covenant and Narrative, God and Time," *JETS* 53, no. 3 (September 2012): 556–59.

rebellious vassals; they also document his conquests, which lead to further treaties—that is, new suzerain–vassal relationships.

These two categories of history writing largely define all biblical history writing as well, so that all biblical historiography may rightly be said to originate in the relationship of the suzerain, in this case the Great King, or God, to his vassals. In other words, all biblical historiography is covenantal.

We discuss this proposition in greater detail later, as we consider the divine–human covenants and their associated literature. For now, the following schema broadly illustrates the idea:

Biblical Data	Covenant/Covenantal History
Genesis 1–2	Adamic/Creation covenant
Genesis 3–5	Life under that covenant
[Genesis 3–Revelation 20	The same, more broadly considered]
Genesis 6–8	Historical background to the Noahic covenant
Genesis 9	Noahic/Re-Creation covenant
Genesis 10–11	Life under the Adamic + Noahic covenants
[Genesis 10–Revelation 20	The same, more broadly considered]
Genesis 12–14	Historical background to the Abrahamic covenant
Genesis 15	Abrahamic covenant
Genesis 17, 22	Further torah of the Abrahamic covenant
Genesis 15–Exodus 19	Life under the Abrahamic covenant
[Genesis 15–Matthew 27 (and parallels)	The same, more broadly considered]
Exodus 3–19	Historical background to the Mosaic covenant
Exodus 20–24	Mosaic covenant preliminary stipulations, ratification (Exod. 24:8), and covenant meal (Exod. 24:9–11)
Exodus 25–Leviticus 27	Further torah of the Mosaic covenant
Numbers	Life under the Sinai covenant and further Mosaic covenant torah
Deuteronomy	Mosaic covenant renewal at Moab (Deut. 29:1)
Joshua	Suzerain's conquests
Joshua–Matthew 27	Life under the Mosaic covenant (now = Sinai + Moab covenants)

(continued)

Biblical Data	Covenant/Covenantal History
Matthew 1–26	Historical background to the New covenant + preliminary stipulations to the same
Matthew 26	New covenant meal
Matthew 27–28	New covenant ratification
Acts	Suzerain's conquests
Romans–Jude	Further torah of the New covenant
Acts–Revelation	Life under the New covenant

The schema shows that all of humanity continue to live under the legal package formed by the Adamic and Noahic covenants (although most of them are unaware of that fact) and will continue to do so until the Lord destroys the old and creates the new heavens and earth.

The Bible may justly be called covenantal literature because God proceeds historically in a series of covenantal dealings with humanity. Through those covenant dealings, God shows—from Genesis through Revelation—what his mode and degree of revelation shall be. That is, he chooses the manner of his self-disclosure and the degree of his propositional revelation in and for each covenant.[10] God has, as we have said, a consistent procedure in all of his covenants. Consequently, his behavior follows a pattern that is foundational to the whole Bible, from start to finish. The pattern of his behavior is as follows:

The Major Paradigm (Provisional Form)

1. *God works*
2. *through the Word/a prophet-figure*
3. *to war against and defeat his foe(s)*
4. *God establishes a covenant with a people*

---

10. I would argue that both God's self-disclosure and the degree of his propositional revelation increase in clarity as we move forward through the Bible from covenant to covenant. That is to say, the *written record* increases in detail and clarity. However, our first parents' *experience* of God was probably more vivid, detailed, and clear (especially before the Fall) than any fallen human experience since.

5. *God's covenant establishes that people as God's people*
6. *God establishes a temple among his people, because he will reside among them*

In a form that can be developed further, this is a foundational pattern that our biblical theology would contribute to the discussion and appreciation of God's Word. The form is provisional because one further element remains to be explained and added. I will make that addition as I outline now the primary elements of the paradigm as they appear in God's first covenant, and suggest how the pattern also informs the later covenants. That discussion will precede the conclusion of our *Prolegomena* and also lay the foundation for the rest of the book—a dynamic exploration of God's covenants and life under them (in other words, of the whole Bible) with the major paradigm in mind.[11]

THE FIRST COVENANT

For some years people have thought the Genesis 1:1–2:3 creation account articulates a covenant between God and humanity. To corroborate this understanding, they have displayed evidence offered by the Noahic covenant, with its remarkable echoes of God's commands to our first parents (Gen. 9:1–3 echoing Gen. 1:28–29).[12] But there is more dramatic evidence for the covenant nature of the creation account. Knowledge from the ancient Near East has now made it possible to understand that the account is cast in the form of a second millennium suzerain–vassal treaty.[13] It articulates major elements of a covenant from that period, including a title, historical prologue, stipulations, witnesses, blessings, and curses, as I have demonstrated with a detailed outline.[14] The covenant nature of the creation account enables us to understand at the outset some essential matters:

---

11. Cf. Niehaus, *ANETBT*, 30–32, 172–76.
12. Cf. William I. Dumbrell, *Covenant and Creation* (Grand Rapids: Baker, 1984), 33.
13. The pioneer of something approaching this understanding, so far as I am aware, was Meredith G. Kline, who taught about the Adamic covenant for years at Gordon-Conwell Theological Seminary and finally published a summary statement of his thought in his work, *Kingdom Prologue* (Overland Park, KS: Two Age Press, 2000).
14. Niehaus, *God at Sinai,* 144–46; Niehaus, "Covenant and Narrative," 238–41. My analysis differs from that of Kline in that it sees the treaty outline in Genesis 1:1–2:3,

1. *God was from the beginning a great king (i.e., a suzerain)*
2. *He created a visible kingdom (the world)*
3. *He installed royalty (the man and woman)*
   as vassal king and queen over that kingdom

The Bible introduces God—as suzerain—in a covenant relationship with the man and the woman who will function as vassal king and queen over the world that God created.

I now pose a question whose answer is fundamental to our biblical–theological paradigm: How did God create the kingdom that then was? The answer is less obvious than may appear, and yet an approach to an answer is possible.

THE SPIRIT AND THE WORD

Genesis 1:2 makes it clear that the Spirit of God was present at the creation. It is not clear, however, what the Spirit was doing there. We know only that "the Spirit of God was hovering over the waters." It may be—as Kline has suggested—that the Spirit was there to ratify the Creation covenant: "This form of divine presence is to be identified with the glory-cloud epiphany. At the ratification of the old covenant at Sinai, this cloud-pillar form of theophany represented God standing as witness to his covenant with Israel." The same glory–Spirit theophany then appears at "the ratification of the new covenant at Pentecost, and finally in eschatological judgment."[15]

The association of God's Spirit presence with a covenantal act (in this case, creation) may imply that the Spirit has the role of a

---

whereas Kline sees elements extending through Genesis 1–3; cf. Kline, *Kingdom Prologue*, 14–21.

15. Kline, *Kingdom Prologue*, 13. Whether the New covenant was ratified at Pentecost or before is a question to be addressed later in this work, but we note now briefly that a covenant is normally ratified by a vassal's symbolic passage between cut animals (hence the idiom כרת ברית, "to cut a covenant") and by an oath. Jesus accomplished the former—the "cutting"—on the cross. The donation of the Spirit at Pentecost was thus not a covenant ratification but rather a fulfillment of a promise made before the covenant was "cut." The promise of the Spirit came *before* the ratification (John 14:16–17). The fulfillment of the promise of the Spirit came *after* the covenant had been "cut" or ratified.

witness—although God (not specified as the Spirit) seems to have that role later in the passage (Gen. 1:31). Maybe the primary role of the Spirit in verse 2 of the account is not that of a witness (although that may be a secondary role).

I believe the role of the Spirit at creation can and should be understood differently. The path to that understanding is through the way the Spirit is portrayed in Genesis 1:2. God's Spirit is said to be "hovering" (מרחפת) over the waters. The verb רחף ("to hover, soar") has avian connotations, as it appears in Ugaritic of an eagle.[16] Only at the baptism of Jesus does the Spirit appear again explicitly in an avian sense: "As soon as Jesus was baptized, he went up out of the water. At that moment, heaven was opened, and he saw the Spirit of God descending like a dove and lighting on him" (Matt. 3:16).[17] It is no accident that both water and the Spirit of God are present at Jesus's baptism, as at Genesis 1:2. Jesus's baptism symbolizes a death to sin and an emergence into a new life. That which is of earth (the man) submerges into a watery death and reappears as a new man, washed clean of sin. Jesus does not need to die to sin, so John the Baptist tries to deter him (Matt. 3:13). But Jesus must be baptized as an expression of his solidarity with humanity. If he is to identify with us, he must go through the actions of a sinful man who requires God's justification ("It is proper for us to do this to fulfill all righteousness").[18] The water at Jesus's baptism is used as a judgment instrument on sin. It symbolizes death to the old self (cf. Rom. 6:1–4). I have discussed in detail the association of water with the powers of death.[19] The relevance of that idea to the creation account will form part of a later discussion. The important point now is the

---

16. Cf. Niehaus, *God at Sinai*, 152.

17. God does speak of how he bore Israel "on eagle's wings" out of Egypt (Exod. 19:4), but he does not say this explicitly of the Spirit, and this metaphor probably is not to be so strictly understood. Cf. Niehaus, *God at Sinai*, 153. All Scripture references and quotations are from the NIV unless otherwise indicated.

18. Once we understand *righteousness* we can understand how Jesus's baptism at John's hands fulfills it. We will discuss righteousness later but, for now, affirm that righteousness is conformity to a divinely revealed standard and thus, ultimately, conformity to God's nature.

19. Niehaus, *God at Sinai*, 111–14, 167–71.

parallel of key elements in the creation account and the account of Jesus's baptism. It is as follows:

Creation Account	Baptismal Account
Spirit of God	Spirit of God
hovers over the waters	descends upon Jesus as dove[20]

We can only understand the importance of these parallels when we also understand from John 1:1–2 that the Word (the Son) "was with God in the beginning," and that "through him all things were made." In other words, God made all things through the Son (the Word). God made the kingdom that then was through that Word. But through the incarnate Word, Jesus, God also proclaimed the "gospel of the kingdom." That is, God declares and advances another kingdom, the kingdom of heaven, through the incarnate Word. He also does signs and wonders through that same incarnate Word as a means of advancing, or (so to speak) creating, that kingdom among humanity.

But the Father and the Word do not work alone. The Father sends the Spirit to work through the Word, to create the kingdom among humans by proclamation and works of power. The Spirit works through the incarnate Word to proclaim and heal. So Jesus can say, "The words I have spoken to you are Spirit" (John 6:63, author's translation), and Paul can say that he speaks "in words taught by the Spirit" (1 Cor. 2:13); so Jesus can say, "If I drive out demons by the Spirit of God, then the Kingdom of God has come among you" (Matt. 12:28), and Paul can attribute the gifts by which God's kingdom is administered and advanced—gifts that Jesus also demonstrated—to the Spirit (1 Cor. 12:1–11).

The pattern of behavior appears to be as follows: the Father causes the Spirit to work through the Son (the incarnate Word) to

---

20. The emergence of the dry land in Genesis 1, the reemergence of dry land in Genesis 7–8, the emergence of Jesus from the water in Matthew 3, the emergence of a baby at birth from the amniotic waters, and the reemergence of a person from baptismal waters present an interesting set of parallels (to be explored later). It need not form part of the present discussion.

produce/advance the kingdom. For that purpose the Spirit appeared in an avian form and descended on the incarnate Word at the outset of his kingdom work.

We propose that—by analogy—one can understand the roles of the Father, the Spirit, and the *preincarnate* Word at the creation. Accordingly, at that time, the Father caused the Spirit to work through the preincarnate Word to produce the kingdom that then was— namely, the visible creation.[21] The Spirit worked through the Word to declare words—words that created the then-kingdom ("Let there be light" and so on). Those words were also manifestations of the Spirit's power.[22] The analogy between the work of the preincarnate Word and the incarnate Word may be illustrated as follows:

	Preincarnate Word	Incarnate Word
1.	*The Spirit works*	*The Spirit works*
2.	*through the preincarnate Word*	*through the incarnate Word*
3.	*to produce kingdom*	*to produce kingdom*
	words/works of power	*words/works of power*

The avian presence of the Spirit of God both at the creation and at the baptism of Jesus—whose work advances God's kingdom and ultimately accomplishes a new heaven and earth (Rev. 21:1)—argues for such an understanding. The mediatorial role of the Word both at the work of creation and at the work of the New covenant (which produces ultimately that same new heaven and earth) argues the same.

---

21. It remains obscure whether God's creative work *as reported in Genesis 1* (i.e., *explicitly*) includes also the creation of all things invisible—that is, the spiritual realm. We shall explore this later. It is not critical to the present discussion.

22. Meredith G. Kline, *God, Heaven, and Har Magedon* (Eugene, OR: Wipf and Stock, 2006), 12, understood this connection too, although he formulated it in a slightly different way: "The Spirit executed in the earth below the fiat of the Logos-Word from heaven above." I suspect rather that the *words* of the Logos-Word were *Spirit* and from the Father, as per John 6:63, 14:10, 24.

EXCURSUS: IRENAEUS ON SPIRIT, WORD, AND CREATION

Long ago, Irenaeus came close to this understanding. In section 5 of his *Demonstration of the Apostolic Preaching*, he wrote as follows:

> And since God is rational, therefore by [the] Word He created the things that were made; and God is Spirit, and by [the] Spirit he adorned all things: as also the prophet says: *By the word of the Lord were the heavens established, and by his spirit all their power* [Ps. 33:6]. Since then the Word establishes, that is, gives body and grants the reality of being, and the Spirit gives order and form to the diversity of the powers; rightly and fittingly is the Word called the Son, and the Spirit the Wisdom of God. Well also does Paul His apostle say: *one God the Father, who is over all and through all and in us all* [Eph. 4:6]. For *over all* is the Father; and *through all* is the Son; and *in us all* is the Spirit, who cries *Abba Father*, and fashions man into the likeness of God.[23]

McDonough gives Irenaeus's statement on creation the best possible interpretation, in my opinion: "Perhaps Irenaeus is working precisely with the words, 'Let there be . . .' of the Genesis text, such that the Son executes the Father's desire that things be, while the Spirit gives them their particular form and expression. If this reading is correct, the executive role of the Son may be said to be broadly 'messianic'"; and again, on Irenaeus's comment in *Demonstration* 54, "For He was named Christ, because through Him the Father anointed and adorned all things; and because on his coming as man He was anointed with the Spirit of God and His Father." McDonough understands Irenaeus to mean that "he [i.e., Christ] pours out the Spirit to inaugurate the first creation, just as the Spirit is poured out on Christ to inaugurate the new creation."[24] We would

---

23. Passage trans. J. Armitage Robinson in Iain MacKenzie, *Irenaeus' Demonstration of the Apostolic Preaching: A Theological Commentary and Translation* (Aldershot: Ashgate, 2002), as quoted in Sean McDonough, *Christ as Creator* (Oxford: Oxford University Press, 2009), 239–40.

24. Ibid., 240.

only say, rather, that in both cases the Father caused the Spirit to work through the Son, to produce the original creation and the new creation, as demonstrated earlier, with parallel divine activity through the ages in all of God's kingdom work.

The Word's incarnate ministry thus offers a model for understanding the way of God's kingdom production and advance. All of the cases the Bible offers are parallel. Just as the Spirit worked through the Son to produce God's original kingdom, the creation, so he worked through the prophets of old and then through the incarnate Word, and so he works today. A schema of this pattern of divine activity is provided in chapter 1, but for now we note as a further basis for it the following facts. The prophet David could declare, "The Spirit of Yahweh spoke through me; his word was on my tongue" (2 Sam. 23:2) when God affirmed the Davidic covenant. The Spirit produced God's words, which confirmed the Davidic covenant and kingdom. But likewise the prophet Agabus could say, "The Holy Spirit says" (Acts 21:11). The Spirit through the prophet produced words of covenant administration—in this case, a prophecy that apprised Paul of a future challenge to his own kingdom work. What was true for Agabus has also been true for all of God's people in the church age: God's Spirit is at work *within us* to advance God's kingdom. That is the work of sanctification. But the Spirit is also at work *through us* to advance God's kingdom. That is the manifold work of the church in evangelization, healing, and prophetic manifestation of God's truth and love. And that work, like all God's kingdom advance, is a matter of warfare. We will affirm now but argue later that, from the Fall onward, God's Spirit has worked through prophet-figures to wage war in order to establish a form of God's kingdom in the world.

Our understanding of God's mode of kingdom creation/advance now enables us to produce a final version of our major paradigm:

The Major Paradigm (Final Form)

1. *God works*
2. *by his Spirit*

3. *through the Word/a prophet-figure*
4. *to war against and defeat his foe(s)*
5. *God establishes a covenant with a people*
6. *God's covenant establishes that people as God's people*
7. *God establishes a temple among his people,*
   because he will reside among them

God conducts warfare through a prophet-figure on the analogy of the Son. Why? Because all prophets through whom the Father worked before the Incarnation were modeled on the Son, although temporally they came before him—inasmuch as eternally he came before them (cf. John 1:30). And all who have the Spirit of Christ after Pentecost are modeled also on the Son, for God's Spirit not only works through us to advance his kingdom (as was the case with the Son) but also works in us to remake us into the Lord's likeness (cf. 2 Cor. 3:18). All of this, further, is but one illustration of a larger and far-reaching principle—namely, that God has patterned things on earth after himself, his ideas, and his ways of working. As we shall see, this is no simplistic form of idealism but a biblically demonstrable truth.

FAITH

It is important for us to understand biblical faith at this point, because faith has an essential role in the way the Spirit works through the Son and through others to advance God's kingdom. It may be presumptuous to suppose that we can understand fully something that is so unseen. But a degree of understanding adequate to the task may be possible.

One who would ask "What is biblical faith?" naturally turns for an answer to the Bible's one propositional statement on the matter. The writer of Hebrews informs us, "Faith is the substance of things hoped for, the assurance of things unseen" (Heb. 11:1, author's translation). A list of illustrations follows, from the days of our first parents to the writer's own day, and so implicitly to our day also, because those illustrations are not only examples: They also challenge us to understand and apply the propositional statement of

Heb. 11:1, a statement that may not have its full impact (and pos-sibly was not meant to) without some probing.

Ancillary to our probe, a prior way is open for us to understand biblical faith. Study of the Hebrew verb הֶאֱמִין ("to believe") offers a perspective that agrees with Hebrews 11 and with all biblical illustra-tions of faith. The root of the Hebrew (Hiphil) form is the verb אָמַן ("to confirm, support"), from which the adverb אָמֵן ("amen," "verily, truly") derives.[25] The basic sense, then, of the Hiphil (הֶאֱמִין, "to believe") is actually, to paraphrase, "to affirm, to agree that it is so."[26] That understanding renders the actual substance of biblical faith.

How can our affirmation or agreement that "it is so" be the same as the faith the Bible portrays? It is the same because biblical faith is in fact, *agreement with what God is doing* (and this is why it is so close to righteousness, which is conformity to God's stan-dard or nature). It is not mere intellectual assent. It is *ownership* of what God is doing. When I believe in or put my faith in Jesus Christ, I actually agree and *own* or *make my own* what God has done, is doing, and promises to do in Christ for me. I conform to God's way of seeing this truth, or to his standard of perception and affirmation. However, this agreement, or *ownership*, is an agreement with—or ownership of—something that is unseen. So, if I "amen" what God has done in Christ, I amen an invisible reality. That is, I can look at the life, death, and even the resurrection of Christ, and yet not know from those data that they have one—and only one at that moment for me—core significance: God's atonement for sin that I may, in effect, apply to myself by amening it. The facts of Jesus's life, minis-try, death, and resurrection have a significance that one apprehends by faith—by amening that significance, or embracing it for oneself.

On such a definition of faith, one may contend that Jesus led a life of perfect faith—and of perfect righteousness. Jesus agreed constantly and totally with what the Father was doing (and so he was "Jesus

25. Cf. Francis Brown, S. R. Driver, and G. A. Briggs, *Hebrew and English Lexicon of the Old Testament* (Oxford: Clarendon Press, 1974), 52–53.

26. Cf. William Holladay, *A Concise Hebrew and Aramaic Lexicon of the Old Testament* (Grand Rapids: Eerdmans, 1971), 20 ("view s.thg as reliable, believe").

Christ the righteous" [1 John 2:1] because he conformed entirely to his Father's character). He could say, "I tell you the truth, the Son can do nothing by himself; he can only do what he sees his Father doing, because whatever the Father does the Son also does" (John 5:19). As we noted, faith is an amening of what is unseen. And although Jesus "saw" in a way that we typically do not, what he saw was invisible to the outward senses, and he had to trust in the reality of that "unseen" that he saw. So Jesus is called "the faithful witness" (Rev. 1:5). That is, he was faithful to, or he amened, what he saw his Father doing.

FAITH AND AGREEMENT WITH GOD

We affirm, then, that faith is—in its simplest form—agreement with God. Although Hebrews 11 does not make this obvious, one event in the ministry of Jesus does bring clarity on this point. Jesus had an encounter with a Roman centurion that can teach us much about faith:

> When Jesus had entered Capernaum, a centurion came to him, asking for help. "Lord," he said, "my servant lies at home paralyzed and in terrible suffering." Jesus said to him, "I will go and heal him." The centurion replied, "Lord, I do not deserve to have you come under my roof. But just say the word, and my servant will be healed. For I myself am a man under authority, with soldiers under me. I tell this one, 'Go,' and he goes; and that one, 'Come,' and he comes. I say to my servant, 'Do this,' and he does it." When Jesus heard this, he was astonished and said to those following him, "I tell you the truth, I have not found anyone in Israel with such great faith." (Matt. 8:5–10)

The centurion says to Jesus, "Just say the word, and my servant will be healed," but how can the Roman know this? He reasons by analogy—that is, he compares Jesus with himself. The centurion has an understanding of his own authority: Whatever he commands must come to pass. He *intuits* that the same is true of Jesus. That intuiting is part of faith.

The centurion understands that Jesus has authority, but he understands much more than that: He understands that Jesus is part of an authority structure. Just as the centurion is under authority, so Jesus is under authority. The centurion is under Caesar; Jesus is under God. Because he is under authority, the centurion can also be sure that his own orders carry authority and must come to pass; moreover, he intuits that the same is true of Jesus. The following diagram illustrates these points:

Caesar	God
Centurion	Jesus
Soldier(s)	Unnamed agent (angel? Holy Spirit?)
Work to be done	Work to be done (healing of servant)

Jesus stands in an authority structure comparable to the centurion's own. How does the Roman know this? We said that he reasons by analogy. But it is better to say that he *senses* an analogy that actually exists. Both authority structures *do exist*, and they are analogous, and the centurion intuits the same. However, although his intuition is true and necessary, it is not, by itself, sufficient. More is required for the centurion's intuition to become faith. First, the centurion must also affirm that his intuition is true. Second, and more importantly, he must apply that truth to his situation; that is, he must "amen" the intuition whose truth he has acknowledged, and he does so by affirming that, because the authority structure he has affirmed is true, Jesus can heal his servant with a word. And Jesus does so.

Jesus's commentary on the centurion, and thus on the whole matter, is decisive: "I tell you the truth, I have not found anyone in Israel with such great faith" (Matt. 8:10). The centurion amens both Jesus's own authority structure and the outcome of it, and Jesus calls that faith. So it is, and the Bible hardly offers a better example. Such an example confirms the understanding of faith offered earlier. *Faith,* then, is *an amening of who God is and what he is doing*—whether one only intuits such matters when they are not in evidence (as in the centurion's case) or one has palpable evidence that invites such an amen (e.g., the testimony of the Bible).

What God is doing (or is about to do) is often unseen; so faith is also called "the substance of things hoped for, the assurance of things unseen" (Heb. 11:1). Faith is the "substance of things hoped for." What one hopes for in faith is indeed substantial. That is because faith intuits what God is doing, and nothing can be more substantial than God and his work. Faith is also the "assurance of things unseen." That is because, although God and his work may be unseen, faith—that *inner amening of who God is and what he is doing*—assures us of the substantial reality and eventuality of all that.

Because faith is the assurance of things unseen, "We live by faith, not by sight" (2 Cor. 5:7). That is, we live by our sure knowledge of God and his work, which includes the ongoing work of the Holy Spirit in our lives. All who follow Christ are called to be like him (Matt. 10:25) and to walk as he walked (1 John 2:6)—that is, "by faith and not by sight." Such a life is also "in step" with God's Spirit (Gal. 5:25). One who lives in that way will more and more know what the Father is doing, and do it, and know what the Father is saying, and say it. As in the case of Jesus, the Spirit will produce his words and deeds.[27]

It follows that every act of God through his servants/children has been made possible by faith—because those people owned and then obediently gave themselves to what God was doing. The owning (faith) comes first, then the act of obedience. That is the logical—and also actual—order. Paul affirms the same, for he calls us "to . . . the obedience that comes from faith" (εἰς ὑπακοὴν πίστεως, Rom. 1:5).

The incarnate Word shows the purest form of faith, for as we said, Jesus led a life of perfect faith. But if the incarnate and now ascended Word, through whom God by his Spirit produces the kingdom among us, led a human life of faith, and if the advance of that kingdom is also by faith, we may pose another question: Was the

---

27. Faith is important not only for life in Christ but also for world history. For example, in the past, God's judgment of Canaan depended on one thing: the faith, or lack of faith, of the land's inhabitants. The counterexample of Rahab shows the same (Heb. 11:31). God's final judgment of the world depends on the same principle (cf. Luke 18:8, "However, when the Son of Man comes, will he find faith on the earth?") Because faith, or lack of it, is so fundamental to human welfare, it becomes very important to understand clearly what faith is.

kingdom work of the preincarnate Word also by faith? For there, too, the Son agreed with what the Father was doing, so that through the Word the Spirit spoke the Father's words, which created the kingdom that then was. Was that creation by faith?

The opening statement of Hebrews 11 may seem to provide an answer. It emphasizes that which is not seen: "Faith is . . . the assurance of things unseen." One could object, then, that faith was not operative at the creation, because the Son surely saw and understood what the Father would do (in creating the world). The Father's plan was not unseen. But this understanding is made impossible by the fact that Jesus also saw what his Father was doing as he walked this earth (John 5:19). And yet, as we have understood, Jesus led a life of perfect faith. That is how he can be called "the faithful witness" (Rev. 1:5). Rather, our understanding of Hebrews 11 must take into account its audience of fallen human beings. The definition of faith in Hebrews is composed for our sake. We often do not see what the Father is doing, and perhaps rarely if ever do we see it as clearly as Jesus saw it, even though Jesus told us that those who believe in him would do the same works he did, and greater works (John 14:12). Yet when we operate in faith we are in a state of agreement with what the Father is doing through Christ, even if we cannot "see" it (or prove it) at the time. That is, we agree with God, who is unseen, and so he works through us.[28]

Finally, it must be added that faith does not preclude sight, even in Hebrews 11, for we read of the saints of old that "all these people were still living by faith when they died. They did not receive the things promised; they only *saw* (ἰδόντες) them and welcomed them from a distance" (Heb. 11:13). Now the epistle to the Hebrews, like the rest of the Bible, is not a logical treatise. It tells us things in parts. Thus it tells us that faith has to do with what is unseen. But it also tells us that the people of old who lived by faith "saw" God's promised things. It does not tell us their mode of seeing, nor whether the

---

28. So Paul, as he contrasts this present life with that to come, says, "We . . . know that as long as we are at home in the body we are away from the Lord. We live by faith, not by sight (εἴδους)" (2 Cor. 5:6–7). That is, our true life is not according to what we see in the world around us but according to faith in what is unseen.

word *saw* is merely figurative in this context. However, we note that the author of Hebrews could make it clear (in the passage at hand) when he was speaking figuratively, for example, "Abraham reasoned that God could even raise the dead, and so *in a manner of speaking* he did receive Isaac back from death" (Heb. 11:19, emphasis added). We conclude, then, that faith can sometimes entail sight, although only in rare cases for fallen human beings. At the creation, Jesus saw what the Father was doing. He was in total agreement with the Father. So the Father, by the Spirit, created the world through the agreeable and faithful Son.

Our understanding of biblical faith (as agreement with who the Father is and what the Father is doing) leads us logically to affirm: By faith the world was created. The preincarnate Word was, by faith, the mediator of creation—he *amened* what the Father was doing; and the incarnate Word was, by faith, the mediator of re-creation (salvation). And since we are told that "the Son is the radiance of God's glory . . . sustaining all things by his powerful word" (Heb. 1:3), we may also conclude that the Spirit works through the Word to produce that word of power that *sustains* the created order that the same Spirit, through the Word, created.[29] So the Father works by the Spirit through the agreeable Son to sustain (cf. Isa. 32:15) and also to save that which he created. By faith the Son has mediated creation, does mediate the continuation of the created order, and mediates also God's great salvation (re-creation) until all those who shall be redeemed have been found. The Son has done—and does—all this *in conformity to the Father's nature*, and so the Son has done—and does—all this in *righteousness* (and also, *by faith*, by amening what the Father does). But we are patterned after that Son through whom the Father so works. So we also, by faith, can be media of God's salvation—his new kingdom work in the world. And as we have said, that work is not accomplished without warfare.

---

29. The Spirit sustains the created order by uninterrupted acts of re-creation from, as it were, nanosecond to nanosecond, and this sustaining process is arguably analogous to God's own aseity. Cf. the argument in Jeffrey Jay Niehaus, *God the Poet: Exploring the Origin and Nature of Poetry* (Wooster, OH: Weaver Book Company, 2014), ch. 1, 25–26, 44–45, restated in part in Appendix A.

WARFARE AND TEMPLE

A pattern of God's kingdom creation/advance has become a part of our major paradigm. According to that paradigm, God's kingdom creation/advance has always, after the Fall, been by way of warfare. God waged warfare first through the preincarnate Son against Satan, then through prophet-figures modeled (as we have said) on the Son, then through the incarnate Son in his earthly ministry, and afterward through the followers of the Son—of whom Jesus said (in a warfare context), "It is enough for the student to be like his teacher, and the servant like his master" (Matt. 10:25). God continues to conduct warfare through his church today.

The explanation of God's warfare against Satan through the preincarnate Son is no easy matter. The biblical data offer scant evidence for it. That does not mean that there is *no* evidence, but the evidence the Bible offers is subject to more than one interpretation. Key passages involved are Isaiah 14:12–15 and Ezekiel 28:12–16 (and perhaps 28:17–19).[30] We discuss this issue later but, for now, affirm that the Father did indeed work through the preincarnate Son to judge the one the Bible calls Satan at the time of the latter's first sin—if only on the basis of the fact that the Father has entrusted *all* judgment to the Son (John 5:22) and the fact that both the Father and the Son are outside time.

I have affirmed that God waged war through the preincarnate Son against Satan. God also chose to wage war against Satan (the serpent, "that ancient serpent, called the devil, or Satan" [Rev. 12:9]) through Adam. Adam—that "son of God" (Luke 3:38) modeled on the Son of God—was also a prophet, a mediator of God's Creation covenant to all humans.[31] Had Adam defeated God's foe, God would have advanced his temple presence beyond Eden to cover the globe through human obedience to the cultural mandate

---

30. I will also address the question of Genesis 1:2, which has been interpreted against the background of Babylonian myth since the days of F. Delitzsch, *Babel und Bibel* (Leipzig: J. C. Hinrichs, 1902).

31. God mediates his covenants through major prophets. Adam was one of six biblical covenant mediators—Adam, Noah, Abraham, Moses, David, and Jesus—who are, for that reason, categorically superior prophets, as we affirm and shall argue.

(Gen. 1:28). A study of eschatological temple data (Ezek. 47:1–12; Rev. 22:1–5), along with other lines of evidence, demonstrate that Eden was that primordial temple.

Adam's failure to defeat Satan was worse than tragic. As a result, Adam and Eve came under Satan's bondage—became virtually his vassals—and Satan became "the prince of this world" (John 12:31), indeed "the god of this world" (2 Cor. 4:4). Satan now is effectively the suzerain of non-Christian humanity until the end, when the Father will put all his enemies under the Son's feet (Heb. 2:5–9).[32]

SCRIPTURE

What is Scripture? Because the Bible is our immediate subject and provides the data we are to explore, this question and its answer are of fundamental importance to our study. What has been said up to this point should make it clear that we affirm the truth of the Bible. That affirmation regards the Bible as true and reliable in matters of history, theology, and praxis. Such an affirmation can be distinguished from a canonical approach that accepts the conclusions of higher criticism or Gunkelian form criticism (e.g., of Genesis) on the one hand and yet, on the other hand, affirms a canonical unity of Genesis or of the Bible. Scholars who do so then proceed to do theology on the basis of that canonical, overarching unity. Such canonical criticism is simply a way for those who accept a disintegrative analysis of the Bible to write theology as though the Bible were, in fact, an organic whole.[33] Put another way, canonical criticism of that

---

32. For a discussion of this idiom, its significance, and its ancient near eastern background, cf. Niehaus, *ANETBT*, 66–69.
33. Cf. Brevard S. Childs, *Introduction to the Old Testament as Scripture* (Philadelphia: Fortress, 1972), 72–73, which notes,

> The major task of a canonical analysis of the Hebrew Bible is a descriptive one. It seeks to understand the peculiar shape and special function of these texts which comprise the Hebrew canon. Such an analysis does not assume a particular stance or faith commitment on the part of the reader because the subject of the investigation is the literature of Israel's faith, not that of the reader. However ... the religious stance of the modern reader can play a legitimate role after the descriptive task has been accomplished, when

sort is, at its root, nothing more than a stratagem or tactic by which someone who does not believe that the Bible records true history or actual acts of God in history can still take the Bible's contents as a viable basis for doing theology.[34]

We can be thankful to those engineers and draftsmen of Napoleon who—in the first overseas archaeological expedition—made scale drawings of the pyramids and the Sphinx, brought them back to France, and electrified all of Europe with their portraits. Since then, archaeology has surfaced important literary data from the ancient Near East that enable one to see how higher criticism and certain other modern approaches to the Bible (and in particular to the Old Testament) are flawed at their foundations. Those records in stone have shown us how the ancients actually wrote. Such data provide stylistic criteria (e.g., how they used divine names and other vocabulary) on the one hand, and form-critical criteria (e.g., the second millennium international treaty form and the covenant lawsuit form) on the other. The former have shown the fundamental flaws of Pentateuchal higher criticism (with respect to the use of divine names and vocabulary as supposed indicators of distinct authors or documents).[35] The latter have shown the fundamental errors of such a hypothetical reconstruction as the "Deuteronomistic history," which turns out to be not a modern discovery but a

---

the reader chooses whether or not to identify with the perspectives of the canonical texts of Israel which he has studied.

34. Cf., in much the same spirit, John F. A. Sawyer, *From Moses to Patmos* (London: SPCK, 1977), 9–10, who in the context of a rejection of Mosaic authorship of the Pentateuch, declares,

"The Mosaic authorship of the Pentateuch" is only one of many examples where we must approach Old Testament tradition at two levels; usually in the development of Christianity and Judaism, the level of the meaning of the text as it stands has been far more influential than the reconstructed original, and must therefore in the context of the study of religion be treated sympathetically. . . . In other words it is the meaning of the text that is important, whether or not it is historically true. It is what the author wants to get across to his readers or listeners that should be the concern of every teacher of the Old Testament.

35. As was recognized over half a century ago by Cyrus Gordon, "Higher Critics and Forbidden Fruit," *CT* IV (1959–1960): 131–34.

modern misunderstanding of OT historiography. That recent construct, given its classical formulation by Martin Noth in 1943, was formed without a proper grasp of how the Hittite treaty genre and the ancient near eastern covenant lawsuit genre inform and condition the material contained in Deuteronomy through 2 Kings.[36] The numerous inscriptions unearthed by archaeology have now put us in a position to understand the Bible in a way that accords not with such fanciful modern reconstructions but with the way people actually wrote—the styles and genres actually used—in the ancient Near East. Scholarship that persists in adhering to the old ways of, for example, Wellhausen or Gunkel and their spiritual descendants thus borders on obscurantism. One who wants to see the Bible for what it is must take a different road.

Only by accepting what Scripture says about itself can we hope to arrive at a proper understanding of what Scripture is. Thankfully, the Bible has not left us without such statements. Once we understand them properly, we can see that God has produced Scripture in a way that very much resembles elements of the Major Paradigm outlined earlier (pg. 13). Two brief statements in the New Testament provide the necessary data for understanding this fact. The first is John 6:63, and the second is 2 Timothy 3:16.

WORDS AND SPIRIT

The first statement comes from Jesus, who tells his followers, "The Spirit gives life; the flesh counts for nothing. The words I have spoken to you are Spirit and they are life" (John 6:63). Because Jesus's words are Spirit, they are life and can impart life. This is a dynamic reality that his followers experience. But the key point to grasp is that his *words* were Spirit—that is, the Holy Spirit taking the form of words. That is why such words could be alive. The author of Hebrews makes a kindred statement: "For the word of God is living and active. Sharper than any double-edged sword, it penetrates even to dividing soul and spirit, joints and marrow; it judges the

---

36. Cf. Martin Noth, *The Deuteronomistic History*, 2nd ed., JSOT supplement (Sheffield: Sheffield Academic Press, 2002).

thoughts and attitudes of the heart" (Heb. 4:12). The "word of God" can be "living and active" and can even "judge" because that word is Spirit, as Jesus has told us. Just as God's spoken word given through Jesus was Spirit, so his written word given through the biblical writers is Spirit.[37] Jesus's words were Spirit because they came from his Father, whose Spirit produced the words. Jesus touched on this truth when he said, "Don't you believe that I am in the Father, and that the Father is in me? The words I say to you are not just my own. Rather, it is the Father, living in me, who is doing his work" (John 14:10), and again, "These words you hear are not my own; they belong to the Father who sent me" (John 14:24b). The proper understanding of Jesus's words, then, is that all three Persons of the Godhead were involved in their creation and articulation: the Father worked in Jesus and the result was that Jesus spoke his Father's words and those words were Spirit.

WORD AND SPIRIT

The second statement comes from Paul, who declares, "All Scripture is God-breathed and is useful for teaching, rebuking, correcting and training in righteousness, so that the man of God may be thoroughly equipped for every good work" (2 Tim. 3:16–17). The key statement here, for our purposes, stands at the beginning of verse 16: "All Scripture is God-breathed." The Greek term that is rendered "God-breathed" (θεόπνευστος) has the word for spirit/Spirit or breath as its root (πνεῦμά).[38] The analogy with what we have noted above is obvious. As we saw there, God's written word given through the biblical writers is Spirit, "God-breathed," just as Jesus's words spoken to his disciples were Spirit. The following simple schema shows the parallel:

---

37. Peter says something similar when he declares, "Concerning this salvation, the prophets, who spoke of the grace that was to come to you, searched intently and with the greatest care, trying to find out the time and circumstances to which the Spirit of Christ in them was pointing when he predicted the sufferings of Christ and the glories that would follow" (1 Pet. 1:10–11), or, as he puts it later, "For prophecy never had its origin in the will of man, but men spoke from God as they were carried along by the Holy Spirit" (2 Pet. 1:21).

38. The corresponding Hebrew term has a similar range of meaning.

Jesus's Spoken Words	God's Written Words
1 *God works*	*God works*
2 *by his Spirit*	*by his Spirit*
3 *through Jesus*	*through biblical writers*
4 *to produce spoken words*	*to produce written words*

The fact of word formation by Spirit is straightforward and clear. It is also the process by which God spoke through the prophets. To cite one example, as noted earlier, David could say, "The Spirit of Yahweh spoke through me; his word was on my tongue" (2 Sam. 23:2). The parallelism of "Spirit of Yahweh" and "his word" is a Hebrew poetical way of saying what Jesus said to his disciples: "The words I have spoken to you are Spirit" (John 6:63).

More importantly, perhaps, the identification of *Spirit* and *words* is also clear, and that is our definition of Scripture. *Scripture* is the Holy Spirit taking the form of words.

The process indicated by the statements of Jesus and Paul also recalls the brief creation process paradigm noted earlier:

Preincarnate Word	Incarnate Word
1 *The Spirit works*	*The Spirit works*
2 *through the preincarnate Word*	*through the incarnate Word*
3 *to produce kingdom*	*to produce kingdom*
words/works of power	*words/works of power*

The similarity arises because God has created by his Spirit through the Word, has advanced his kingdom by his Spirit through that same Word, does now advance his kingdom by his Spirit through humans in his church, and has also produced Scripture by his Spirit through human prophets and writers. Scripture claims, then, to be the Holy Spirit taking the form of words. That is why it is (to use the phrase from Hebrews) living and active.

GOD AND TIME

God is outside time. That is why he says, "I am the first and I am the last" (Isa. 44:6, 48:12), and of all human generations he can say that he has been "calling forth the generations from the beginning . . . I, the LORD—with the first of them and with the last—I am he" (Isa. 41:4).[39] That is, God is "with the first of them and with the last" at one and the same instant. Likewise, in John's Revelation, he says, "I am the Alpha and the Omega, the First and the Last, the Beginning and the End" (Rev. 22:13; cf. "'I am the Alpha and the Omega,' says the Lord God, 'who is, and who was, and who is to come, the Almighty'" [Rev. 1:8]; cf. Rev. 21:6). Another way of putting this is to say that God "inhabits eternity" (Isa. 57:15, KJV, ESV, ASV; Heb. שכן עד; cf. Ps. 102:12 [Heb. 102:13]).[40] One consequence of this fact is that all times are present to God. God existed eternally before he created the cosmos and man and woman in it, and when God created them, God also already dwelt in the eschaton and in eternity beyond the eschaton. That is why Paul can say of God that "he chose us in him before the creation of the world to be holy and blameless in his sight" (Eph. 1:4). God could choose Paul's contemporary believers (and subsequent believers as well) "before the creation of the world" because all of them were present in his view before the creation of the world. So also, at this moment in human time, God is already with his redeemed in our future: "And God raised us up with Christ and seated us with him in the heavenly realms in Christ Jesus" (Eph. 2:6). Paul can say that God has already "seated us with him" in heaven, because,

---

39. The Hebrew of Isaiah 41:4 concludes אני הוא (LXX, ἐγώ εἰμι, "I am"). This is, I propose, the sort of OT statement to which Jesus alluded with he declared, "Before Abraham was, I am" (ἐγώ εἰμι, John 8:58), echoing also LXX of Deuteronomy 32:39 ("See now that I myself am he [MT, אני הוא; LXX, ἐγώ εἰμι, 'I am']! There is no god besides me"). The allusion to Exodus 3:14 (LXX ἐγώ εἰμι ο ων, lit., "I am the [One] Being") is less direct, although also implied. We will discuss this further when we come to the Mosaic covenant.

40. NIV renders the phrase in question in Isaiah 57:15 as "he who lives forever." It seems to me that this translation is less likely to be correct than the one we have adopted, if only because the Hebrew verb carries more of a sense of "inhabit" than merely to "live," but since it is viable we have here, at the very least, a case of fruitful ambiguity or *double entendre*, a literary reality to which the Old Testament is no stranger.

although for Paul it was future, for God it was past—and for God, outside time, it remains future, present, and past.[41] Finally, since we know that we live in a space–time continuum, it follows that if Genesis 1:1 is true, and God created both the heavens and the earth and all that is in them (that is, the creatures and their contexts, as clarified and amplified by Exod. 20:11), then by definition God is outside time, for he was outside whatever he created (including the space–time continuum, which is the overarching context of all the creatures). He always existed before whatever he created—before, in the words of Genesis 2:1, "the heavens and the earth were completed in all their vast array."[42]

GOD, THE NEW COVENANT, AND HISTORICITY

For God, then, any event is at once future, present, and past. So, for example, the institution of the New covenant was, for him, at once future, present, and past. That is why John can say the Son is "the Lamb slain from the foundation/creation of the world" (Rev. 13:8). This does not mean that the Son was slain when the world was created. The Son was crucified at one point in human time, long after the creation. Yet for God that point in time was a present reality, and also a future reality, when he created the world. But the crucifixion was also a past reality when God created the world, because God was also the Omega when he created the world, for he is always the Alpha and the Omega.

---

41. Not long after writing this, I came upon the following lines from George Gordon, Lord Byron:

> "We are immortal, and do not forget;
> We are eternal; and to us the past
> Is, as the future, present"
> (*Manfred*, Act 1, Scene 1, lines 149–51)

Sadly, Byron put these words, which would be appropriate coming from an omniscient God, into the mouth of a pagan spirit. But then, he was a typical Romantic. See Lord Byron, *Childe Harold's Pilgrimage and Other Romantic Poems*, ed. Samuel C. Chew (New York: Odyssey, 1936), 356.

42. We will have more to say about this matter in our second volume, but for now, note the relevance of such passages as 1 Corinthians 2:7, 2 Timothy 1:9, and Titus 1:2.

Just as the Lamb of God was slain at one point in time on earth, so the New covenant was instituted among people at one point in time on earth. Jesus instituted that covenant proleptically at the Lord's Supper. The covenant was actually "cut," to use OT parlance, when Jesus fulfilled the symbolic and prophetic (but somewhat questionably titled) "oath-passage" of the Abrahamic covenant on the cross, followed by his prophetically promised resurrection on the third day (cf. Hos. 6:1–2).[43] Those events brought the covenant into being among humans, after which the promise of the covenant— eternal life—began to be fulfilled at Pentecost.

It is important to understand the significance of such facts if we are to understand how the New covenant can be called the "Everlasting covenant" (as when the author of Hebrews invokes "the God of peace, who through the blood of the eternal/everlasting covenant [ἐν αἵματι διαθήκης αἰωνίου] brought back from the dead our Lord Jesus, that great Shepherd of the sheep," Heb. 13:20). Jesus instituted the covenant in human time. But for God, as the Alpha, that act of institution was a present reality at the creation, and also prior to the creation, so that for God it was a present future event (i.e., a future event for earth, but an event present before God outside time at and before the creation)—just as for God, as the Omega, it was a present past event (i.e., a past event for earth, but an event present before God outside time at, say, the eschaton and beyond). So, in human time, and from God's point of view outside time, there were eons during which the New covenant had not yet come into existence, and yet the moment of its coming into existence was eternally present before him. Once the New covenant had come into existence between God and humans, however, it would never pass away— hence it is justly called the Everlasting covenant. It was instituted within human history, and before that it did not exist within human history, but once instituted it would endure beyond human history for eternity, because it institutes our fellowship with God, which can never pass away.

---

43. For a good discussion of the NT use of such OT passages, cf. Richard Longenecker, *Biblical Exegesis in the Apostolic Period* (Grand Rapids: Eerdmans, 1975), 96–103, esp. 98–99. We discuss the concept of the "oath-passage" of Genesis 15 in volume 2.

The foregoing observations not only clarify the meaning of the phrase "the everlasting covenant" (as it applies to the New covenant) but also enable us to understand that God can endow his word with historicity. He is outside history (although he also informs it, as he informs all time and space; cf. Heb. 1:3). He knows the flow of events thoroughly and perfectly. Indeed, because he alone is omniscient and sees all things exactly as they are, his is the only comprehensively objective point of view in the universe. Consequently, he is able to produce a Bible endowed with historical accuracy. And not incidentally, he can easily foretell, through prophets, what is to come with as much detailed accuracy as suits him, since anything that is future for the prophet and his audience is eternally present before God and may be viewed by him exactly as it is and communicated through his prophets with accuracy. This is the implication of the statement "with the first of them and with the last—I am he." That is, God is with the first and the last—he is the Alpha and the Omega—at one and the same instant.

CONCLUSION

We have suggested that a major paradigm articulates God's behavior from Genesis through Revelation. God operates consistently from before the creation onward. In particular, after the Fall, the Father wages war by his Spirit through the Son or through a prophet-figure to defeat his foe(s). He makes a covenant through that same prophet and so constitutes a people among whom he will dwell in a temple. The Son or prophet allows the Spirit to work through him by faith. By faith—by amening God's nature and what he is doing—the world was created, is sustained, and shall be redeemed. So we also live by faith.

The pattern we have articulated is consequently foundational to the whole Bible. That does not mean that every element is present in every covenant. In the Creation covenant, there was no warfare. There are covenants in which God does not elect to have a temple because his time has not come to dwell among a people—for instance, in the covenants with Noah and Abraham (although even in those covenant narratives there are adumbrations of temple realities, as we will discuss). But our paradigm does present the *dynamic* of God's behavior in every covenant. It remains to understand and display how, in each case, the dynamic plays out. We set ourselves that task, among others, in the rest of this work.

SOME FINAL REMARKS

Temple

One point perhaps not sufficiently emphasized in the closing part of these *prolegomena*, which yet plays a major role among the work's conclusions, is the importance of the goal of God's overarching covenantal program: to reestablish his temple presence among humans so that he may indeed dwell among them and be their God.[44] The age must come when God has returned and made all things right—when God, his people, his new creation, and his temple presence are coextensive. At that time, he will truly be all in all. This is the deeper implication of Revelation 21:22: "I did not see a temple in the city, because the Lord God Almighty and the Lamb are its temple," as Beale has suggested.[45] It is also implied by Ezekiel 1:28, where the human form on the chariot throne, seen by the prophet, is "the appearance of the likeness of the Glory of the Lord." As I will argue later, this statement declares the human form to be the form of the Spirit and so also is tantamount to saying that the Lord is a temple of his own Spirit, or, of himself. When God is all in all, the state of affairs will be that "the temple of God has been transformed into God, his people and the rest of the new creation as the temple."[46] Fuller discussion of the guiding role of that final goal in the formation of God's revelation throughout the Bible will form a later part of our biblical theology.

---

44. This is the so-called covenant formula, which articulates God's ultimate goal for us. Cf. Rolf Rendtorff, *The Covenant Formula: An Exegetical and Theological Investigation*, trans. Margaret Kohl (Edinburgh: T & T Clark, 1998). Rendtorff identifies and tracks the elements of the formula in the Bible in commendable detail, although in the context of a higher critical approach.

45. G. K. Beale, *The Temple and the Church's Mission* (Downers Grove, IL: InterVarsity Press, 2004), 376.

46. Ibid., 393.

THE COMMON GRACE COVENANTS
AND THE SPECIAL GRACE COVENANTS

The Common Grace Covenants

We have spoken of "God's overarching covenantal program," and we take a moment here to make it very clear, in a summary statement, what we mean. The view taken in this biblical theology is that God has proceeded through human history with a program of salvation, a program that implemented Common Grace covenants as a foundation for the salvific, Special Grace covenants.

Once our first parents had sinned, God established the covenantal foundation of that program in two ways. First, he graciously continued the Adamic or Creation covenant so that humans could continue to exist, procreate, and fulfill the cultural mandate even though they were in a fallen state. Second, when human sin had reached such proportions that God's justice (and merciful provision for a possible human future) compelled him to bring judgment in the form of the Flood, God made a covenant with and through Noah that renewed the Adamic covenant. From that point onward in human history, the Adamic and Noahic covenants have constituted one legal package under which all humans have lived and will continue to live until the eschaton. So, for example, humans continue to be fruitful and multiply, to exercise rule over the earth and the creatures, and to die.

The Special Grace Covenants

At the appropriate time, God revealed himself to Abram and eventually (in Gen. 15) "cut" or made with him the first Special Grace covenant. We discuss that covenant in volume 2.[47] God's covenant with Abraham entailed promises and blessings that foreshadowed the other Special Grace covenants—the Mosaic, the Davidic, and the New covenants—and those Special Grace covenants, though distinct and having distinguishable (as well as overlapping) provisions and

---

47. Those who wish a preview of our discussion of the Abrahamic covenant can find it in Jeffrey J. Niehaus, "God's Covenant with Abraham," *JETS* 56, no. 2 (2013): 249–71.

requirements, constituted God's Special Grace program of salvation, which produced the bulk of the *Heilsgeschichte* recorded in the Bible. This understanding of God's manner of working with humans through history to accomplish the salvation of at least some people is diagrammed in a chart at the end of these *prolegomena*. The chart contradistinguishes our understanding of the biblical divine–human covenants and their place in God's plan for history from other proposals that have been made, including the classic formulation of traditional covenant theology.

With all that we have said about faith it probably goes without saying, but we make the following affirmation now. We consider that at any time in human history after the Fall, and whatever covenant any of God's people may have been under at any time, salvation has been through faith alone, whatever some of the members of God's covenant communities may have thought, and whatever the degree of God's propositional and personal revelation may have been under any of those covenants. *Amening*—that is, believing or having faith in—who God is and what he is doing, so far as those things could be grasped by a person who desired God under any of the covenants, and bearing the fruit that shows one's faith is true have always marked such a person as one of God's elect. The fact that salvation has always been by faith no matter what covenant one was under does not, of course, mean or imply that all the covenants are "one," although they do interrelate and are all part of God's one program of redemption—all of which we will discuss later.

Traditional Covenant Theology (E. J. Young [*The Study of Old Testament Theology Today*], M. G. Klinee [*Kingdom Prologue*])

Covenant of Works	Covenant of Grace
Adamic (Creation) Covenant	Noahic (Re-Creation) Covenant
	Abrahamic Covenant
	Mosaic Covenant
	Davidic Covenant
	New Covenant

J. Walton (*Covenant*)

Common Grace	"The Covenant" = One Special Grace Covenant
Noahic (Re-Creation) Covenant	Abrahamic Covenant
	Mosaic Covenant
	Davidic Covenant
	New Covenant

W. Dumbrell (*Covenant and Creation*), S. Hafemann (*The God of Promise and the Life of Faith*)

One Overarching Covenant Relationship

Adamic - New Covenant

Proposed:

One Overarching *Program*, employing distinct but interrelated covenants

Two Common Grace Covenants	Four Special Grace/Revelation Covenants
Adamic (Creation) Covenant*	Abrahamic Covenant ⟶ New Covenant
Noahic (Re-Creation)Covenant*	↘ ↘ ↗
	Mosaic Covenant ⟶ Davidic Covenant
	(Dt. 17) (2 Sam. 7; Ps. 2)

The Creation Covenant might be called both **Special Grace/Revelation**, as made with God's peculiar people, and **Common Grace**, as made with all people on earth at the time. The same might be said, initially, of the Noahic Covenant. By contrast, the subsequent covenants are strictly **Special Grace** covenants, that is, covenants with a special people, who constitute a subset of all people at the time the covenants are made.

CHAPTER ONE

THE CREATION COVENANT

"mi parve pinta de la nostra effige"
—Dante[1]

THE IDEA OF COVENANT

As my own thinking on covenant has evolved, I have taken a—to the best of my knowledge—somewhat different road from the ones followed by other scholars who have written on the topic. This evolutionary process began as a result of reading and disagreeing with two scholars, and led to my composing several articles, including the article, "Covenant: An Idea in the Mind of God." In that article, I proposed that the second millennium B.C. covenant idea and form as we find them in the ancient Near East did not simply arise in a process by which family relations were taken as a model for treaties between states, as has sometimes been argued. The use of familial terms in ancient near eastern treaties makes it seem rather obvious

---

1. The poet sees God who "seemed to me painted with our effigy" (Dante Alighieri, *The Divine Comedy: Paradiso,* Canto XXXIII, line 131). Cf. later discussion of the *imago Dei.* Cf. Niehaus, *God the Poet,* 54–55.

that some such development of the treaty concept took place over time (say, over a millennium or so). But there is, I believe, a deeper root explanation for the covenant concept, and that is that both authority and kinship *within the family*, and authority and legal "kinship" *between partners in a covenant*, arose out of human nature as a reflection of God's nature.[2]

I would now put the matter in the following way: A suzerain–vassal covenant is an expression of the elements of a *power relationship*, and the original of this pattern resides with God, who instituted a power relationship with creation and its inhabitants when he created it and them. This idea applies to both the invisible and the visible "registers" (to use Meredith Kline's term) of the created order.

Any power relationship, then, will contain the most important elements of a covenant.[3] For example, if one has a job, the following "covenantal" elements are in place: one has a *suzerain* (a boss or employer), who promised to provide certain good things for the *vassal-to-be* (the employee-to-be) and to expect certain things from the vassal-to-be (again, the employee-to-be) before the contract was signed, and such is the historical background, and also the stuff of the classic "historical prologue," of the covenant or treaty; one has certain tasks to perform on the job and certain rules that must be obeyed and not broken, and these correspond to the "stipulations" of the covenant; the employee will be *blessed* if he or she does the work assigned *as* assigned and obeys whatever rules are in place, or the employee will be *cursed* (e.g., be demoted, suffer a pay cut, or be fired) if he or she fails to do so. Although, then, scholars distinguish between treaties and contracts in the ancient Near East because of the presence or absence of certain recorded elements, it remains true that a contract between a boss and a worker in any age and culture will contain the essential elements of a covenant, as

---

2. There is good reason to use the terms *treaty* and *covenant* to distinguish between international (or intranational) suzerain–vassal *treaties* on the one hand, and biblical *covenants* on the other. Since this work deals almost entirely with the biblical covenants, I note the distinction now in passing but may discuss both types under the heading "Covenant" for convenience, as indeed I have in the Prolegomena.

3. In the subsequent remarks, I use *covenant* to denote more specifically a "suzerain–vassal" type covenant.

indicated earlier. The covenant *idea* is the idea of *a power relationship*, and this idea is rooted in the very nature of God and finds expression in any relationship between God and his creatures, and in any power relationship between humans, because humans are made in the image of God, and thus will, out of their own natural constitution, form and formulate power relationships that echo the covenantal nature of God.

Put another way, *covenant* is an expression of God's nature as a great suzerain who provides good things for his vassals, who imparts standards for their way of life, who will bless them for obedience and curse them for disobedience, and who is the eternal witness to these facts. Form critically speaking, these are the relational elements that appear in second millennium BC Hittite suzerain–vassal treaties. They also appear in the creation account, Genesis 1:1–2:3. The creation account that contains all of these elements is thus an expression of God's nature and also has formally the constituent parts of a covenant and thus shows us that God's nature is what people would later call *covenantal*. Since God also has *ideas* of his own nature and of the legal forms that nature's expression will take as he makes covenants with people in human history, covenant is also, as I have called it, "an idea in the mind of God." God's nature is covenantal, and as he is supremely self-aware, he has an accurate idea of his own nature.

It follows from our observations on the nature of a divine–human covenant as a power relationship that, when a covenant is reported in a biblical narrative, the report need not include certain technical elements, such as a recorded oath or a ratification ceremony—or even the very term *covenant*—in order for the narrative of the institution of the relationship to be a narrative of a covenant's first appearance.[4] So, Genesis 1:1–2:3 can portray the institution of relations between God and humans as he creates the world and them in it, and the pericope can be the narrative account of a relationship that is covenantal between God and humans without using the term *covenant* and without recording any oath or ceremony of institution.

---

4. I say "the narrative of a covenant's first appearance" because for God, who is outside time, all of the biblical covenants perpetually exist as past, present, and future realities and did so before the creation of all things.

THE CREATION COVENANT
AND ITS FORMS OF REVELATION

On such an understanding we affirm that, from the beginning, God has been in covenant with all creation. Moreover, both Old and New Testaments attest to this fact.[5] The Old Testament in particular makes it clear that God had, from the beginning, a Creation covenant that he renewed in his covenant with Noah. God caused both covenants to be composed as narratives that have the form of second millennium BC international treaties. His purpose in doing so was to communicate to humanity that he was indeed in covenant with them, and to communicate that fact even through a narrative such as Genesis 1:1–2:3, which does not contain the actual term *covenant*. The church has long understood, and some modern scholars have affirmed, the reality of a Creation covenant, and also recognized that the Noahic covenant was a re-Creation covenant—that is, a covenant that reinstated humanity as vassal rulers over the created order on earth after the Flood.[6]

I will review some evidences for a Creation covenant later in this chapter. Before that is done, however, it is worthwhile to understand and to display the fact that the Genesis creation account (Gen. 1:1–2:3) also partakes of two other literary forms: the form

---

5. I affirm here the fact of a Creation covenant, for which ample evidences have been published by myself and by others before me; cf. further discussion below. Some dispute the reality of such a covenant, but as has been noted, "God's relationship with his creation, including the man and the woman he made in his image, was implicitly—to use a term we now know—covenantal" (Niehaus, "Covenant: An Idea," 246). I hope any fair-minded reader will acknowledge that all the *constituent elements* of what was later called a *covenant* are present in Genesis 1:1–2:3. Since the elements define the relationship, and the elements here are formally covenantal, we justly term the *relationship*, in effect, covenantal; now, covenantal relationships are created by and exist *within covenants*, and so, again, we do no violence to the data to speak of a Creation covenant.

6. Of course, the fact that "the church has long understood" something does not ipso facto mean that her understanding has been correct. In this case, however, I believe she has been correct, even if not unqualifiedly so—for example, the Westminster divines thought correctly in terms of a Creation or Adamic covenant (*WC*, VIII.ii), even though they characterized its place imperfectly in a larger covenant scheme (*WC*, VII. iii–vi). Cf. Jeffrey J. Niehaus, "An Argument against Theologically Constructed Covenants," *JETS* 50, no. 2 (June 2007): 260–62; Niehaus, "Covenant: An Idea," 230.

of an ancient near eastern list (e.g., the Sumerian King List) and a structurally balanced form of domains and dominators sometimes referred to as the "Framework Hypothesis," after its articulation as such by Meredith Kline. Both of these forms are important and not incidental. If all scripture is "God–breathed," then the literary and/or legal forms into which the Spirit has cast items of revelation must of themselves be important and communicate things of value. Form criticism on this understanding contributes to the content of theology.

THE ANCIENT NEAR EASTERN LIST FORM

The creation account, Genesis 1:1–2:3, has the form of an ancient near eastern list, a form attested through three millennia in the ancient world. A very good example that can ground the present discussion is the Sumerian King List. A comparative analysis of the beginning of that list with Genesis 1:1–2:3, and with the tabernacle offering list of Numbers 7 (added for further illustration) makes it clear that the creation account under consideration was cast in that ancient literary form. Two other passages, not considered here, also share the form: the conquest summary of Joshua 10:16–43 (especially vss. 29–43) and the Egypt oracle of Ezekiel 32:17–32.

The comparison on the next page makes it clear that the creation account in Genesis 1:1–2:3 is cast in the form of an ancient near eastern list. It is a uniquely elegant and (without contradiction) rich articulation of that form when one considers the content. But the fact that it has the form tells us something irrespective of the content, and that is that the maker of the list has authority over the content of the list. That is so for anyone who produces a list. A person who crafts a list has authority over the words in the list: to introduce them, to alter them, to relocate them, and so on, as that person deems best. But the list of Genesis 1:1–2:3 is a list of words that God has spoken, and the words he has spoken have created in reality the items in the list. The list form, then, implies the authority of the one who produced the list over the contents of the list, and *in the case of a God-breathed list such as this*, the same God has authority not only over the words of the written list, but also over the cosmic materials created by the *fiats* and portrayed in the list. God has enlisted for us an ordered cosmos.

Ancient Near Eastern List Form

Theme	Sumerian King List	Genesis 1:1–2:3	Numbers 7:1–88
Narrative introduction	II.1–7	1:1–2	7:1–11 (days)
Intermediate sections with opening and closing formulas	II.8–17 (Bad-tibira)	1:3–5 (day 1)	7:12–17 (day 1)
	II.18–23 (Larak)	1:6–8 (day 2)	7:18–23 (day 2)
	II.24–29 (Sippar)	1:9–13 (day 3)	7:24–29 (day 3)
	II.30–35 (Shuruppak)	1:14–19 (day 4)	7:30–35 (day 4)
		1:20–23 (day 5)	7:36–41 (day 5)
		1:24–31 (day 6)	7:42–47 (day 6)
			7:48–53 (day 7)
			7:54–59 (day 8)
			7:60–65 (day 9)
			7:66–71 (day 10)
			7:72–77 (day 11)
			7:78–83 (day 12)
Narrative conclusion	II.36–39	2:1–3 (day 7)	7:84–88

THE *FRAMEWORK HYPOTHESIS*

All of the literary forms enshrined in Genesis. 1:1–2:3 communicate God's authority over what he has made. The list form, as it turns out, is the weakest of these witnesses, although it is potent enough. The second form to consider is what has been termed the *Framework Hypothesis*, after the work of Meredith Kline. It is to be noted that Kline was not the first to perceive the essential components of this structure. Augustine noted them, and they have since been addressed by other, modern scholars. But Kline has given the form its most mature and best articulation to date, and it is as follows:

Created Domains	Creature Kings
Day 1 light and dark	**Day 4** luminaries
Day 2 firmament: seas, atmosphere	**Day 5** sea creatures, birds
Day 3 land and plants	**Day 6** earth creatures, human
Day 7 Sabbath	

What Driver referred to as two sets of days—days of *form* (days 1 through 3) and days of *fullness* (days 4 through 6), respectively—Kline has shown to embody a principle of domains and dominators, or of kingdoms and creature kings. The veracity of the proposed form is affirmed by the contents, because we read that God created the greater and lesser lights to "rule over" the day and the night, and that he created the man and woman with the command to "subdue [the earth] and rule over [the animals]" (Gen. 1:28). Bracketed by such institutions of authority, the principle may reasonably be inferred for day 5, in which the sea creatures rule the seas and the birds rule the air.

Further evidence of God's authority is the command–fulfillment pattern that informs the list. The pattern is well attested in ancient near eastern inscriptions (an outstanding example is the "Kirta" or "Keret Epic" from the second millennium BC city-state of Ugarit) and both Old and New Testaments. The pattern consists of commands followed by statements that the commands have been fulfilled. The fulfillments are often reported in virtually the same terms as the commands. The purpose of such reportage is to illustrate the authority of the one who gives the commands: His authority is such that the commands must be carried out to the letter. The creation list of days is dense with command–fulfillment language.

Command–Fulfillment Pattern

Day	Verse	Command		Fulfillment
1	1:3	"Let there be light"		"and there was light"
2	1:6	"Let there be a firmament"	1:7	"and it was so"
3	1:9	"Let waters be gathered"		"and it was so"
	1:11	"Let earth put forth vegetation"		"and it was so"
4	1:14	"Let there be lights"	1:15	"and it was so"
5	1:20	"Let waters bring forth swarms and let birds fly"	1:21–1:22	fulfillment
6	1:24	"Let earth bring forth living creatures"	1:24	"and it was so"
	1:26	"Let us make man ..."	1:27	man made
		"Let them have dominion"	1:28	fulfillment

Other passages in the Old Testament, and in the Pentateuch itself, attest the command–fulfillment pattern, as Cassuto has noted. Perhaps the most outstanding, apart from the Genesis 1 creation account, is the tabernacle instruction and fulfillment material in Exodus (Exod. 25–39). In any case, the creation account here is replete with such language, and its purpose is to emphasize, again and again, that God has complete authority. His word is authoritative: What he commands must come to pass. An ancient near eastern reader of Genesis 1 would have recognized the same, and even for modern readers who are unfamiliar with ancient near eastern literature, the impact of the repeated commands and fulfillments can hardly be lost.

EXCURSUS: GENESIS 1:1 AND 2:1 IN LIGHT OF NEHEMIAH 9:6

A few remarks are in order a propos of the character of Genesis 1:1—what it communicates, and what its role is in the Genesis 1:1–2:3 account. We turn first to Nehemiah 9:6, which tells us the following: "You are He, Yahweh, alone. You made the heavens, the heavens of heavens, and all their host, the earth and all that [is/are] upon it, the waters and all that [is/are] in them, and you made them all live, and the host of the heavens bow down in worship to you" (author's translation). It would seem from this statement that the "host of the heavens" is the angelic host. This host would also seem to be included in the statement, "You made the heavens, the heavens of heavens, and all their host." It may be that the "heavens" here are the visible heavens and that the "heavens of heavens" are the invisible heavens (cf. 1 Kings 9:27). But since it is the "host of the *heavens*" that worship the Lord, it seems clear that the "heavens" and the "heavens of heavens" are used somewhat interchangeably in Nehemiah's statement. If we apply these data to Genesis 1, it would follow that the heavens the Lord made in Genesis 1:1 may not be the visible heavens (or at least not *only* the visible heavens), and the host that the Lord made is not the stars (or at least not *only* the stars), since the stars, although they can be called the host in other contexts that mention heaven (e.g., Ps. 33:6, Isa. 40:26), do not bow down to the Lord in worship.

The same ideas occur in Psalm 89:5–8, 11 (Heb. 89:6–9, 12), which reads:

> The heavens praise your wonders, Lord,
>   your faithfulness too, in the assembly of the holy
>   ones.
>
> For who in the skies above can compare with the LORD?
>   Who is like the Lord among the heavenly beings?
> In the council of the holy ones God is greatly feared;
>   he is more awesome than all who surround him.

Who is like you, LORD God Almighty?
>> You, LORD, are mighty, and your faithfulness sur-
>> rounds you.

The heavens are yours, and yours also the earth;
>> you founded the world and all that is in it.

The "heavens" (vs. 5, שמים) here are in parallel with "the assembly of the holy ones" (קהל קדשים), which are the angelic host. They are the "heavenly beings" of verse 6 (בני אלים, as at Ps. 29:1). The supernal heavens are thus clearly meant. On the other hand, verse 11 presents us with the same apparent ambiguity that we find at Genesis 1:1. In both Genesis 1:1 and here, the heavens are mentioned along with the earth. In both statements the "heavens" could refer either to the invisible or to the visible heavens (or to both). Clearly, then, in OT phraseological usage, both the "heavens" and the "heaven(s) of heavens" can be used to signify the supernal, invisible heaven.

Such later OT theological commentary on God's creative act in Genesis 1 ought to have a bearing on our understanding of Genesis 1:1 (and 1:2) and 2:1: "In the beginning God created the heavens and the earth" (Gen. 1:1; we add here that Gen. 1:2 describes the state of the created earth before God began to modify or "complete" it), and "he completed the heavens and the earth and all their host" (Gen. 2:1). The latter statement seems to summarize the former (i.e., Gen. 1:1) and render an *inclusio* effect for the intervening material— material which tells how God "completed" the earth by bringing it from a relatively formless state (Gen. 1:2) to the finished condition that God as witness called "very good" (Gen. 1:3–31).

Genesis 2:1, however, also gives us important information evocative of Nehemiah 9:6 (and Ps. 89:5). The word *host* is used for the first time in Genesis 2:1, and it may refer to the luminaries mentioned in the preceding verses. Since Nehemiah 9:6 later informs us that Yahweh "made" (עשית) the "heavens, the heavens of heavens, and all their host" (as well as the earth and waters and all that are in them), and since Nehemiah 9:6 also informs us that the "host of the heavens" worship Yahweh (cf. Ps. 89:5), it seems reasonable to take this as supplemental information, which therefore tells us that the host first mentioned in Genesis 2:1 could include a host capable of worshiping the Lord—that is, the angelic host. Job also indicates the prior creation of angels. In a rhetorical question, God asks Job where he was when God created the world (and, in context, the angels), speaking of creation "while the morning stars sang together and all the angels [Heb. 'sons of God'] shouted for joy" (Job 38:7).

It follows that the creation stated in Genesis 1:1 (and declared as finalized in Gen. 2:1) included the creation of the heavenly host, or *angels* (the "assembly of the holy ones," the "heavenly beings" of Ps. 89:5–6). Although their creation is not described in Genesis 1, we understand from later data that it is included implicitly. Since they and their realm are invisible, Genesis 1:1 apparently tells us that God created all things visible and invisible ("the heavens and the earth," Gen. 1:1, similarly Ps. 89:11)—compare Colossians 1:16: "For by him all things were created: things in heaven and on earth, visible and invisible, whether thrones or powers or rulers or authorities; all things were created by him and for him." The heavens in Genesis 1:1–2:3, then, can refer either to the visible heavens (as in, for example, Gen. 1:30, "the birds of the heavens") or to the invisible heavens (as in Gen. 1:1).

The structure of the Genesis 1:1–2:3 creation account may thus be outlined as follows:

Genesis 1:1	Creation of heaven [and angels] and earth
Genesis 1:2	Spirit and waters (cf. Matt. 3:16–17)
Day 1	Light and dark
Day 2	Water and atmosphere
Day 3	Land and vegetation
Day 4	Luminaries to govern
Day 5	Inhabitants
Day 6	Inhabitants male and female to rule
Genesis 2:1	Conclusion of creation—*inclusio*
Genesis 2:2–3	Day 7, rest and blessing

It is worth noting that the Spirit comes in Genesis 1:2 to begin the work of completing the still relatively formless world—that is, forming it into a cosmos that is also a kingdom—and the Spirit descends on Jesus also in avian fashion to begin the work of forming God's kingdom on earth through the ministry of the incarnate Son. The Spirit, through the preincarnate Son, in Genesis 1 forms the words and works of power that created the kingdom that then was, and the Spirit, through the incarnate Son, forms the words and works of power that create God's kingdom among people—in a world that also found itself in a condition of some chaos (cf. discussion below).

Because the Framework Hypothesis gives an outline of the six days of creation, with the first three days forming a set of domains or kingdoms and the second three days forming a set of dominators or creature kings that rule over those kingdoms, it follows that the "days" are not literal days. They are structuring devices. The creation account is designed to tell us many things, and one of them is the authority structure that God has built into the created order. Consequently also, Genesis 1:1–2:3 gives us no "timeline." The world could be four billion years old and the universe could be seventeen billion years old, and that would present no problem for the truthfulness of Genesis 1, which is in fact not designed to tell us anything about the age of the world or the cosmos.[7]

THE CREATION, OR ADAMIC, COVENANT

THE CLAIMS OF GENESIS 1:1

Another feature of this remarkable narrative, and one that would also not have been lost on an ancient near eastern reader, is the claim it makes in the opening verse. Of course, that verse declares, "In the beginning, God created heaven and earth." But in that statement there rests another claim, one that modern readers unacquainted with the

---

7. Cf. Meredith G. Kline, "Space and Time in the Genesis Cosmogony," *Perspectives on Science and Christian Faith* 48 (1996): 1–22. Cf. further the discussion regarding heavenly time and space and their earthly counterparts in Appendix B.

ancient Near East could miss. A religiously aware ancient near east-ern reader would have understood that this verse claims suzerainty over the universe for the God it names. That is so because, in the ancient world, the creator god was also suzerain over all that he had created. Consequently, the statement that God created heaven and earth implies that he is in covenant with both and, moreover, that he is the source of all authority for any beings in heaven above or on earth below.

THE LEGAL FORM OF THE NARRATIVE

The legal form of the creation account also indicates the presence of a Creation covenant. As has been demonstrated elsewhere, Genesis 1:1–2:3 has the form of a second millennium international Hittite treaty—that is, it has the elements that are basic to such a document. Of course, it is not a written treaty, because God was not composing a legal document to which the man and the woman were to agree, as though they were independent monarchs choosing to come under the protection and administration of a great emperor. Rather, it is a narrative cast in the form of a treaty, in order to signal to know-ing readers that God was, in creation, bringing the universe into a covenantal relationship with himself as it came into being, and also more particularly bringing the human vassal king and queen whom he had created into such a relationship with himself.

SCRIPTURAL ALLUSIONS TO A CREATION COVENANT

Scripture subsequently suggests that there was such a covenant by brief but telling allusions. So the Lord refers to "my covenant with [lit., 'of'] the day and my covenant with [lit., 'of'] the night, so that day and night no longer come at their time/season" (Jer. 33:20; author's translation) as a form of assurance of his faithfulness to the Davidic covenant (vs. 21); and he further compares his faithfulness to the Davidic covenant (vs. 26) with his faithfulness to his "covenant with [lit., 'of'] day and night and the ordinances of heaven and earth" (Jer. 33:25; author's translation). Both allusions are significant. The first declares that the Lord, as suzerain over heaven, has appointed the sun, moon, and stars for days, nights, and times/seasons (cf. Gen. 1:14–19) and, implicitly, appointed the laws of planetary motion by which day and night can occur on an orbiting and rotating earth. The second refers to the same ideas and uses another explicit covenant term: the word *ordinances* (חקות), a standard term in the covenantal legal repertoire (cf. Exod. 12:24, Deut. 4:1, passim). The Lord asserts his faithfulness to the Davidic covenant in both cases: There will be "a descendant to reign on his throne" (vs. 21), and "one of his sons to rule over the descendants of Abraham, Isaac, and Jacob" (vs. 26). Moreover, the allusion to the Creation covenant also grounds a reference to the Mosaic covenant context, for the Lord promises not to break "my covenant with the Levites who are priests ministering before me" (vs. 21). Further, there is an implicit reference to the Abrahamic covenant when he says, "I will make the descendants of David and the Levites who minister before me as countless as the stars of the sky and as measureless as the sand of the seashore" (vs. 22), echoing the Lord's promises of descendants to Abraham (cf. Gen. 15:5, for stars; Gen. 22:17, for sand and stars).[8] The Lord makes it clear enough by such references that he is in covenant with the created order. He also indicates that the Special Grace covenants—the Abrahamic, Mosaic, and Davidic—are somehow fundamentally connected and, perhaps, fundamentally related to the Creation covenant, a concept that is true and that we will explore later.

The Creation covenant entails a relation between God and the heavens and earth, but also a relation between God and humans. Hosea may allude to that covenantal relationship in a fallen context when he declares of Israel, "Like Adam, they have broken the covenant" (Hos. 6:7). Hebrew readers will know that the word *Adam* may instead be rendered *mankind/humanity*.[9] However, even if that is the

---

8. The Lord makes the same comparisons in the confirmations of the Abrahamic covenant with Isaac ("stars," Gen. 26:4) and with Jacob ("sand," Gen. 32:12). The comparison with stars is attested in ancient Assyria, and the comparison with sand is attested in ancient Egypt. It is poetically fitting that the Lord, making promises to Abraham in Canaan, would draw on both east and west for comparisons.

9. The term *Adam* may also refer to the town of that name, especially given the conclusion of Hosea 6:7, "they were unfaithful to me *there*." The full verse reads, "And/but they like Adam have broken the covenant; *they were unfaithful to me there.*" The "like Adam"

right understanding (and the term remains genuinely and maybe even fruitfully ambiguous), the end result is the same: Humans are declared to be in some universal covenant relationship with God, and that can only be through the Adamic/Creation covenant (and through its renewal, the Noahic/re-Creation covenant, to be discussed later).[10]

Finally, the language of Genesis 9:1—"And God blessed Noah and his sons, and said to them, 'Be fruitful and multiply, and fill the earth'"—deliberately echoes (as has long been recognized) Genesis 1:28—"And God blessed them and God said to them, 'Be fruitful and multiply, and fill the earth.'" On the strength of this comparison alone, many have long and rightly understood that there must have been an original Creation covenant, which God is now renewing with Noah.[11]

In sum, there are major lines of evidence for a Creation covenant in the Old Testament. These are: the implicit claim of Genesis 1:1 to the universal suzerainty of God the creator, the legal elements

naturally makes a reader think of the first man; the conclusion of the verse make the reader think of—or wonder about—another possible interpretation. This seems to me a case of *double entendre*, and a fruitful one, even if we no longer know what sort of covenant breaking took place at the town Adam (supposing that any took place).

10. Dumbrell, *Creation and Covenant*, 25–26, has argued another line of evidence. According to him, a technical term (the verb, קוּם [Hiphil]), used in the establishment of the Noahic covenant, is used for covenant perpetuations. The use of this term, then, would indicate that the Noahic covenant continues the Adamic covenant. The term is usually translated "establish," as in "I now establish my covenant with you and with your descendants after you and with every living creature that was with you—the birds, the livestock and all the wild animals, all those that came out of the ark with you—every living creature on earth" (Gen. 9:9). However, it has been argued that the verb in question is used with regard to other covenants that are not continuations. If that were correct, it would be a mistake to claim that it has that significance ipso facto in any situation without other evidence to indicate that the covenant in view is continuing an earlier covenant. Cf. further Paul R. Williamson, *Sealed with an Oath: Covenant in God's Unfolding Purpose* (Downers Grove, IL: InterVarsity Press, 2007), 70–73; cf. discussion in Niehaus, "An Argument," 264–69.

11. The command in Genesis 1:28, to rule over the earth and subdue the creatures, has as its counterpart in Genesis 9:2–3 a different divine provision: God will put the fear of humans on the animals. There is a reason for this change, and we will discuss it in chapter 6, where we take up the Noahic covenant as a re-Creation covenant, with both its provisions and its eschatological implications.

and form of the creation narrative itself, and, finally, terminological evidence that is brief but telling in its implications.

The fact of a Creation covenant also and alone makes sense of biblical eschatology with its new heavens and earth and new humanity. For truly *Endzeit* recalls and renews *Urzeit*, and we will see later, when we discuss the Noahic covenant in detail, how fundamentally biblical eschatology is rooted in these two major Common Grace covenants.

Our study of the Genesis 1:1–2:3 creation account has shown that it partakes of three literary forms: a list form found in the ancient Near East and in the Old Testament, a balanced structure of days of domains and days of dominators (or days of kingdoms and days of creature kings), and the form of a second millennium BC international treaty. All three forms communicate, in one way or another, the authority of God over what he has created, whether as composer of the ordered and enlisted cosmos, ordainer of the kingdoms and their kings, or suzerain in the suzerain–vassal relationship that we have called the Creation or Adamic covenant. It now remains to consider some matters within Genesis 1:1–2:3 that have further significance for biblical theology.

PROPHETIC CREATION AND THE *IMAGO DEI*: THE MAJOR PARADIGM

GENESIS 1:2 AND THE SPIRIT OF GOD

We observed in our Prolegomena how the Word and the Spirit were at work in creation. We arrived at that understanding on the basis of a sure (although not exhaustive!) knowledge of how the Spirit was at work in the ministry of the incarnate Word. We reasoned by analogy on the basis of Genesis 1:2 and John 1:1ff. and came up with a simple paradigm:

	Preincarnate Word	Incarnate Word
1	*The Spirit works*	*The Spirit works*
2	*through the preincarnate Word*	*through the incarnate Word*
3	*to produce kingdom*	*to produce kingdom*
	words/works of power	*words/works of power*

Further analogous reasoning led to the understanding that a similar paradigm applied to the work of the prophets in the Old Testament and the church in the New. That led to the following, more ample paradigm:

The Major Paradigm (Final Form)

1 *God works*
2 *by his Spirit*
3 *through the Word/a prophet-figure*
4 *to war against and defeat his foe(s)*
5 *God establishes a covenant with a people*
6 *God's covenant establishes that people as God's people*
7 *God establishes a temple among his people,*
   because he will reside among them

It is now possible to illustrate, in the following simple diagram, basic parallels between the major stages of God's work:

Kingdom Creation Paradigm

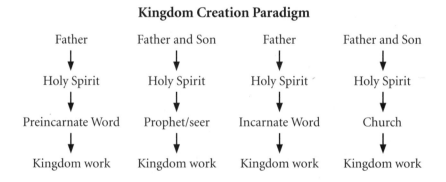

Father	Father and Son	Father	Father and Son
↓	↓	↓	↓
Holy Spirit	Holy Spirit	Holy Spirit	Holy Spirit
↓	↓	↓	↓
Preincarnate Word	Prophet/seer	Incarnate Word	Church
↓	↓	↓	↓
Kingdom work	Kingdom work	Kingdom work	Kingdom work

The Father caused the Spirit to work through the preincarnate Word to produce the words and works of power that were the creative fiats and their created results. Likewise, the Father caused the Spirit to work through the incarnate Word to produce the words and works of power that were Jesus's words (cf. "The words I have spoken to you are Spirit, and they are life" [John 6:63]) and signs and wonders (e.g., "if I drive out demons by the Spirit of God, then the kingdom of God has come upon you" [Matt. 12:28]). On the other hand, once Jesus ascended to be with the Father, together they sent the Spirit to dwell in, work in, and work through all believers (John 14:16, 15:26; cf. Luke 11:13).[12] By analogy, we suggest that the Father and the Son likewise sent the Spirit to work through (although not yet dwell in) God's people in OT times.[13]

THE *IMAGO DEI* IN GENESIS 1

GENESIS 1:26–27 AND THE *IMAGO DEI*

Much has been written about the *imago Dei*, yet one of the most basic facts of the matter has been often overlooked, and that is the terminology employed by the author of Genesis 1:26–27 and what that terminology would have conveyed to an ancient near eastern reader. The words in question are *image* (צלם) and *likeness* (דמות). The former appears abundantly in ancient near eastern inscriptions over three millennia, especially those from Mesopotamia. It is used to describe statues of governors, of kings, or of gods. The latter term occurs less frequently, and most anciently (to this date) in an Assyrian inscription from around 1000 BC; along with the word for *image*, which is in the same inscription, it refers to the statue on which it is

---

12. The Spirit (John 14:26), "whom the *Father* will send in my name," Jesus says, is also the Spirit "whom *I* will send to you from the Father—the Spirit of truth who goes out from the Father" (John 15:26).

    Jesus's words establish the following parallel:

a	b	
the Father sends the Spirit	in the Son's name	(John 14:26)
a'	b'	
the Spirit goes forth from the Father	and is sent by the Son	(John 15:26)

    Note that Jesus first says the Father sends the Spirit and next says the Son sends the Spirit. I think the sequence is important: If we remember that, on earth, Jesus *did* what he saw the Father *doing*, then we see the Father initiates and the Son follows. So here, the Son *does* what the Father is *doing*: The Father sends the Spirit, and then so does the Son. There can be a sequence of actions in heaven just as there is on earth.

13. Important lines of evidence indicate that the Holy Spirit did not indwell any of the Lord's people under the Mosaic covenant, and these will be taken up in chapters 2 and 4.

inscribed—a stone statue of an Assyrian provincial governor.[14] So, both terms are used of a stone statue, made to resemble the provincial governor. It should be clear from such data that the words in question were used to convey an idea of formal representation. A statue of a king or a governor would have a head, a torso, arms and hands, and legs and feet, in formal resemblance to the original of which it was a copy. Statues may be poorly executed, or they may be idealized, but in such matters, they are essentially the same in outline or form as the original they were made to represent. Likewise, God made humans in his image and likeness, to represent himself both formally and functionally on the earth over which they were to rule.

One does not need, however, to cast one's net as far as Assyria to reach such a conclusion. The beginning of the account of Adam's line presents a parallel that makes the same conclusion very obvious.

Genesis 5:1, 2	Genesis 5:3
When God created man,	When Adam had lived 130 years
he made him in the likeness	he had a son in his own likeness
(דמות) of God.	(דמות)
	in his own image (צלם)
And . . . he called their name "man."	and he called his name Seth

Adam produces a son, and the language purposefully echoes the terms of Genesis 1:26, in which God planned to create humans in his image and likeness. The parallels illustrated above purposefully show what it means to be in the image and likeness of a parent: Adam's son, a human with the same form as his father, is said to be in Adam's image and likeness. The same is true of Adam with respect to God. So also, Luke's genealogy can refer to Adam as a "son of God" (Luke 3:37).

---

14. Cf. A. Abou-Assaf, P. Bordreuil, and A. R. Millard, *La Statue de Tell Fekherye et son inscription bilingue assyro-araméenne* (Paris: Études Assyriologiques, Cahier 7, 1982)—the *editio princeps*.

EXCURSUS:
OT APPEARANCES OF GOD

One line of evidence that should not be ignored as regards the *form* of God is the way he sometimes appeared to humans. Those appearances indicate that, at the very least, God and the human form were not incompatible, a truth we see most obviously in the Incarnation. I would categorize the OT appearances in two ways: appearances of God as a man and appearances of God as an exalted man. We should note at the outset that such appearances cannot be anthropomorphisms, because an anthropomorphism is an implicit comparison of two things, one of them human, one of them not human (e.g., Ps. 11:4, KJV, "The LORD is in his holy temple, the LORD's throne is in heaven: his eyes behold, his eyelids try, the children of men"). Rather, the OT appearances of God in human form either are accurate (though not exhaustive) descriptions or simply show God accommodating himself to those to whom he reveals himself.

GOD APPEARS AS A MAN

God appears as a man to Abraham before the trees of Mamre, and we read, "The LORD appeared to Abraham near the great trees of Mamre while he was sitting at the entrance to his tent in the heat of the day. Abraham looked up and saw three men standing nearby" (Gen. 18:1–2). We later learn that one of these men is the Lord and that the other two are angels who go to warn Lot of God's impending judgment on Sodom and Gomorrah.

God later appears to Jacob, with whom he wrestles. When Jacob succeeds in pinning him down and can wrest a blessing from him, we read, "Then the man said, 'Your name will no longer be Jacob, but Israel, because you have struggled with God and with humans and have overcome' . . . So Jacob called the place Peniel, saying, 'It is because I saw God face to face, and yet my life was spared'" (Gen. 32:28, 30). Jacob names the place Peniel (meaning "face of God") because he understands that he has wrestled with God. Here again,

God either appeared in a form compatible with himself because it conformed to his own supernal image or outline, or he appeared in a form that Jacob could recognize (and even wrestle with!) as an accommodation to the patriarch's humanness.

APPEARANCES OF GOD AS AN EXALTED MAN

The first recorded appearance of God as an exalted man to a human (after Eden) occurs when the Lord appears to Moses and others in what is arguably a covenant ratification meal: "Moses and Aaron, Nadab and Abihu, and the seventy elders of Israel went up and saw the God of Israel. Under his feet was something like a pavement made of lapis lazuli, as bright blue as the sky. But God did not raise his hand against these leaders of the Israelites; they saw God, and they ate and drank" (Exod. 24:10–11). The expression "God did not raise his hand against" may simply be a way of saying that God did not chastise them for their approach to his holy self, even though, in fact, God does not literally have a hand. But since his "feet" are also mentioned with a supernal pavement under them, it does seem that we are given here a picture of God with human features, though only hands and feet are mentioned. This would be consistent with the laconic nature of reportage in the early pages of the Bible, a principle we have already noted and may expect to see in play subsequently.

The Lord also appears in a dream vision to Daniel in the last of what might be called the "throne appearances" of God (the others being in Isaiah 6 and in Ezekiel 1, the latter of which we consider below), and here the exalted man aspect is most clear:

As I looked,
thrones were set in place,
    and the Ancient of Days took his seat.
His clothing was as white as snow;
    the hair of his head was white like wool.
His throne was flaming with fire,
    and its wheels were all ablaze.
A river of fire was flowing,
    coming out from before him.

Thousands upon thousands attended him;
    ten thousand times ten thousand stood before him.
The court was seated,
    and the books were opened. (Dan. 7:9–10)

We know that "one like a Son of Man" approaches the Ancient of Days in this scene (Dan. 7:13). We also know that the risen and exalted Son does indeed have a spiritual body upon his ascension (cf. 1 Cor. 15:35–49). It would follow that the scene Daniel portrays is a vision of heavenly reality, in which the "body" of the Ancient of Days is as real as the glorified body of the Son of Man. Both are, then, "spiritual bodies," to use Paul's term.

The popular concept of the *imago Dei* has been poorly informed, perhaps because of Jesus's statement that "God is Spirit" (John 4:24), or perhaps because of a well-intended but erroneous way of honoring God's transcendence. After all, how can the Former of the universe be said to have a form? Yet the New Testament makes it clear that the risen and ascended Christ has a glorified, spiritual body (1 Cor. 15:44–49), even though it is also true that he is omnipresent (Eph. 1:22–23; cf. Isa. 6:3, Ps. 139:7–10). If the "Lamb slain from the foundation of the world" (Rev. 13:8) has a spiritual "human" body after his ascension, he can have had a spiritual "human" form before his incarnation.

Paul's teaching about a spiritual body is also telling in this matter. He says that, in heaven, we will each have a spiritual body (1 Cor. 15:44) and "so shall we bear the likeness of the man from heaven" (1 Cor. 15:49). That means that the man from heaven, Christ, has a spiritual body. But a spiritual body is a body of the Spirit. And that is exactly what Ezekiel saw in his inaugural vision in Ezekiel 1:26–28, a passage that also presents God as an exalted man but that we consider separately because of its unique importance for understanding the *imago Dei*.

THE *IMAGO DEI* IN EZEKIEL 1
AS IT RELATES TO GENESIS 1

EZEKIEL 1:26–28 AND THE *IMAGO DEI*

When God appeared to Ezekiel in that inaugural vision, Ezekiel the man was overwhelmed. But Ezekiel the prophet was able, subsequently, by the power of the Holy Spirit, to produce an accurate account of what he saw. He described what he saw as "a figure like that of a man." The Hebrew says literally, "a likeness like an appearance of a man." Here again we meet that word, *likeness* (דמות), which is so evocative of Genesis 1:26. The same term is used earlier in the verse to describe "what looked like a throne," literally, "a likeness of a throne." In both cases, it apparently means something with the outline, the form, of the object of comparison: What looked like a man sat on what looked like a throne. This is not impressionistic language. The prophet is declaring the formal outlines of what he saw. It is important to recall at this point that the term employed (דמות), or its cognate, was used in the ancient Near East to describe a statue that was crafted to have the same form as its living original.

Ezekiel has yet more to tell us about what he saw, however, and his next comparison ought to make the verse in which it appears rank among the most revelatory verses of the Bible when it comes to any discussion of the *imago Dei*. In verse 28, after describing the radiance of the "likeness like an appearance of a man" and the light associated with him, Ezekiel goes on to declare that what he saw was "the appearance of the likeness of the glory of the Lord." One might paraphrase, "how the likeness of the glory of the Lord appeared," or "what the likeness of the glory of the Lord looked like." Here again is the word *likeness* (דמות), and this time it is used to describe the "glory of the Lord." In other words, if the glory of the Lord has any likeness, any formal resemblance or outline, it is this human outline or form. But what is the "glory of the Lord"? Peter identifies it more precisely than any other biblical writer with the phrase, "the Spirit of glory and of God" (1 Pet. 4:14). That is, the "Spirit of glory," or, as Kline has aptly phrased it, the "Glory-Spirit," is the Holy Spirit himself. John's gospel in particular attests to this fact by referring to Jesus's glory in association with his miracles, which are works of the same Spirit.[15] In any case, the conclusion to be drawn is this: If the Holy Spirit has any likeness, any formal outline, it is this form that Ezekiel sees on the throne, full of light and power, and that, for want of a better term, we call the *human* form. Kline understood this same truth and so gave his book on the *imago Dei* the title *Images of the Spirit*.[16]

The proper understanding of Ezekiel 1:26 and especially 1:28 leads inexorably to another conclusion. If the *human* form of God contains his Spirit, then that form must also be a *temple* of God's Spirit. The Hebrew word for temple (היכל) is actually a loan word from Sumerian, *É.GAL*, which means "big house." That is why the word *house* is often used in Akkadian (*bitu*) and in Hebrew (בית) as a substitute for *temple* (היכל, Akkadian *ekallu*). The fundamental meaning of a temple in the ancient world, and still today, is a house in which a god lives. Of course, Solomon was quite right when he declared of the temple he had built in Jerusalem, "The heavens, even the highest heaven, cannot contain you. How much less this temple (בית, 'house') I have built?" (1 Kings 8:27). Yet God did presence himself in the temple, to reside there, and with such a glory theophany that "the priests could not perform their service because of the cloud, for the glory of the Lord filled his temple" (1 Kings 8:11). God's Glory-Spirit invested the structure and

---

15. Cf. Appendix D.

16. Although without basing his conclusion on Ezekiel 1:28 but, rather, on other biblical considerations. Cf. Meredith G. Kline, *Images of the Spirit*, rpt. (Eugene, OR: Wipf and Stock, 1999). Irenaeus, in a comment on Genesis 1:26, came close to this insight when he argued that God did not need to employ angels in any creative act, because he had the "two hands" of the Son and the Spirit

> as if he did not possess his own hands. For with him were always present the Word and Wisdom, the Son and the Spirit, by whom and in whom, freely and spontaneously, he made all things, and to whom he speaks, saying, "Let us make man after our image and likeness," taking from himself the substance of the creatures formed and the patterns of things made, and the type of all the adornments of the world. *Adversus Haereses* 4.20.1 as referenced in McDonough, *Christ as Creator*, 241.

Irenaeus also touches on a broader pattern of heavenly-earthly correspondences mentioned in our Prolegomena and explored further in this work. Cf. *ANETBT*, 83–115.

made it a temple indeed, a house in which God dwelt in order to be among his people.

It is clear that the place in which God resides is, ipso facto, a temple—that is, a residence. That is why, after Pentecost, human beings are called temples of the Spirit for the first time, for only after that event has the Spirit come to dwell in human beings. But the same Spirit who dwells in believers has also dwelt in God all the time, just as our human spirits dwell in us.[17] And so God is and always was a temple, a residence, of his own Spirit. Consequently, that too is what it means to be made in the image of God. The form in which humans were made was always meant to contain that Holy Spirit, of whom it is the outline, or to use the biblical term, the *likeness* (Gen. 1:16, Ezek. 1:28).

It is not clear that humans contained that Spirit from the beginning, however. We are told that God breathed into the man's nostrils the "breath of life" (Gen. 2:7). The word *breath* (נשמה) is sometimes used in parallel with the Hebrew word for *spirit* (רוח), so the one might be used for the other in Genesis 2:7. On the other hand, the author could easily have used the word for *spirit* and avoided all ambiguity. It is certainly true that the "breath" made the man become a "living being." But it is also true that there are many humans who are living beings on the earth, but who are not temples of the Holy Spirit. God's statement in Genesis 6:3, which has been rendered either "My Spirit will not contend with man forever," or "My Spirit will not dwell in man forever," will be of help in deciding the question, because a better translation, "My Spirit will not dwell with man forever," is possible, as we will discuss later. On purely logical grounds, it would seem unlikely that the Holy Spirit, who was given to sinful humans only after the death, resurrection, and ascension of Christ, would have remained in sinful humans after the Fall. (Any such argument must remain inconclusive, however, because it is based on plausible reasoning and not on clear data of scripture. We will see that there are sufficient data to support the view that our first

---

17. Cf. 1 Corinthians 2:10–11: "The Spirit searches all things, even the deep things of God. For who knows a person's thoughts except his own spirit within him? In the same way no one knows the thoughts of God except the Spirit of God."

parents were not temples of the Spirit.) As we affirm now, and will discuss later, the weight of likelihood favors the view that the Spirit did not dwell in humans, even at the beginning, and not subsequently between Genesis 2:7 and Genesis 6:3. God did enliven the formed clay, and that was most likely a work of the Spirit. The Spirit sustains and renews life all over the earth. He can enliven the various plants and animals (cf. Isa. 32:15), but that does not mean he dwells in them and thus makes temples of them.

GENESIS 1:27 AND THE *IMAGO DEI*

The creation of humans as male and female is celebrated in the first poetry the Bible records. The poem of Genesis 1:27 is significant not only for being a small specimen of Hebrew poetic art but also for what it tells us about biblical anthropology. A structural analysis is necessary in order to understand the poem's anthropological message. The biblical verse is actually three verses in the structure of the Hebrew poem. Each of the verses is a bicolon. None of the bicola contain parallels within themselves, but they do contain parallels between each other—a phenomenon sometimes referred to as *external synonymous parallelism*. Conclusions are warranted regarding biblical anthropology because of the parallelism between the bicola. A simple analysis demonstrates these facts:

c	b	a
בצלמו	את־האדם	ויברא אלהים
b'	a'	c'
אתו	ברא	בצלם אלהים
b"	a'	c"
אתם	ברא	זכר ונקבה

Set forth in translation, the verse reads and is diagrammed as follows:

a	b	c
And God created	the earthling	in his image

c'	a'	b'
In the image of God	he created	him
c"	a'	b"
male and female	he created	them

The poem is both elaborate and simple, and therein lie its magnificence and its beauty. The creation of humans is emphasized by an interlocking pattern of chiasms between the first two cola (a b / b' a' and a c/ c' a'). The third colon follows with more synonymous parallelism (c' a' b'/c" a' b"). The chiastic pattern and the threefold declaration of God's creative act emphasize what he has done. They place the creation of humans at a high level, at the apex of God's creative acts in Genesis 1:1–27, both positionally and aesthetically. The poem employs the term *image* (צֶלֶם), so important for understanding the *imago Dei*. But it also tells us by its parallelisms that "male and female" are both made in God's image. The parallelism is set up to tell us that fact (c // c' // c").

We know that to be "in God's image" has a formal aspect. The repeated use of the word *image* in Genesis 1:27 reminds us of that fact. That is, both male and female share the outline or form of God. The data available to us so far do not tell us more than that. We must read further, both in Genesis 1 and in the Bible, if we are to understand what else, besides formal resemblance, constitutes the *imago Dei*. The importance of such an approach cannot be overemphasized. It is unwarranted, for example, to read into such a verse as Genesis 1:27, with its limited information, implications for one view or another on the issue of biblical manhood and womanhood. Our little poem can be interpreted in ways compatible with both egalitarian and complementarian biblical anthropologies, as indeed it has been. The reason for that lies largely, perhaps, in the very generality of the data it presents—data unspecific enough to enable more than one school of interpretation. The broad simplicity here—in which the *imago Dei* is stated in terms of a well-understood word (*image*, צֶלֶם) but is not more precisely defined—is in fact characteristic of early biblical statements or portrayals, as we will see a number of times. The Bible sometimes proceeds, or progresses, in its revelation by producing laconic articulations of data or doctrines in the earlier material. Each successive articulation of the datum or doctrine contains more information in terms of which the earlier articulations can then be better—more accurately and deeply—understood.

GENESIS 1:28 AND THE *IMAGO DEI*

The consequence of such considerations is that we choose to limit any affirmations about male and female that one might base on Genesis 1:27 to the established fact that both partake of the form of God. Any further interpretations based on that verse alone make the verse bear more weight than it fairly can or should. But the passage does contain more data about the man's and the woman's participation in the *imago Dei*, and, as it happens, close at hand. God commands the two to be fruitful and multiply and so establishes their roles in procreation, and he commands them to populate the earth by so doing and subdue it (Gen. 1:28). Here again, the laconic nature of early narrative is apparent. The command to fill the earth clearly enough implies a role differentiation (e.g., only the woman can become pregnant and bear a child). But information is lacking with regard to the presence or absence of specific roles to be filled by the man or the woman in the work of subduing the earth—for instance, whether the woman in any way has a role subordinate to the man. But something very important is established: Both partake of God's royal nature and are to rule over the earth under the authority of the God who has commanded them to do so. In other words, the very fact that they can rule over the earth makes them parallel in some respect to God, who, as all of the authority elements in the account have clearly established, certainly does rule over all that he has created. God's command to rule thus makes it clear that the man and the woman not only partake of God's form, they also partake of his nature, at least with respect to the faculty for royal dominion. Because they are to rule under God, it seems reasonable to infer that their faculty for rule would include qualities that parallel or image forth God's own faculty for rule—for example, intelligence, imagination, sensibility, and the ability to subdue or subordinate things to themselves—for God also subordinates all things to himself and, after the fall of

Lucifer (to speak in temporal terms), also shows himself able to subdue whatever would prove resistant to himself. Since rule is also a function—both a function of the royal nature and a function to be carried out by that nature—God's command thus makes it clear that there also exists a functional aspect to the *imago Dei*.

GENESIS 1:28–29 AND THE *IMAGO DEI*

Another functional aspect of the *imago Dei* is couched in God's address to the man and the woman. It is not readily apparent, but we mention it now because it is present, and the Bible later gives it a name. Both the man and the woman hear from God and receive instructions from him about the administration of his kingdom on earth. A person who is in such a position, and who receives such instruction (such torah) from God, is later called a prophet. We will discuss the nature of the prophetic office and the very meaning of the word *prophet* in more detail later. For now, it is enough to note that our economical passage communicates the *substance* of a prophetic relationship between God, on the one hand, and his royal vassal king and queen, on the other, without yet giving that relationship a name—just as the Genesis 1:1–2:3 creation account contains the elements of a second millennium BC suzerain–vassal treaty/covenant without yet using the word *covenant*. Both are examples of the principle we have stated: that the earliest formulations of an idea or a doctrine in the Bible are expressed laconically, with more detail to follow in the subsequent pages of revelation. We can affirm, then, a second functional aspect to the *imago Dei* from the beginning, and that is a prophetic aspect or role. It might seem somewhat speculative to argue whether, had the man and woman not sinned, they alone or primarily would have heard from God for others, as first citizens, so to speak, of God's newly fashioned earthly kingdom. On the other hand, we might not unreasonably suspect that, had the Fall never taken place, Moses's ancient wish would have been fulfilled from the beginning, and all of God's people would have been prophets. So we can and do tentatively, and yet with some confidence, affirm a prophetic role as a second functional aspect of the *imago Dei* in general, although after the Fall the function was largely lost among humans, even though the innate capacity for it continues to this day and will continue as long as humans are born.

AUTHORITY AND *IMAGO*

Our survey to this point has established three form-critical conclusions about the Genesis 1:1–2:3 creation account. In so doing, it has also brought forth an understanding of the divine authority implicit in those three literary forms. Moreover, our consideration of the creation of humans in God's image and likeness has yielded both a fundamental formal understanding of the *imago Dei* and two functional aspects of the same *imago*, namely, a royal aspect and a prophetic aspect. The latter, although not stated explicitly, was seen to be implicit in God's donation of torah to his vassal king and queen.

What is sometimes called the second creation account, in Genesis 2, gives yet more valuable information about the functional aspects of the *imago Dei*. We turn now to that "second account," and will consider both its form-critical aspects and the implications of its content for the *imago Dei* discussion, as well as other matters. As we proceed, we will always attempt to allow Scripture to interpret Scripture and do our best to avoid any tendentious interpretation, committed to the principle that our accurate grasp of the matter at hand is more important than any human agenda.

CHAPTER TWO

THE CREATION
COVENANT UNFOLDS

THE "SECOND CREATION ACCOUNT":
FORM-CRITICAL CONSIDERATIONS

Many scholars over the last two centuries have seen Genesis 2 as a
second creation account. This second account has a different style
from that of the first account (Gen. 1:1–2:3) and contains material that supposedly contradicts statements in the first account. For
such reasons, the majority of scholars consider that the two accounts
must have been written by two (or three) different authors or represent data handed down from two (or three) different sources. Usually, these are reckoned to be the *P* source for the first account and a
combination of the *J* and *E* sources for the second account. However,
such hypothetical divisions were developed before much was known
about how people in the ancient Near East actually wrote, and today
the source division arrived at by critical scholarship can easily be
shown to be—at the very least—highly unlikely.

First, it is clear that the second account has a different style from
that of Genesis 1:1–2:3. That is because, as we have noted, the first
account is a list and the second account is a flowing narrative. Ancient
near eastern lists could be very formalized, as we have seen. When one

reads along in a narrative and suddenly encounters a list, one realizes very soon that one has left the narrative flow and entered into that more formal genre. Anyone who has read Numbers 7:12–88 in its context has had this experience. The difference between the narrative and the list, however, is a difference between genres, not ipso facto a difference between authors or sources. Several royal annals from the ancient Near East contain lists amid flowing narratives of royal conquests, but no one has thought to attribute the lists and the narratives to different authors. Assyriologists and Egyptologists know better than to make such conjectures. For the ancients, and for us today, one and the same person could compose both a list and a narrative.

The second account, Genesis 2:4–25, is a narrative and more than a narrative.[1] It is a detailed account of some things already presented more generally in the first account. In the first account, we read that God created the man and the woman in his image and that he gave them certain commands. That brief summary is somewhat proleptic. It anticipates what the second account tells us in much greater detail about the creation of the man and the woman and God's initial dealings with them. Prolepsis is known in the ancient Near East, and it may have already occurred in the first account in Genesis 1:1, which could be seen as a proleptic statement subsequently unfolded in Genesis 1:2–2:3.[2] The same proleptic relationship exists between Genesis 1:26–30 and 2:4–25. What we are told in Genesis 1:26–30 is enough to establish the creation of humans and their dominion over the created order on day 6 of the creation list. Subsequently, we are told more about their creation (Gen. 2:7, 21–22) and God's dealings with them in the detailed narrative of

---

1. The first words of Genesis 2:4, "These are the generations" (אלה תולדות) indicate that it starts a new pericope. For discussions of the ten *toledoth* (תולדות) sections of Genesis and their role in structuring the book, cf. most Genesis commentaries. We note that the term תולדות literally means "generations"—that is, "things that came forth from, were generated from"—and this precisely suits what happens in Genesis 2:5ff.
2. This can be so, even if, as we believe, Genesis 1:1 narrates the creation of the supernal heavens and the earth, as we have argued (cf. chapter 1, "Excursus: Genesis 1:1 and 2:1 in Light of Nehemiah 9:6"). By using the term *heavens* in conjunction with *earth,* an *allusion* to the creation of the physical heavens is made proleptically (since the creation of the physical heavens over the earth is narrated subsequently).

Genesis 2:4–25, which expands on the proleptic statement in Genesis 1. The pattern of a proleptic statement followed by an unfolding narrative that gives more details about, or focuses in on, the subject of the prolepsis has been noted by scholars and is well established.[3]

The difference between the list and narrative genres also accounts for supposed chronological discrepancies between the two accounts. Ancient near eastern writers would sometimes sacrifice chronology to other considerations they thought were more important.[4] So, for example, the first account portrays the creation of plants and trees on the third day before the creation of humans on the sixth day, whereas Genesis 2:5–7 makes it clear that God created the man before he created plants in the wide world, although he had already created Eden with its many plants and trees (Gen. 2:8–9). As Kline has pointed out, the different order is a function of the naturalistic portrayal of matters in the second account.[5] To that we add the dischronology produced by the list genre in the first account. A related and supposed discrepancy is that between the creation of animals first (Gen. 1:24–25) and then humans (Gen. 1:26–27), and the creation of man first (Gen. 2:7) and then animals (Gen. 2:19) in the first and second accounts, respectively.[6] There is actually no difference of order in this case, however. Any apparent difference is erased once we understand that the operative verb in Genesis 2:19, "formed" (וַיִּצֶר), may also be translated as a pluperfect "had formed" (cf. NIV). We learn in Genesis 2, then, that God "had formed" the animals already, before he created the man, and so they were available to the man for naming.

This work is not an apologetic. In this particular case, we have taken the trouble to address some misconceptions that have had a long standing in modern scholarship—and are still very popular and

---

3. The technique has been noted by biblical scholars and was also practiced by ancient near eastern composers of royal annals.
4. Cf. W. J. Martin, *"Dischronologized Narrative" in the Old Testament*, VTSup 17 (Leiden: Brill, 1969).
5. Meredith G. Kline, "Because It Had Not Rained," *WTJ* 20 (1958): 146–57.
6. Cf. S. R. Driver, *The Book of Genesis*, 3rd ed., Westminster Commentary (London: Methuen, 1904), 35, 42.

will probably continue to be so—because they produce a mistaken understanding of the relationship between the two creation accounts.

We are now in a position to see these two passages in their proper relationship to one another thanks to form-critical light shed on that relationship by other ancient near eastern data. Consequently, we understand that we are not dealing in Genesis 1 and 2 with two conflicting accounts coming from different documents handed down from separate sources. Rather, we are dealing with one general account, the first account, which employs prolepsis in both Genesis 1:1 and 1:26–30, followed by the second account, which is an unfolding of the first report of the creation of humans with more detail in a naturalistic narrative.

THE DUST OF THE GROUND
AND THE BREATH OF LIFE

We are told that God formed the man out of the dust of the ground and breathed into him the breath of life (Gen. 2:7). The meaning of the first phrase, *dust of the ground*, seems clear enough. But the meaning of the second, *breath of life*, is not so clear. Since the Holy Spirit is associated with life, does this mean that God put his Spirit into the man so that the man became a temple of the Spirit? It is not clear that such was the case. The term for *breath* (נשמה) is sometimes used parallelistically with the word for *Spirit* (רוח). But that in and of itself is not proof that the breath of life is the Holy Spirit coming to *dwell* in the man. One might turn to Genesis 6:3 for help in deciding this question, but the help it can offer is qualified. In that verse, God declares (according to many translations), "My Spirit will not contend with man forever, for he is mortal; his days will be a hundred and twenty years." The phrase translated "contend with" has also been translated "remain in" and, we suggest, is better translated "remain with" (see discussion in chapter 6). The limitation of human lifespan to one hundred and twenty years (if that is the correct understanding of the clause) does seem to be related to a work of the Spirit according to this verse. But that work might simply be one of *sustaining* human life, and not one of dwelling in human beings.

We noted that *breath* and *Spirit* are sometimes used in parallel, and one such case would seem to bear on our question. Job 33:4 declares,

a	b
"The Spirit of God	has made me;
a'	b'
the breath of the Almighty	gives me life."

The parallel cola make it clear that the Spirit (רוח) of God has made Elihu, and the breath (נשמה) of the Almighty gives him life (lit., "makes me alive," the verb from which the word *life* in Gen. 2:7 is derived). The latter is the same breath (נשמה) of life that gave the man life in Genesis 2:7. But Elihu is in a fallen state long before Pentecost, and since we know that humans after the Fall but before Pentecost were not temples of the Spirit, it follows that Adam was also not a temple of the Spirit even before the Fall, since the same phraseology is used both of Elihu and of Adam when the Spirit's role in giving life to a human is described. Consequently, one may go so far as to affirm that the Spirit was the breath of life by whom God gave Adam life, just as he was later with Elihu, but that, as Adam and Elihu are parallel in this, they are also parallel in not being temples of the Spirit. One may object that Elihu is only expressing his opinion on a matter about which he could not have definitive knowledge or even claim to be divinely inspired, and such may be the case, although his statement is nowhere disapproved.[7] But Isaiah's statement on the matter is not open to such an objection:

This is what God the LORD says—
The Creator of the heavens, who stretches them out,
Who spreads out the earth with all that springs from it,
Who gives breath (נשמה) to its people,
And life (רוח) to those who walk on it.

(Isa. 42:5)

---

7. Cf. Elihu's similar remark, "But it is the spirit (רוח) in a person, the breath (נשמה) of the Almighty, that gives him understanding" (Job 32:8), a statement that applies to everyone under Common Grace.

Here again, we find *breath* and *spirit/Spirit* (NIV, "life") in parallel, as at Job 33:4, and in this case we are dealing, not with Elihu's opinion (however debatably well or ill informed), but with a word from the Lord through his prophet. As the parallel is the same, the same arguments would seem to apply and lead to the same conclusion—namely, that the Spirit had a sustaining role (as arguably he still does; cf. later, chapter 4) with regard to human life, but that he did not and does not indwell nonbelievers; since the same terms are implicated in Genesis 2:7, the same was most likely true for Adam—namely, that the Spirit enlivened and sustained him, but did not indwell him.

EXCURSUS: THE HOLY SPIRIT AND OT BELIEVERS

We take this opportunity to consider, in an anticipatory way, the role of the Spirit in believers under the Mosaic covenant.[8] The OT data support the idea that the Holy Spirit did not *dwell in* believers under the Old covenant and before the New covenant. There are several lines of evidence that indicate this conclusion. Among the relevant data the terms "in," "filled," "dwell," and "temple" are significant in the discussion. Our exploration of these terms is not exhaustive at this early, anticipatory stage but, rather, representative and indicative.

IN

It seems significant that virtually no one under the Old covenant is expressly said to have the Spirit *in* him or her. The prepositions used are almost always "on" or "upon/to." So, for example, we read of the Lord's Spirit on (עַל) Moses and the elders (Num. 11:17, 25, 26, 29), Othniel (Judg. 3:10), Jephthah (Judg. 11:29), Ezekiel (Ezek. 11:5), and even Balaam (Num. 24:2).[9] The same is even true (with

---

8. We will explore this issue more completely in volume 2 (forthcoming). For now, we indicate the trajectories of the discussion.

9. Curiously, externally, we also read that the Spirit "clothed" (לבשה) Gideon (Judg. 6:34).

the analogous preposition אל) of David, about whom we read, "So Samuel took the horn of oil and anointed him in the presence of his brothers, and from that day on the Spirit of the LORD came powerfully *upon* David" (lit., "*to* David" [1 Sam. 16:13]). We are not told the Spirit dwelt in David. We are told the Spirit came *to* him daily, presumably for the tasks of kingship that lay before him day by day. Even when the Spirit later enters Ezekiel, it is to help him recover from a theophanic encounter so he can prepare to minister: "As he spoke, the Spirit came into me (בי) and raised me to my feet, and I heard him speaking to me" (Ezek. 2: 2; cf. 2:3–10ff; cf. 3:24–27). The reported opinions of pagan rulers in the Old Testament do not contradict these data. Pagan rulers may opine that a divine spirit is in someone, and perhaps they think that spirit dwells within that person, but they speak without knowledge of the true God (e.g., Pharaoh regarding Joseph [Gen. 41:38], and the queen to Belshazzar regarding Daniel [Dan. 5:11]). In sum, the routine prepositional usage of the Spirit's coming or being *on* or *upon* (or coming *to* or *clothing*) someone under the Old covenant would be consistent with the Spirit's not dwelling *in* anyone under that covenant.

FILLED

There are several passages that say the Spirit filled someone under the Old covenant, but we are not told that the Spirit *dwelt* in anyone. So for instance, in the case of Micah, we read the following:

> But as for me, I am filled with power,
> with the Spirit of the Lord,
> and with justice and might,
> to declare to Jacob his transgression,
> to Israel his sin. (Mic. 3:8)

Micah was filled with the Spirit for a certain *task*. We are not, however, told that the Spirit remained dwelling within him always. We find, in fact, that the filling with the Spirit under the Old covenant is always for some particular task or tasks the Spirit will enable. The same may be said of other passages in which someone is said to be *filled* with God's Spirit. Such are Bazalel (filled "with the Spirit of God, with skill, ability and knowledge in all kinds of crafts" [Exod. 31:3; 35:31]) and other skilled men of whom God says, "Tell all the skilled men to whom *I have given wisdom* [lit., 'I have filled with the spirit/Spirit of wisdom'] in such matters that they are to make garments for Aaron, for his consecration, so he may serve me as priest" (Exod. 28:3).[10] Incidentally, we may well believe that the Spirit who filled certain OT believers for certain tasks also influenced their character for good, but there is never mention of the indwelling Spirit in an ongoing and sanctifying role under the Old covenant such as we find under the New covenant.

DWELL AND TEMPLE

We limit for now our discussion of these terms, partly because we will devote more space to the overall issue in volume 2, but partly also because the terms *dwell* and *temple* are never used of the Spirit in his relation to believers under the Old covenant, nor indeed of anyone in the Old Testament. If OT writers could say the Spirit *filled* someone (for a task), they could just as easily have said the Spirit *dwelt* in someone if such were the case. Likewise, since we know that a *temple* is a dwelling place of a god, it follows that we should expect *someone* in the Old Testament to be called a temple if the Spirit of God dwelt in him; however, such is not the case. Given the expanse

---

10. John the Baptist may at first seem an exception, for we are told that "he will be filled with the Holy Spirit even before he is born," but a better translation is, "He will be filled with the Holy Spirit even *from/out from/away from his mother's womb*" (πνεύματος ἁγίου πλησθήσεται ἔτι ἐκ κοιλίας μητρὸς αὐτοῦ), which may be more ambiguous. In any case, even this powerful statement does not conclusively state that John always had the Spirit *dwelling* in him. Even here, the filling with the Spirit is connected not to a reborn condition (and so Jesus can say that the least in the kingdom of heaven is greater than John the Baptist—precisely, we would submit, because that "least" one has the Spirit indwelling—Matt. 11:11) but to *tasks* for which the Spirit will endow him, namely, "And he will go on before the Lord, in the spirit and power of Elijah, to turn the hearts of the parents to their children and the disobedient to the wisdom of the righteous—to make ready a people prepared for the Lord" (vs. 17).

of the Old Testament, the lack of these expressions regarding the Spirit's relation to believers under the Old covenant becomes more than a questionable argument from silence.

OTHER EVIDENCE

The statement of Ezekiel 26:27 would seem to be decisive on the issue: "And I will put my Spirit in you and move you to follow my decrees and be careful to keep my laws" (cf. Ezek. 11:19; 36:26; 37:14). Ezekiel's forward-looking statement (or rather, God's forward-looking statement through him) to people under the Mosaic covenant clearly indicates a time when the Spirit not only will *fill*, be *on*, *come upon*, or *clothe* certain individuals for some external task, as he did under the Old covenant and as we noted earlier, but will now be *put in* God's people for an inner work of sanctification or transformation (a Spirit-motivated obedience to God's standards; cf. Rom. 8:1–4)—but that time is not yet. Jesus does tell his disciples that time is about to come, however: "And I will ask the Father, and he will give you another advocate to help you and be with you forever—the Spirit of truth. The world cannot accept him, because it neither sees him nor knows him. But you know him, for he lives *with you* [παρ᾽ ὑμῖν] and *will be in you*" (ἐν ὑμῖν ἔσται; John 14:16–17, emphasis added). Jesus's disciples enjoy a condition that is the best someone under the Old covenant could enjoy: The Spirit was *with* them (indeed, even working through them and enabling them to heal the sick, cast out demons, and proclaim the Gospel). But the state they would soon enjoy, and the state all believers under the New covenant would enjoy, is much better: The Spirit would now dwell *in* them (in fulfillment of Ezek. 36:27).[11]

Once the Spirit does come to inhabit God's people under the New covenant, then those people become *temples* (i.e., dwellings)

---

11. We note the OT use of *filled with* seems to contrast with Jesus's *with*, but the OT usage is explained by the contexts in which it occurs, which, as we have seen, indicate that the Spirit entered or *filled* someone to enable some task. Again, we are never told in the Old Testament that the Spirit *dwelt* in anyone, and the Old Testament's silence on this matter is consistent with the Old Testament's statements about the Lord's *filling* someone with the Spirit—for example, a Bezalel or a prophet—for some external work.

of the Spirit (e.g., 1 Cor. 6:19), a term applied to no one in the Bible before Jesus (John 2:19–21) who had the Spirit without measure (John 3:34), our great forerunner.

There is further evidence that suggests that Adam was not a temple of the Holy Spirit. That evidence comes by way of analogy between the work of the first Adam and the work of the second, to be considered next.

THE GARDEN, TWO TREES, AND A RIVER

We subscribe to the view that the Garden of Eden was the first earthly temple of God. The presence of gardens associated with temples in the ancient Near East would be consistent with this concept, but there are biblical parallels that point to it more clearly. The first is found in Ezekiel 47 and the second in Revelation 22, both with parallels to Genesis 2:9–10.

Theme	Ezekiel	Revelation
Water flows from temple/throne of God and Lamb	47:1	22:1
Fruit trees/tree of life grows along the river	47:12	22:2
Leaves will not wither nor fruit fail	47:12	22:2
Will bear every month, because water from the sanctuary flows into it	47:12	22:2
Fruit for food [implicitly], leaves for healing [of the nations; Revelation]	47:12	22:2

Both Ezekiel and John record the same revelation of a heavenly reality. Ezekiel sees it in the context of an eschatological temple presence. John sees it in the context of an eschatological reality in which there will no longer be a temple, because the Lamb himself has become the temple and all things are contained in him. The latter is a refinement of the former on the principle already noted: Earlier biblical portrayals of certain truths can be laconic, with more detail provided by later statements or revelations of the same truths.

In addition to being parallel with each other, these two prophetic passages are parallel with the earlier account of Eden:

Theme	Ezekiel	Revelation	Genesis
River flows from temple/Lamb's throne	47:1	22:1	2:10
Tree of life	47:12	22:2	2:9

Once again, the earlier account is laconic, but the elements that are present, though few (namely, the tree of life and the river that flows from the inner place), are so important that the parallels should not be overlooked. Because Christ comes to "restore all things," it is an established biblical principle that *Endzeit* parallels or alludes to *Urzeit*. Even the Egyptians understood this, since it was the primary task of every Pharaoh to restore all things "as at the beginning."[12]

Eden was, then, the first earthly temple of God. The parallels we have considered support this concept. The very idea of *temple* also supports it because, as we noted in chapter 1, a temple in the ancient world was understood to be a house—that is, a dwelling in which a god lives. That is how a person can be called a temple of God's Spirit when God's Spirit dwells in that person, and by the same token, Eden could have been a temple of God provided only that God took it for an earthly residence. The Edenic data later paralleled by Ezekiel 47 and Revelation 22 indicate that he did. Moreover, we live in an "already not yet" phase of history in which the Eden temple has been lost and the eschatological temple presence not yet gained. In that interim, we are temples of God's Spirit, who flows from us like a river, as Jesus said: "Whoever believes in me, as the Scripture has said, streams of living water will flow from within him" (John 7:38); and as John comments, "By this he meant the Spirit, whom those who believed in him were later to receive. Up to that time the Spirit had not been given, since Jesus had not yet been glorified" (John 7:39). Moreover, these living temples from whom living water flows also produce healing, like the trees of Ezekiel's vision and John's vision, whose leaves are for healing (Ezek. 47:12; Rev. 22:2). We are thus in a better position than even the godly man of Psalm 1, who meditated on the Lord's word day and night and could want to do so because he had been "transplanted by streams of living water," which allude

12. Cf. Niehaus, *ANETBT*, 171–72.

to the Spirit (Ps. 1:3).[13] Nourished in such a way, his leaves would not wither nor his fruit fail.

The parallels noted earlier highlight the importance of the tree of life and the river that flows from the temple. There is another important tree in Genesis 2 that does not appear in Ezekiel or Revelation—the tree of the knowledge of good and evil.[14] It does not appear in the eschatological visions because it has been supplanted in history by the cross of Christ. The original tree was a judgment tree at which our first parents ought to have judged the serpent by renouncing him and his claims. The first Adam failed to do this, so there was need of a second Adam who would accomplish that judgment. The second Adam—Jesus—did accomplish it by having all sins judged in his person at the second tree, the cross of his judgment. Both Paul and Peter address the cross as a tree and enable us to make this connection. Paul states that "Christ redeemed us from the curse of the law by becoming a curse for us, for it is written: 'Cursed is everyone who is hung on a tree'" (Gal. 3:13, quoting Deut. 21:22–23). Peter adds, "He himself bore our sins in his body on the tree, so that we might die to sins and live for righteousness; by his wounds you have been healed" (1 Pet. 2:24). The latter signifies, of course, our healing from the rule of sin, so that we might "die to sins and live for righteousness."

THE PURPOSES AND THE COMMANDS: WORKS AND GRACE

When God gave the man tenure of Eden he had two purposes in mind: He was "to work it and to keep it" (Gen. 2:15). As others have

---

13. The proper translation of the verb (שׁתוּל) *transplanted*, rather than merely *planted*, is significant. The idea is of a tree that had been in a less favorable environment but that has been transplanted so as to be close to the life-giving waters. The tree is a person, his or her former environment was a life apart from God, and God has transplanted him or her into proximity to God's Spirit—that is, God's Spirit-breathed word—and that Spirit enables him or her to love God's word and bear good fruit. We discuss this further in volume 2.

14. Or, as some might understand it, the tree of omniscience, taking "good and evil" as a merismus indicating all things.

noted, the verbs used here are also used later with respect to the Levitical service in the Mosaic tabernacle. The Levites are to "do the service" (i.e., "work") of the tabernacle (e.g., Num. 4:26, 28, 31, 33), and they are to "care for" (i.e., "keep") it (e.g., Num. 1:53, 3:25). The close relationship between the verb *to work* (עבד) and the derived noun *service/worship* (עבדה) points to a theology of work as service to God or worship of him, and the church has long understood this, as is evidenced by its maxim, *laborare est orare* ("to work is to pray"). The second verb, *to keep* (שמר), can have overtones of guardianship as well as care, and we soon learn in Genesis 3 that there is a reason to guard the garden.

God has positive commands for the man in Eden, but he also gives, in this passage, the one negative command of the Adamic covenant. Adam must not eat of the tree of the knowledge of good and evil, for when he eats of it, he will surely die (Gen. 2:17). Here, as in the decalogue later, both positive and negative apodictic commands appear. The positive commands were stated in Genesis 1:28, and more of them are implied in the purposes of Genesis 2:15, perhaps even in the license God gives Adam to eat of any other tree of the garden (Gen. 2:16). Consequently, it is clear that Adam's enjoyment of the covenantal blessings depends on his obedience to God's commands and, in particular, to his nonviolation of the command of Genesis 2:17.

The same—that is, the presence of conditionality—is true of anyone under the Mosaic covenant. We will later argue that the same is true, either implicitly or explicitly, for all of God's covenants. In that sense, one may say that all God's covenants are "covenants of works." On the other hand, God graciously initiates every human–divine covenant, and all of those covenants are therefore acts of his grace. And because he always seeks to forgive and restore what was lost, each covenant contains the element of forgiveness, either implicitly or explicitly, and each covenant—after the Fall—aims to restore what was lost, and that restoration can only come about by God's gracious gift. So, in another sense, all of the divine–human covenants are covenants entailing grace, or "of grace," or gracious covenants. In this we agree with Hafemann: The long-standing division between covenants of works and covenants of grace is an erroneous division. All covenants involve works, and all come about and are maintained only by God's grace. Some further comments on works and grace in God's first two covenants with humans are now in order.

We have seen already that the Adamic or Creation covenant entails works. It is also a gracious covenant because God has graciously—that is, as a gift—created both the vassals and their kingdom environment (the world) and provided everything needed for their life and prosperity. God's grace comes through yet again when he deals with Adam and Eve in their sin. At that time, the figurative meaning of the word "day" in the sentence "for in the day you eat of it you shall surely die" (Gen. 2:17) becomes clearer, since Adam and Eve do not die on that day. God allows their lives to continue for some time, and that continuance allows scope for his grace to be made manifest. Once God has pronounced judgment on the humans and on the serpent, he does a remarkable thing. God clothes the man and the woman with animal skins (Gen. 3:21). Although this verse falls outside the passage we are considering, it deserves attention as an aspect of grace in the present discussion. It now becomes clear that God has been gracious not only in his covenant making but also with his vassals in their covenant breaking. The church has long understood the skin garment episode as an adumbration of Christ and his sacrifice, in much the same way as the later Levitical animal sacrifices anticipate that of the Son. Surely this is correct, but it is not an exhaustive explanation of the significance of Genesis 3:16. The act that God commits when he clothes Adam and Eve can and should, like much else in these early chapters, be understood in the context of the ancient near eastern world in which Moses wrote. And whatever else the act may signify, an ancient near eastern person would most likely have understood it to be an investiture in office or station. Assyrian suzerains, for instance, regularly invested vassal officials with certain robes of state, sometimes also giving them a ring of office.[15] Such practice, incidentally, may go far to explain a hitherto unappreciated aspect of the prodigal son parable. When the father

---

15. Cf. Jeffrey M. Bradshaw and Ronan James Head, *The Investiture Panel at Mari and Rituals of Divine Kingship in the Ancient Near East*, unpublished manuscript, October 24, 2013, 1–90. http://templethemes.net/publications/131024-TheInvestiturePanelat Mari-long.pdf.

gives his younger son a ring and a robe he, in effect, welcomes him back into the family: It is an act of investiture that restores the son to his station or position in the household. The father does not restore his inheritance, of course, since that has been squandered, so he can say to his older son, "Everything I have is yours" (Luke 15:31). But he does restore the prodigal son to his place in the household. That is like what God did with Adam and Eve, his prodigals: They had forgone (or "squandered") the garden that God had given them, but God restored them to their position in his household, a restoration that included a reconfirmation of their royal office and the blessing of fecundity.[16] The latter may easily be surmised from the fact that humans did continue to be fruitful and multiply, and did begin to rule over the earth and subdue it, as we continue to do to this day.

But what can explain God's gracious act? His grace does not avert justice, because the man and the woman would still die. God must remain true to all of his covenantal commitments because doing so actually means that he remains true to his own nature, out of which covenantal relationships and commitments arise. But he also does the one thing that his covenant does not require: He reinstates his fallen vassals so that the covenant might continue. And so it did, with humans ruling and multiplying, although in a sinful and fallen world. On such grounds (as well as those noted earlier), it becomes clear that the Adamic or Creation covenant cannot simply be called a covenant of works. The continuation of the covenant clearly does not depend on the obedience, or the successful work, of the vassals, for the covenant has continued in spite of their disobedience—because God himself has graciously continued it. The Noahic covenant, which (as we discuss later) is a renewal of the Adamic covenant, only fortifies this position, since it guarantees further the continuance of the key provisions of the Adamic or Creation covenant. We therefore submit again that, on such grounds, the concept of a *covenant of works* is not adequate to explain all the aspects of the Adamic covenant. It cannot account even for the most fundamentally important fact about the covenant—namely, that it

---

16. Subsequently, it took a second Adam—one without sin—to win Paradise back for the sons of Adam and the daughters of Eve.

continued after the Fall and continues to this day. Therefore, this foundational covenant is no covenant of works but, rather, a covenant of grace *and* works. We will see that the same is true, *mutatis mutandis*, of all the divine–human covenants.

THE CONCLUSION OF GENESIS 2

The conclusion of Genesis 2 has occasioned a good deal of controversy because of its importance for biblical anthropology. At least four major issues of interpretation arise: the question of what "a helper suitable" might mean (Gen. 2:18; cf. vs. 20); the significance of naming, as Adam names the animals (Gen. 2:19–20) and the woman (Gen. 2:23); the derivative manner of the woman's creation (Gen. 2:21–22); and the family or relational implications of the male–female union (Gen. 2:24).

Complementarians and egalitarians view these matters in ways that both disagree and overlap. Both schools of thought can affirm, for example, the concept of "one flesh" declared by Genesis 2:24, although the two schools nuance the nature of that oneness because of other considerations. Our goal is not to advocate one view or the other but to understand what we may fairly understand from the passage. The same opportunities and the same limitations that we encountered in Genesis 1:26–27 appear again in Genesis 2. The fundamental interpretive problem remains the same here as it was there: the laconic nature of the very earliest biblical statements of any idea or doctrine. We are likely to conclude that the present pericope does not furnish adequate information *in and of itself* to produce a firm and unequivocal stand on matters of equality or complementarity when it comes to the male and female created in God's image.

A HELPER SUITABLE

The first question to face is the meaning of the phrase *a helper suitable* or even simply the word *helper* (Gen. 2:18.20). Despite much that has been written, neither of these terms indicates clearly that the woman is subordinate to the man or that the man and woman are equal with respect to ontology or roles. Traditionally the church has considered the woman, as helper, to be in a subordinate role. Moreover, since the man seems to have been incomplete without her ("It is not good for the man to be alone," vs. 18), the woman has been seen as an adjunct (an important one, to be sure), one of whose purposes is to render the man complete. On the other hand, some have pointed out that the term *helper* is used of God with respect to his vassals. Moreover, the man's lack of completeness indicates a deficiency that only the woman can remedy. Such considerations could almost reverse the interpretation of the passage, and make the woman superior to the man in some ontological way or with regard to her role, just as, indeed, God is superior as a helper and completer of his people.[17] But the term can also be used of human help that is subordinate.[18] The polyvalence of the term *helper* takes away with one hand what it gives with the other, because it renders both interpretations equally possible. The data provide no clear result.

THE SIGNIFICANCE OF NAMING

The authority given Adam to name the animals presents the same sort of difficulty. The creation account (Gen. 1:1–2:3) has already associated the act of naming with the possession of authority, because God gave names to some of the things he created: the light and the darkness (Gen. 1:5), the expanse above the waters (Gen. 1:8), and the dry ground and the gathered waters (Gen. 1:10). The ancient concept of a "name" was that it defined or stated the essential nature of the thing or being named. So when God gave names to things, he was defining and articulating the nature of those things. God then gives Adam the same privilege. Adam may name the animals, and whatever he names them, that communicates what they are

---

17. See, for example, Exodus 18:4, Deuteronomy 33:7.26.29, and Psalm 33:20.
18. Cf. Ezekiel 12:14 (helpers of Israel's prince, who goes into Babylonian exile): "I will scatter to the winds all around him—his staff and all his troops [עזרה וכל־אגפיו]" (lit., "his help and all his band/group"). The contexts in which the term occurs may suggest a military nuance, and the fact that a cognate exists in Ugaritic (*gzr*) with the meaning, "power" or "strength" may support such a nuance. Whatever they may seem to suggest, however, the data cannot be conclusive, because a term can occur only once with a different nuance from the one it carries elsewhere.

(Gen. 2:19). Because a name is an expression of the nature of an object or subject, what Adam truly did was to articulate—prophetically, as it were—the nature of each animal. We can imagine that, could we have heard those names, we would agree that each name perfectly described or suited the animal that bore it.

The foregoing instances of naming portray the significance of the naming act up to this point. They are important for biblical anthropology because Adam will soon name his wife Eve "because she would become the mother of all living" (Gen. 3:20). If, as we have seen, the act of naming connotes the authority of the namer over the named—as God has authority over the created order, parts of which he has named, and as Adam has authority over the animals he has named—it seems to follow inevitably that the man has authority over the woman whom he has named. Those who disagree with this line of reasoning are quick to point out that the idiom used in all three cases is not the same. The idiom used when God names things (in Gen. 1:5.8.10) is a combination of the verb *to call* (קרא) and the preposition *to* (ל). The same idiom is used when Adam names the animals (Gen. 2:19). However, when Adam names his wife, the idiom is different: a combination of the verb *to call* and the word *name* (שם) in construct with the word *woman/wife* with the pronominal suffix—hence literally, "he called the name of his woman/wife." Further study of this Hebrew idiom, which is used many times, seems to support that idea that the namer has authority over the entity named. For instance, it is used in the naming of children, for example, Ishmael (Gen. 16:11) and Esau (Gen. 25:26); it is used in the naming of cities or locales, for example, Babel (Gen. 11:9) and Massah (Exod. 17:7). It is used by Yahweh when he gives Sarai the name Sarah ("You shall not call her name Sarai, for Sarah [is] her name," Gen. 17:15); it is used when God renames Jacob, Israel: "And God said to him, '. . . your name shall no longer be called Jacob, for Israel shall be your name, and *he called his name* Israel.'" An almost identical idiom (קרא שם ל) is used of Yahweh when he names his servants in Isaiah 65:15:

> Adonai Yahweh will put you [the disobedient] to death
> But to his servants he will give another name.

In all these cases, the act of naming indicates that the one who names has the authority to do so. The idiom used in Genesis 3:20 suggests, then, that Adam's naming of Eve indicates his authority over her. Moreover, it is later paralleled in both the idiom and the associated blessing when Yahweh renames Sarai (and Jacob). Adam gives Eve her name because she shall become the mother of all living (Gen. 3:20); Yahweh renames Sarai and then declares that "I will bless her so that she will be the mother of nations; kings of peoples will come from her" (Gen. 17:16).

One other observation may be made, and that is that Adam gives Eve her proper name after the Fall. This second act of naming might be seen as an act of usurpation, an unrighteous claim to authority over her. On the other hand, Adam named womankind in general when he first saw Eve, and that was before the Fall (Gen. 2:23, emphasis mine):

> The man said,
> This is now bone of my bones
> and flesh of my flesh;
> she shall be called *woman*
> *for she was taken out of man*

The idiom used here is the same one employed when Adam named the animals (Gen. 2:19) and when God named certain features of creation in Genesis 1 (Gen. 1:5, 8, 10). Here again the idiom seems to imply authority, and the name *woman* derives from the noun *man* just as the woman herself derived from the man (as God created her out of the man's rib or side, Gen. 2:21–22).

Although the considerations noted earlier regarding naming seem to have some force, and certainly should not be ignored or downplayed, two further facts about naming need to be understood. The first is that the naming idioms in play seem to be essentially the same in meaning. This fact may somewhat diminish the force of the egalitarian argument that the idiom employed in Genesis 3:20 is not the same idiom used when Adam named the animals or when God named certain features of creation. The second consideration is more significant, however: One does not have to look very far into

Genesis to discover that the same idiom used when Adam gives his wife her proper name (Eve; Gen. 3:20) is also used by Hagar to name the Lord: "She gave this name to the Lᴏʀᴅ who spoke to her: 'You are the God who sees me,' for she said, 'I have now seen the One who sees me'" (Gen. 16:13). No argument is needed to help us appreciate that Hagar has no authority over Yahweh, and her act of naming him does not indicate or establish any such authority—nor is it arguably an attempt to usurp such authority. Furthermore, if the naming idioms overlap in usage, as they seem to do, it follows that the act of naming in general, although it is associated with the authority of the namer *in most instances,* is not of itself sufficient to prove that someone who bestows a name has authority over the recipient of the name.

The result of such considerations would seem to be that the act of naming, although it usually indicates the authority of the one who gives the name over the one who is named, does not always indicate the presence of such authority. Consequently, Adam's naming of his wife, whether we consider the common noun (*woman*) by which he names her (and her gender) before the Fall, or the proper noun (Eve) by which he names her after the Fall, does not per se demonstrate that he has authority over her. Furthermore, it cannot per se demonstrate that he has usurped authority over her after the Fall. The data we have on naming leave us an ambiguous picture regarding authority or equality between the first man and woman, both before and after the Fall.

A DERIVATIVE CREATION

The creation of the woman is another significant but laconic event in Genesis 2. God creates the man from the dust of the ground (אדמה), and as a result he is called Adam (in effect, *earthling* in the most fundamental possible sense; Gen. 2:7). God also forms the animals from the ground (vs. 19). But God creates the woman from the man. He takes a rib (or perhaps merely a "part of the side," cf. NIV) from the man and makes (lit., "builds") a woman out of it (Gen. 2:21–22). The woman is clearly a derivative creation. But that does not in itself have negative connotations. It is not possible from the passage alone to conclude that the woman is somehow beneath the man because she was made out of him. After all, the animals were made out of the ground, but they are not inferior to it; also, the man himself was made out of the ground, and yet he is so far from being inferior to it that God appoints him to rule over the whole earth. The passage alone does not warrant our drawing any conclusions about hierarchical significance when it comes to the derivative or secondary creation of woman. Any such conclusions, if they are legitimate, must come from a future stage of biblical revelation, one that is not as laconic as Genesis 2.

The laconic nature of early biblical narrative has been a factor— or, rather, a virtual roadblock to a more detailed understanding—in several cases of interpretation we have examined, and the same is true when we turn to the union of the man and the woman. Adam declaims the first poetry spoken by a human in the Bible when he declares the woman God has presented to him to be "bone of my bone and flesh of my flesh" (Gen. 2:23a). He follows that bicolon with a second, in which he affirms the derivative nature of the woman's creation: "She shall be called woman, for she was taken out of man" (Gen. 2:23b). Here we have the first brilliant example of Hebrew wordplay in the Bible: *woman* (אשה) as a pun on *man* (איש). (Writers of the English Renaissance employed a different pun using the same two words. They liked to comment that *woman* was aptly named— *woe* to *man*.) An English translation reflects the Hebrew wordplay very well. The wordplay itself does not necessarily indicate equality or lack of it, however. One must resist the temptation to conclude some degree of female subordination in terms of either ontology or roles because of her derivative nature *as stated in this passage* and without warrant from any subsequent biblical data. On the other hand, the fact that the man, in effect, names her, or at least names her gender, in his short outburst of poetry does suggest he has authority to do so, and it could consequently be the first hint or implication of male authority over a woman before the Fall.[19] And it may not be incidental that the first poetry we encounter in the Bible was the statement that God made the humans in his image. Both instances of

---

19. Of course, in situ, it could simply be an accurate acknowledgment of the facts of the case. Certainly, it is a celebration of those facts.

poetic expression (in Gen. 1 and 2) celebrate the creation of a being
or beings in God's image, whatever the implications of authority in
each case. However, the fact that Adam's reaction to his first sight of
the woman is a poetic outburst suggests a different emphasis: He is
so happy to see this person, this one who shares his very own nature
("flesh of my flesh," "bone of my bones"), that his whole being is
caught up into a loftier form of expression than mere prose could
afford. One may recall Coleridge's affirmation that a poet (and hence
poetry) "brings the whole soul of man into activity."[20] It is very
touching that the introduction of the woman forms the subject of
the first poetry spoken by a human in the Bible. The next poetic outburst regrettably celebrates a degraded subject by way of contrast.

The penultimate comment on the man and woman in Genesis 2 tells us that "a man will leave his father and mother and be
united with his wife, and they will become one flesh" (Gen. 2:24).
The rationale for such union is that the woman is bone of the man's
bone and flesh of his flesh (vs. 23)—the referent for the opening
phrase of the verse "For this reason." They are of the same genus
(homo) and species (sapiens), and so they can be joined in marriage.
The verse thus builds on the biological data affirmed by Adam's
statement. But it also furnishes new social information: Now a man
will leave his father and mother and join with a woman to form
a new social unit, a household. At the outset, then, human marriage and the formation of a family grounded in the union of a man
and a woman are affirmed. The verse alone does not tell us more.
However, if we permit ourselves a longer view, we can recall how
the figure of marriage is used to portray the relationship of God to
Israel and of Christ to his church. Both of those subsequent uses of
the marriage figure involve concepts also to be encountered later—
namely, federal headship and corporate solidarity—and those will
receive more extensive comment in their place. At this point we
indulge a brief look ahead, because what is later revealed illumi-
nates what is primordial.

---

20. S. T. Coleridge, *Biographia Literaria*, vol. II, ed. J. Shaw Cross (Oxford: Oxford University Press, 1967), 12.

EXCURSUS: A BRIEF LOOK AHEAD— CHRIST AND THE CHURCH

What is arguably the most definitive doctrinal biblical statement on marriage, Ephesians 5:22–33, also shows how marriage parallels the relationship between Christ and the church. We repeat here the relevant section and follow it with a brief discussion and illustrative chart (emphases added):

> Wives, submit to your husbands as to the Lord. For the husband is the head of the wife as Christ is the head of the church, his body, of which he is the Savior. *Now as the church submits to Christ, so also wives should submit to their husbands in everything.* Husbands, love your wives, just as Christ loved the church and gave himself up for her to make her holy, cleansing her by the washing with water through the word, and to present her to himself as a radiant church, without stain or wrinkle or any other blemish, but holy and blameless. In this same way, husbands ought to love their wives as their own bodies. He who loves his wife loves himself. After all, no one ever hated his own body, but he feeds and cares for it, just as Christ does the church—for we are members of his body. *"For this reason a man will leave his father and mother and be united to his wife, and the two will become one flesh."* This is a profound mystery—but I am talking about Christ and the church. However, each one of you also must love his wife as he loves himself, and the wife must respect her husband. (Eph. 5:22–33)

Just before the pericope comes the injunction of verse 21, in which all church members are encouraged to "submit to one another out of reverence for Christ." This introduces the command of verse 22, "Wives, submit to your husbands as to the Lord." Translations usually obscure the fact that there is no verb in verse 22, since the participle in verse 21 does double duty (21 Ὑποτασσόμενοι ἀλλήλοις ἐν φόβῳ Χριστοῦ, 22 αἱ γυναῖκες τοῖς ἰδίοις ἀνδράσιν ὡς τῷ κυρίῳ = "21 *submitting* to one another in the fear of [reverence for] Christ, 22 wives to their husbands as unto the Lord," or "wives [*submitting*] to their husbands as [*submitting*] to the Lord"). The parallelism stated in verse 22, that wives should be submitting to their husbands as they (the wives) should be submitting to the Lord, is obvious. It cannot be undone by arguing that somehow the first use of the participle (in vs. 21) involves mutual and equal submission, so its implied use (in vs. 22) must also involve mutual and equal submission. Such an implied nuance could be carried over from verse 21 into verse 22 if there were no other qualifying statement, but here the explicit statement of verse 22, "as unto the Lord," rules it out.[21] This is not to say that Christ does not somehow submit himself to the church or to each one of us, because in a sense, he does: He always serves us—as indeed he serves the world by maintaining its existence (as the Spirit works through him to do so). But nonetheless, he is Lord, and we are not, and our submission to him is different from his submission to us. The following chart shows the parallels that Paul states:

The Parallelisms of Ephesians 5:22–33

Head	Servanthood	Body	Obedience
Christ vs. 23b	Christ vss. 25b–26, 29	Church vs. 29b	Church vs. 24a
Husband vs. 23a	Husband vss. 25a, 28, 33a	Wife vss. 28–29a	Wife vss. 22, 24b

God has created a dynamic and wonderful parallel between two relationships: The husband relates to the wife as Christ does to the church. Obviously, the roles in these relationships cannot be reversed (as would be the case for the partners if the relationships were equal): If they were equal, and thus reversible, the church could be the head of Christ so that Christ obeyed every word of the church. Christ serves the church and the church serves Christ, but Christ remains the head, in authority over the church, just as, in human anatomy (from which the analogy that governs the passage is drawn), the head directs the body and indeed even serves the body

---

21. In fairness, though, we must admit that, even in the church, submission may be mutual yet not always involve role equality: A pastor or an elder submits to church members in various forms of service, yet such church officers are shepherds in authority over the sheep. This is evident in cases such as that of Timothy in the early church and, of course, in Jesus's final command to Peter.

by informing what is called the autonomic nervous system, which keeps the body's organs functioning. So likewise, the husband is the head of the wife, and the wives are appropriately counseled: "Now as the church submits to Christ, so also wives should submit to their husbands in everything" (vs. 24).[22]

What God has done with Christ and the church is, in the profoundest sense, grounded in the relational nature of God. Paul shows in this passage how human marriage correlates to the relationship God has with his people in the New covenant. Because the New covenant aims to restore all things, the relationship between God and his people in that covenant suggests what the relationship between God and our first parents, and then also between God and their offspring had there been no Fall, was meant to be: a relationship with God as the head and his unfallen covenant people as the body—or, as Revelation would have it, the Lord as the husband who returns eschatologically to take his bride unto himself (cf. Rev. 21:2).

As we return to Genesis 2, it is worth noting that Genesis 2:23–24, and especially verse 24, strongly affirm the corporate solidarity of the man and the woman in marriage. As they are of the same flesh and bone originally by creation, they now become one flesh in marriage.

The final statement of Genesis 2 could only be read with equanimity by a world fatally desensitized to the nature of sin and to its own condition. We are told simply, "The man and his wife were both naked, and they felt no shame" (Gen. 2:25). Shame in the Bible normally has to do with an appropriate sense of guilt because of sin. Conviction produces shame, and conviction comes by judgments of God. This is clear in the Old Testament when nations are said to bear

---

22. It should be obvious that a different interpretation of *head* (e.g., as "source") in the pericope does nothing to unhinge or cancel the force of verse 24. It is also worth noting that the other uses of the term *head* in Ephesians have the same sense as the use here: the capital part of the anatomy (cf. Eph. 1:22, 4:15). This is not decisive for its meaning in Ephesians 5, but it is the understanding most consistent with the explicit statements of Ephesians 5:22, 24.

their shame as a result of God's judgments on them. So, for example, in the great prose poem oracle against Egypt in Ezekiel 32 (also patterned after the ancient near eastern list form discussed in chapter 1), Elam, and indeed all those who "go down to the pit" (Ezek. 32:24–25) including Assyria (32:22–23), Meshek and Tubal (32:26–27), Edom (32:29), all the princes of the north and the Sidonians (32:30), and Pharaoh and all his army (32:31–32), "bear their shame" as verses 24 and 25 insist, having been brought to nothing by the God who rules over human events. Later, under a more gracious covenant, it is the Holy Spirit who will come to "convict the world of guilt in regard to sin and righteous and judgment" (John 16:8). When the Spirit acts to convict in our age—the church age—he does so in order to produce a salutary shame, a "godly sorrow," meant to bring people to Christ and into a new covenant relationship with God. Conviction and shame in the Old Testament come with divine judgments on a national scale and are features characteristic of the human condition after people have broken God's Special Grace covenant, the Mosaic covenant (in the cases of Israel and Judah), or his Common Grace covenants, the Adamic and the Noahic (as we will discuss later). So in the Old Testament, shame comes from judgment, but in the New Testament, shame is meant to avert judgment by inducing repentance and then faith and the covenantal obedience that comes with faith (cf. Rom. 1:5).

The fact that both the man and the woman are naked is also a wonderful truth. It could not have taken much imagination in Moses's day, nor does it take much imagination in ours, to sense that more than physical nakedness is implied in this simple description. If physical nakedness entails shame in a fallen world, it is because one's proper sense of self as a sinless being before God has been taken away. Indeed, for all of humanity after the Fall, it has never been there.[23] Only Adam and Eve ever experienced it, and for how long we do not know. Without sin there is no sense of inadequacy or insecurity, because one's security is God, and with him one is adequate for anything he might require or command. Adam and Eve were in that state,

---

23. Jesus being the one exception, as the only person after the Fall without sin (cf. 2 Cor. 5:21).

perfectly secure in God and perfectly suited to and adequate for the tasks that God had set them in Genesis 1:28. They were also perfectly suited for each other, and because God is truth and they were made in his untarnished image, they too were truthfully made, made for truth, embodied truth, and could *be* true—thus spiritually, emotionally, and intellectually "naked" with each other—and feel no shame.

ONE FLESH, THE *IMAGO DEI*, AND THE TRINITY

Whatever we have understood about the *imago Dei* from the first two chapters of Genesis, many questions remain unanswered because of the laconic nature of the early biblical data. One aspect of the *imago* that deserves further attention in Genesis 1, however, has little to do with the verses that actually talk about humans and more to do with data concerning God. The first datum comes in Genesis 1:1, where we are told, "In the beginning, God created the heavens and the earth." Here we have the grammatical anomaly of a plural noun form, *Elohim* (a masculine plural in Hebrew), matched with a singular verb *created* (third-person masculine singular in Hebrew). The verb (ברא), as scholars have noted, is used only of divine activity in the Old Testament. But how can a plural noun be the subject of a singular verb? Some suggest that the plural, which functions syntactically as a singular, should be understood without any plural implications (as in such usage throughout the Old Testament it seems to have been). One explanation offered is to take it as an intensive plural and, in effect, a singular that emphasizes God's power (the root apparently means "to be strong"), and this is the usual explanation. A similar approach understands the noun as a plural of *majesty*, a rare but attested OT phenomenon.[24] Both solutions are attractive, and both aspects are possible. Another possibility, however, is that the plural implies the Trinity. If that is correct, we would have another case of a laconic statement early in the Bible: The God who is both a plurality and a unity has created the cosmos. From a NT perspective (in particular, Matt. 28:19, "Therefore go and make disciples of all nations, baptizing them in the name of the Father and of the Son and

---

24. Cf. Driver, *The Book of Genesis*, 14.

of the Holy Spirit," that is, one *name*—one essential nature—and three persons), and even from data in the Old Testament (e.g., Isa. 9:5), a trinitarian perspective is possible. The objection that such an interpretation is eisegetical or unscientific is, in fact, no objection for anyone who believes in one God-breathed Scripture and in the possibility of doing biblical theology on that basis. The Bible is one God-breathed work, organically whole and alive (cf. Heb. 4:12) because its words are, in fact, Spirit (analogous to Jesus's words; cf. John 6:63).

Further evidence exists for a trinitarian perspective in Genesis 1. The plural used in Genesis 1:26, "Let us make man in our image," seems to imply the same, especially as it is followed by a fulfillment in the singular "So God created man in his own image" in the next verse. If "our image" and "his image" are parallel (not poetically parallel, since Genesis 1:26 is not poetry, but parallel in their roles in the respective verses), an equivalence of the plurality of the former and the unity of the latter is more or less explicit given the nature of parallelistic thought in Hebrew. A different interpretation suggests that the "our" of verse 26 refers to the divine council, so that humans are created in the image of God and angels. This perspective may find some support in the LXX translation of *Elohim* as "angels" in Psalm 8:5 (cf. NIV, "heavenly beings"), which is picked up in Hebrews 2:7. This interpretation for Genesis 1:26 is not as farfetched as may first appear, since angels routinely appear in *human form* in the Bible, and even the cherubim of Ezekiel's experience are basically human in form, despite the addition of wings and, of course, the outlandish four-facedness of the "living creatures" (Ezek. 1:4–9, 10:1; cf. Rev. 4:6–8).[25]

Given the laconic nature of the verses in question and the suggestiveness (and yet inconclusiveness) of the later biblical data, it seems wise to allow for both possibilities: Elohim in Genesis 1 generally may allude to the Trinity, and in Genesis 1:26 in particular it may also include "heavenly beings" other than God—that is, angels. One need not insist on an either/or approach. In fact, such an approach

---

25. The inclusion of angels in the "Let us make" part of Genesis 1:26 is still difficult, however, because there is no evidence that angels actually participated in the creation of human beings in God's image. One may imagine a triune God addressing angels ("Let us make") but reserving the actually "making" to himself.

can sometimes be counterproductive, since it can vitiate some passages of an ambivalence that is full of meaning and fruitful.

If we then proceed on the assumption that the Trinity is implied in uses of Elohim in Genesis 1, what does that further imply about humans and the *imago Dei*? First, we ought to admit that any suggestions about a trinitarian or multiple aspect to an individual *imago*—that is, a person—has no apparent foundation in the Bible. Moreover, certain kinds of experiential data are not revelatory. For instance, the bizarre fact that traumatized humans sometimes manifest multiple personality disorder has no implications for or parallelism to the Trinity, for the Trinity is not the result of trauma. If there is any parallel to be found, it could be in the fact that two persons, the man and the woman, can become one flesh, with all the unity and mutuality that such a condition implies. Some scholars have seen an implicit parallel because of this fact. However, such a direct parallel should probably be held tentatively, because the one parallel the Bible actually draws to the man and the woman in marriage is not the Trinity but the relationship between Christ and the church (Eph. 5:23–33), a comparison that does, as noted, explicitly reference Genesis 2:24 as a foundational part of its argument (Eph. 5:31). Accordingly, Genesis 2:24 and the "one flesh" relationship between husband and wife do not allude directly to the Trinity but, rather, foreshadow the relationship between Christ and the church.

Having said as much, it is nonetheless incumbent on us to recognize that as humans are explicitly made in the image of God, so marriage and the possibility of human relationships in general are also implicitly grounded in the relational aspect of the Trinity. That is to say, because the Father, Son, and Holy Spirit do always relate to one another as distinct persons of one substance within the Godhead, so a man and a woman can relate to one another as of the same substance ("one flesh"), and paramountly, humans in any relationship can relate to one another as distinct persons who share the same Spirit. Although these wonderful truths are not at all apparent in the early chapters of Genesis, they are indicated clearly enough by Jesus's so-called high priestly prayer in John 17, for example, when Jesus asks his Father for the benefit of his followers, "that they may be one as we are one" (John 17:11)—a prayer that anticipates the doctrine

of the one body, the church, made up of many members but uni-
fied by the one Spirit (cf. 1 Cor. 12:13). More broadly speaking, one
may even suggest that human society of any sort, even fallen and
without the Spirit indwelling, is grounded in the relational nature
of the Trinity, without whom human relationships and even human
existence would not be possible.[26] Ultimately, of course, all things are
grounded in God and, in some way or other, partake of his nature.
So C. S. Lewis was right when he wrote of God's presence, "only by
being like this had anything existed."[27]

Tragically, the simple and sinless nakedness we encounter in
Genesis 2:25 and all that it implies—a lack of guilt and a corresponding lack of self-centered inhibitions and fears—gave way to a very
different sort of life. The narrative has prepared us for the unhappy
transition to that fallen state of affairs—ironically by using the word
naked (ערום), which is identical in form to a key word in the verse
that follows: "Now the serpent was more *crafty* (ערום) than any of the
wild animals the Lord God had made" (Gen. 3:1).

---

26. Cf. Niehaus, "Covenant: An Idea," 228–29.
27. C. S. Lewis, *That Hideous Strength* (New York: Macmillan, 1965), 318.

CHAPTER THREE

THE CREATION COVENANT IS THREATENED

THE ELEMENTS OF GENESIS 3

There is no warfare without a foe, and until now in the Genesis narrative there has been no foe. But the third chapter of Genesis contains a major threat to the man and the woman, and thus also to the Creation covenant. The foe is introduced promptly, and the scene is set immediately for a contest that has many implications. This chapter contains the serpent's challenge, the resultant human failure and disobedience, and the many consequences of their act, including relational implications for humans and God as well as suzerain–vassal implications for humanity and Satan.

As we consider these major topics, we again discover that the narrative is laconic in nature and thus open-ended to some extent. Such cases naturally leave room for speculation, and the only control available is later commentary on unclear passages by relevant subsequent revelation. We will draw on such revelation as it seems economical and appropriate to do so, knowing we can also return to any topic again when the subsequent revelatory data are taken up and studied in their own right.

THE CLEVER SERPENT AND HIS CLEVER WAYS

Some facts are important to grasp if we are to understand the nature of the serpent's attack. The first thing we read about the serpent is that he was "more crafty than any of the wild animals the Lord God had made" (Gen. 3:1). As we noted, the word *crafty* is a Hebrew homonym of the word *naked* at the end of chapter 2. The author apparently uses this homonym and its wordplay purposefully: It is precisely the sinless quality of physical and spiritual nakedness without shame that is about to be lost as a result of the serpent's craftiness. The serpent is also later identified as "that ancient serpent called the devil, or Satan, who leads the whole world astray" (Rev. 12:9). He leads astray by means of lies, and he is in fact the "father of lies" (John 8:44). He trades in sin, which is deceptive (Heb. 3:13). Moreover, whatever is not of faith is sin (Rom. 14:23). These facts are germane to the narrative and essential to understanding it.

The serpent's attack is not only on the man, the woman, and their happy estate. The serpent also attacks the word of God. We recall that faith is the act of "amening" what God has said and/or done—whatever he has revealed about himself and his ways. That amening means not only acknowledging intellectually, but also—and even more—embracing and making one's own or *owning* what God has revealed, with the result that one "walks" by it (i.e., lives by it), to use a biblical idiom. So we are told that "Man does not live on bread alone, but on every word that comes from the mouth of God" (Deut. 8:3, Matt. 4:4). This quote, from Jesus's response to Satan's first temptation, is significant as we consider Genesis 3 because it is precisely the second Adam (1 Cor. 15:45–47) who refutes "that ancient serpent . . . the devil," a rejection the first Adam failed to accomplish. Moreover, he rebuffs Satan on the basis of God's word—the very thing that the serpent attacked when he tempted the woman.

The serpent's challenge is, at its root, a challenge not only to God's vassals but also to God's word, and if that word is truth (John 17:17), then the challenge is a lie. The foe would subvert truth itself: He portrays what is true as though it were false, and what is false as though it were true—and that is the nature of the "deceptiveness of sin." The serpent starts with an apparently harmless question, "Did

God really say, 'You must not eat from any tree in the garden'?" (Gen. 3:1). The question seems innocent, but it is barbed. The emphatic "Did God *really* say" (אַף כִּי אָמַר) lays the groundwork for further questioning of God's word. The serpent next misquotes God: "You must not eat from *any* tree in the garden?" The word translated "any" (כֹּל), and in fact the whole phrase "from any tree in the garden," is identical to what God had told the man before: "You may eat from any (כֹּל) tree in the garden" (Gen. 2:16). The only difference is that the serpent has turned God's permission on its head, making it a negative command—"You may *not* eat from any tree in the garden." The reversal softens the ground for his further suggestion that God does not have human interests at heart, since it already suggests that God has denied some good things to the humans—the fruit of *any* tree in the garden. The fact that the woman knows the serpent's statement is not true does not matter; a seed has been planted.

The woman responds quite accurately that she and her husband may indeed eat from the trees in the garden (Gen. 2:2), but she also says more, and some have seen her next statement as a false addition to what God said. She repeats God's original command about the tree in the middle of the garden (Gen. 2:3a) but then adds, "and you must not touch it" (Gen. 2:3b). It would be a mistake, however, to see this as an unwarranted addition.[1] Such an addition—that is, additional words that she attributes to God even though he did not say them—would be an act of *sin* on her part: It would be a misrepresentation of what God actually said, in other words, a lie. Nothing in the narrative or any later biblical revelation suggests this is the case. Her addition, therefore, is better understood as a consequence of the (again, laconic) nature of the foregoing narrative. In other words, the prior material in Genesis 2 does not tell us that God prohibited even touching the forbidden tree, yet apparently he did, because we now have that information from the woman, who is not yet in a state of sin and who does not report untrue things about God. Her statement simply supplies data not given in the earlier account.

---

1. As do, for example, Geerhardus Vos, *Biblical Theology: Old and New Testaments* (Grand Rapids: Eerdmans, 1948), 35; Gordon Wenham, *Genesis 1–15*, WBC 1 (Waco, TX: Word, 1987): 75; Kline, *Kingdom Prologue*, 124.

The serpent's next statement reveals his nature and intent without further delay: "You will not surely die" (Gen. 3:4). There is no way to know how long the conversation between the serpent and the woman took place. C. S. Lewis, with perhaps a stroke of sanctified imagination, portrayed the Venusian Eve involved in a days-long conversation with Satan in human form, a prolonged conversational assault by which the foe gradually wore her down almost to the point of agreeing with his false portrayal of things, thus sinning against her God.[2] We cannot know whether the serpent spent days, hours, or only minutes in his deception of the woman in Genesis 3, and here again the laconic nature of the narrative is the reason. He is portrayed as setting to work quickly, and his opening salvo is a direct refutation of God's word and with it the veracity of God himself. If he said nothing more, he would be confronting the woman with a bald choice: Believe him or believe God. Because he was crafty in his assault on her spiritual nakedness, he did not stop there.

"YOU WILL BE LIKE ELOHIM"

The serpent's temptation now comes to the fore. He tells the woman, "On the day you eat (אכלכם) of it your eyes will be opened, and you will be (והייתם) like God, knowing [lit., 'knowers of'—that is, 'those who know'] good and evil" (ידעי טוב ורע, Gen. 3:5). The serpent's address to the woman uses plural forms (as he did in vs. 4, "you shall not surely die"), which raises some interesting questions. By using the second person plural address, the serpent enhances the attractiveness of his temptation by (implicitly) including the woman's husband: She need not and would not be alone in defying God for such knowledge. By the same token, he shows he has in mind the subversion of both the woman and her husband as he implies that both should partake of the forbidden fruit.[3] A second significant issue in this verse is the serpent's use of the term *elohim*, typically translated

---

2. C. S. Lewis, *Perelandra* (New York: Macmillan, 1944), 125–50.

3. The fact that the woman reports God's command and warning in the plural ("we may eat," vs. 2; "You shall not eat of it, neither shall you touch it, lest you die," vs. 3) does not change the implications noted above.

"God" here. Although ancient and modern translators have rendered it "God," it may be that *elohim*, in this case, does include angels, as discussed earlier with regard to Genesis 1:26. The reason is that the referent for the participle, "knowers," is ambiguous: The participle is masculine plural and could thus refer either to *elohim* or to the man and woman. If it refers to *elohim* as a plural, the meaning would be something like "heavenly beings" (cf. Ps. 8:5, אלהים [MT], αγγελους [LXX], hence "heavenly beings," NIV).[4] So the man and the woman could become like the "heavenly beings, [who are] knowers of good and evil." Or if, as is typically thought, the referent is the first couple in Eden, the promise then is that the man and the woman could become "knowers of good and evil" like God. The moral nature of holy angels and their ability to discern between good and evil will be discussed later. For now, it is enough to affirm that they do indeed "know" the difference between "good and evil," and they regularly reject what is evil and choose what is good.

THE FALL

The fall of humankind is narrated in one brief verse: "When the woman saw that the fruit of the tree was good for food and pleasing to the eye, and also desirable for gaining wisdom, she took some and ate it. She also gave some to her husband, who was with her, and he ate it" (vs. 6). These two sentences contain more information and more ambiguity.

The first sentence presents a sequence important for our under-standing of sin and human nature. First we are told that the woman "saw"; then that she saw the tree was "good"; finally, we are told that she "took." Her road to sin thus begins with seeing. The very first human sin begins with what John would later call "the lust of the

---

4. We note that *elohim*, by itself, is not normally used for angels in the Old Testament (when it is used, it typically appears in the phrase, "sons of God," for example, Job 1:6, 2:1, 38:7, and Genesis 6:2 [to be discussed later]). In one case, however, *elohim* alone is used for angels, although translations obscure it: "There he built an altar, and he called the place El Bethel, because it was there that God revealed himself (נגלו אליו האלהים, lit., "the *elohim* [i.e., 'angels/heavenly beings'] revealed *themselves*") to him when he was fleeing from his brother" (NIV, Gen. 35:7, referring to Gen. 28:12).

eyes" (1 John 2:16). Moreover, what the woman sees with her eyes is good—that is, attractive because it had good in itself and could confer some good on the one who ate it. These are true facts, nonetheless so because God has forbidden their eating of it. The evil lay not in the object but in the disobedience that moved the woman, and then the man, to take the object. Moreover, what is forbidden may seem to confer some good, but only in a warped manner. There is pleasure in sin for a season, but the pleasure comes from an abuse of human capabilities—that is, a use God never intended. The woman has embarked on a course that leads to disobedience, first by eyeing the forbidden object, then by allowing/indulging thoughts of its desirability, and finally by taking and consuming it. As though to underscore the sinfulness of her progress, a later account has manifestly evil agents following the same pattern of behavior. In Genesis 6, the sons of God "saw" that the daughters of men were "beautiful" (lit., "good," the same Hebrew adjective as in Gen. 3:6), and they "married" (lit., "took," the same verb as in Gen. 3:6) any of them they wanted. We will discuss later who the "sons of God" may have been, although we may say now that the body of evidence suggests they were fallen angels. Whoever they may have been, though, their behavior is presented in the context of a sinful world about to be judged, and it is presented as inordinate even in that context. So we may conclude, not that it is sinful in the absolute to "see" that something is *"good"* and "take" it, but that, in the two proximate cases in which those terms are used in that sequence, they portray a sinful act, so that the one reinforces the other for any reader who is familiar with both.[5]

The second sentence of the verse in question presents another ambiguity: "She also gave some to her husband, who was with her, and he ate it" (vs. 6). The English poet, John Milton, who sought to "justify the ways of God to men" in his great epic poem, portrayed the serpent as one who craftily waited until Eve was alone before attempting a seduction. Many scholars have held such a view, conjecturing that the serpent, being a crafty tactician, would seek to

---

5. The same sequence occurs in the sin of Achan when he violates God's ban against taking any plunder from captured Jericho (cf. discussion later). The sequence seems to be paradigmatic of the lust of the eyes leading to a sinful "taking."

subvert humanity by going after its weaker member—that is, avoiding Adam and seeking out Eve. Whatever the merits of such a view, and whatever NT texts may say or imply about it, it is difficult to reach such a conclusion on the basis of the data in Genesis 3. The narrative says she gave some to her husband, "who was with her" (NIV). That translation, however, is not as definitive as one may think. The Hebrew simply says "to her husband with her." The Hebrew phrase *with her* may indicate immediate presence but need not, for later on in the same chapter Adam refers to Eve as "the woman you put here with me" (Gen. 3:12), which refers back to God's creation of the woman as a help meet for the man.[6] The Hebrew reads literally, "the woman whom you gave/put with me." It does not take much imagination to realize that for God to "put" or "give" the woman to be with the man in the garden does not ipso facto mean that she was with him *every minute*. So this latter use of the phrase *with me* makes it clear enough that the phrase can be used in different senses. The same is true in English. It is true that the man was "with" the woman, as we read in Genesis 3:6. But that could mean that he was with her at the very moment of her temptation and fall; that he was with her afterward, and she gave the fruit to him then; that he was generally with her in the garden but not at the moment of her temptation and fall, and so she gave him the fruit later; or finally, that once he partook of the fruit he had joined her—was *with her*—in sin.

The ambiguity of the statement means that two possibilities should be envisioned. Either the man was with the woman at the moment of temptation or he was not. If he was, then he was culpable of two things: not intervening to prevent the woman, if possible, from taking the fruit, and not resisting or dealing with the serpent

---

6. The preposition used in Genesis 3:6 is עמה, "with her"; the preposition in Genesis 3:12 is עמדי, "with me." The two overlap in meaning, with the possible nuance that the latter, used by the man, is more emphatic—that is, something like "with me as a close companion"—for instance, Luther ("Die Frau, die du mir zugesellt hast") and Jerome ("Mulier, quam dedisti mihi sociam"). It is clear, one would hope, to any fair-minded reader that the prepositions have a range of possible interpretation, as we argue here. Without other qualifying data, we cannot insist on one interpretation in either verse when the prepositions themselves leave open more than one equally possible scenario in both cases.

on his own account. His blame for these two failures is unavoid-able, whether one thinks of him as being in authority over his wife or not. Whether or not he was in authority over her, he had a moral responsibility to try to protect her from the enemy's attack. He was not free to say, as Cain did later, "Am I my brother's (or sister's, or wife's) keeper?" Moreover, one of his two assigned tasks in the gar-den was to *keep*—that is, protect—it. So on any view of male author-ity, the man failed. But what of the other possibility? What if the man was not present when the woman was tempted and fell? One might argue that his absence was tantamount to criminal negligence, since he ought to have been present to protect his wife or to stand with her. But such a view (to which Milton's presentation of the matter has, incidentally, some affinity) is possible only if one assumes that the man and woman already knew that a foe was about, and (*pace* Milton) there is no evidence of that.

So then, if the man was not present when the woman was tempted but rejoined her only to discover that she had transgressed God's command, what should he have done? We could imagine—assuming a highly authoritarian view—that he should have judged her and handed her over to God. Or we could imagine that he would have interceded for her, just as the second Adam has interceded for many. One might even imagine that he would have offered his own life in place of hers in a truly Christological act.[7] Considering these possibilities, one might say it is doubtful the man should have had a role in judging the woman, since we have it as a principle that judg-ment belongs to God. On the other hand, it is also true that God appointed judges for his people later under the Mosaic covenant, and eschatologically humans will judge angels, and the second Adam will judge both humans and angels. The one thing we can affirm is that there is no evidence that the man had a judicial function with respect to the woman. The more likely thing may be that he should have left her judgment to God, whatever else he might have done. In the subsequent narrative, God appears as both prosecutor and judge.

---

7. A sentiment somewhat akin to the expressed wish to God of another covenant media-tor prophet, Moses, in Exodus 32:32 and also to the sentiment of the apostle Paul in Romans 9:1–4a.

Another thing we can affirm, however, is that the man should have been true to his charge to keep the garden. Whatever it would have meant for him to protect the garden from the serpent, he should have done it. The presence of the foe presents the human with an opportunity to wage war. This too, then, appears to be an aspect of the *imago Dei*—the ability to wage war against evil. To be sure, it is a latent quality of the *imago* that would (presumably) never have been called into play had no provocation been present; however, since the foe did appear, the human ought to have warred against him. The proper form of that warfare would have been, initially at least, the rejection of the serpent's assault. The man's "shield of faith" in this case would have been his *amening* of what God had said. He would have quoted the word of God against the foe, just as the second Adam later did when the same foe tempted him. His repudiation of the serpent would have judged the serpent, and that judgment would have had to do with the tree that formed the subject of the enemy's temptation. So Kline has rightly labeled the tree of the knowledge of good and evil a "judgment tree."[8]

Since the first Adam failed to make use of that judgment tree in defeating the foe—that is, since he failed to take the subject of the serpent's temptation (the tree) and turn it against him to defeat him—the second Adam had to accomplish that defeat on a second tree, the cross, which was his "judgment tree." (Interestingly, the first Adam was tempted to *access* the tree, but the second Adam's temptation was to *avoid* the tree [the cross]; cf. Matt. 26:39.) So Peter can say, "He himself bore our sins in his body on the tree, so that we might die to sins and live for righteousness" (1 Pet. 2:24), and Paul can affirm, "Christ redeemed us from the curse of the law by becoming a curse for us, for it is written: 'Cursed is everyone who is hung on a tree'" (Gal. 3:13, quoting Deut. 21:22–23).

---

8. Since God gave the command regarding the tree, it is reasonable to ask why he did so. If, as we believe, the fall of Lucifer took place after the creation of Eden (cf. Ezek. 28:13), it may be reasonable to infer that God intended the tree as probationary—if the man and woman had not failed, they would have had access to more heavenly knowledge—and this has been a long-held view. Cf. Vos, *Biblical Theology*, 31–32.

WHAT MIGHT HAVE BEEN

Suppose the man and the woman had defeated the serpent—what then? One could suggest a scenario on the basis of what the second Adam accomplished, understanding the suggestion is speculative.

The man and woman renounce the serpent and his claims, so all his efforts come to nothing. The consequences and the benefits that accrue to humanity as a result of the second Adam's life, death, and resurrection are thus secured much sooner and without a world of human agony. God himself comes in judgment against "that ancient serpent" and throws him and his angels (wherever they may have been at the time) into the lake of fire. The man and woman can go on to fulfill their mandates in sinless freedom. At some point, perhaps immediately after their successful rejection of the serpent or perhaps much later, they receive the Holy Spirit and become temples of the Spirit, who was with them but now is in them. And sooner or later, God's purposes with the physical earth are fulfilled/consummated, and an eschatological transformation takes place in which all of humanity receive glorified bodies and dwell with God in a supernal heavens and earth, of which the original heavens and earth were only copies. Alternatively, just as the humans would be glorified, so would the visible heavens and earth be transformed/glorified so that God's heaven—the archetype of the created cosmos—and the created cosmos would become one, with God being all in all.[9] Such possible scenarios arise out of NT events and eschatology, drawing also on heavenly temple and heavenly Jerusalem typology. They are only scenarios, however, and the truth of human history presents a very different picture, and that picture begins to develop in Genesis 3.

---

9. Cf. Meredith G. Kline, "Space and Time," 3: "Redemption is a way of achieving the original telos of creation despite the Fall. A successful probation by the first Adam would have led through a cosmologically two-register history to an eschatological climax at which Eden's Glory would have been absorbed into the surpassing heavenly Glory. At the dawning of the eternal Sabbath for humanity, all space, without distinction any longer of upper and lower cosmological levels, would have become a consummate revelation of the Glory of heaven's King. Because of the Fall, that eschatological omega-point had to be won by the second Adam."

WHAT ACTUALLY WAS

What actually happened, of course, was very different. God comes now to judge, but not to judge the serpent on the heels of a successful rejection of him by the man and woman. He comes to judge all three, and our first parents are the first to experience God's advent in a frightful way. Kline has brilliantly characterized God's judgment advent as "primal *parousia*"—that is, a first advent of God in judgment that will be paralleled by his second Advent at the end of days. He translates Genesis 3:8 in a way consistent with his understanding: The man and the woman hear the sound of the Lord God walking in the garden "in the Spirit of the Day." That is, God comes in the Spirit of that final day of judgment.[10] Kline's interpretation is theologically informed, but lexical data may lead in another direction. Evidence from Akkadian, the language of ancient Assyria and Babylon, now makes possible a different and, I would argue, better translation: The man and the woman heard the sound of the Lord God walking in the garden "in the wind of the storm." As I have made the case for this translation elsewhere, I will only pursue the implications and consequences of it here.[11]

God now appears in a judgment theophany—the first storm theophany. The *voice* of God that the man and the woman hear is better rendered "thunderous voice" and is the same term (קוֹל) used for the thunders on Mount Sinai (Exod. 19:16, 19; 20:18). The verb *walking* (הלך, Hithp.) means going back and forth, perhaps rapidly, and is also used to refer to lightning flashes (Ps. 77:17, where God's "arrows" are lightning). Finally, "the wind of the storm" completes the picture of a stormy advent. Here again the laconic nature of the narrative plays a role. The account uses terminology that indicates the nature of the event, yet it stops far short of the sort of full-blown description we later encounter of Yahweh's descent on Sinai. This is the nature of early biblical narrative, and Genesis 3:8 is a good example of it.

---

10. Kline, *Kingdom Prologue*, 47.

11. Jeffrey J. Niehaus, "In the Wind of the Storm: Another Look at Genesis iii 8," *VT* 44, no. 2 (April 1994): 263–67; Niehaus, *God at Sinai*, 155–59.

What are the implications of such an advent? We know from the Sinai experience that God concealed himself in a dark cloud (Exod. 20:21; Deut. 4:11; cf. 1 Kings 8:12). Had he not done so, the sinless glory of his presence would have destroyed the Israelites—as they themselves declare (Exod. 20:18–19; Deut. 18:16–17). If Genesis 3 reports such a theophany, we can well understand why the man was afraid (Gen. 3:10), just as Israel would later be afraid. We may also reasonably infer that his sense of nakedness was not only physical: He was a sinner exposed to the presence of a holy God. He was spiritually naked, just as we are. Because all sinful humans are spiritually naked, the man's fearful reaction has become characteristic of all human reaction to God whenever he appears in something of his true glory. Humans fear his advent not because he is powerful but because he is holy. His very presence judges us.

The Lord comes now to judge the man and the woman, and the fact that they hide from his advent already confesses their fallen condition. They have lapsed into sin and cannot endure the holy presence of God's glory without fear. Accordingly, God comes in a storm cloud that hides his glory, so that the sinful couple may endure his presence during his judgment process.

GOD'S JUDICIAL PROCESS

God's stormy entrance into the garden is a judgment advent, and he brings with him a judicial procedure that is the precursor and archetype on earth of the covenant lawsuit form as we find it in both the prophets and the OT historical narratives, as well as in ancient near eastern annals and poetry that deal with divine treatment of rebellious vassals. We will examine that form and its implications later when we turn our attention to Deuteronomy and in particular Deuteronomy 32, which is the first full-blown example of the genre under the Mosaic covenant.[12] We note here, however, that theologians old and new who reckon the Creation or Adamic covenant to cover Genesis 1–3 have

---

12. Cf. G. Ernest Wright, "The Lawsuit of God: A Form-Critical Study of Deuteronomy 32," in *Israel's Prophetic Heritage*, ed. Bernard W. Anderson and Walter Harrelson (New York: Harper, 1962), 26–67.

misunderstood the nature of Genesis 3. Genesis 3 begins to tell us of the life of the man and woman under the Adamic covenant—after that covenant has come to be—and is not material of the covenant itself, which is reported in Genesis 1:1–2:3, with Genesis 2:4–25 playing the supplemental, "zooming in" role we discussed in chapter 2. Moreover, anything that smacks of covenantal material in Genesis 3 appears there not because Genesis 3 is part of the *covenant itself* but because Genesis 3 enshrines God's first *covenant lawsuit* among people. A covenant lawsuit refers to the original covenant because its indictments are rooted in the stipulations of the covenant, but it is nevertheless separate from the covenant and comes after it—once the vassal has broken the original covenant and the suzerain brings charges against him.[13] The primordial covenant lawsuit in Genesis 3 takes the form of a judicial engagement between God—who is apprehending officer, prosecutor, and judge—and the culpable man and woman.

God enters the garden in storm theophany, and when the man and woman are not in plain sight (although of course they are not hidden from God), he enquires as to their whereabouts, calling specifically for the man (Gen. 3:9). The fact that God calls initially for the man, in the singular, may support the earlier idea that the woman and the man were not always together in the garden; on that understanding, the serpent may have approached the woman when she was alone, although, again, there can be no proof of this, either from the proximate data or, we would submit, from subsequent biblical revelation.[14] Furthermore, it may support the idea that the man was the head of the marriage, and thus the one God first called on to respond (akin to the principle we refer to legally as *respondeat superior*).

---

13. The covenant lawsuit in Deuteronomy 32 is an exception because it is a prophecy: a prediction of the covenant breaking Israel *will do* (but has not yet done) once they have settled in the Promised Land.

14. Although 1 Timothy 2:14 ("Adam was not the one deceived; it was the woman who was deceived and became a sinner") may seem to suggest the woman was alone, it actually does not. The verse simply tells us that the woman was deceived, whereas, apparently, the man was not deceived when he partook of the fruit. If he was with her and yet not deceived, we might agree that he sinned egregiously by not trying to intervene in some way. Of course, he may have been with her and intervened, and the fact was left unreported, but that would be a rather glaring omission even in a laconic style of reporting.

God next inquires whether the man has broken covenant—that is, "Have you eaten from the tree that I commanded you not to eat from?" (Gen. 3:11). Adam shows his fallen nature by shifting the blame to his wife: "The woman you put here with me—she gave me some fruit from the tree, and I ate it" (Gen. 3:12). The implication, as many have noted, is that God somehow is at fault for providing Adam with a woman who would mislead him—as though the man himself lacked the wits or the knowledge required to avoid eating the forbidden fruit. According to the text, God does not respond to the man's implication, but rather questions the woman, who declares, "The serpent deceived me, and I ate" (Gen. 3:13). The verses cited highlight the deceptiveness of sin (mentioned above) in two ways. First, the woman is quite correct in saying the serpent deceived her. The fact that she chose to take the fruit in no way diminishes this truth. For, as we noted, the nature of sin is deception: The enemy makes what is bad look good, for he knows that we are made for what is good, and if he can trick us into thinking that what is bad is good, then we will do the rest of his work for him and choose what is bad. Second, the man himself now shows his sinful nature by practicing deception, or by trying to. He shifts the blame not merely to the woman but to God himself, almost as though the man were quite ignorant of the nature of the fruit, and thus imposed upon by a faulty woman who was given to him by her Creator, as though God could make a faulty human—he who, when he summarily considered all he had made, including the humans, declared it to be "very good" (Gen. 1:31).

There is a bigger picture to be considered here, and that is the formal nature of the judicial enquiry we have been considering. It is worth examination as God's primordial covenant lawsuit with humans. (We cannot speak of his prior judicial dealings with Satan, whatever form they may have taken as a result of the latter's rebellion, since those judicial dealings have not been revealed).[15]

---

15. Although Jesus declared, "I saw Satan fall like lightning from heaven" (Luke 10:18), it would seem that what he saw must have happened, at the very earliest, after the scene we are given in Job 1–2, where Satan is among the "sons of God" challenging God about Job. Jesus's statement is probably proleptic, a revelation of what happens to Satan once the Son has accomplished his work on earth and has ascended to heaven (cf. Rev. 12:9).

Moreover, it can be compared with the one other public judicial enquiry made by God in the Bible: the judicial process involving Achan in Joshua 7. Remarkably, Achan confesses to the same process of being led into sin that the woman has experienced. We recall that she *saw* that the fruit was *good* and also *desirable*, so she *took* it. Achan later must confess the same: He *saw* the forbidden objects of Jericho, including a *beautiful* (lit., "good," as noted earlier) Babylonian robe, he *coveted* them, and he *took* them (Josh. 7:21). The terms exactly parallel the woman's experience: the verb *see* (ראה; Gen. 3:6, Josh. 7:21), the term *good* (טוב; Gen. 3:6, Josh. 7:21), the term *desirable* (נהמד; Gen. 3:6; the verb from the same root in Josh. 7:21 is translated "coveted/desired"), and the final, fatal verb *took* (לקח; Gen. 3:6, Josh. 7:21). In each case, the lesson to be learned is the same: The "lust of the eyes" can lead us to take what is not right for us to take— with disastrous consequences.[16] The parallelism of the sinful progress of, first, the woman and, later, Achan is met by parallel judicial processes initiated by God in both cases, as the following simple chart illustrates:

Theme	Genesis 3	Joshua 7
God / God's agent apprehends the guilty	3:8–10	7:13–18
God / God's agent interrogates the guilty	3:11	7:19
The guilty confess(es)	3:12–13	7:20–21
God / God's agent pronounces judgment	3:14–19	7:24–26

Here we have two microcosmic examples of what most likely will be God's eschatological judicial process when he returns to judge the world. Appropriately, the second Adam will conduct that process to its conclusion—one that will cleanse the cosmos of sin. That cosmic judgment is indicated by Isaiah 24, which we study in greater depth later. There we read, "In that day the Lord will punish / the powers in the heavens above / and the kings on the earth below" (Isa. 24:21). The cosmic judgment and cleansing will result in a new and sinless

---

16. One may wonder, then, at the virtual eruption of visual media in our culture and increasingly in the world—at the content of the same and its implications for the spiritual good and future of humanity.

humanity dwelling in a new heavens and earth (Isa. 65:17, 66:22; Rev. 21:1). The result for humans will be that they can stand before and endure the unmitigated holy presence of God: "For Yahweh of hosts will reign / on Mount Zion and in Jerusalem / and before its [or "his"] elders: Glory" (Isa. 24:23, author's translation). God will no longer need to conceal himself in "dark cloud," as he did, for example, at Sinai, so that his people could endure his holy presence. Now his glory can be fully manifest before his people, because sin has been done away with. God can once again dwell among his people, and they can dwell with him without fear, reflecting his glory and shining like the sun in his presence (Matt. 13:43). Thus *Endzeit* parallels *Urzeit*—Eden is, in effect, restored, lost by the first Adam but regained by the second. Much must happen before that happy event, however, and the Bible is the record of foundational parts of that history. But now, before us, are God's judgments on those who have rebelled against him.

DUST, PAIN, AND SWEAT

Yahweh God now pronounces judgment on the three who have disobeyed him. He hands down three judgments, and they apply to the ones who have disobeyed in the order of their disobedience. Each judgment presents, in effect, a reversal or a subversion of the condition of the accused. God as judge turns the tables on—or rather, in some sense, overthrows—those who sought to overthrow his truth. His judgments are in accord with a basic premise or principle of divine judgment, perhaps best stated in Isaiah 2, a poem that seems to be eschatological in most of its aspects: "The Lord Almighty has a day in store / for all the proud and lofty, / for all that is exalted (and they will be humbled)" (Isa. 2:12; cf. vss. 11, 17). God's judgment will come down on all that exalt themselves against him—that is, against all who would "be like *Elohim*." He will humble them, bring them down, so that "the Lord alone will be exalted in that day" (Isa. 2:11). God will not give his glory to another (Isa. 42:8), and on that basis he proceeds now in judgment against the serpent, the woman, and the man.

THE SERPENT

God starts with the serpent, and his judgment has more than one aspect. First, he pronounces the serpent *more* accursed than any livestock or wild animal (Gen. 3:14). This is a remarkable statement, since it indicates that the creatures God created are now also under a curse. (We understand from later revelation that all creation is under a curse because of what the man and the woman, king and queen over creation, have done.) After that general statement of the serpent's cursed condition, God makes clear the details of that condition. The serpent will crawl on its belly and eat dust. This seems to imply that it was not always so, and Milton assumed the same, portraying the serpent as a gorgeous convoluted reptile able to stand on its tail and speak face to face with the woman. Whatever its original condition, the serpent is now made the lowest of the low, so to speak, with the further result that humans will tread on it. That is one way to understand the result of the enmity that God puts between the woman and the serpent and between the offspring of the serpent and the offspring of the woman (Gen. 3:15). As often happens in OT typology, however, what is said of men or humans in general may later be epitomized in the second Adam. So, for example, man generically is regarded as little lower than *elohim* in Psalm 8:5, but the same verse is later applied specifically to the one man, Christ, who was made "for a little while lower than angels" (Heb. 2:7, 9).[17] So here, God pronounces what has long been understood to be the first statement of the Gospel, or the *protevangelium*: "He will crush your head, / and you will strike his heel" (Gen. 3:15b). Although there appear to be two different verbs in this English translation, the verb is the same in both cases. Consequently, we may understand that, just as the serpent's strike is fatal, so too the strike administered to the serpent's head is fatal. As the author of Hebrews says, "Since the children have flesh and blood, he too shared in their humanity so that by his death he might destroy him who has the power of death—that is, the devil" (Heb. 2:14).

---

17. Such Christology, and Christology under the Mosaic covenant generally, will be taken up in volume 2 of this work, where the Mosaic covenant comes under consideration with the other Special Grace covenants.

At this point, we digress briefly and discuss the consequences of the serpent's success with our first parents. The reason for doing so will soon become apparent. As we recall, the woman and then the man transgressed the one negative stipulation of their covenant with God. But their act was not simply an act of disobedience; it had legal consequences beyond the consequence of covenantal judgment (they would surely die) that must come into play. By choosing to obey the word of the serpent rather than the word of God—by accepting the serpent's torah—they, in effect, submitted themselves to a new suzerain. Of course, God remained and remains suzerain over all, and, as Abraham would later say, the "Judge of all the earth" (Gen. 18:25). But the humans chose to follow another leader, and, by doing so, gave him and his angels legal entrée into the world. That is why, much later, Paul can refer to the devil as "the god of this world" (2 Cor. 4:4). He is so and will remain so until the second Adam returns to judge him and end his suzerainty over earth.

Psalm 110 portrays that triumph in brief, with terminology evocative of Genesis 3:15:

> He will judge the nations,
> heaping up the dead
> and crushing the rulers of
> the whole earth. (Ps. 110: 6)

The New International Version does us a disservice by this translation, however, because the final line actually reads, "He will crush the head (sing., ראשׁ, as in Gen. 3:15) *over* great earth" (על־ארץ רבה). Now the *head* over "great earth" is Satan, the god of this world, and the Messiah will indeed "crush his head," according to Psalm 110:6 and Genesis 3:15.[18] So we see that the curse pronounced on the serpent in

---

18. The Hebrew verb in Psalm 110:6 translated "crush" (מחץ) is different from the word in Genesis 3:15 for "strike" (שׁוף). Such a variation is normal in the use of stock or allusive phraseology in the ancient Near East and makes no significant difference here. Cf. the similar, "You crushed the leader of the land of wickedness," lit., "You crushed the head of the household of wickedness" (ראשׁ מחצת מבית רשׁע, Hab. 3:13b), said of the Lord's

Genesis 3 implies and anticipates biblical eschatology even as that eschatology is articulated later within the Old Testament.

We noted that God's first pronouncement on the serpent was that he would be more cursed than any other animal. God's second pronouncement against the serpent was that the woman's offspring would strike his head. It turns out that God's statements against the woman and man are also two-part pronouncements, and all these "pronouncements" are judgments. The first judgment in each case has to do in some way with a major aspect of the defendant's life or milieu—or, as we will say, field of endeavor. We put it so generally in order to accommodate the statements in a parallelism that really does exist and that we can demonstrate with a schema. The second part of each judgment seems to home in more specifically on the issue of authority, and in each case, the authority the individual had, or pretended to have, is overturned. It should be noted before we go on that the specific term *curse* is applied only to the serpent (Gen. 3:14) and to the ground (Gen. 3:17). God does not say that the woman or man is cursed. We discuss the significance of this later.

In the serpent's case, the first judgment is that he will be made lower than all the domesticated and wild animals (Gen. 3:14). The judgment applies to his future in the field, but it also contains a special irony: The serpent was more crafty than the wild animals (Gen. 3:1), but now he is made more accursed than they are. The second judgment places him beneath the feet of humans, with all that this implies messianically as we have noted. The second judgment thus symbolically reverses the suzerainty over humans at which the serpent aimed and did indeed achieve; that suzerainty continues to this day and will only end when the offspring of the woman, Christ, returns to end it—at which time the symbolic reversal will be fully realized and final. Of course, those who put their faith in the Messiah already experience a significant foretaste of that reversal in their own lives.

---

triumph over his foe, which he accomplished "to deliver your people, to save your anointed one" (lit., "your messiah," מְשִׁיחֶךָ, Hab. 3:13a).

THE WOMAN

The two judgments on the woman seem to follow a parallel pattern. The first addresses her experience of pregnancy and childbirth, and these are surely a significant part of her life and would have been even if the Fall had never occurred. That is, the woman uniquely would have had a major role in fulfilling the first mandate given by God: "Be fruitful and multiply" (Gen. 1:28). Of course, both the man and the woman would have been involved in that project, but it was the woman who would have to carry the child to term. She will still now fulfill that mandate, but with pain and suffering.

The second judgment has more specifically to do with authority. In order to understand this better, we look ahead to verse 17. In that verse, God says to the man, "Because you listened to your wife and ate from the tree about which I commanded you, 'You must not eat of it.'" An important Hebrew idiom is glossed over by this translation. A better translation than "listened to the voice of" would be "paid heed to the voice of" (the Hebrew idiom is שמע לקול). This is a very significant difference, because the Hebrew idiom employed here is also employed later in God's covenantal dealings with Israel, who are to "pay heed to" Moses's "voice"—that is, obey him. It first appears when God tells Moses that the elders of Israel will accept his prophetic authority once he has told them of the mission God has given him (Exod. 3:18).[19] An implication of the idiom employed here, one that would not be missed by a Hebrew reader, is that the man treated the woman as though she were in authority over him, or at least as one with an authoritative word for him, by accepting the fruit from her. The idiom makes it clear that her voice was involved—that is, that she *said* something to him about eating the fruit—since God says his eating of it was subsequent to his "paying heed to her voice." He therefore, in effect, received *torah*, or instruction, from her

---

19. God tells Moses, "The elders of Israel will listen to you (lit., "pay heed to your voice" [שמע לקול]). Then you and the elders are to go to the king of Egypt," and so on (Exod. 3:18). But Moses then complains, "What if they do not believe me or listen to me?" (שמע בקול, Exod. 4:1). In both cases the parallel idioms mean that the elders will (or will not) follow Moses's leadership or, to put it another way, accept his prophetic authority and go along with what he says God wants them to do. Cf. *BDB*, 1034.

as to the fruit—possibly as to its desirability or its now (by her) experienced knowledge-enhancing effects.[20] In any case, it appears that the man knew what he was doing and chose to sin. This conclusion is suggested by the fact that there is no statement to the effect that his wife deceived him (as contrasted with the woman's statement that the serpent deceived her; cf. later 1 Tim. 2:14). He had received torah/instruction from God about this fruit, but he chose to "pay heed to" his wife's voice/torah rather than to God's.

The point at issue is the authority structure implied by the idiom, which states that the man "paid heed to the voice of"—that is, recognized as authoritative for himself—the words of his wife, just as later the elders of Israel would "pay heed to" or recognize the prophetic authority of Moses's message for them. Now by contrast, God's pronouncement puts the man in authority over the woman: "He will rule over you" (מָשַׁל; Gen. 3:16, the same verb used at Gen. 1:28 for human rule over the creatures and at Gen. 4:7 for Cain's obligation to rule over [NIV "master"] sin). The verb used seems to imply nothing other than *rule*. The quality of the rule in this case, however, is suggested by the statement that prefaces it: "Your desire will be for your husband, but he will rule over you" (Gen. 3:16). NIV translates "*and* he will rule," but the conjunction may (and, in this case, we suggest should) be translated as adversative, because a contrast is in effect: The woman will desire her husband, *but* he will rule over her. The term for *desire* (תְּשׁוּקָה) used here is only used on two other occasions in the Bible: It characterizes sin's desire for Cain (Gen. 4:7) and the lover's desire for his beloved (Song of Sol. 7:10). In the case of Cain, the same adversative structure appears: "[Sin] desires to have you [lit., '*its* desire is for you'; cf. 3:16, '*your* desire will be for your husband'], *but* you must master it [lit., '*but* you must rule over it']." The term translated *desire* seems to imply a longing for intimacy. So the irony is that the woman will long for intimacy with

20. It is worth noting that this statement by God, as evidence of the laconic nature of the earlier report of the same event (which did *not* report the woman's saying anything when she gave the fruit to Adam), is consistent with what we have said of her account of God's injunction—not adding to what God said but supplying further information about what God said that was *not* reported earlier.

her husband, which would include being understood and loved on the deepest levels, but instead of providing that, the man will rule over her. "Lord it over" might better capture the sense. God's pronouncement at this juncture, incidentally, fits the pattern that would emerge under the Mosaic covenant and that Hillers has aptly termed *futility curses*, in which the desire or effort of the person who has broken covenant is subjected to futility—to an impossibility of being fulfilled.[21] The principle is clearly stated early in the body of curses in Deuteronomy 28: "The Lord will send on you curses, confusion and rebuke in everything you put your hand to, until you are destroyed and come to sudden ruin because of the evil you have done in forsaking him . . . You will be unsuccessful in everything you do; day after day you will be oppressed and robbed, with no one to rescue you" (Deut. 28:20, 29). Specific examples in Deuteronomy illustrate the futility genre; for example, "You will be pledged to be married to a woman, but another will take her and ravish her. You will build a house, but you will not live in it. You will plant a vineyard, but you will not even begin to enjoy its fruit" (Deut. 28:30). Against such exemplars, the genre of Genesis 3:16b becomes clear: "Your desire will be for your husband, but he will lord it over you."[22] We noted earlier that God does not curse the woman and man as he does the serpent and the ground. We will address this difference later, but suffice it for now to note that there is a difference between being cursed forever, as the serpent is, and having covenant curses descend on one with a hope of restoration, which is the case for the woman and the

---

21. Delbert R. Hillers, *Treaty Curses and the Old Testament Prophets* (Rome: Pontifical Biblical Institute, 1964), 78–79; cf. D. Stuart, "Curse," in *Anchor Bible Dictionary*, vol. 1: 1218–19.

22. We noted that the verb translated "lord it over" or "rule" in Genesis 3:16 is Hebrew מׁשל, a verb commonly used for royal rule; the same verb is used in Genesis 1:16.18 for the greater and lesser lights that are made to rule over day and night. So it is not a concept that appears only in a fallen world. A different verb (Hebrew רדה) is employed in Genesis 1:26.28 and is also translated as "rule." This verb is also used of royal rule, for example, of Solomon's rule (1 Kings 4:24 [Heb., 1 Kings 5:4]). The verbs seem to overlap in meaning. Clearly, both are used not only after but also before the Fall. This would suggest that neither of them intrinsically contains a nuance of arbitrary, authoritarian, or ungodly rule. Any nuance of that sort must be inferred—when it can be legitimately inferred—from the context in which the verb functions.

man (and their domain, the land, or even more broadly, the created order; cf. Rom. 8:21, which anticipates the day when "the creation itself will be liberated from its bondage to decay and brought into the freedom and glory of the children of God").

THE MAN

So far, we have seen a parallelism between the judgments on the serpent and the woman, and the same parallelism appears with the judgments on the man. The first judgment addresses a major area of his life: his husbandry, which is both an exercise of the cultural mandate given in Genesis 1:28 and, quite simply, a necessary way of providing food for survival. Apparently, then, the woman and the man would (very naturally, in God's arrangement of things) have specialized somewhat in their joint rule over earth and fulfillment of the cultural mandate. Both, of course, would have been involved in being fruitful and multiplying, but naturally the woman would bear the greater burden of that work, as we have noted, since she would have to carry a child to its term. On the other hand, both might do certain kinds of agricultural work, but it would seem that, ultimately and inevitably, a larger share of that labor would fall to the man, especially as the woman advanced in pregnancy. There is nothing wrong with such a natural allocation, and it certainly implies nothing about authority. By God's grace those roles and characteristic callings were allowed and enabled to continue, since the man and the woman did not die on the very day of their sin but were allowed to live, procreate, and carry forth their rule of earth, and God enabled them to do so as he continued (and continues) to sustain all things (cf. Heb. 1:3). The second judgment on the man, however, implies an overthrowing, or perhaps better, a reversal, of his authority over earth. For he will one day degenerate into the dust of earth from which he was taken and formed. In that sense, the dust will have the last say and triumph over the one who emerged from it into a higher state of being.[23]

---

23. The same might be said, in a sense, of the woman, who ends up under the authority of the one from whom she was made. It occurs that another parallel may have existed

SUMMARY OF THE JUDGMENTS

Our analysis has shown a pattern that appears in all of God's judgments in Genesis 3. The pattern includes two types of judgment in each case: one on the individual's field of endeavor, and one on the individual's authority. The pattern may now be displayed with a simple chart:

Judgment	Serpent	Woman	Man
On field of endeavor	3:14	3:16a	3:17b–19a
Reduction of obtained or implied authority	3:15	3:16b	3:19bc

God's approach in each case is to pronounce futility or frustration over the individual in his or her characteristic or major field of endeavor and then to pronounce a reversal, or reduction, of authority for each individual. The latter judgments are consistent with what we see later in the Mosaic covenant (as noted in Deut. 32), in the prophets of that covenant (as we noted from Isa. 2), and also with what Jesus taught about God's way of dealing with pretenders to authority: "Whoever exalts himself will be humbled" (Matt. 23:12a; and cf. the curse on Capernaum, Matt. 11:23).

THE SECOND NAMING

God's judgments are followed by a very significant event touched on earlier: Adam names his wife, Eve. His act may indicate the restoration of his own role from Genesis 2:19—the one who would name the living creatures—and thus may be a subtle hint at his own redemption. Although Adam's naming of Eve is consistent with other acts of naming in the Old Testament, there are two things that draw special attention to this event. The first is that Adam's naming of Eve is juxtaposed with his own name and God's wordplay associated with it in Genesis 3:17–19: Whereas Adam's name is associated with

---

before the Fall: As the earth sustains or provides a foundation for the man who was formed from it, so the man was meant to sustain or provide a foundation for the woman who was formed from him. In both cases, the provided foundation would contribute to blossoming and fruitfulness.

death ("until you return to the ground [אדמה], since from it you were taken," Gen. 3:19), Eve's name is associated with life ("Adam named his wife Eve, because she would become the mother of all the living," Gen. 3:20). Second, the woman now has in effect two names: Her first name, "woman" (Gen. 2:23), underscored the woman's relationship with the man ("bone of my bones and flesh of my flesh"); her second name underscores her relationship with humanity (the "mother of all living"). In addition, the first name looked back to the woman's origin, but the second name looks forward to the woman's role in world history.[24] Her new name may seem to elevate her, somehow giving her a new and higher status. And it is important to note that Adam's act here—whether or not it is an assertion of authority over her by naming her (a possibility noted earlier)—is a prophetic act. Thus we see another aspect of restoration in Adam's life: the prophetic dimension. And this must have come by some spiritual encouragement from God: Adam does not say he *hopes* she will become the mother of all living. Although he has been told that "on the day" he ate of the fruit he would surely die, he is bold (by faith, I would submit) to trust that he will live some "days" yet with the newly named Eve, and she will indeed become the "mother of all living."

CURSES!

It has often been noted that, while God curses the serpent and the ground, he does not curse the woman or the man, and much has been made of this apparent difference; however, closer scrutiny casts doubt on the significance of the difference. It appears that God cursed more than people give him credit for in this passage. Before we examine the data offered by Genesis 3, however, it is important to understand the nature of curses better.

Stuart has, in my opinion, done us a service by analyzing in detail the curses that appear in Leviticus, Deuteronomy 28, and the prophets. Although he differentiates among the curses in those corpora (he gives us, in effect, a taxonomy of curses), the fundamental

---

24. Of course, the first name is also a common noun, the second a proper noun—her personal name.

quality the curses share is a sense of futility or frustration, as noted earlier with regard to Deuteronomy. We saw several examples of this from Deuteronomy 28. Indeed, such is the inevitable nature of a curse, since it overturns or prevents what otherwise would be a healthy course of events or a healthy condition. So curses are fundamentally ironic.

A closer look at Deuteronomy 28 is helpful when we consider Genesis 3. In particular, it helps us understand that there is no significant distinction between a curse threatened and a curse fulfilled, except that the one is threatened and the other fulfilled. So, for example, God warns Israel that, if they do not obey all his commands and decrees, "all these curses will come upon you and overtake you" (Deut. 28:15b). He then portrays the result as follows: "You will be cursed in the city and cursed in the country" (Deut. 28:16), and so on. The statement "You will be cursed" is identical in Hebrew to what God says to the serpent in Genesis 3:14, "Cursed are you." The Hebrew is a verbless clause (ארור אתה) in which the verb *to be* must be supplied in the appropriate tense for the context: "Cursed you [are]" (Gen. 3:14); "Cursed you [will be]" (Deut. 28:16).

Consequently, God pronounces the serpent accursed. But he does so in a way that tells us that the serpent is not alone in being cursed. God says, "Cursed are you *more than* [Hebrew comparative מן] all the livestock and all the wild animals" (Gen. 3:14). As we noted, this comparative makes it clear that the animals are also cursed—otherwise, the serpent could not be more cursed than they. We now consider their accursed condition in light of the futility curse concept and, in so doing, revisit Paul's statement: "The creation was subjected to frustration, not by its own choice, but by the will of the one who subjected it, in hope that the creation itself will be liberated from its bondage to decay and brought into the glorious freedom of the children of God" (Rom. 8:20). God subjected the whole creation, including the animals, to frustration—the frustration of the futility curses we have discussed—and he has done so even as he also subjected humanity to frustrations (the judgments of Gen. 3). However, for both humans and the created order, there is hope of liberation from bondage to that decay through the second

Adam, for through him come the new humanity (2 Cor. 5:17) and the new heavens and earth (Rev. 21:1). There can come even (apparently) new hope for animals, since Isaiah portrays a future for them that is not unattractive (Isa. 11:6–9). For the serpent, however, there is no such hope of redemption.

That is the difference between what God says to the serpent and what God says to the man and the woman. It is not that one of them is cursed and the others are not. They are all under curses, according to what we now understand of God's implementation of covenant curses. But the serpent is offered no redemption out of his fallen condition, whereas the man and the woman are offered such redemption, as Genesis 3:15 first signals.

In sum, we recognize that the text refuses to apply the word *curse* to every single statement of a curse (Deuteronomy 28 likewise begins with a few curse statements, but then proceeds to declare many curses that are not individually called curses in the passage). Such was Moses's method, and in this, he resembles composers of those other ancient near eastern treaties/covenants that could also list curses but not call them curses.

GARMENTS OF SKIN

God's redemptive intentions toward the man and woman are illustrated further by his next act: He makes garments of skin for them. The church has long understood the skins to anticipate the Mosaic sacrificial system and, ultimately, the sacrifice of Christ, because "without the shedding of blood there is no forgiveness of sins," and blood had to be shed for the skin garments to be prepared. Surely, this understanding has merit. God's provision of garments can have other connotations as well, however, which we can now understand from the Bible and the ancient Near East. For one thing, a garment can signify inheritance. In that case, God is symbolically restoring the inheritance to our first parents. However, since it is ultimately the second Adam who accomplishes that restoration of all things, this act is symbolic and anticipatory at best. Another understanding, well known from the ancient Near East, is that a garment can signify office or position. So, for example, Assyrian rulers bestowed robes and rings on those they appointed to certain offices.[25] The Parable of the Prodigal Son may echo this practice, since the father bestows on him a robe and a ring. The robe and the ring do not signify inheritance, since the prodigal has squandered his inheritance, and his father tells the older son, "Everything that I have is yours" (Luke 15:31). But the robe and the ring do signify position: The father is restoring the son to his place in the family. And that, we may suggest, is one thing God does by clothing Adam and Eve. He restores them to their royal position (their vassal dominion over earth) and also prospectively, so to speak, to their place in a godly family—to what becomes the elect lineage of Genesis 5.

CHERUBIM AND THE TEMPLE

God, not willing that the man and woman should access the Tree of Life and thus live eternally in a fallen state, evicts them from the garden and stations cherubim to guard the way back (Gen. 3:22–24). This is the first appearance of cherubim in the Bible, and their function is clearly to guard the Eden–temple. Cherubim appear later in the Old Testament as guardians, at least symbolically, of the Mosaic tabernacle and the Solomonic temple. We find cherubim figures woven into the tabernacle curtains (Exod. 26:1) and cherubim figures incised on the inner walls of the temple (1 Kings 6:29.32). We will study these creatures in more detail later, but note now that Genesis 3 presents them in one of their two major roles, that of temple guardian. Because they do have that function, it is reasonable to ask whether they guard the temple now—that is, individual believers who are temples of God's Spirit. There are NT statements that are suggestive—but *only* suggestive—of such an idea. Jesus says of his followers, "their angels in heaven always see the face of my Father in heaven" (Matt. 18:10). But even if those angels stood before the Father to receive orders for ministry to Jesus's followers, those followers were not yet temples of the Spirit. The author of Hebrews asks rhetorically, "Are not all angels ministering spirits sent to serve those who will inherit salvation?" (Heb. 1:14). But to minister to and to

25. Cf. chapter 2, n. 15.

guard are not necessarily the same thing. Our best conclusion then is modest: By analogy, we suggest that individuals have guardian angels and, in particular, cherubim protecting them. If so, those guardians are formidable indeed, according to Ezekiel's account of them.

CONCLUDING OPTIMISTIC OBSERVATION

We noted earlier that, when he entered Eden to confront our first parents with their sin, God appeared as "apprehending officer, prosecutor, and judge." Although that is true, his subsequent provision for them shows another aspect or role. At some unspoken point, God was also their advocate. Without advocacy in God, no provision for a future, no mercy, would have been shown. Genesis 3 does not show us the Godhead's inner workings during that judicial process, but the outcome for the man and woman finds reasonable explanation in the future roles of the incarnate Son and the Spirit. The incarnate Son came not to judge the world but to save it (John 12:47), and of him, we are told, "But if anybody does sin, we have an advocate with the Father—Jesus Christ, the Righteous One" (1 John 2:1). Moreover, Jesus promised his followers, "I will ask the Father, and he will give you another advocate to help you and be with you forever—the Spirit of truth" (John 14:16–17a). Any who have two such powerful advocates with the Father need not fear his condemnation, and we submit that the Son and the Spirit, who are now our advocates both from and with the Father, were also the sort of advocate most needed by our first parents—and within God's own Being, their advocacy would have been heard.

CHAPTER FOUR

THE SIN AND HERITAGE OF CAIN

THE ELEMENTS OF GENESIS 4 AND GENESIS 5

The next chapter of Genesis deals largely with the start and early progress of the nonelect line—that is, the line of Cain. In this chapter, we encounter more laconic passages that, for all their brevity, contain important information on the nature and progress of evil. Issues that arise include the birth of Cain, the nature of God's warning to him, the nature of his sin, and the outworkings of his own nature, including the erection of the first city and the quality of his progeny. For all that, Genesis 4 begins on a more positive note.

THE BIRTH OF CAIN AND ABEL

Cain's birth appears to be auspicious on two counts. First, we read, "Eve . . . became pregnant and gave birth to Cain" (Gen. 4:1). There is no mention of Eve's pains in pregnancy or childbirth, and though one assumes she had them (since God said she would), our attention is quickly drawn in a different direction, for the next thing we read is, "With the help of the Lord I have brought forth a man" (Gen. 4:2). The Hebrew is more pregnant with meaning (with apologies for a fitting wordplay) than the NIV translation conveys, as we discuss in a moment. Before we do, we note that Eve *acknowledged the Lord's help* in the pregnancy and birth process. In terms of faith, she is *agreeing with God* and what he has done. It may have been this very faith that brought her safely through her first pregnancy, and one may recall Paul's statement, "But women will be saved through childbearing—if they continue in faith, love, and holiness with propriety" (1 Tim. 2:15).

Eve's statement appears to be more fruitfully ambiguous than translations typically suggest. The Hebrew reads literally, "I have gotten/acquired a man with Yahweh," or "I have gotten/acquired a man, [namely] Yahweh" (קָנִיתִי אִישׁ אֶת־יהוה). The ambiguity arises because the preposition *with* (אֵת) and the direct object marker (אֵת) are identical in Hebrew, so that the phrase that follows "a man" in Eve's statement could be read in two different ways. Translators have normally assumed the particle is the preposition and trans-lated something like, "*with* [the help of] the Lord."[1] However, if the particle is the direct object marker, then the phrase becomes an appositive, "I have gotten a man, [namely] the Lord." It seems Luther may have understood the phrase this way, for he originally rendered it "Ich hab kriegt den man des Herren" ("I have gotten the man of the Lord," or "I have gotten the Lord's man").[2] But even Luther's rendering is a paraphrase, meant to indicate that Eve thought she had already given birth to *the man*, the offspring prom-ised in Genesis 3:15, who would now soon crush the serpent's head. The Hebrew itself is even richer with meaning if the phrase in ques-tion is understood as a direct object, for then it declares, "I have gotten a man, [namely] Yahweh." In other words, Eve's statement means she has given birth to the incarnate Lord. Ultimately, one can affirm both meanings. That is, an unbiased reader of Hebrew could naturally see both meanings at the same time when he or she read the text. It is important to be able to see this ourselves, irrespective

---

1. So the Vulgate, "Possedi hominem per Deum"; and the 1984 Deutsche Bibelgesell-schaft edition of Luther's translation, "Ich habe einen Mann gewonnen mit Hilfe des Herrn," which is somewhat more periphrastic. Cf. English language translations.
2. Cf. Martin Luther, *Die Luther–Bibel von 1534 Vollständiger Nachdruck* (Köln, Ger-many: Taschen, 2002).

of the history of interpretation of the verse. The Hebrew is what it is, and this is one of those biblical statements that are genuinely and fruitfully ambiguous. One may say on the authority of the Hebrew text alone that Eve got Yahweh's help in giving birth (and acknowledged that help), and that she either purposefully said, or unwittingly implied, that the child she had birthed was Yahweh himself, "[namely] the Lord." In that case, she forecast the Incarnation and may have *said more than she knew*—maybe the first time, but certainly not the last time in biblical or human experience, that such a thing has occurred.

We next learn that she gave birth again, to Cain's brother Abel, and that Abel was a shepherd and Cain worked the land (Gen. 4:2). Since it is the righteous shepherd, Abel, who is murdered, there is a certain Christology in his pastoral calling. Jesus may have implied the same when he declared of the generation that would persecute and crucify the prophets, sages, and teachers he would send (and who, of course, would do the same to him), "And so upon you will come all the righteous blood that has been shed on earth, from the blood of righteous Abel to the blood of Zechariah son of Berekiah" (Matt. 23:35). The shepherd typology of the Bible also appears in the ancient Near East and is a standard figure for rulers and those over whom they rule (their "sheep").[3] Jesus appropriates this figure to himself (cf. John 10) after God had already done so (e.g., through the prophet David; cf. Psalm 23). Here, we see the symbol *in potentia*: the literal calling of Abel, later to be used as a potent figure when the Spirit breathed forth the prose and poetry of the prophets.

OFFERINGS AND ADMONITION

The exaltation of self (which we may call *pride*, wounded or otherwise) is the occasion of sin, and Cain's behavior is the first example of it in a fallen line. We are told of two offerings to the Lord, hence the first practice of sacrifice in the world. Cain brought some of the fruits of the soil, but Abel brought some fat from the firstborn of his flock (Gen. 4:3–4). Interpreters have often and rightly noted

---

3. Cf. Niehaus, *ANETBT*, 34–55.

that Abel's choice of the firstborn is the better offering because it involves a deeper level of trust in God. To offer God something once one is sure of the produce—be it animal or vegetable—is one thing. To offer him something when one cannot yet be sure there will be enough coming later for oneself is quite another. But that is what Abel apparently does, and that is why God approves his offering rather than Cain's offering (Gen. 4:4). Cain's downcast response, one may reasonably suggest, is the result of wounded pride.

God asks Cain why his face is downcast, and his question naturally echoes the judicial process that he earlier undertook with the man and the woman. It implies already that Cain is in the wrong, and God's next statement declares the same: "If you do what is right, will you not be accepted?" (Gen. 4:7). The laconic nature of the text becomes apparent. We are not told outright that Cain has done something wrong by the nature of his offering, but God's statement assumes he has: We know his offering has not been accepted (vs. 5), so it follows that he has done something wrong, as God inversely declares, "If you do what is right, will you not be accepted?" The wrong he has committed is not stated plainly. Since the only data we have involve the offerings, any answer we may get from the text apparently lies in that area. We are clearly told two things: the nature of the offerings, and the fact that the Lord looked with favor on Abel's offering but not on Cain's (Gen. 4:5). Interpreters have traditionally found the answer in what we have already said about the contrast between the offerings. It comes down to this: Cain's offering did not indicate trust in the Lord, but Abel's offering did. Put another way, Cain's offering was not out of faith but out of duty. Abel's offering, on the other hand, may have recognized a duty, but it was made in faith—an amening of the nature of God that understood and embraced a truth about God: God would provide what Abel needed. Jesus, in the Sermon on the Mount, makes a strong statement of this truth about the reliability of God as a provider. Cain, however, lacks the fundamental ability, or orientation of soul, to understand and embrace the loving nature of God. Instead he makes sure of his own provision, and only then makes an offering to God. So it proves true in this early passage that "everything that does not come from faith is sin" (Rom. 14:23).

SIN CROUCHING AT THE DOOR

The Lord issues a remarkable warning to Cain, and its meaning is best understood in the broader context of biblical revelation. God has already told Cain that he will be accepted if he does what is right (Gen. 4:7a). He then goes on to warn Cain, "But if you do not do what is right, sin is crouching at your door; it desires to have you, but you must master it" (Gen. 4:7b). There are both translation issues and issues of biblical theology to be addressed in order to understand this verse properly.

The translation issues have to do with the parallelism between certain statements in this verse and earlier statements in Genesis 1 and 3. We have noted above that the NIV rendering, "it desires to have you," obscures the fact that the Hebrew here is identical to the Hebrew in Genesis 3:16 and that it should be rendered in a way that shows that parallelism: "Your desire will be for your husband" // "it's [sin's] desire is for you." Likewise, the verb in the phrase "you must master it" is identical with the verb in Genesis 1:28, where the man and woman are to "rule over" the earth, and also with the verb in Genesis 3:16, where the husband will "rule over" his wife. In each case, God is declaring rule and a context of rule: originally, sinless human rule over earth; in a fallen state, the man's rule over his wife (which we rendered as "lord it over" to capture something of the futility aspect of the judgment on the woman); and again in a fallen state, an indication of the necessity that Cain completely control sin—"rule over" it in that sense—so that it might not possess or devour him.

We use that last phrase, "devour him," deliberately. It is part of an overall picture framed or indicated by the allusive terms of this verse—a picture of the nature of sin and, even more, of the tempter. The first clue to the portrait appears in the verb *crouching* (רבץ), which is used for the way a lion crouches in its lair.[4] Later in Genesis, we read, "You are a lion's cub, Judah; you return from the prey, my son. Like a lion he crouches (רבץ) and lies down, like a lioness—who dares to rouse him?" (Gen. 49:9).[5] Apparently, we are dealing here

---

4. Hence *BDB*, which translates Genesis 4:7, "at the door sin makes its lair," 918.

5. As *BDB* (ad loc.) notes, the verb is also used several times of inoffensive animals, but we need no dictionary to tell us that sin in Genesis 4:7 is not portrayed as inoffensive.

with a zoomorphism in which sin is implicitly compared to a lion. But it is more than a local zoomorphism—that is, one whose sole significance is as a figurative touch in this verse. For we later read a warning to believers that is very similar to what God warned Cain: "Be alert and of sober mind. Your enemy the devil prowls around like a roaring lion looking for someone to devour" (1 Pet. 5:8). The warnings are parallel: Cain must rule over sin, and believers must be alert and of sober mind against it (which amount to much the same thing); sin crouches [like a lion] at his doorstep, and the devil prowls around like a lion; sin's desire is for Cain, and the devil looks for someone to devour. The parallels imply that Genesis 4:7 is doing more than simply portraying sin in a zoomorphism: It portrays sin as an active entity whose identity is made clear in 1 Peter. This is not to say that sin equals Satan but that the term *sin*, in this case, is being used as a metonymy (of an effect for a cause). Nor is it to say that all sin is caused directly by Satan. The Lord is simply pointing here to the one who wants to produce sin in Cain (and in us).

The term *desire* in Genesis 4:7 only enhances this picture. That term is used of the woman's desire for her husband in Genesis 3:16 and also of the lover's desire for his beloved in Solomon's Song. We noted that the term suggests a longing for intimacy with the desired person. In this case, then, *sin* or the devil (or a demon, one of the devil's angels who were allowed legal entrée in our world because of our first parents' covenant breaking) desires intimacy with Cain. Just as the desire of a woman for her husband, or of a lover for his beloved, implies or includes both physical and spiritual intimacy, so *sin* or the enemy desires the same with Cain. If we ask where we can find any human in such a condition—that is, a condition of intimacy with an evil spirit—the answer is not far to seek. The New Testament provides a number of accounts of individuals who had evil spirits dwelling within them. Demons are not the devil himself, of course, but they are apparently his angels (or messengers), and we know from the Gospel accounts that demons have inhabited individuals. A more intimate form of relationship can hardly be imagined, since it is a satanic counterpart to what all humans were made for: to be temples of the Holy Spirit, with God's own Spirit dwelling within them in intimate and redemptive relationship. Moreover, those demonic possessions have found their epitome in one case of genuine *satanic* possession: when Satan himself entered Judas in order to strike the heel of the woman's offspring, the second Adam (John 13:27). As we discuss later (in volume 2), the aforementioned demonic intimacy also goes far to explain the sexual language used for idolatry later in the Bible.

THE SIN OF CAIN

Cain does not pay heed to God's warning but invites his brother out to the field and kills him. The text is laconic and does not spell out Cain's motives, but we would be completely without imagination if we did not appropriately infer that wounded pride moved him to his act. In the same way the serpent, fallen through pride (cf. Ezek. 28:17), sought to bring down someone else in revenge. The serpent could not attack God (who rejected him), but he could attack God's image in the man and woman. Similarly, Cain cannot attack God (who rebuked him), but he can attack God's image in his brother. It is clear that such is the nature of his crime because the renewal of the Adamic covenant, the Noahic covenant, stipulates that those who shed human blood have assaulted God's image (Gen. 9:6). Cain's attack on Abel is really an indirect attack on God. Such is the nature of murder, and it is rooted in the devil, so Jesus makes the point that Satan "was a murderer from the beginning" (John 8:44).

Cain has another point of affinity with the enemy: Cain's sin is predicated on deception. He sets the scene for murder by deceiving his brother with an invitation: "Let's go out to the field" (Gen. 4:8). The passage does not tell us what reason, if any, Cain may have provided when he asked his brother into the field. It seems clear enough that he issued what seemed a harmless invitation in order to accomplish his goal. Maybe he wanted to be sure the two of them were out of sight or hearing of their parents. In any case, his act of deception aligns him with Satan, who deceived our first mother and who "is a liar and the father of lies" (John 8:44).

Because Cain is aligned with Satan in two major aspects—deception and murder—he has always and rightly been reckoned to be the sire of a nonelect line, and we will discuss this concept further below. We proceed now to God's judicial enquiry, which pursues the sin of Cain as it did the sins of his parents.

JUDICIAL PROCESS AND JUDGMENT

God comes onto the scene and initiates a judicial process against Cain. We are not told how God appeared but it is clear he has arrived, and he immediately asks Cain, "Where is your brother Abel?" (Gen. 4:9a). Cain's reply deepens or more deeply reveals (or both) his deceptive character, since he now tries to deceive God: "I don't know" (Gen. 4:9b). Cain has already sunk below the active awareness that God is indeed one who knows "good and evil" without exception—every good thing and every evil thing in the universe—that is, all things. (We submit that there is nothing that is neither good nor evil in the created order, because a thing is either in conformity with the nature and will of God [and thus good] or not in conformity with the nature and will of God [and thus evil], just as whatever is not of faith— that is, amening the nature and will of God—is sin.) Cain's response illustrates at a very early stage in human history the truth articulated by Paul much later in Romans 1: Humans in their sinfulness historically grew further and further from the knowledge of God and what he is truly like. Moreover, Cain challenges the moral authority of God when he asks, "Am I my brother's keeper?" (Gen. 4:9b), as though God were making an unjust demand of him by asking Abel's whereabouts. We understand and affirm that a person may ask questions, even angry and complaining questions, of God as part of a life of faith. God honors such people because he knows that, out of their human finitude and imperfect knowledge, they are being genuine with him and honestly challenging and wrestling with him in the boldness of faith—that is, *agreeing with God* that he is a God with whom one can so deal. Job may be the supreme biblical example of such an attitude, although it can also be seen more mildly in Mary's questioning of the angel Gabriel (Luke 1:34). As has been noted, she has apparently the same sort of conversation with the angel that Zechariah did (Luke 1:18), namely, a question how such a birth can happen, followed by a physical reason it could not—for example, "I am a virgin," cf. "I am an old man and my wife is well along in years"—yet her question is carefully answered, whereas Zechariah's only got rebuke. The reason for the difference (one can only infer) is that she asked in the obedience of faith, whereas he did not.[6]

God's judicial process with Cain resembles the process he undertook with Cain's parents. In that process, the man and woman confessed their sin, although they did try to pass the blame. In this case, however, God meets not with confession but with a false profession of ignorance on the part of Cain. The following simple schema displays the similarities and differences:

Theme	Genesis 3	Genesis 4
God apprehends the guilty	3:8–10	4:9a
God interrogates the guilty	3:11	4:9a
The guilty confess(es)	3:12–13	
The guilty tries to deceive the judge		4:9b
God states the truth, establishes his case		4:10
God pronounces judgment	3:14–19	4:11–12

We noted that Cain's replies to God illustrate an ignorance about God's true nature and, specifically, about his omniscience. That ignorance arises because his mind has become darkened by sin, or as the author of Hebrews put it, his heart had been hardened by sin's deceptiveness (Heb. 3:12–13). So it is that those who deceive others also deceive themselves more profoundly because they are out of touch with the gravity, or even the true nature, of their sin.

God opposes Cain's lies with the truth by declaring that Abel's blood cries out to him from the ground. He then pronounces judgment, and his judgment is parallel in character with the judgments he pronounced earlier on the serpent, the woman, and the man:

Judgment	Serpent	Woman	Man	Cain
On field of endeavor	3:14	3:16a	3:17b–19a	4:11
Overturning of obtained or implied authority	3:15	3:16b	3:19bc	4:12

---

6. Cf. Niehaus, *God at Sinai*, 354–57.

The curse on Cain's field of endeavor is clear enough: God drives him from the ground that would otherwise have nourished him with its produce. God further overturns Cain's authority over the ground by declaring, "When you work the ground, it will no longer yield its crops for you" (Gen. 4:12a). Before this curse, Cain shared in the Creation covenant's cultural mandate to rule over the earth and subdue it. Now he is told that the earth will, in effect, no longer submit to him. A similar judgment, although less drastic in its extent, was placed on Adam, who was told that the ground would produce thorns and thistles for him, thus making the fulfillment of the cultural mandate more difficult. God's curse on Cain takes place because Cain abused his authority over the land and made it swallow his brother's blood (Gen. 4:11). Cain also took authority over his brother by deciding the time of his death. Murder is perhaps the ultimate usurpation of authority, because death is God's judgment on fallen humans, and its timing should belong to him alone. It is intriguing that, when Paul much later forbids a woman to have authority over a man, apparently in a church context, he uses a verb that sometimes in Hellenistic usage connoted the act of murder (αὐθεντεῖν, 1 Tim. 2:12). Murder is the ultimate usurpation of authority, and that is what Cain has committed.

The second part of God's judgment involves Cain's security on the land. He is both driven from the land (Gen. 4:11) and made to be "a restless wanderer on the earth" (Gen. 4:12b). Cain reacts to this curse with some complaints, all of which impugn God's justice and also have to do with Cain's survival. It is appropriate to see these complaints as parallel:

Verse	Complaint
4:14a	Today you are driving me from the land
4:14c	I will be a restless wanderer on the earth
4:14b	I will be hidden from your presence
4:14d	Whoever finds me will kill me

Each pair of complaints constitutes a cause and an effect. God is driving Cain from the land with the result that he will be a restless wanderer; Cain will be hidden from God's presence with the result that anyone who finds him will kill him. As we have argued elsewhere, God's presence (lit., "face") is the source and sustainer of life. So later, when God warns or judges Israel, a fundamental judgment is that he will hide his face (i.e., "presence") from them so that they perish (cf. Deut. 32:20).[7] The opposite of this cursed condition is expressed in the Aaronic blessing (Num. 6:24–26):

a	b
The Lord bless you	and keep you;
a'	b'
the Lord make his face shine upon you	and be gracious to you
a"	b"
the Lord turn his face toward you	and give you peace

The blessing emphasizes the relationship between the Lord's "face" (often translated "presence," as at Gen. 4:14) on the one hand and a condition of blessedness on the other. The last bicolon is especially significant. It caps the blessing and makes it clear that, when the Lord turns his face *toward* one, a condition of wholeness or soundness is the result, because the word *peace* (שׁלום) here actually means "wholeness." So later, when Jesus promises his peace (John 14:27), he is not promising what the world thinks of as peace, and he is certainly not promising an absence of persecution or conflict since he has already told his followers that they are blessed when they are persecuted for his sake (Matt. 5:11–12). Rather, he is promising an inner *shalom*, quite literally the presence and work of the Holy Spirit, who starts the process of renewing the one who receives him by making him or her into a new—a whole—creature in Christ (2 Cor. 5:17). That blessed condition is the opposite of Cain's lot.

Cain does not like what he hears from God, and his response is accusatory: "My punishment is more than I can bear. Today you are driving me from the land" (Gen. 4:13–14a). His first statement amounts to a criticism of God's justice or mercy, or even of God's

---

7. For fuller discussion, cf. Niehaus, *God at Sinai*, 310–15.

omniscience, as though God either does not know how harsh his curse has been or, worse, knowing how hard it is, imposes it anyway without good judgment or compassion. Cain's second statement highlights God in much the same way Adam did when he responded to God's judicial inquiry (Gen. 3:12). There, Adam complained, "The woman *you* put here with me—she gave me some fruit from the tree," implying that somehow God was at fault because he provided someone for Adam who would cause him trouble. Cain complains, "Today *you* are driving me from the land," implying that God's judgment, by depriving him of a source of livelihood, is somehow too hard or disproportionate. Both complaints, impugning God's omniscience and/or the wisdom and/or goodness of his judgment, are distorted insinuations of God's nature and are thus lies, since God is both omniscient and just.

God is not without an answer, but he responds to Cain with something Cain does not deserve—namely, grace. God gives Cain both a promise and a mark: a promise that Cain will be avenged seven times against anyone who kills him and "a mark on Cain so that no one who found him would kill him" (Gen. 4:15). God makes provision for the nonelect line of Cain before it has even begun—indeed, so it may begin. Cain will go on living and enjoying the potential for his own fulfillment of the provisions of the cultural mandate: He will be able to be fruitful and multiply and also, in some fashion or other, rule over the earth and subdue it.

CAIN AND CULTURE

Cain is condemned to be "a restless wanderer on the earth" (Gen. 4:12). The word *wanderer* (נוד) is of the same root that now appears again in Cain's destination: We read that "Cain went out from the Lord's presence and lived in the land of *Nod*" (נוד; lit., "Wandering," Gen. 4:16). As he knew he would be, Cain is now indeed separate from the "presence" or "face" of the Lord. This little statement is of great importance. The Lord's presence is not only the source of life, as we have noted, but also the proper source of human security. Much later, in the New covenant, Jesus promised that the Spirit of truth would be with his followers forever, and that same Spirit is the one who brings the inner soundness and peace of which we spoke earlier (cf. Matt. 28:20). As Paul later stated in a slightly different phrase, "If God is for us, who can be against us?" (Rom. 8:31).

Humans separate from God today do not have such assurances or such peace, however, and that has been the condition of most people throughout human history. Anyone who lacks a relationship with God in Christ today does not have the Holy Spirit who brings such peace. And anyone who lived before the New covenant not only lacked the Holy Spirit within (since the Spirit did not dwell in people until after Pentecost, a point already noted and to be discussed more fully later)—most of them also lack God's presence under any Special Grace relationship. We can affirm that Adam and Eve did have some special relationship with God, because we have already seen that God reinstated them as vassal rulers over earth, and also that God made a strong messianic promise to the woman. So theologians have rightly understood them and their line to be elect, even within the context of a covenant that rapidly became a Common Grace covenant for a fallen world as the humans under it advanced in sin and degradation—as Paul aptly noted (Romans 1). The distinction we made in the Prolegomena between Common Grace covenants and Special Grace covenants is taken up more fully later.

Cain, apart from God's presence, now operates out of insecurity. Because of this he is the first one to build a city, which he names after his son, Enoch (Gen. 4:17b). It must be affirmed at the outset that although Cain, who was evil, built the first city, the idea of a city is not in itself evil. After all, God inhabits a celestial city, the heavenly Jerusalem (Revelation 21). Moreover, that heavenly city may be an archetypal city—a concept that the ancients in Mesopotamia and Egypt embraced and that was later implied in Platonic idealism. We address this concept in an Excursus below. But the Hebrew word for city may come from a root that means "to be vigilant or on watch" (עיר), and such a concept would be very consistent with Cain's present condition. He is apart from God and insecure. Even though God has placed a mark on him to prevent his murder, that is not enough for Cain. He wants to take his defense into his own hands. The birth of his son is significant because it is the first fruit of God's protection, so that Cain would be able to carry forth the cultural mandate, as we have noted. So Cain has already had palpable proof of God's faithfulness to his promise: Cain has lived long enough to marry and have a son. But humans in a fallen condition are by nature insecure, and fall into the temptation of providing for themselves both materially and defensively, without reference to God. That is what Cain does when he builds the first city on earth.

EXCURSUS: HOW COULD CAIN BUILD A CITY?[8]

The statement that Cain built a city (Gen. 4:17) may invite one to wonder how alone or with what help Cain was able to accomplish such a large task. But it also implies another and more important question—namely, where did Cain get the idea—that is, what put it into his head to undertake such a work? That question may form the starting point for our inquiry, which would explore the role of God's *presence* in the realm theologians often call the realm of Common Grace. We take up the issue now because it pervades all of history from this point on, and evidences relevant to it appear under both the Old and the New covenants.

I would submit that God's presence had much to do with Cain's undertaking, despite the fact that Cain could (accurately) complain, "Today you are driving me from the land, and I will be hidden from your presence (lit., "face"); I will be a restless wanderer on the earth, and whoever finds me will kill me" (Gen. 4:14). Cain's fear for his life shows his motivation for building a city, which could provide a form of defense (the word for *city* [עיר] might even evoke a near homonym, "to be watchful, vigilant" [עור] for a Hebrew reader). Fear may well have been his *motivation* to build a city, but what was the source of his *idea* of a city? It may be that the existence of a supernal city

---

8. The material of this Excursus substantially reproduces a paper presented at a conference, "God with Us: The Theme of Divine Presence in Scripture," held in honor of Dr. Gary Pratico at Gordon-Conwell Theological Seminary, October 17–18, 2013.

(the heavenly Jerusalem) argues for God as the source of Cain's idea of a city and also, directly or indirectly, of all human ideas of cities. Before we explore this concept, it will be useful to establish the role of the Holy Spirit in the realm of Common Grace.

GOD'S COMMON GRACE PRESENCE: THE HOLY SPIRIT

Although the first part of Cain's statement is true, "I will be hidden from your face," that does not mean that God, who is omnipresent, would not be present in some way with Cain. Cain would not enjoy anything like a direct experience of God's presence—an experience that could occur only if God chose to reveal himself to Cain as he subsequently did at times to chosen ones. But God can be present without disclosing his presence. Indeed, Hebrews 1:3 says, "The Son is the radiance of God's glory and the exact representation of his being, sustaining all things by his powerful word." Moreover, Job 34:14–15 tells us,

> If it were his intention
> and he withdrew his spirit and breath,
> all humanity would perish together
> and mankind would return to the dust.

Paul likewise says, "he himself gives everyone life and breath *and everything else*" (Acts 17:25, emphasis added), and "For in him we live and move and have our being" (Acts 17:28, agreeing with the Cretan philosopher, Epimenides). From these statements we may understand that God, and in particular God the Son and God the Spirit, are involved in sustaining all things. Although we cannot understand the *mechanism*, so to speak, by which they do so, there is some sort of *connection* between God the sustainer and whatever is sustained.[9] We affirm, then, God's omnipresence and the

---

9. The connection would seem to be one of cause and effect, which we can affirm despite the fact that Hume could not quite accomplish a philosophical affirmation of it. The proper answer to problems that mere empiricism cannot answer is inevitably idealism

sustaining work of that presence in the world before Cain, during Cain's life, and after Cain.[10]

The Spirit sustained Cain and was his breath of life, as he was Adam's breath of life and also the breath of life for everyone after Adam (cf. again Job 34:14–15). Since the Spirit is so present, one may further ask if the Spirit had, or has, or can have any other sort of "work" to do with people. Put another way, does the Spirit only sustain life among us? I would affirm here, as I have argued elsewhere, that God is not only the source (and sustainer) of life but also a source of *ideas*. Paul's statement that God gives "everyone life and breath *and everything else*" leaves room for such a concept.

GOD: A SOURCE OF IDEAS FOR EVERYONE

I hope we can take it as axiomatic that, if one is going to make something, one must have some idea of what that thing will be. So if Cain set about to build a city, as we are told he did, he had some idea of that city before he built it. I would not go so far as to say he had a "vision" of what he would build because the term *vision* is probably used more freely than it should be. But let us agree that he must have had an *idea* of what he would build—some general outline or concept of its form, nature, and purpose. He then set about to build

---

rightly understood: for God is biblically the source of all things, things that correspond to his plans or *ideas*. Cf. below.

10. The same is affirmed poetically not only for humans but for all creatures and their environments in Proverbs 8:27–30:

> [27] All creatures look to you
>   to give them their food at the proper time.
> [28] When you give it to them,
>   they gather it up;
> when you open your hand,
>   they are satisfied with good things.
> [29] When you hide your face,
>   they are terrified;
> when you take away their breath,
>   they die and return to the dust.
> [30] When you send your Spirit,
>   they are created,
>   and you renew the face of the ground.

a city—with whatever help and materials—that would fulfill his idea of a city. But where did Cain's idea come from?

A foundational principle must be affirmed in order to answer this question. We must affirm that Cain, fallen though he was, was still made in the *imago Dei*. As such, his ability to imagine what he would build is rooted in that same *imago*. Created in God's image, Cain, like us, had an imagination that could produce an idea. But this implies that God, who made us in his image, also has a power of ideation or imagination, and this is, in fact, a concomitant to his being able to create.

If we understand something of how God creates, we can also understand something of how a person creates and, in particular, the role of ideation or imagination in the creative process. Here I take leave to quote from a recently published book, *God the Poet: Exploring the Origin and Nature of Poetry*:

> In order to understand what we may reasonably hope to understand about God and his poetic nature, it is important to be able to affirm not only that God created the visible and invisible realms, but also that God is a *planner*—that he can plan and has indeed planned—and the Bible is clear enough on this matter.[11] If God is one who can plan, however, that means he has ideas of what he intends to do before he does them. It follows that when he created the cosmos, he did so according to his plans or ideas. [12]

If God had ideas of what he would create before he created them, one may make such statements as the following:

> God knows all things beforehand, and this is no new idea. But among the things he has known are those things he would create. This is implicit in the statement, "In him we were also chosen, having been predestined according to the plan of him *who works everything in*

---

11. So David says, "But the plans of the LORD stand firm forever, / the purposes of his heart through all generations" (Ps. 33:11), and we read of "God's deliberate plan and foreknowledge" that had to do with salvation (Acts 2:23) and similarly how "God had planned something better for us" than he had revealed to OT believers (Heb. 11:40).

12. Niehaus, *God the Poet: Exploring the Origen and Nature of Poetry* (Wooster, OH: Weaver Book Company, 2014), 16.

conformity with the purpose of his will" (Eph. 1:11). God had an idea
(a "plan") of the cosmos before he chose or willed to create the cosmos,
and God had an idea of man before he created man. Before he created a
plant, God had the idea of that plant. Before he created an animal, God
had the idea of that animal. Put in terms of Eph. 1:11, if God *purposed*
to create a thing, he had an idea of that thing. In that sense, each created thing had its archetypal idea in the mind of God. These statements
are not a form of unbiblical idealism but are the implications of what
Paul has written: God works everything in conformity with the purpose of his will. One might add that Rom. 4:17 implies the same. There
we read that God "calls things that are not as though they were." God
could not call things that are not as though they were, unless he had an
idea of them before he called them.[13]

God has made us in his image and likeness. Among other things this
means that, like God, people can have plans and ideas of what they
would make. Cain was no different from any human in this regard,
for we recall that even fallen humans are made in God's [image and]
likeness (cf. James 3:9, "With the tongue we praise our Lord and
Father, and with it we curse human beings, who have been made in
God's likeness" [καθ' ὁμοίωσιν θεοῦ; and cf. LXX Gen. 1:26]). Now,
although a human mind can have ideas of what it would make and in
this way bears a likeness to God, it does not follow that every human
idea has its source in the mind of God. Humans can imagine and
plan much evil that God did not intend. But when a human idea
partakes of a divine archetype—that is, what was originally an idea in
the mind of God—it may be reasonable to conclude that the human
idea, being rooted in a supernal reality, somehow has come from God.

An idea may come from God in two ways.

An idea may occur on the basis of an observed phenomenon, as
Descartes says we can only imagine things that we have seen, even if
what we imagine is a composite of what we have seen. What we have
seen, however, has been created by God, and so indirectly the idea of
what we have seen comes ultimately from God.

---

13. Niehaus, *God the Poet*, 16–17, quoting Niehaus, "Covenant: An Idea," 245–46. All of
this understands that God is outside time, something also known by, for example, Paul
and Augustine.

An idea may also occur on the basis of something unseen—that is, on the basis of some inspiration. But such an inspiration comes from a spiritual source. If it is a bad inspiration, it comes from the enemy. Nonetheless, because evil spirits are creatures, even their ideas are somehow rooted in what God has created, be it earthly or heavenly. So for instance, although pagan religions are demonically inspired (cf. Deut. 32:16ff., 1 Cor. 10:20, and even 1 Tim. 4:1, which warns the church against the "doctrines of demons"), they all echo in various particulars what we know biblically to be true religion.[14] However, if a spiritual inspiration is a good inspiration, it comes from God. If it comes from God, such an in*spiration* is the Spirit informing and moving someone in some way.

When God's Spirit informs he gives ideas. So we are told of David's plans for the future temple and its furnishings: "Then David gave his son Solomon the plans for the portico of the temple, its buildings, its storerooms, its upper parts, its inner rooms and the place of atonement. He gave him the *plans* of all that *the Spirit had put in his mind* for the courts of the temple of the LORD and all the surrounding rooms, for the treasuries of the temple of God and for the treasuries for the dedicated things" (1 Chron. 28:11–12, emphasis added). God's Spirit may have given David ideas, but we know that the Spirit did not dwell in David, for we are told, "So Samuel took the horn of oil and anointed him in the presence of his brothers, and *from that day on* the Spirit of the LORD *came* powerfully *upon* David" (1 Sam. 16:13, emphasis added; cf. discussion in chapter 2). If the Spirit *came upon* him daily, the Spirit *most likely* did not dwell in him—for if he had, the biblical writer could easily have written that, rather than, or in addition to, what he wrote. With David (and anyone other than Jesus under the Old covenant), it was as Jesus said to his disciples of the Spirit, "And I will ask the Father, and he will give you another advocate to help you and be with you forever—the Spirit of truth. The world cannot accept him, because it neither sees him nor knows him. But you know him, for he lives *with you* [παρ' ὑμῖν] and *will be in you*" (ἐν ὑμῖν ἔσται; John 14:16–17, emphasis added). The world that cannot accept the Spirit whom Jesus and the

---

14. Cf. Niehaus, *ANETBT*, passim.

Father *will send* is the world that would not and will not receive the Son (cf. John 1:10–11). However, we have already established that the same Spirit sustains all life, including humans, whether or not they accept him as a dynamic, indwelling blessing of the New covenant through faith in Christ, the mediator of the New covenant.

If the Spirit can give ideas or plans to someone in whom the Spirit does not dwell, as was the case with David, and if the Spirit gives life and breath to all people created in God's image, can the Spirit also give plans or ideas to people under Common Grace? The Bible appears to answer this question in the affirmative.

SPIRIT ANOINTING UNDER COMMON GRACE

There are two very noteworthy examples of anointing under Common Grace in the Old Testament: the anointing of Hazael commanded by the Lord to Elijah, and the anointing of Cyrus (apparently by the Lord without any prophetic intermediary). We take the more explicit one first.

The Lord refers to Cyrus prophetically through Isaiah, who reports as follows:

> This is what the LORD says to his anointed [Heb. משיחו],
>   to Cyrus, whose right hand I take hold of
> to subdue nations before him
>   and to strip kings of their armor,
> to open doors before him
>   so that gates will not be shut:
> I will go before you
>   and will level the mountains;
> I will break down gates of bronze
>   and cut through bars of iron.
> I will give you hidden treasures,
>   riches stored in secret places,
> so that you may know that I am the LORD,
>   the God of Israel, who summons you by name.
> For the sake of Jacob my servant,
>   of Israel my chosen,

I summon you by name
and bestow on you a title of honor,
though you do not acknowledge me [lit., "know
me," Heb. ידעתני].
I am the LORD, and there is no other;
apart from me there is no God.
I will strengthen you,
though you have not acknowledged me [lit., "know me,"
Heb. ידעתני]
so that from the rising of the sun
to the place of its setting
people may know there is none besides me.
I am the LORD, and there is no other.
I form the light and create darkness,
I bring prosperity and create disaster;
I, the LORD, do all these things. (Isa. 45:1–7)

Amid strong affirmations of the Lord's sovereignty in the realm of
Common Grace, we are told that, although Cyrus did not know the
Lord in that realm, the Lord could refer to Cyrus as his "anointed"
(i.e., "messiah"). We understand that to be *anointed* by the Lord is to
have the Holy Spirit come upon one and inform and empower one
for whatever work the Lord has in mind.[15]

In a less explicit and powerful report, the Lord tells Elijah, "Go
back the way you came, and go to the Desert of Damascus. When
you get there, anoint Hazael king over Aram" (1 Kings 19:15). The
Lord also tells Elijah to anoint Jehu as king over Israel and Elisha as
prophet to succeed him (1 Kings 19:16).

Anointing with oil was symbolic of and perhaps meant to be
evocative of anointing with the Holy Spirit. So when Samuel anoints
Saul (1 Sam. 10:1–11) and David (1 Sam. 16:13), the Holy Spirit
comes *upon* them (על, 1 Sam. 10:6.10; אל, 1 Sam. 16:13) and

---

15. We note also that there is no prospect in the passage that Cyrus will ever know the
Lord. The Lord says he will grant Cyrus various forms of conquest and success, so
that Cyrus may know *that* [the God of Israel] is "the Lord" (vs. 3). But knowing *that*
Yahweh is God is not the same as *knowing* Yahweh/the Lord.

empowers them to do works of God's kingdom as both prophets and kings. So later in the church, we are instructed by the Lord through James, "Is anyone among you sick? Let them call the elders of the church to pray over them and anoint them with oil in the name of the Lord. And the prayer offered in faith will make the sick person well; the Lord will raise them up" (James 5:14–15a). Interestingly, James speaks of believers ("anyone among you" in the church) who already have the Spirit dwelling within them, and yet anointing with oil, as symbolic of the Spirit, would mean the Spirit would come to them in a particular act of power to heal them. We note also that it is the "prayer offered in faith" and not the symbolic anointing that "will make the sick person well," even though the anointing is a symbolic recognition that it is the Spirit who will come and do the healing. Jesus already proclaimed the substance of which anointing with oil is the symbol when he declared of himself (quoting Isa. 61:1–2):

> The Spirit of the Lord is on me,
>> because he has anointed me
>> to proclaim good news to the poor.
> He has sent me to proclaim freedom for the prisoners
>> and recovery of sight for the blind,
> to set the oppressed free,
>> to proclaim the year of the Lord's favor. (Luke
>> 4:18–19)

It is important to note that the anointing of the Spirit is for both words ("to proclaim good news … to proclaim freedom") and miraculous works ("recovery of sight for the blind, to set the oppressed free"), although the latter could and probably should be taken in more than one sense.

What matters for our purposes is that the Spirit with whom Jesus is endowed is a Spirit who can give counsel and authority.[16] Indeed, the Spirit of God gives us the authority to become children of God:

---

16. Cf. also Isaiah 11:1–3:

> "A shoot will come up from the stump of Jesse;
>> from his roots a Branch will bear fruit.

"Yet to all who did receive him, to those who believed in his name, he gave the right [better, 'he gave them authority,' ἔδωκεν αὐτοῖς ἐξουσίαν] to become children of God—children born not of natural descent, nor of human decision or a husband's will, but born of God" (John 1:12–13). But those given such authority to become children of God become so by the Spirit, for they are born of the Spirit, as Jesus says to Nicodemus, "Very truly I tell you, no one can enter the kingdom of God unless he is born of water and the Spirit" (John 3:5).

The Spirit is the one who endows with authority. He is the one who endowed Cyrus with authority—with counsel and power for conquest and for statecraft—and perhaps the same applies throughout history.

THE SPIRIT AS GIVER OF AUTHORITY UNDER COMMON GRACE

All humans live in the realm of Common Grace, a realm sustained by the Spirit through the Word. The Spirit who sustains the universe also endows with authority. Cyrus, anointed with the Spirit, had authority for conquest and rule, and Paul affirms the same truth for all earthly authority: "Let every person be subject to the governing authorities. For there is no authority except from God, and those that exist have been instituted by God" (Rom. 13:1, ESV; Πᾶσα ψυχὴ ἐξουσίαις ὑπερεχούσαις ὑποτασσέσθω. οὐ γὰρ ἔστιν ἐξουσία εἰ μὴ ὑπὸ θεοῦ, αἱ δὲ οὖσαι ὑπὸ θεοῦ τεταγμέναι εἰσίν).

Just as authority (ἐξουσία) was associated with becoming a child of God—and we know that only happens via a rebirth by the Spirit—so here authority (ἐξουσία) is implicitly associated with the presence of the Holy Spirit for endowment. Such was manifestly the case with Cyrus (God's "messiah" or "anointed") and also the case with Hazael (who was to be "anointed"). The Holy Spirit can endow a pagan ruler

---

The Spirit of the Lord will rest on him—
    the Spirit of wisdom and of understanding,
    the Spirit of counsel and of might,
    the Spirit of the knowledge and fear of the LORD—
and he will delight in the fear of the LORD."

with abilities and perhaps even, by affecting those he rules or would conquer, pave his way as a conqueror and ruler. Such spiritual realities may underlie what we read of Assyria in Isaiah 10:5–15:

> Woe to the Assyrian, the rod of my anger,
>   in whose hand is the club of my wrath!
> I send him against a godless nation,
>   I dispatch him against a people who anger me,
> to seize loot and snatch plunder,
>   and to trample them down like mud in the streets.
> But this is not what he intends,
>   this is not what he has in mind;
> his purpose is to destroy,
>   to put an end to many nations.
> "Are not my commanders all kings?" he says.
>   "Has not Kalno fared like Carchemish?
> Is not Hamath like Arpad,
>   and Samaria like Damascus?
> As my hand seized the kingdoms of the idols,
>   kingdoms whose images excelled those of Jerusa-
>   lem and Samaria—
> shall I not deal with Jerusalem and her images
>   as I dealt with Samaria and her idols?"

When the Lord has finished all his work against Mount Zion and Jerusalem, he will say, "I will punish the king of Assyria for the willful pride of his heart and the haughty look in his eyes. For he says,

> "'By the strength of my hand I have done this,
>   and by my wisdom, because I have understanding.
> I removed the boundaries of nations,
>   I plundered their treasures;
>   like a mighty one I subdued their kings.
> As one reaches into a nest,
>   so my hand reached for the wealth of the nations;
> as people gather abandoned eggs,
>   so I gathered all the countries;

> not one flapped a wing,
>> or opened its mouth to chirp.'"
> Does the ax raise itself above the person who swings it,
>> or the saw boast against the one who uses it?
> As if a rod were to wield the person who lifts it up,
>> or a club brandish the one who is not wood!

Beyond the figurative language of this passage lies a spiritual reality: Somehow God endowed Assyria with the abilities—the military acumen as well as the resources for and skill to develop an army and favorable opportunities to employ them—to conquer and subdue. Since, as Paul says, God "himself gives everyone life and breath *and everything else*" (Acts 17:25, emphasis added), we refer again to our argument that the Spirit who imparts life and sustains it could also have imparted the authority and gifting to build an empire—in this case, the Assyrian empire. The same may be said of Babylon (Hab. 1:6–7):

> I am raising up the Babylonians,
>> that ruthless and impetuous people,
> who sweep across the whole earth
>> to seize dwellings not their own.
> They are a feared and dreaded people;
>> they are a law to themselves
>> and promote their own honor.

What we said of Assyria may also apply here. God is "raising up the Babylonians." In both cases, the Lord empowers and employs an empire as a judgment instrument against his own covenant-breaking people. In both cases, he will also judge the judgment instrument, and for the same reason: Neither acknowledges the source of its authority; both are "a law unto themselves."

The irony is instructive. God may empower a ruler and the empire under him for certain works of judgment by God; however, the endowment with authority is one thing, and the use of it another. Being lawless themselves, the gifted and empowered rulers go beyond what God intended, and God will judge them for it.

Even though the Spirit may be the endower of the human, the human may continue to be a lawless person, or a "law unto himself."

He may accomplish the judgment God intends but also do those things God never intended. He thus abuses the authority God has given him. We may apply this concept in subsequent cases.

SATAN'S THIRD TEMPTATION OF CHRIST

What we have said naturally invites a question regarding Satan's claim for himself. When he offers Jesus the kingdoms of this world if only Jesus will fall down and worship him, he makes the following claim: "The devil led him up to a high place and showed him in an instant all the kingdoms of the world. And he said to him, 'I will give you all their authority and splendor; it has been given to me, and I can give it to anyone I want to. If you worship me, it will all be yours'" (Luke 4:5–7).

I believe these lines imply a level of spiritual reality that we cannot discern with certainty. What is clear from other passages of the Bible is that all authority comes from God. If that means, as we have suggested it does in several passages, that God by his Spirit endows certain ones with authority to conquer and to rule, and if that is *always* the mode of God's impartation of authority, then Satan's words to Jesus are a lie. That would be no surprise. If, however, God has chosen, or does sometimes choose, to allow Satan the impartation of authority in one "kingdom" or another, then Satan's statement to Jesus could sometimes apply—but not always.[17] It is hard to imagine, for example, that God allowed *Satan* to give Cyrus his authority, when God calls Cyrus *my messiah* (i.e., God's *anointed one* by God's Spirit). If we may apply Occam's razor here, the simplest explanation would be that Satan lied to Jesus, and that, in fact, the authority of the kingdoms of this world *always* did come, does come, and will come from God alone—even if sometimes, and apparently at the end, evil powers achieve authority not by God's endowment

---

17. However, it is hard to imagine God's Spirit being involved in the dynamic of Satan's impartation of any authority. Rather, it would seem God's Spirit would not stand in the way, as it were, of Satan's empowering and moving an earthly being. This, I suspect, is what will happen toward the end, as Paul says in 2 Thessalonians 2:7, "For the secret power of lawlessness is already at work; but the one who now holds it back will continue to do so till he is taken out of the way."

(as by the Spirit) but only by his permission (his allowing the enemy to do things). Then again, the very being of evil spirits only continues because God sustains them as he sustains all things: "by the word of his power" (Heb. 1:3).

Although, then, all authority comes—directly or indirectly— from God, evil spirits may be involved with those who receive it. And now it may be useful to distinguish between positional authority and spiritual authority.

We posit that God may give positional authority and yet not impart his Spirit to one who holds a given position. In the cases of Hazael and Cyrus, it seems relatively clear from the mere terminology that God's Spirit was at work on and through those rulers, whom God also made to be kings. However, it may also be that God gives positions to people and yet does not anoint them with his Spirit, even though that same Spirit keeps them alive, as he keeps us all alive.

If God gives a position to someone but does not give spiritual gifting beyond the mere position, what source might there be of spiritual dynamism in the chosen ruler? This is an important question to ask, because we do live in a spiritual universe, and the Holy Spirit is not the only spirit around. We know, for example, that a Philippian slave girl could foretell things by a demon within her: "Once when we were going to the place of prayer, we were met by a female slave who had a spirit by which she predicted the future. She earned a great deal of money for her owners by fortune-telling" (Acts 16:16). If prophetic gifting can be imitated by a demon, perhaps other giftings can as well.

I venture now to consider a case about which and a person about whom not all will agree. But the case of the person in question has strong spiritual implications and is worth looking at, if only for the questions it may raise.

Most people will allow that Adolf Hitler was a strongly charismatic person, even if they disagree on what they mean by such a statement. The testimony of Hitler and others about this aspect of his presence is worth noting. Hitler once described his own experience, before giving a speech, as a spiritual event in which the power from above came down on him. A party colleague, Otto Strasser, described Hitler's speechmaking as follows:

Hitler responds to the vibration of the human heart with the delicacy of a seismograph, or perhaps a wireless receiving set, enabling him, with a certainty with which no conscious gift could endow him, to act as a loudspeaker proclaiming the most secret desires, the least admissible instincts, the sufferings and personal revolts of a whole nation . . . I have been asked many times what is the secret of Hitler's extraordinary power as a speaker. I can only attribute it to his uncanny intuition, which infallibly diagnoses the ills from which his audience is suffering. If he tries to bolster up his argument with theories or quotations from books he has only imperfectly understood, he scarcely rises above a very poor mediocrity. But let him throw away his crutches and step out boldly, speaking as the spirit moves him, and he is promptly transformed into one of the greatest speakers of the century. . . . Adolf Hitler enters a hall. He sniffs the air. For a minute he gropes, feels his way, senses the atmosphere. Suddenly he bursts forth. His words go like an arrow to their target, he touches each private wound on the raw, liberating the mass unconscious, expressing its inmost aspirations, telling it what it most wants to hear.[18]

The description is remarkable for its spiritual implications, and not merely because of a possible allusion to the healing of cripples by Jesus or in Jesus's name. Just as Jesus could know by the Spirit what was in a person's heart, so here, perhaps, a man could know by demonic inspiration what his audience wanted to hear.

Such reflections may never rise above the level of speculation, but they may not be out of place in a world that has witnessed demonic signs and wonders by Pharaoh's magicians, and that will someday witness them by the Antichrist and his prophet.

Penultimate Word

I hope that the note on which the earlier remarks concluded has not disqualified our excursion from being a work of some, however modest, scholarly merit. We hope they will invite worthwhile thought on some matters of spiritual importance.

18. Allan Bullock, *Hitler: A Study in Tyranny* (Old Saybrook: Konecky and Konecky, 1962), 373–74.

What can be known and affirmed with greater certainty is the role of God's Spirit in sustaining life and all things. The same Spirit also, arguably, has played a role in the endowment of some people with a dynamic authority to advance a kingdom—even a pagan kingdom—and rule, as it suited God's purposes to do.

We may reprise, as we return to our opening question—how could Cain build a city, or, more precisely, how could he have had an idea of a city?—that wherever an archetypal idea is concerned, God is the source. The idea of a city is one such idea, and we may say so without doubt because we know that God has a supernal city, whose architect and builder is God, that awaits its day on earth—on a new earth under a new heaven.

Moreover, God's imagination and its ability to form plans or ideas is the foundation of an echoing imagination and ability of the *imago Dei* to do the same, though always with a lesser scope and lesser power. Perhaps this thought may serve to moderate hubris as we consider that, in the profoundest sense, no one is an original thinker or artist or creator, but that anyone who is gifted is *gifted*, and has nothing which he or she has not received, and moreover been formed by God to be *able* to receive—that is, the person has been given a capable mind and imagination as a spiritual entity. So we can do what dogs cannot, and so too, as the decidedly non-Christian poet William Blake could nonetheless truly aver,

> "There is NO Natural Religion"
> [a],
> "Conclusion. If it were not for the Poetic or Prophetic character
> the Philosophic & Experimental would soon be the ratio of all
> things, & stand still unable to do other than repeat the same dull
> round over again."[19]

But these things come to all people, whether under Common Grace or Special Grace or both, by God's Spirit.

---

19. William Blake, "There Is NO Natural Religion," in *The Poetry and Prose of William Blake*, ed. David V. Erdman (New York: Doubleday, 1965), 1.

CAIN'S GENEALOGY AND LAMECH

A brief passage presents us with the line of Cain, and this brevity sets the pattern for all subsequent nonelect genealogies. Just as the Bible in general tells us much more about God's kingdom than it does about Satan's kingdom, so the Genesis genealogies tell us more about the elect line than they do about the nonelect. What we do learn is important, however, because it illustrates further God's protection of Cain and his line under Common Grace so that they may fulfill the cultural mandate after their fashion. So we are told the sixth generation from Cain produces the start of nomadic culture (Jabal; Gen. 4:20), musical technology (Jubal; Gen. 4:21), and metal-work in brass and iron (Tubal-Cain; Gen. 4:22). It is appropriate that a nomadic culture arises in Cain's line, since he was condemned to be a restless wanderer. He was also, however, the first to build a city, and we see important technologies arising in his line, technologies that have been a blessing to humans through many generations. It is important to recognize the hand of God's grace in such inventiveness. Later, God gives the Spirit, who makes the creativity and technical skills of Bezalel and Oholiab possible when they start work on the tabernacle (Exod. 35:30–35). It may be (on the understandings forwarded in "Excursus: How Could Cain Build a City?") that the same Spirit was involved in the creativity of a Jubal or a Tubal-Cain. At the very least, as humans made in God's image, those individuals were able to understand things about the world God had made and thus learn how to manipulate and configure materials in order to produce desired products and effects.

Lamech appears fifth in the genealogy, and we read that he took two wives, Adah and Zillah (Gen. 4:19). This small laconic statement contains a cosmos of rebelliousness (if that phrase is not an oxymoron). Lamech violates God's original intent for marriage—that one man and one woman shall become one flesh (Gen. 2:24)—an intent Jesus later affirms (Matt. 19:5–6). Lamech's move smacks of self-aggrandizement and uncontrolled appetite. The same qualities appear more explicitly in his short poem (Gen. 4:23–24), which is a masterpiece of thematic illustration (NIV translation, with phrases offset to highlight the parallelisms):

Adah and Zillah,	hear my voice
Wives of Lamech,	give ear to my utterance
For I would slay a man	for wounding me
a youth	for bruising me
If Cain is avenged	seven times,
then Lamech	seventy seven times

It has been noted that Lamech's poem begins with stock word pairs in parallel.[20] Canaanite poetry employed many such stock pairs (e.g., "heavens and earth," "day and night"), as did biblical poetry, which employed the same techniques as its pagan counterparts in Egypt, Ugarit, and Mesopotamia. The pairs "Adah and Zillah" // "Wives of Lamech" (proper noun paralleled by common noun) and "hear" // "give ear" are standard types of parallel in OT poetry. However, after those pairs, Lamech's poem begins to employ parallels that are non-standard. "Man" is never paralleled by "youth" in biblical poetry, nor is "wounding" paralleled by "bruising." Finally, Lamech employs a device known as *step parallelism*. In such usage, numbers in succession are made parallel—for example, "three" // "four," "six" // "seven," and so on. When one employs double digits, the step is higher—for example, "seventy seven" // "eighty eight." From this brief discussion, it should be clear that Lamech violates poetic convention by creating a step parallel between "seven" (which should be followed by "eight") and "seventy seven" (which should be preceded by "sixty six"). For a reader of ancient near eastern poetry, this last violation of poetic convention may have come across as the grossest. It caps off a series of broken rules that are all significant because the poem is a statement of Lamech himself—that is, an outflowing of his own nature. As such it reveals both his sentiments and his character. What comes out of his mouth is an utterance that breaks all poetic law and shows Lamech himself to be a lawless man. Just as poetry is a heightened form of language or expression, so this poem is a heightened illustration of what Jesus meant when he said, "It is what comes out of a man that makes him [that is, shows him to be] unclean" (Matt. 15:11).

---

20. Cf. Stanley Gevirtz, *Patterns in the Early Poetry of Israel* (Chicago: University of Chicago Press, 1963).

Lamech started by violating God's intent for marriage. He now also decides to take vengeance into his own hands. God promised Cain that *God* would avenge Cain's death sevenfold, as a deterrent that would protect Cain's life. Lamech, however, leaves no room for God in the picture. He now declares that—for a mere bruise—*he* will do extravagantly more by way of revenge: seventy seven times.[21] Lamech's threat shows a murderous character that has come down to him from Cain, and we note again that it shows the influence of Satan, who was a murderer from the beginning. It is also noteworthy that Jesus overturns the standard set by Lamech when Peter comes to him with a question about forgiveness. Peter asks, "Lord, how many times shall I forgive my brother when he sins against me? Up to seven times?" (Matt. 18:21). Peter asks if he must forgive as many as seven times—the perfect number, which would imply, perhaps, not perfect forgiveness but at least a complete discharge of his obligation to pardon. But Jesus responds, "I tell you, not seven times, but seventy seven times" (Matt. 18:22). Jesus's reply not only shows Peter how magnanimously we must be prepared to forgive, as God forgives us; it also overturns the standard set by Cain. Cain was emphatically vengeful. Jesus is emphatically forgiving.

As we consider the character of Cain, it is also important to remember that he is a vassal to the god of this world. Satan and his angels have gained legal entrée into the world. He now holds sway over, and his demons may influence, those who do not choose to align themselves with the Lord.

Those of Adam's lineage through Seth do align themselves with the Lord, as Genesis 4:25–26 informs us. Eve names her third son Seth (after the Hebrew verb meaning "to place, set") because the Lord has placed another son in her family to replace Abel, whom Cain slew. We are told further that people then "began to call on the name of the Lord" (Gen. 4:26). Joel reveals an eschatological scenario in which, after the "great and dreadful day of the Lord," that final day of his coming in stormy judgment, all those who call upon

---

21. Likewise Cain built a city to provide for his security apart from God's provision, and Lamech carries that ethos further by threatening to murder anyone who even bruises him, irrespective of any provision or protection by God.

the name of the Lord will be saved (Joel 2:32). His use of the phrase "to call upon the name of the Lord" echoes its well-established use in the literature of the Mosaic covenant—that is, of Israel under that covenant—so it indicates the behavior of those who recognize God as their suzerain and call upon him for help and deliverance. Adam and his line through Seth are of that sort, and on that note, the sin-racked history portrayed in Genesis 4 comes to a hopeful conclusion.

ADAM'S GENEALOGY AND NOAH

Adam's genealogy begins on a positive note entirely lacking in the genealogy of Cain. It is also much longer. Both of these facts indicate the greater prominence given to the elect line, the line of those who "call upon the name of the Lord," as is appropriate. Those who "call upon" his "name" are, in effect, appealing to God on the basis of who he truly is, and this is akin to faith—an amening of God's nature.

The *name* in the ancient Near East signified the essential nature of the one who bore it. That is why it was deemed so important to know the names of the various gods and goddesses. So later, in Athens, people built a monument to an "unknown god" (Acts 17:23) as their best way of appealing to and appeasing any deity whose name they did *not* know. The Lord, however, has revealed his name to his covenant people at various stages of his covenantal dealings with them. That name appears in a way that reveals more of its significance later, when God makes Moses his covenant mediator and tells him the divine name (Exod. 3:14), and we will discuss that name and its significance in volume 2.[22] Jesus is himself the fullest revelation of the divine name when he promises his followers, "Until now you have not asked for anything in my name. Ask and you will receive, and your joy will be complete" (John 16:24). A proper understanding of Jesus's promise tells us that we will receive whatever we ask for if what we ask for is consistent with his character and nature. If we do so our joy will be complete, because we will have the joy of

---

22. For now I refer the reader to the very good discussion in Duane Garrett, *Rethinking Genesis: The Sources and Authorship of the First Book of the Bible* (Grand Rapids: Baker, 1991), 18–22 (esp. 20–21).

knowing we are in step with the Spirit and at one with God in what he is being and doing (or put another way, amening who he is and what he is doing).

Adam and his offspring are not in that condition, but they can nonetheless call upon the Lord's name. And the emphasis now shifts entirely to the line—the elect line—that does so. The account begins with the wonderful reminder that man and woman have been created in God's image (Gen. 5:1–2, echoing Gen. 1:26–27). That reminder is not nostalgic but forward-looking. Just as God has created beings in his image, so Adam and Eve can procreate beings in their (and God's) image and likeness. And in a sense, each male born could, and probably would, be a reminder of the messianic promise of Genesis 3:15, as Eve's remarkable but premature statement at the birth of Cain anticipated ("I have gotten a man with the Lord," or "I have gotten a man, [*namely*] the Lord"; Gen. 4:1). A further positive aspect of Adam's genealogy is that Abel and Cain are not mentioned. Abel died without progeny, and Cain has gone away, initiator of the nonelect line. The focus now is entirely on the positive: a line of descendants who implicitly "call on the name of the Lord" and whose line of descent produces Noah and his sons.

SOME SUMMARY OBSERVATIONS

The fourth chapter of Genesis is largely an account of a sinful line and its progress. It begins with the birth of Cain, whose significance Eve understandably misconstrues with a messianic hope that may be profound in its intuition and yet proves vain in the short term. Cain will not be the incarnate Lord and will not strike the serpent's heel. Rather, he will fail to guard his door against sin and will allow it to become master over him. Given the demonic implications of Genesis 4:7, it may be that Cain, by failing to rule over the tempter, fell under the influence of evil spirits or of Satan himself (who was "a murderer from the beginning," apparently via his influence through Cain or perhaps by virtue of his success with our first parents, encouraging transgression that resulted in their deaths), and Cain rose up and murdered his brother accordingly. In any case, his spiritual qualities were, in some sense, passed on to his offspring (cf. Exod. 34:7) so that by the sixth generation we find Lamech threatening to outdo God in vengeance ("seventy-seven times" as opposed to God's "seven times"), and kill a man, even a youth, for merely bruising him.

The account concludes on a hopeful note, however, as we are told that Eve had another son, Seth, that Seth had a son, Enosh, and that "men began to call on the name of the Lord." That statement with its redemptive covenantal implications (as understood later) is then followed by the account of Adam's offspring with its hopeful opening reminder that humans are made in the image and likeness of God. The one who does what Cain could not—who does what Adam did not—the second Adam, who strikes the serpent's head, will come from that lineage. He will bring a judgment more complete and more final than the Noahic Flood. He will also bring a new heaven and earth and a new humanity—of which the heaven and earth restored to Noah and his offspring, and the human line preserved in and through Noah, could only be pale anticipations.

CHAPTER FIVE

NOAH AND THE REASON FOR THE FLOOD

GENESIS 6:1–4 AND THE FLOOD

The next three chapters of Genesis present the account of Noah and the Flood. They begin with a portrait of the condition of fallen humanity before the Flood, a portrayal that explains the reason for God's judgment on humanity, and they end with an account of the Noahic household redeemed from and through the Flood. This episode may be said to conclude properly with the Noahic covenant presented in Genesis 9, but that will form the subject of another chapter.

The Babylonian flood account, often cited as a parallel and a model for the Genesis account, also gives a reason for the Flood: the chief god Enlil (the storm god) could not sleep because of the din made by a human population that was on the increase, so he decides to wipe out humanity. But when humanity is destroyed, the gods become desperate because they now have no one to offer them food as sacrifices. Once the Flood is over and Atrahasis (the counterpart of Noah in the myth) makes a burnt offering, the hungry gods smell the fragrance and gather like flies over the offering.[1]

---

1. Cf. W. G. Lambert and A. R. Millard, *Atrahasis: The Babylonian Story of the Flood* (Oxford: Clarendon Press, 1969; repr., Winona Lake, IN: Eisenbrauns, 1999).

This is not the place for a polemic about the merits or lack thereof in characterizing the biblical account as secondary and derivative from the Babylonian. Good arguments against such an approach have already been made. But it is important to note that, unlike the gods of pagan myth, the God of Genesis is not capricious, impulsive, or shortsighted. God knows exactly what he is doing when he resolves to judge the earth, he knows that the reason for his judgment is just, and he knows exactly what the outcome will be. And although Noah does indeed offer a sacrifice of thanks when the Flood has receded and the earth can again be inhabited, it is not a sacrifice that God needs in order to sustain himself (cf. later, "Excursus: Noah's Sacrifice and What It Is Not"), since we already know from Genesis 1:1 that he created all things. There was a "time"—or a state of affairs—when the whole cosmos did not exist, and there is no evidence that God could not and did not manage perfectly without it.

THE REASON FOR THE FLOOD

After the enigmatic opening of the chapter (Gen. 6:1–4), which we discuss later, the narrative states the reason for the Flood clearly and unequivocally: "The Lord saw how great man's wickedness on the earth had become, and that every inclination of the thoughts of his heart was only evil all the time. The Lord was grieved that he had made man on the earth, and his heart was filled with pain. So the Lord said, 'I will wipe mankind, whom I have created, from the face of the earth—men and animals, and creatures that move along the ground, and birds of the air—for I am grieved that I have made them'" (Gen. 6:5–7). The reason for judgment is clearly stated: the increase of sin among humans on earth. That increase (and not an increase of noise) causes God pain, and he is grieved that he made humans. Since nothing is amiss with God, his grief is not misplaced, and it requires action. Although there is no doubt that anthropomorphic language is used here (the Hebrew reads literally, "It repented God that he had made the human[s] on the earth"), God in fact does not change his mind as humans do (cf. 1 Sam. 15:29) unpredictably in the flow of time, because his thoughts take place in the overall context of his own eternity. That is, God knew that this day would come long before he created the earth and humans on it. He also looks back on the Flood from all future days and beyond, and the Flood is also always present to him. For him, outside time, all things can be and are past, present, and future. That is why predictive prophecy is no problem for God (although it has often been a problem for scholars who do not believe it is possible). God knew when he created humans that they would sin and bring him sorrow, but he still created them and a world for them out of his great love. The eternal, loving, yet also just being of God is the proper context for understanding the statement "it repented God" that he had made man on the earth. We may allow that God is complex enough to have feelings of regret that he always knew he would have—and indeed always did have in his own eternal nature—yet still choose to create the world and humans on it, with a plan already fulfilled at the end of time (and whose fulfillment was already present before him and also past for him in Noah's day) to redeem what was lost through human sin.

We have noted the reason for the Flood—namely, the increase of human sin on the earth (Gen. 6:5), and it is important to recognize this cause for another reason. Some have imagined that the events recorded in Genesis 6:1–4 present the reason for the Flood. Since the reason is actually (and clearly) stated in Genesis 6:5, that interpretation cannot be correct. Rather, the first four verses of Genesis 6 present a unique scenario that does indeed show us events and behaviors that occurred in the antediluvian world; the state of humans as reported in Genesis 6:5 is one that accommodated all sorts of evil, including the sort presented by Genesis 6:1–4. We now turn to consider just what the nature of that evil may have been.

THE CHALLENGES OF GENESIS 6:1–4

The pericope before us has been the subject of much controversy and not a few surprising arguments by commentators. We read that, as humans began to multiply on the earth and daughters were born to them (Gen. 6:1), "the sons of God saw that the daughters of men were beautiful, and they married any of them they chose" (Gen. 6:2). Because we believe that some things about this verse can be rightly understood, we can also be bold to say that the verse has been the subject of much right and wrong understanding. It is especially a case in which the strictest rules of evidence ought to apply as far as possible. Personal preference should not cloud the waters as we seek to interpret this or any challenging passage, and we do our utmost here to present data as data with all proper respect to their significance and to the likelihood of their bearing on the question. Challenges to understanding arise in every verse of this small pericope, including the role of the Spirit and the significance of the 120 years (vs. 3) as well as the identity of the Nephilim (vs. 4). Some of these challenges may be resolved; others may remain unresolved. But (at the risk of sounding sententious) it truly is wholesome to admit when we cannot find an answer, rather than convincing ourselves, and trying to convince others, that we have found one.

THE SONS OF GOD AND THE DAUGHTERS OF MEN AND WHO TOOK WHAT

We read, "The sons of God saw that the daughters of men were beautiful, and they married any of them they chose" (Gen. 6:2). Two things are immediately clear in this verse: Men had daughters, and the "sons of God" made unrestricted choice among them ("any of them they chose"). Who those sons of God may have been is, after centuries, still the subject of disagreement; moreover, the verb translated "married" (NIV) actually means "took" (Heb. לקח) and is thus ambiguous. We turn now to these matters.

There have been three major schools of thought about "the sons of God." One school maintains that they were from the line of Seth: men of the elect line who trespassed the boundaries of their righteous company and took wives from the nonelect line of Cain. A second school maintains that they were ancient near eastern kings who multiplied the sin of Lamech and took not only two wives but as many wives as they wished. The third school of interpretation, and apparently the most ancient, holds that they were fallen angels who somehow managed to take human women and produce giant offspring (according to the LXX translation of Nephilim as γιγαντες, "giants").[2]

The first school of interpretation has some formidable advocates among its ranks, including Saint Augustine, Martin Luther, and John Calvin. Augustine states the position well: "By these two names [the sons of God and the daughters of men] the two cities are sufficiently distinguished. For although the former were by nature children of men, they had come into possession of another name by grace . . . When they [the godly race] were captivated by the daughters of men, they adopted the manners of the earthly to win them as their brides, and forsook the godly ways they had followed in their own holy society."[3] Luther likewise declares, "the Sons of God are those male descendants who have the promise of the *protevangelium*" (Gen. 3:15).[4] And Calvin distinguishes the sons of God and the daughters of men nicely:

> Moses, then, does not distinguish the sons of God from the daughters of men, because they were of dissimilar nature, or of different origin; but because they were sons of God by adoption whom he has set apart for himself; while the rest remained in their original condition. . . . It was therefore base ingratitude in the posterity of Seth, to mingle themselves with the children of Cain, and with other profane races; because they voluntarily deprived themselves of the inestimable grace of God. For it was an intolerable profanation, to pervert, and to confound, the order appointed by God.[5]

The Sethite interpretation, as this school of thought is called, has the advantage of understanding the sons of God in familiar and

---

2. A minor variant on this theme suggests that fallen angels (demons) possessed human males and took the women as they pleased.

3. James Montgomery Boice, *Genesis 1:1–11:32*, vol. 1 of *Genesis* (Grand Rapids: Zondervan, 1982), 245; cf. Augustine, *The City of God* (New York: Random House, 1950), 510–14.

4. Cf. W. A. Van Gemeren, "The Sons of God in Genesis 6:1–4 (An Example of Evangelical Demythologization?)," *WTJ* 43 (1981): 335.

5. John Calvin, *The First Book of Moses Called Genesis* (London: Banner of Truth, 1965), 283.

acceptable human categories: They were men, and they were, more-over, men of a chosen line who, in their folly, crossed the bounds of holy society and took wives from the sinful Cainite line.

This approach has serious problems, however. For one thing, it does not do justice to the use of the phrase "sons of God" in the rest of the Old Testament. The phrase is used only of angels else-where in the Old Testament (Job 1:6, 2:1, 38:7, and cf. the similar Pss. 29:1, 89:6). Our verse, Genesis 6:2, would be the one exception if the "sons of God" were Sethites. Of course, that is possible, but there is more evidence that points in another direction (as we shall see). The second problem with the Sethite interpretation is its arbi-trariness. It claims that the "sons of God" were Sethites who trans-gressed a boundary by marrying into a sinful line; however, there is no command against intermarriage with Cainites given to Sethites in the previous chapter of Genesis. The claim is eisegetical. It imports an idea that would later be part of the Mosaic covenant, which for-bade Israelites to marry Canaanites. But there has been no command prior to Genesis 6 that Sethites may not marry Cainites.

The second school of thought advocates a royal interpretation. The proponents of this school argue that the sons of God are mon-archs of antiquity who took to themselves harems. This interpreta-tion has been advocated more in modern times than in ancient. Paul Hershon commented over a century ago, "And the princes and magistrates saw the beautiful daughters and took them away from their husbands to be wives for themselves."[6] This understanding depends a great deal on one fact: Some ancient kings did claim to be divine offspring. However, it should be taken into account that ancient pagan kings as a group are never referred to as "sons of God" or "sons of a god" in any extant ancient near eastern inscrip-tion. They are also not described with that phrase in the Bible. Con-sequently, the royal interpretation, like the Sethite reading, runs counter to the actual use of the phrase "the sons of God" in the Old

6. Paul Isaac Hershon, *A Rabbinical Commentary on Genesis* (London: Hodder and Stoughton, 1885), 40. We note that the text does not mention the "sons of God" taking other men's wives, although the phrase "any they chose" (Gen. 6:2) seems to leave such a possibility open.

Testament. Moreover, there are no phraseological parallels in the ancient world to support it.[7]

The third interpretation is that the sons of God are angels. That would be consistent with the way the phrase is used elsewhere in the Old Testament, as we have noted. If they were angels, though, they must have been fallen angels, since they did something lawless. This, too, would be consistent with biblical usage of the phrase, for we read of Satan, the lawless one: "One day the sons of God came to present themselves before the Lord, and Satan also came in their midst" (or, "and Satan came also among them," Job 1:6; cf. 2:1). The sons of God in context are clearly angels and, with the exception of Satan (who seems to be one of them), holy angels. We affirm here what we argue at length later: Satan himself was and is a fallen angel and most likely a fallen cherub who once had sacred duty in Eden (cf. Ezek. 28:13–14). In any case, the phraseological evidence, though not conclusive, points toward the sons of God being fallen angels.

The phrase "the sons of God" also appears to be set in deliberate contrast to "the daughters of men," as though the two were of different genera. Gerhard von Rad remarks, "The *b'ne ha elohim* (L[uther]: *Kinder Gottes*, "children of God") here, by the way, clearly contrasted to the daughters of men, are beings of the upper heavenly world."[8] The Sethite argument is weak at this point, since the Sethites were also men, and it is not clear why, if they were called sons of God, the women should be called daughters of *men* (i.e., *in general*) when

---

7. One famous OT passage refers to a group of people as God's sons, but differently: Psalm 82:6 says of Israelite magistrates, "all of you are sons of the Most High"—but these are not kings, and the phrase is not the same. An individual can be referred to as God's son in the Old Testament. God says of Solomon's offspring, who will build the temple, "I will be his father, and he will be my son" (2 Sam. 7:14), but this is an adoptive sonship for David's son in particular. The Lord says to his Messiah, "You are my son. This day I have begotten you" (Ps. 2:7), but this is again (probably) the Davidic son—namely, Solomon—in the first instance and is ultimately applied to Jesus, the Messiah and Son of God par excellence (cf. Heb. 1:5). Again, the phrase "sons of God" is not applied to humans in the Old Testament, unless our passage is the exception. As we argue, there is a better understanding of the phrase "sons of God" (or its singular, "son of God") as a *terminus technicus*.

8. Gerhard von Rad, *Genesis: A Commentary*, trans. John H. Marks (London: SCM Press, 1961), 110.

a better contrast would have been "daughters of Cain" or some such more specific indicator.

These fallen angels, then, "married" or, to be more precise, "took" women—as many as they chose. The verb employed here, *to take* (לקח), is also used of Shechem's rape of Dinah: "And when Shechem the son of Hamor the Hivite, prince of the country, saw her, he *took* her, and lay with her, and defiled her" (Gen. 34:2). That is, Shechem raped Dinah, with fatal consequences for himself and his people (Gen. 34:5–29). Since the context of Genesis 6:1–4 does not provide sufficient data, we cannot insist that the sons of God raped the daughters of men when they *took* them; on the other hand, it is not clear that they married them. The point may have to remain obscure, although there is evidence from the New Testament that appears to shed some light on it.

RELEVANT NT DATA

Jude compares the sin of Sodom and Gomorrah with the sin of angels in a way that seems to reflect on our passage:

> Jude 6: "And the angels who did not keep their positions of authority but abandoned their own home—these he has kept in darkness, bound with everlasting chains for judgment on the great Day."

> Jude 7: "In a similar way, Sodom and Gomorrah and the surround- ing towns gave themselves up to sexual immorality and perversion. They serve as an example of those who suffer the punishment of eternal fire."

The Greek translated "in a similar way" (NIV) actually reads "in a way similar to these" (τὸν ὅμοιον τρόπον τούτοις). The word *these* (τούτοις) is masculine plural and should have a masculine plural antecedent. The only masculine plural antecedent is "angels" in the preceding verse.[9] So Jude appears to be saying that, like the angels,

---

9. Those who argue otherwise seem not to take account of the gender issue involved here. As Victor P. Hamilton has noted, "If we identify the antecedent of *toutois* [these] as Sodom and Gomorrah, we need to read and punctuate as follows: 'as Sodom and Gomorrah, and the surrounding cities in like manner with them, gave themselves . . .' We know that *toutois* (masc.) cannot refer back to *poleis*, 'cities' (fem.), unless we have here a case of gender confusion. If we identify the antecedent of *toutois* as the angels

the men of Sodom and Gomorrah "gave themselves up to sexual immorality and perversion" (Jude 7). Moreover, this perversion constituted an abandoning of their proper place (cf. Jude 6). Since the transgression of those men was homosexuality, that makes perfect sense: Men abandoned the proper use of women—that is, their proper place with respect to women sexually—and went after men instead (cf. Rom. 1:26–27).

What we know of holy angels is consistent with such a picture. Angels can do physical things and can assume physical, human form. For instance, angels appear to Abraham looking like men (Gen. 18:1), and they eat what Abraham gives them (Gen. 18:8). The angels who go to rescue Lot and his family also eat what Lot gives them (Gen. 19:3), and they are so physically attractive that the men of Sodom and Gomorrah want to have sex with them (Gen. 19:5).[10] Paul may be alluding to the danger of angelic temptation when he says, "For indeed man was not created for the woman's sake, but woman for the man's sake. Therefore the woman ought to have a symbol of authority on her head, *because of the angels*" (1 Cor. 11:9–10; emphasis added), although the passage remains obscure on this

---

of verse 6, then Jude must be seeing in Genesis 6:1–4 not marriage, *but rape and fornication, and titanic lust, an interpretation favored by pseudepigraphical literature.*" As Hamilton notes further, it is quite obvious that Jude was very familiar with the book of 1 Enoch. Not only did he quote directly from it (Jude 14 and 15 are from 1 Enoch 60:8), but he also used phrases that have parallels in 1 Enoch. For example, in the incident under discussion (the fallen angels), compare the following:

1 Enoch	Jude
[The angels] have abandoned the high heaven, the holy eternal place (12:4)	And the angels that did not keep their own position but left their proper dwelling (6a)
Bind Azaz'el hand and foot (and) throw him into the darkness (10:4)	have been kept by him in eternal chains in the nether gloom (6b)
that he may be sent into the fire on the great day of judgment (10:6)	until the judgment of the great day (6c)

Cf. further Victor P. Hamilton, *The Book of Genesis, 1–17*, NICOT (Grand Rapids: Eerdmans, 1990), 261–71.

10. Manna is even referred to as "food from heaven" and "the bread of the mighty ones [i.e., angels]," Psalm 78:24–25, but we cannot know whether this is a figurative or a literal statement.

point. In any case, the biblical data we have noted are consistent with a scenario in which fallen angels assume human form and carry out unlawful acts with women.[11]

Peter also seems to refer to the Genesis 6 passage when he says, as the first part of a long protasis, "For if God did not spare angels when they sinned, but sent them to hell, putting them into gloomy dungeons to be held for judgment" (2 Pet. 2:4). This statement sounds very much like what Jude writes about fallen angels that are "kept in darkness, bound with everlasting chains for judgment on the great Day" (Jude 6). Moreover, Peter follows that protasis with a second one that refers to the days of Noah and the Flood, and then by a third that refers to the condemnation of Sodom and Gomorrah (2 Pet. 2:5, 6, respectively). Thus his reference to the fallen angels precedes those two events in a timeline, just as the vignette of Genesis 6:1–4 precedes them: first, the fallen angel episode; second, the Flood; third, the Sodom and Gomorrah episode.[12]

It is important to understand exactly what this enigmatic vignette accomplishes, and understanding it will also contribute to our discussion of the identity of the sons of God. Our short pericope is so stark and dramatic—and laconic—in its appearance that it can seem almost out of place, and it has seemed out of place to some scholars. Hermann Gunkel, in his Genesis commentary, referred to it as a "torso"—a mythological fragment that a biblical editor attempted to incorporate into the surrounding narrative.[13] Julius Wellhausen reached a similar conclusion, calling the passage

---

11. We note here, as regards the sin of the men of Sodom and Gomorrah, that homosexuality was as sinful in God's eyes then as it was later defined to be under the Mosaic covenant, since the covenant was an articulation of God's eternal nature (as are all divine–human covenants).

12. Derek Kidner has noted the same and aptly comments, "Possible New Testament support for 'angels' may be seen in 1 Peter 3:19,20; also in 2 Peter 2:4–6, where the fallen angels, the Flood, and the doom of Sodom form a series that could be based on Genesis, and in Jude 6, where the angels' offence is that they 'left their proper habitation.' The craving of demons for a body, evident in the Gospels, offers at least some parallel to this hunger for sexual experience." Derek Kidner, *Genesis: An Introduction and Commentary* (London: Tyndale, 1967), 84.

13. H. Gunkel, *Genesis übersetzt und erklärt* (Göttingen, Germany: Vandenhoeck & Ruprecht, 1901), 59.

a "cracked erratic boulder."[14] S. R. Driver thought it was a piece of Hebrew folklore attempting to account for a race of prehistoric giants.[15] All these scholars took a much more liberal view of Scripture than the one taken here; however, they may not have been mistaken in connecting our passage with pagan folklore. It seems most likely that Genesis 6:1–4 gives us a true, although short, account of a sinful descent of fallen angels to copulate with women. The result of their unions might have been giants (LXX γιγαντες) or at least very violent men (another meaning of the Greek term). Those angelic acts then gave rise to pagan folklore about gods coming to earth and taking human women, accounts that recalled and recorded the very events of which we speak, although in a darkened and polytheistic form. Indeed, those fallen angels may even have persuaded the humans that they were gods come to earth. This understanding is consistent with Paul's statement about the pagan gods—namely, that they were in fact demons (1 Cor. 10:20)—an observation already made long before him by Moses (Deut. 32:16–17; cf. Ps. 106:36–39).

On this understanding, our passage gives us a small picture of angelic actions that gave rise to many pagan myths. One thing the passage does not do, however, is give us the reason for the Flood. An era in which fallen angels could come to earth and pass themselves off as gods and then take whatever women they pleased must have been a truly corrupt era, and that is just the sort of human cultural environment Genesis 6:5–7 portrays. But Genesis 6:5 makes it very clear that God brought the Flood because of human sin, just as he will bring a judgment of fire at the eschaton for the same reason. The passage thus gives us the occasion for the Flood, and it was not what the angels did but what the humans were doing. A parallel may be seen when the Lord returns to judge the earth at the eschaton. He will return to judge human sin, which will have become so universal and profound that people will be entirely open to believing any deception and to the work of Satan through his Antichrist—who, as Antichrist, will pretend to be the son of God. Nonetheless, it will

---

14. Julius Wellhausen, *Prolegomena to the History of Israel*, trans. J. S. Black and A. Menzies (Edinburgh: Adam and Charles Black, 1885), 317.

15. Driver, *The Book of Genesis*, 83.

be the universal and intractable presence of human sin (which gives the Antichrist his opportunity for successful and open action among people) that occasions the *parousia*.

Finally, there is one major, or at least common, argument that has been leveled against the fallen angel interpretation, and it deserves our attention. Scholars often refer to what Jesus said about angels and marriage and assert that it refutes the idea that the sons of God in Genesis 6:2 could be angels. Jesus was contradicting the Sadducees, who believed there was no resurrection. The Sadducees built a logical argument against resurrection by proposing a case in which a man died and his six brothers, in succession, all married his wife (according to the Levirate law, Deut. 25:5–6) and then also died, thus creating the apparently untenable scenario in which, at the resurrection, they all ought to have her since they had all been married to her (Matt. 22:23–30). But Jesus declares that they are in error, not understanding the Scriptures or the power of God, and that "at the resurrection people will neither marry nor be given in marriage; they will be like the angels in heaven" (Matt. 22:30). Some conclude from Jesus's statement that angels cannot marry; however, it ought to be clear that Jesus only spoke about holy angels. He said what holy angels do not do, not what fallen angels could or could not do. This is another case in which the data set clear limits to interpretation. In this case, Jesus's words cannot be shown to have anything to do with fallen angels. Consequently, they cannot be shown to have anything to do with the fallen-angel understanding of the sons of God in Genesis 6:2.

Scholars and theologians who reject the angelic interpretation seem to do so in much the same spirit as Calvin, who remarked, "The ancient figment, concerning the intercourse of angels with women, is abundantly refuted by its own absurdity, and it is surprising that learned men should formerly have been fascinated by ravings so gross and prodigious."[16] Calvin's objection is based solely on his opinion that it is absurd. His assertion is polemical and may be effective as such—and perhaps some of its power has derived from the fame of its advocate—but it is not likely to guide us well when it

---

16. Calvin, *The First Book of Moses*, 238.

ignores so many relevant data. Duane Garrett, in his study on angels, has made the following pertinent remarks about Genesis 6:2 and its interpretation:

> In short, the ancient Hebrew would take this to mean that angelic beings somehow took on corporeal form as males and had sexual relations with women, and this is how the ancient Jewish interpreters all took it. This does not really contradict the teaching of Jesus that angels to not marry (and thus are presumably without gender), since clearly what the angels do here is illicit and represents an abandoning of their proper place. I suspect that the real reason modern people reject this interpretation is that they just find it too far-fetched.[17]

Our passage does seem to be one that challenges the worldview of modern interpreters. Perhaps it challenges our worldview more than it challenges our research capabilities. The data in this case all apparently point in the same direction. Uncomfortable as it may be to some, Genesis 6:2, understood in the light of other biblical passages, does seem to be saying that fallen angels—that is, the devil's angels—had abandoned their proper station with God in heaven and misused their powers in order to appear as men (perhaps men with extraordinary powers, hence, gods in the eyes of people around them) and take whatever human women they chose. God in turn punished these angels most severely, keeping them bound in dark dungeons against the Day of Judgment.

THE SPIRIT AND THE 120 YEARS

On the understanding reached previously, we can say the Lord condemned the sons of God—certain fallen angels—to bondage in darkness until the final judgment. The Lord also reacted to the commerce between fallen angels and human women by declaring, "My Spirit will not remain with the human forever, for he is mortal; his days will be a hundred and twenty years" (Gen. 6:3, author's translation). The key phrase in this verse has sometimes been translated, "My Spirit will not contend/strive with" (e.g., KJV, ASV, NASB, NIV;

---

17. Duane Garrett, *Angels and the New Spirituality* (Nashville: B & H Books, 1995), 47.

cf. Luther 1545, "Die Menschen wollen sich von meinem Geist nicht mehr strafen lassen"), but the translation offered here is more likely and is reflected in some modern versions (HCSB, NRSV; cf. ESV).[18] Although the preposition (בְּ) is usually translated "in," the use of this preposition need not raise the question of the indwelling of the Spirit before the New covenant when we recognize the construction (יָדוֹן בְּ) as a phrasal one where the preposition (בְּ) is transitive (cf. the verb used at Gen. 3:3, "to touch," נגע בְּ), so that the translation is "remain with" rather than "remain in."[19] The alternate and more common translation, "contend with," is similar in concept, though of course with a different meaning. Finally, even if we allow that either translation has merit, both involve God's "remaining with" the human, for he must remain with the human in order to contend with him or her, especially since the "contending with" has to do with the Spirit's frustration as he remains with (and thus sustains even as he contends with) the rebellious human.

If, as appears likely, the translation "My Spirit will not remain with" is accurate, it would be consistent with the evidence reviewed earlier: People in the Old Testament did not have the Spirit dwelling constantly within them (a condition that only became possible after Jesus ascended and, with the Father, sent the Spirit to dwell in his followers).[20] More broadly considered, if even godly people under the Mosaic covenant—the fullest stage of God's special revelation to fallen humans prior to the New covenant—did not have the Spirit dwelling within them (cf. the promises of Ezek. 36:27, John 7:38–39), it is not very likely that humanity before the Mosaic covenant, having only a Common Grace covenantal relation to God, had the Spirit dwelling within.

So then, God declares that his Spirit, who has been instrumental in the creation and who works through the Word to sustain all things, will no longer sustain rebellious humans to the degree he had before. The withdrawal of God's Spirit, or at least the reduction

---

18. Cf. earlier LXX (Οὐ μὴ καταμείνῃ τὸ πνεῦμά μου ἐν); cf. with cognate evidence favoring "remain with," Wenham, *Genesis 1–15*, 142.

19. For נגע בְּ, cf. *BDB*, 619; for בְּ meaning "with," cf. *BDB*, 89–90.

20. Cf. earlier, chapter 2.

of the Spirit's activity in sustaining human life, has a consequence for human longevity: "His days will be a hundred and twenty years" (Gen. 6:3, and cf. Job 34:14–15). Humans, in general, will live to a maximum of 120 years. It is no argument against this understanding that most humans do not attain that age or that some humans live longer. God is laying down a general standard here, and humans all over the globe live and die under its aegis and will until the Lord returns. Finally, another school of thought argues that the 120 years have nothing to do with human lifespan but, rather, designate the time of human life remaining on earth before God sends the Flood. Such an interpretation could fit the overall Flood narrative, but it does not seem to be the more natural and straightforward reading of Genesis 6:3. Since it is possible, however, we can be content to live with ambiguity in this case, rather than insisting on one of two possibilities. And finally, given the nature of biblical narrative, both possibilities may be intended.

THE NEPHILIM AND THEIR ORIGIN

The final enigma of our passage is the nature and origin of the Nephilim. The Hebrew term seems to come from a root that means "to fall" (נפל). Nephilim is a passive form, so if it is from that root, it ought to mean something like "fallen ones." The Greek Old Testament translated it as *gigantes*, as noted earlier—either "giants" or "violent men." The verse reads, "The Nephilim were on the earth in those days—and also afterward—when the sons of God went to the daughters of men and had children by them. They were the heroes of old, men of renown" (Gen. 6:4).

The first statement seems deceptively clear: "The Nephilim were on the earth in those days—and also afterward" (Gen. 6:4). We know that the same term, *Nephilim*, was later applied to giants in Canaan in the days of Moses and Joshua. When Joshua and the other scouts return from exploring the Promised Land, they report, "All the people we saw there are of great size. We saw the Nephilim there [the descendants of Anak come from the Nephilim]. We seemed like grasshoppers in our own eyes, and we looked the same to them" (Num. 13:32–33; cf. Num. 13:22.28, Deut. 1:28, 9:1–3). So the Nephilim were "on the earth . . . also afterward"—that is, after the Flood. But the question naturally arises: How can that be? After all, the Flood destroyed all animal and human life on earth except for those saved by the ark (and also probably with the exception of many aquatic creatures). One can only guess, but one guess may be that a later race of giant people was called by the same generic name as those earlier giants by association. To cite a small modern example of such association, people in England have often referred to vacuum cleaners as "Hoovers," whether or not they were made by Hoover (and they have referred to vacuum cleaning as "hoovering," whether or not one does it with a Hoover). Likewise, some Americans in the 1950s still called a refrigerator an "ice box" even though ice boxes were a thing of the past. If the biblical usage is of this sort—and on the reasonable assumption that human nature has continued much the same—it may indicate that the original Nephilim were, like their later counterparts, giants and not simply "violent men," although one suspects that violence was part of their nature whatever they were.

The same verse tells us that the Nephilim were on the earth "when the sons of God went to the daughters of men and had children by them" (Gen. 6:4). Commentators have normally taken this to mean that the Nephilim were the offspring of those unions between the sons of God and the daughters of men. That, however, is not stated. It may be a reasonable inference since there is no apparent reason for mentioning both things contiguously unless they are meant to be related; however, such an interpretation remains an inference and unprovable. If it is true, then it may explain the heroes of ancient mythology, such as Ulysses, Achilles, or Aeneas (or Hatshepsut?), who were claimed to be offspring of unions between deities and mortals. Indeed, the next thing we are told is that "they were the heroes of old, men of renown."

It has been speculated that the fallen angels took human women as part of a satanic plot. The serpent knew that, someday, the woman's offspring would crush his head. So he engineered the scenario in Genesis 6:2 in order to thwart that promise. Fallen angels would produce gigantic offspring from unholy unions with women and gradually corrupt the human genetic line so it would be incapable of producing the promised savior. However attractive this interpretation may be to some, it is conjectural. The only reason the passage gives for the behavior of the sons of God is that "the daughters of men were beautiful" (Gen. 6:2). So the only explanation offered by the text is the sheer attraction the sons of God felt for the women—an attraction most likely understood as lust, since the polygamy or promiscuity involved suggests unbridled appetite.

EXCURSUS: "SONS OF GOD" AS A TERMINUS TECHNICUS

A brief survey of the biblical use of the phrase "sons of God" (and also its singular form, "son of God") seems to indicate that it is a *terminus technicus*, meaning one born of God by a *special creation*. The phrase occurs in the Old Testament only four times, three in Job and one in Genesis 6:2. A related but not identical phrase is the "sons of God/gods/the mighty" in Psalm 29:1—possibly, as Cross has suggested, to be understood as "sons of El" (i.e., "God"), thus the same in meaning, if not quite the same in form, as the phrase in question.[21] The occurrences in Job all refer to angels (Job 1:6, 2:1, 38:7). The occurrence in Genesis 6, of course, seems unclear and has given rise to much debate and our discussion.

The use of what appears to be the equivalent Greek phrase in the New Testament may clarify the core meaning of this curious OT phrase. We read at the beginning of John's Gospel, "But as many as received him, to them gave he power to become the sons of God, even to them that believe on his name: Which were born, not of blood, nor of the will of the flesh, nor of the will of man, but of God" (John 1:12–13, KJV). John speaks of the miraculous birth accomplished by the Spirit (who, we have argued, is the "authority" [ἐξουσία] by whom believers become born anew) in new believers. In other words, they—we—become sons of God by an act of special

---

21. Cf. Frank Moore Cross, *Canaanite Myth and Hebrew Epic* (Cambridge: Harvard University Press, 1973), 152.

creation by God: "Therefore if anyone is in Christ—a new creation [καινὴ κτίσις]" (cf. 2 Corinthians 5:17; author's translation). Finally, if we may press into service the singular form of the phrase, we read in Luke's genealogy of Jesus that his earliest human ancestor was "Adam, the son of God" (Ἀδὰμ τοῦ θεοῦ [Luke 3:38]).[22] That is, Adam was "born of God," with God as his father in the genealogy. Adam was a result of a special creation by God, as are the angels, as are those people who have been "born again."

If our understanding is correct, the phrase "sons of God" would be a *terminus technicus* in the Old Testament and would mean one who has become a son of God by an act of special creation by God. It is possible that the occurrence of the phrase in Genesis 6:2 is an exception, because exceptions, even individual exceptions, to normal meanings do occur in Hebrew and in every language, but it seems fair to say that such does not seem likely in Genesis 6; perhaps better, the burden of proof would rest with those who do not want to see the sons of God in Genesis 6:2 in the same way—that is, as (fallen) angels.

NOAH AND CHRIST

When God decides to judge the earth, we learn about Noah. There are four statements about Noah that may remind us of Christ: "Noah found favor in the eyes of the Lord" (Gen. 6:8); "Noah was a righteous man, blameless among the people of his time" (Gen. 6:9); and "he walked with God" (Gen. 6:9). The same three things are true of Jesus. We read that Jesus was in favor with God and humans (Luke 2:52); he is called "Jesus Christ the righteous" (1 John 2:1), and his walk with God was such that he could say, "The words I say to you are not just my own. Rather, it is the Father, living in me, who is doing his work" (John 14:10), and moreover we read of him that he

---

22. Ἀδὰμ τοῦ θεοῦ is short for Ἀδὰμ υἱος τοῦ θεοῦ; cf. Jesus in the genealogy as υἱός, ὡς ἐνομίζετο, Ἰωσὴφ τοῦ Ἠλὶ, and so on—in other words, Jesus "son, as was thought, of Joseph (son) of Heli," and so on.

could only "do what he sees his Father doing" (John 5:19). Finally, God says to Noah, "Go into the ark, you and your whole family, because I have found you righteous in this generation" (Gen. 7:1). God's instructions to Noah are in the singular: "go into" (בא, imv. sg., and then the action includes his family, "you and all your family," vs. 1), and "I have found you righteous" ("you" is the second person singular pronoun). In other words, God is telling Noah that he and his family can be saved in the ark because God has found Noah *singularly* to be righteous. By the righteousness of one, the many are saved—a salvific arrangement that clearly anticipates the saving work of Christ.

Noah was a righteous man, and his family was saved through his righteousness; even so, the Christology we associate with him is not technically grounded in his character. Christology is a matter of the office, not of the person. So, for example, Ahab is a Christological figure or a "type of Christ," not because he was a righteous man, which he wasn't, or because he "walked with God," which he didn't. Rather, he is a Christological figure because he was a king. As a holder of that office, he anticipates (however poorly in his character and behavior) the royal office of Christ. Christology is therefore to be found in those figures who held offices also held by Christ, irrespective of their character, moral stature, or behavior. Those OT figures who were kings, priests, or prophets are therefore types of Christ. Among prophets, covenant mediator prophets are more particularly "types of Christ" because Christ was the mediator of that "new covenant" with the "sprinkled blood that speaks a better word than the blood of Abel" (Heb. 12:24). Noah, then, is a type of Christ primarily because he is a covenant mediator prophet, and the covenant he mediates is, in fact, a renewal covenant—that is, a covenant that renews for humanity the stipulations and provisions of the original Adamic or Creation covenant.

EXCURSUS: NOAH'S SACRIFICE AND WHAT IT IS NOT

Although we take up matters concerning Genesis 7 and 8 in the next chapter, we make some remarks here on Noah's sacrifice at the end of Genesis 8. We do so as a follow-up on our comments at the beginning of this chapter. Some have suggested that the sacrifice might have to do with ratification of the Noahic covenant. Since, however, Noah's sacrifice comes *before* the covenant narrative, it is very unlikely that it has to do with covenant ratification, any more than Abraham's sacrifice in Genesis 22 ratifies the Abrahamic covenant (which the Lord ratifies by passing between the pieces in Genesis 15). In OT narratives that have to do with God's covenants, any ratifying sacrifices (when they occur or are reported) follow the articulation of at least the essence of the covenant in question, as in the cases of the Abrahamic covenant (Gen. 15:18) and the Mosaic covenant (e.g., Exod. 24:3–8). This is so even though supplemental torah may follow the ratification, as does happen with the Abrahamic and Mosaic covenants in the narrative material that follows the covenant institution in each case.

What, then, is Noah's sacrifice at the end of Genesis 8? At the beginning of this chapter, we called it a sacrifice of thanksgiving, and in the context of the reported events, this seems most likely since Noah offers it once he, his family, and the animals have come out of their long sojourn in the ark and are again free to stand on dry ground with a prospect of a resumed life with all that may entail. We note that the Lord's reaction to the offering is one of pleasure:

> Then Noah built an altar to the LORD and, taking some of all the clean animals and clean birds, he sacrificed burnt offerings on it. The LORD smelled the pleasing aroma and said in his heart: "Never again will I curse the ground because of humans, even though every inclination of the human heart is evil from childhood. And never again will I destroy all living creatures, as I have done.

As long as the earth endures,
seedtime and harvest,
cold and heat,
summer and winter,
day and night
will never cease." (Gen. 8:20–22)

First, as we noted at the beginning of this chapter, the Lord does not need to be sustained by human offerings because he created all things and also existed forever before that creation with no need of material sustenance. Just as we inferred the motive for Noah's sacrifice, we are bold to infer the motive for the Lord's reaction to it: He finds the aroma of the sacrifice "pleasing" because the offering it comes from is a tangible expression of an invisible reality—namely, a genuine, humble, and appropriate gratitude on the part of Noah for the deliverance and provision the Lord has shown him. God is not contradicting his earlier reason for sending the Flood when he says "every inclination of the human heart is evil from childhood" (Gen. 8:21; cf. Gen. 6:5). The world culture (so to speak) produced by such humans before the Flood led to a condition that would have so corrupted humanity that no place would have been left for faith—much as things will be when Christ returns (Luke 18:8). Now, however, although humans would still be born with sin in their hearts, the pace of corruption would take some centuries to reach anything like the heights it reached when the Lord chose to send the Flood. One reason for the slower advance of evil after the Flood may be the elimination of such egregious demonic influences as those reported of the sons of God in Genesis 6:1–4.

Nonetheless, although the Lord would continue to sustain life on earth, as he declares in Genesis 8:22, he would do so only "as long as the earth endures," and we know from subsequent revelation that the earth will not endure forever. The Lord will indeed never again destroy all living creatures *as he has done* in the Flood (Gen. 8:21); he will destroy the world and its life not by a Flood but by fire, as Peter declares: "The heavens will disappear with a roar; the elements will be destroyed by fire, and the earth and everything done in it will be laid bare" (2 Pet. 3:10), and again, "That day will bring about the destruction of the heavens by fire, and the elements will melt in the heat" (2 Pet. 3:12).

CONCLUSION

A survey of Genesis 6:1–4 leads us to conclude that, although it presents a pre-Flood scenario of unusual power and distinctness, it does not give us the reason for the Flood. Rather, we see here the unhallowed behavior of fallen angels, the sons of God, who "take" any human women they want (whether by marriage or by rape is ambiguous). They may well have passed themselves off as gods, and if so, their behavior gave rise to the many pagan accounts of gods who came to earth, took human women, and sired "the heroes of old, men of renown" (Gen. 6:4). Whether the Nephilim, also mentioned in the passage, were giants or only violent men, and whether they were offspring of the angelic–human unions or were merely around at that time (as vs. 4 states), remains unclear. The fact that giants in Canaan were later called Nephilim seems to support the "giant" interpretation for the Nephilim in Genesis 6:4; the existence of many pagan accounts of gods producing heroic offspring by human women seems to support the idea that the Nephilim were products of those unions recorded in Genesis 6:2.

There are times when an ambiguous conclusion is the best that interpretation can produce. Such a result does not close the door to future discovery and new understanding, but for some, it may close the door to speculation—to the natural human yearning to be able to say that we have solved a problem or answered a question when we actually have not. Maybe one of the best things a proper study of Genesis 6:1–4 can do for us is encourage humility.

The passage we have studied does not give us *the reason* for the Flood. Genesis 6:5 does that clearly enough, and its data are reinforced by what follows in Genesis 6:11–13—namely, that God brings the Flood as a judgment on human corruption and violence—a context in which the scenario of Genesis 6:1–4 would be at home, whoever the sons of God were. God's judgment also brings blessing, however, for it affords the opportunity for a second biblical covenant and another covenantal community. God makes that covenant with and through Noah, who thus becomes the second covenant mediator prophet in the Bible. As we have said, the Noahic covenant is a renewal of the Adamic covenant: The two together form one legal package under which all people continue to live and will live until the eschaton. We turn now to consider that covenant, as well as its eschatological implications, more closely.

CHAPTER SIX

THE FLOOD AND THE NOAHIC COVENANT

THE FLOOD ACCOUNT AS HISTORICAL BACKGROUND

The narrative, Genesis 6:9–8:22, functions as a historical background to the institution of the Noahic covenant reported in Genesis 9. We will examine the account in that light, also understanding its role as a type of the judgment to come that both Jesus and the NT writers affirm. As we note now, and discuss later, the pattern established here—a narrative that functions as historical background to a covenant-making or "cutting"—recurs in God's precovenantal dealings with Abram (from Genesis 12 to 14), with Moses and Israel (from Exodus 3 to 19), and also in the Gospels.

The narrative that lies before us is lengthy and both copious and repetitive in its details. It shares those qualities with other specimens of ancient near eastern literature, which could sometimes be laconic but, when they chose to be generous, could also indulge in repetitive statements or repeated use of stock phraseology. Traits like these are not highly prized in modern literature, and because they are somewhat alien in spirit to our literary practices, modern scholars have attributed such passages in the Old Testament to oral tradition or to a plurality of documentary sources. The same stylistic features, however, are now well documented in second millennium BC inscriptions from, for example, Assyria and Egypt, which were not the product of either oral tradition or documentary splicing. The ancients wrote so, and Moses was no exception. The Flood account thus contains repetitions, but those are the result of stylistic choice, not oral or documentary origin.

The fulsome account that we have makes a significant contribution to the overall establishment and literary presentation of the Noahic covenant and begins with some very important data. The first datum is that Noah was "righteous and walked with God" (Gen. 6:9). We have here the first occurrence of the word *righteous* (צדק) in the Bible, and the immediate context illustrates what the term means: the fact that Noah "walked with God" shows that he was righteous. The term *righteous* means "in accord with an established standard."[1] In Aramaic inscriptions, for example, when a king is called righteous, it means not that he is a moral or ethical person but that he is the *legitimate* heir to the throne.[2] That is, his accession to and session on the throne are *in accordance* with the accepted *standard* by which one inherits the throne. Therefore, Noah's righteousness is shown by the fact that he "walked" (= "lived") with God—that is, according to God's will or standard. The NT way of saying this for beneficiaries of the New covenant is, "Since we live by the Spirit, let us keep in step with the Spirit" (Gal. 5:25).

Moreover, Noah's righteousness can only come by faith, since he "walks with God," who is unseen; furthermore, he believes what God says about the coming Flood and does what God commands regarding the ark—two matters for which there was no visible warrant whatsoever. What is explicitly said of Abram, that "he believed the Lord and the Lord credited it to him as righteousness" (Gen. 15:6), is also

---

1. Cf. Wenham, *Genesis 1–15*, 170, on Noah's righteousness, "So in describing Noah as righteous, he is being pointed to as a good man who lived *according to God's standards of behavior*" (emphasis added).
2. Cf. H. Donner and W. Röllig, *Kanaanäische und Aramäische Inschriften* (Wiesbaden, Germany: Harrasowitz, 1971 [vol. I], 1973 [vol. II], 1976 [vol. III]), vol. I, 10; vol. II, 60.

true of Noah even though it is not explicitly said of him.[3] Both men amened the Lord and what he was doing, although the Lord and what he was doing were unseen (cf. Heb. 11:1)—thus they exercised faith. This is another example of the laconic nature of the Bible, according to which things may be present in an earlier account although not expressly mentioned or given a name but only explicitly designated or explained later.

EXCURSUS: LOOKING AHEAD— WRIGHT AND JUSTIFICATION

Because the subject of righteousness has implications that resonate through the Bible from Genesis 6:9 onward, I submit the following reflections on the topic at this point. Since NT scholar N. T. Wright has presented a very different view of righteousness, and since that view has attracted a significant following, I take occasion to disagree with it now at the outset of our discussion, not out of a polemical desire but out of a concern to make clear and indeed contradistinguish the understanding that pervades this biblical theology. What follows is a selection of thoughts and arises out of reading chapter 6 of Wright's book *What St. Paul Really Said*.[4] Wright develops an understanding of righteousness based on a law court setting, and I believe this interpretive construction illustrates a serious misunderstanding. Closely associated with the misunderstanding is Wright's failure to understand something about God and covenant, as I hope to explain.

Wright defines God's righteousness as having a twofold aspect: "God's righteousness is thus cognate with his trustworthiness on the one hand, and Israel's salvation on the other," and again, "In the Septuagint, the phrase means, most naturally, God's faithfulness to

---

3. The role of faith in Noah's life is not explicitly stated until Hebrews 11:7, "By faith Noah, when warned about things not yet seen, in holy fear built an ark to save his family. By his faith he condemned the world and became heir of the righteousness that is in keeping with faith."

4. N. T. Wright, *What St. Paul Really Said* (Grand Rapids: Eerdmans, 1997).

his covenant with Israel, as a result of which he saves her from her exile in Babylon."[5]

God's faithfulness to his covenant, however, is actually his faithfulness to *himself*, since, as I have argued, covenant is an idea in the mind of God, and any covenant God makes is also an expression of the nature of God.[6] Because God is faithful to *himself*—true to his own nature—he is also faithful to any covenant he has made, which is an expression of that nature and, consequently, in Israel's case, also faithful to redeem them out of exile according to promises he made within the Mosaic covenant.

A corollary truth is this: To be righteous is to be faithful to God's nature. In a divine–human covenant relationship, it means (for the human vassal) to be faithful to God's nature as he has revealed that nature within the framework of life created by the covenant. In other words, the vassal's covenant faithfulness, naturally and derivatively, means faithfulness to the *standards* of the covenant—which, again, articulate something of God's nature.

If we understand these facts, we are in a position to see clearly the inadequacy of what Wright says about righteousness in court. He asks regarding the forensic context, "What does it mean to use the language of 'righteousness' in this context? It means something quite different when applied to the judge to what it means to either the plaintiff or the defendant."[7] However, this is, in the deepest sense, mistaken, as a careful analysis can show.

Wright correctly says, "Applied to the judge, it means (as is clear from the Old Testament) that the judge must try the case according to the law."[8] However, he does not acknowledge that for the judge to try the case according to the law means that he is trying it according to, and in agreement with, God's revealed nature.

Of the plaintiff and defendant, he says that to be righteous does not mean they are, "before the case starts, morally upright and so

5. Ibid., 96–97.
6. Niehaus, "Covenant: An Idea," 225–46; cf. chapter 1. It is also true that God has a perfect idea of his own nature.
7. Ibid., 97.
8. Ibid.

deserving to have the verdict go their way. No, for the plaintiff or defendant to be 'righteous' in the biblical sense *within the law court setting* is for them to have that status *as a result of the decision of the court*."[9] There are two problems with these statements, and the first is that Wright sets up a straw man as a foil to make his own case seem more plausible. With regard to that, the issue, then, is not whether the plaintiff or defendant is "morally upright and so deserving to have the verdict go their way." This phrasing makes the straw man. It rightly says the fact that the plaintiff or defendant may be morally upright *in general* does not make his or her claims right—or should not incline the judge in his or her favor—*in this case*. But no one would doubt this. The issue is whether they are righteous—that is, in agreement with God's law and thus with God's nature *in this particular case*—in the matter before the court right now. Second and much more important, and related to what we have just said, when the court declares either the plaintiff or the defendant to be righteous, that declaration confers a public or forensic "status" of righteousness on them and thus effectively concludes the case, but the judge's declaration that they are righteous only acknowledges *a righteousness that was already there* before anyone came to court. The plaintiff or the defendant was *righteous before the case was taken up*. That is, one or the other of them *had already behaved in faithfulness to God's law*, or to God's revealed nature, in the particular matter that subsequently comes before the judge. Righteousness, therefore, is the *state of being in conformity to God's law and revealed nature*. The declaration of righteousness by the judge is simply a *public acknowledgement of that preexisting righteousness* that the court process has now discovered—or shown to have preexisted—in either the plaintiff or the defendant.

It follows that, *in the deepest sense*, righteousness is in fact, and contra Wright, the same for the judge, the plaintiff, and the defendant, because righteousness is conformity to God's revealed standard and to God's revealed nature in *any* matter. The judge is righteous if he tries the case according to God's law or revealed nature. The plaintiff is righteous if he brings a case which it is appropriate to

---

9. Ibid., 97–98.

bring to court because he has a claim against the defendant that is a true claim—according to God's law or revealed nature, the standard of truth of which the applicable law is an expression. The defendant is righteous if he acted according to God's law or revealed nature (and thus should not have been brought before the judge as though he had acted otherwise).

We have said, "Righteousness, therefore, is the *state of being in conformity to God's law and revealed nature.*" When it comes to a faith that saves one, it seems to me the matter is this: Anyone who *amens* (drawing again on the Hebrew term for faith; cf. Gen. 15:6) what God has done in Christ *conforms to God's revealed law* (in this case, the law of salvation—for example, "Believe in the Lord Jesus, and you will be saved" [Acts 16:31]), which includes affirmation of God's revealed nature as Savior of the world in and through his Son (cf. Rom. 10:9).

FINAL COMMENTS ON THE COURTROOM AND STATUS DISCUSSION

Wright makes the following comments toward the end of his court-room analogy and covenant-related discussion:

> If and when God does act to vindicate his people, his people will then, metaphorically speaking, have the status of "righteousness" . . . *But the righteousness they have will not be God's own righteousness.* That makes no sense at all. God's own righteousness is his covenant faithfulness, because of which he will (Israel hopes) vindicate her, and bestow upon her the status of "righteous," as the vindicated or acquitted defendant. But God's righteousness remains, so to speak, God's own property. It is the reason for his acting to vindicate his people. It is not the status he bestows upon them in so doing.[10]

God's righteousness is indeed his own property, but it is also a communicable attribute that the Holy Spirit works in believers; so Paul wants "the righteousness that comes from God and is by faith" (i.e., by amening who God is and what he has done in Christ, Phil. 3:9;

10. Ibid., 99.

it "comes from God" because the Spirit works the amen conformity in the person). Wright continues to think of righteousness as
a *status*, whereas it is a *state of being* in conformity with God's law
and revealed nature. Wright says, "God's own righteousness is his
covenant faithfulness." More deeply understood, as we have said,
God's righteousness is not merely his faithfulness to his covenant
but his faithfulness *to his own nature*, of which his covenant is a
partial expression. Consequently, *Israel's* righteousness will indeed
be *God's own righteousness*, to the extent that Israel can be faithful
to—conform to—the covenant that is an expression of God's own
nature, including his righteousness. Wright says that God bestows a
status of righteousness on someone. It is more accurate, I suggest,
to say that God *declares* the person righteous, and that declaration
is an affirmation of the righteousness the person already has. But
again, the person can only have *any degree* of righteousness because
that person has been faithful to the nature of God as revealed by
God—to whatever extent he has revealed it. So Abraham, when he
amened the Lord (Gen. 15:6), owned and was true to what the Lord
had thus far revealed to Abraham of himself and his intentions.
Finally, since no one can fully be faithful to God's revealed nature,
God has provided a way so that we can have *credited* to us the righteousness to which we cannot attain, and that way is belief in the
one he has sent, his Son who fulfilled the law for us, Jesus Christ the
righteous (cf. 1 John 2:1).

The second datum of our fulsome account (Gen. 6:9–8:22) is the
proper introduction of Noah and his sons Shem, Ham, and Japheth
(Gen. 6:10), who figure so importantly in the history that is to come.
The introduction is prefaced by a formulaic phrase used throughout
Genesis to introduce genealogies: "This is the account of Noah" (lit.,
"these are the offsprings/generations [תולדת] of Noah," Gen. 6:9a).
After this brief but significant introduction, the Flood account
proper (Gen. 6:11ff.) begins. That account further emphasizes and
establishes God's reason for bringing the Flood (cf. Gen. 6:5–7.11),
as we have noted, but it also provides other important data.

God's Purposes and Provisions

God intends to wipe out life in general from earth, but he also intends to preserve a remnant, Noah and his family. He begins with instructions for the ark, and it is of passing interest that the type of wood chosen (גפר, transliterated "gopher"), although of uncertain kind, has consonants consistent with a known type of tree, the cypress. Some translators identify it as such (e.g., NIV), and if they are correct, there is an apparent connection with the pagan association between the cypress tree and death.[11]

God gives Noah the instructions for his ark, and Noah, who walks with God (Gen. 6:9), obeys. God follows his architectural instructions with the promise "I will carry out/put into effect my covenant with you" (Gen. 6:18, author's translation), and the verb "carry out/put into effect" (קום, Hiphil) can be used when one is reconfirming or sustaining an existing covenant but also when one is promising to put into effect a covenant to be made sometime in the future (as at Ezek. 16:60.62).[12] In this case, there is a preexisting covenant under which Noah and his contemporaries live—namely, the Adamic or Creation covenant. The parallelism between Genesis 1:28 and 9:1–3 is consistent with our understanding that the Noahic covenant renews that prior arrangement, as we consider in more detail later.

God also provides for the renewal of animal life on earth by instructing Noah to bring on board the ark "two of all living creatures, male and female, to keep them alive with you" (Gen. 6:19). He also provides for a future sacrificial system by instructing Noah to bring on board "seven of every kind of clean animal, a male and its mate" as well as "two of every kind of unclean animal, a male and its mate" (Gen. 7:2). Here we find both the ancient near eastern love of repeated phraseology and a greater specificity as the narrative progresses. God also anticipates the later, more fully revealed sacrificial requirements of the Mosaic covenant.

---

11. Cf. most popularly Ovid, *Metamorphoses*, trans. Rolfe Humphries (Bloomington: Indiana University Press, 1955), 237–38.
12. Cf. Volume II, chapter 5 of *Biblical Theology* for further discussion of the covenant making/sustaining idioms.

THE FLOOD AND STORM THEOPHANY

Debate has arisen about the extent and nature of the Flood.[13] The biblical account, however, does not seem to leave much room for doubt as to the Flood's extent. We read of the waters that "they rose greatly on the earth, and all the high mountains under the entire heavens were covered" (Gen. 7:19). The waters did not merely cover the mountains: "The waters rose and covered the mountains to a depth of more than twenty feet" (Gen. 7:20). The predictable result was that "everything on dry land that had the breath of life in its nostrils died" (Gen. 7:22). The clear and simple language of this account does not naturally lend itself to an interpretation that would make the Flood a local rather than a global phenomenon. Objections have been brought forth because such a flood is not within the experience of modern scientists and interpreters and, thus, seems impossible to them.

Good studies have been done that advocate both a universal Flood and an ark that was capable of preserving the species needed to account for the varieties of life that now populate the earth, and we do not repeat those arguments here. It is significant, though, that, in biblical theological terms, a global Flood makes sense. Jesus and the NT writers make a point of drawing parallels between the Noahic Flood and the eschatological judgment (e.g., Matt. 24:36–41, Luke 17:26–27). According to them, the Second Coming will be like the coming of the Flood: sudden and unexpected, global, and a judgment on all God's enemies.[14]

The Noahic Flood is a divine judgment, and there are overtones in the narrative suggesting that, like the *Parousia*, it has a theophanic aspect. George Mendenhall, who did pioneering work on the covenant form in the ancient Near East and the Old Testament, has remarked, "The translation, 'When I bring clouds over the earth' [Gen. 9:14] . . . is completely inadequate, since it does not convey the sense that the Hebrew word for 'cloud' here (עָנָן) is first

---

13. The bibliography provides a sampling of scholarship on this issue.
14. The theological parallel invites an understanding of a global Flood but would not be seen by all as determinative for interpretation of the Flood's extent. However, the theological parallel is consistent with the actual statements of Genesis 7.

and foremost a theophany in the form of a storm-cloud."[15] Kline has likewise suggested that "the thundering storm clouds of the flood may themselves be regarded as an extended manifestation of the Glory-cloud of the Lord God, riding over the earth in judgment."[16] Psalm 29 reflects on the Flood event as well; in fact, it is the only other place in the Bible outside Genesis that we find the word for the Flood (מבול).[17] Since Psalm 29 is a paean to the Lord in theophany and celebrates his supremacy over the Flood—"The Lord sits enthroned over the Flood" (Ps. 29:10)—it seems to be a subsequent act of biblical interpretation telling us that the Lord was theophanically involved in the Flood.[18] The same will be true, of course, at the *Parousia*, when, as Jesus tells the Sanhedrin, "You will see the Son of man sitting at the right hand of the Mighty One, and coming on the clouds of heaven" (Matt. 26:64). He will come "in his glory," "sit on his throne in heavenly glory," and "separate the people one from another as a shepherd separates the sheep from the goats" (Matt. 24:31–32). The Lord comes in storm theophany to judge those who have rebelled against him. He did so in the garden after the Fall, and he does so again in the world of Noah. That latter judgment adumbrates the eschaton, as we have noted and explore more completely when we turn our attention to the Noahic covenant proper in Genesis 9.

THE END OF THE FLOOD

The Flood has an end in two senses. It has an end or a goal in view: the extermination of all God's foes and of the environmental system (the world) that sustained them. But it also has an end in the sense that it comes to an end. And when it does, the dry land emerges once again, just as it did in Genesis 1. The parallel is real and not merely literary. When God brought the Flood, he returned the globe

---

15. George Mendenhall, *The Tenth Generation: The Origins of the Biblical Tradition* (Baltimore: Johns Hopkins University Press, 1973), 57, n. 58.
16. Kline, *Kingdom Prologue*, 219; cf. Kline, *Images of the Spirit*, 101.
17. The occurrences are Genesis 6:17; 7:6, 7, 10, 17; 9:11, 15, 28; 10:1, 32; and 11:10 and Psalm 29:10.
18. Cf. Niehaus, "The 'God of Glory' and the Noahic Flood," in *God at Sinai*, 160–71.

to a preemergent state—that is, the state in which it found itself
before God caused the dry land to emerge from the waters. Only
after the land emerged did life appear on it. By bringing the Flood,
God has reversed the condition of the earth and made it what it
originally was. So now, again, there are no land creatures in existence except for Noah "and those with him in the ark" (Gen. 7:23).
When God causes dry land to reemerge from a global ocean, it will
be an act of re-creation, a making of a new earth, and this act is
introduced with an evocative term: "But God remembered Noah
and all the wild animals and the livestock that were with him in the
ark, and he sent a wind over the earth, and the waters receded" (Gen.
8:1). The term for *wind* here is the word that can also mean "spirit/
Spirit" (רוח), and it appears in the creation account when the "Spirit
of God" hovered over the face of the deep before God separated the
land from the water (Gen. 1:2). The narrative seems to allude to
God's original act and thereby indicate the "new creation" aspect of
the Flood waters' retreat.

God may indeed make a "new earth" after the Noahic Flood,
but that earth is not pristine. It still groans in a fallen condition:
The original futility curses on man and woman are in place as is
the original curse on the ground. That ancient serpent, called the
devil or Satan (Rev. 12:9), is still the god of this world (2 Cor. 4:4),
and humans are still under the influence of the devil and his angels.
The episode with Ham, soon to follow, illustrates clearly enough that
such is the case. We know that a truly new "heavens and earth" will
only occur as a result of the work of the second Adam. Still, God has
accomplished much with the Flood: He has rinsed the earth clean
and given humanity a new start, a start from a family progenitor who
is righteous. He has thereby ensured that humanity will not so corrupt itself that a messianic advent would be thwarted in its effective-
ness, as will be the case at the end of time, when humans will be so
corrupt that there will be no more faith—apparently, no possibility
of faith—in the earth (Luke 18:8).

As though to endorse both the Flood's historicity and its effec-
tiveness, the New Testament makes it explicitly parallel with baptism, as Peter recalls: "God waited patiently in the days of Noah
while the ark was being built. In it only a few people, eight in all,

were saved through water, and this water symbolizes baptism that now saves you also—not the removal of dirt from the body but the pledge of a good conscience toward God" (1 Pet. 3:21). Peter parallels the Flood and Christian baptism and thus indicates that, just as the Flood cleansed the earth of sinners, so baptism cleanses the believer and "saves" him or her through water. The parallel is symbolic and must be understood as such if it is to be understood properly. In reality, of course, baptism does not remove sin from the believer any more than the Flood removed sin from the earth. Paul's comment on baptism brings out a further dimension of this parallel: "What shall we say, then? Shall we go on sinning so that grace may increase? By no means! We died to sin; how can we live in it any longer? Or don't you know that all of us who were baptized into Christ Jesus were baptized into his death? We were therefore buried with him through baptism into death in order that, just as Christ was raised from the dead through the glory of the father, we too may live a new life" (Rom. 6:1–4). Where Peter drew a parallel between the Flood and baptism, Paul draws a parallel between baptism and the death and resurrection of Christ. Both parallels draw on a powerful and ancient cluster of ideas that associate death and water (in Ugaritic myth, for example, Yamm, the sea god, and Mot, the god of death, were close friends and allies). The biblical and pagan ideas probably go back to a primordial reality: There was no human life before the land was separated from the waters. Consequently, waters can stand for a preemergent state, or a state of "nonlife," for earth creatures. The Flood palpably underscored this symbolic value of water when it literally eliminated all land-based life except for the humans and animals preserved in the ark. So the Flood and baptism—and the cross—can be connected as symbols of death from which new life can emerge. If we add Jesus's comment to Nicodemus that one cannot enter God's kingdom unless he is "born of water and the Spirit" (John 3:5), we have another symbolic component. The water may be baptismal water or the waters of birth, but in either case, they partake of the same symbolic system, which we can illustrate with a schema:

Scripture	Water		Spirit/Wind	Consequence
Gen. 1:2ff.	Water, preemergent state	+	Spirit (רוח)	yield dry land
Gen. 6–8	Water of the Flood (= return to preemergent state)	+	wind (רוח)	yield dry land
John 3:5	Water of childbirth (= preemergent state)	+	Spirit (cf. Job 34:5)	yield human
Rom. 6:1–4	Water of baptism (= return to preemergent state = symbolic death to sin)	+	Spirit	yield human born of water and Spirit

The difference in the last two cases, of course, is that the human born of both water and the Spirit is "born again," or "born from above" (John 3:7), and has begun to become a "new creation" in Christ (2 Cor. 5:17). There is a clear parallel, however, between the birth of the original land out of water and its rebirth out of the Flood waters by the *wind* (רוח), on the one hand, and the birth of a person out of water and that person's rebirth out of the waters of baptism by the Spirit (πνεῦμα, with a similar range of meaning to the Hebrew רוח, both meaning "wind," "spirit," or "Spirit"), on the other hand. So when Peter draws a comparison between the waters of the Flood and the waters of baptism, he implies more than he says.

The end of the Flood, then, is a cleansed earth, emerging out of the judgment waters and ready for a new life with redeemed humans on it. The end of baptism, likewise, is a cleansed human (אדם, "earthling," from אדמה, "earth") ready for a new life as a redeemed human.

GOD REMEMBERS

When the time comes for the Flood to recede, we read, "God remembered Noah and all the wild animals and the livestock that were with him in the ark" (Gen. 8:1). The meaning here is not that God forgot or could forget anything he then later remembers. Rather, the phrase is a covenantal one, which indicates that God has now taken up the subject of Noah and the animals and that it is time to do the next thing with and for them. We read the same of God's dealings with others who are in covenant with him: "And God remembered Abraham" and brought Lot out of the catastrophe of Sodom and Gomorrah (Gen. 19:29) just as he remembers Noah and brings him out of the catastrophe of the Flood; "and God remembered his covenant with Abraham, with Isaac, and with Jacob" (Exod. 2:24; cf. Exod. 6:5) when he hears the groaning of Israel and begins to work their deliverance through Moses. So we find that the phrase can appear in signal cases when God is about to begin some (redemptive) act on the basis of a covenantal commitment.[19]

GOD'S COVENANT WITH ADAM RENEWED WITH NOAH

God does indeed deal with Noah on the basis of a covenant, so the first occurrence of the phrase "And God remembered [someone]" sets a pattern of subsequent usage with God as subject. However, God establishes his covenant with Noah in Genesis 9. Therefore, if the phrase has here, as subsequently, a basis in prior covenantal relations, God is dealing with Noah on the basis of an already-existing covenant—just as he later does when the same phrase is used with regard to Abraham (Gen. 19:25) and the patriarchs (Exod. 2:24). In all these cases, then, the appeal is to a covenantal relationship already in existence. The same possibility was indicated by the phrase "to establish covenant" in Genesis 6:18, where a

---

19. Cf. "He has remembered his covenant forever" (Ps. 105:8; cf. Ps. 98:3 [with "love and faithfulness" as synecdoche for covenant]; Ps. 105:42 [his "holy promise given to . . . Abraham" and its beginning fulfillment in the Exodus]; Pss. 106:45, 136:23 [both Mosaic covenant references]; and Lamentations 2:1 [adversely: "How the Lord has covered Daughter Zion with the cloud of his anger! He has hurled down the splendor of Israel from heaven to earth; he has not remembered his footstool in the day of his anger"] with reference to Jerusalem under the Mosaic covenant). The phrase is also used in two personal cases, when the Lord remembers [the prayers of] Rachel (Gen. 30:22) and Hannah (1 Sam. 1:19) and blesses each with a son—cases of individual mercy under the Abrahamic and Mosaic covenants.

better translation than "establish" would be "to carry out/put into effect," a translation that may make the prior existence of the covenant clearer.[20] Other lines of evidence that point to the fact of an Adamic or Creation covenant are, as we have noted, the second millennium treaty form that structures the creation narrative (Gen. 1:1–2:3) and the fact that the second Adam mediates a covenant that eventuates in a new heaven and earth and a new humanity, thus establishing a natural parallel to the themes of Genesis 1:1–2:3 and implying the covenantal nature of that passage and the covenant mediator status of the first Adam.

When God deals with Noah, he therefore deals with him as a person already in covenant with God. But in this respect, Noah is no different from all the sinful people on earth at the time. All were in covenant with God because they lived, were fruitful and multiplied, ruled over the earth and subdued it, and died—all under the Creation covenant. God singled Noah out as a righteous man, and God made him a prophet. But even as a prophet, Noah was not yet a covenant mediator prophet. Noah became a prophet when God first spoke to him and constituted him (as we read in 2 Pet. 2:5) a *preacher of righteousness*—that is, a man who spoke for God with words from God for the people around him. Our understanding of Peter's characterization is that Noah did hear words from God that spoke to and were meant to convict his generation. But even if we cannot document that particular prophetic revelation, it is clear that God spoke to Noah and gave him revelations of his purposes and instructions for his and his family's salvation, and all of that constitutes torah—that is, instruction. As a recipient of torah—even if only for himself and his family—Noah was a prophet. But he was not yet a covenant mediator prophet. God dealt with him first as a subject of the Adamic covenant, but from Genesis 9 onward God would deal with him as the mediator of the second biblical covenant, which has been named after him: the Noahic covenant.

---

20. We allow, however, that both of these terminological data are indicative and suggestive but not absolutely conclusive.

THE MAJOR PARADIGM
AND THE NOAHIC COVENANT

We now display briefly what we have called the *major paradigm* as it applies to—or expresses the dynamic creation of—the Noahic covenant:

1. *God works*	Gen. 6:13ff.
2. *by his Spirit*	(cf. John 6:63, Gen. 8:1)
3. *through the Word/a prophet-figure*	Noah (Gen. 6:9–7:5)
4. *to war against and defeat his foe(s)*	Humanity (Gen. 7:5–8:14)
5. *God establishes a covenant with a people*	Noah/family (Gen. 9:1–17)
6. *God's covenant establishes that people as God's people*	
7. *God establishes a temple among his people, because he will reside among them*	NOT YET

A few words are necessary regarding the table. First, as we noted regarding Adam, one who hears from God, as Noah manifestly does, is ipso facto a prophet. Since he heard God's words, which are Spirit, the Spirit was involved with Noah's calling and, presumably, also his task. God would have given him wisdom (as well as or via divine instruction) to construct the ark and make all necessary preparations. As a recipient of torah from the Lord, he is, again, a prophet. Since he did mediate a covenant for others, he is also a covenant mediator prophet as Adam was, and as Abraham, Moses, David, and Jesus would be.

THE NATURE OF THE NOAHIC COVENANT

The covenant with Noah (whose name, incidentally, means "rest") is a renewal covenant. It is the sort of covenant a suzerain in the ancient Near East would make with the son of a vassal king, when that vassal king had died and his son had succeeded him to the throne. In the present case, the sons, who are royal descendants of Adam and are ruling over the earth, are going to be judged and destroyed by their suzerain—with the exception of Noah and his household, who will be the new royalty. That new royalty will carry on the work of ruling over the earth and subduing it once the judgment has taken hold and accomplished its goals. When that time comes, the suzerain will make a new covenant with those royal vassals. But as in the ancient Near East, the new covenant will, in fact, be a renewal covenant: It will reestablish the terms of the original covenant but with some minor modifications appropriate to the new conditions or circumstances. The renewal nature of the Noahic covenant becomes clear when we compare the stipulations of the Adamic/Creation and Noahic/Re-Creation covenants:

THE ADAMIC/CREATION COVENANT IN GENESIS 1:28–29

"*And God blessed them and God said to them,* '**Be fruitful and multiply, and fill the earth** and subdue it; and have dominion over the fish of the sea and over the birds of the air and over every living thing that moves upon the earth."

THE NOAHIC/RE-CREATION COVENANT OF GENESIS 9:1–3

"*And God blessed Noah and his sons, and said to them,* '**Be fruitful and multiply, and fill the earth**. The fear of you and the dread of you shall be upon every beast of the earth, and upon every bird of the air, upon everything that creeps on the ground and all the fish of the sea; into your hand they are delivered."

These commands or stipulations are identical except for one significant alteration. The command to subdue the earth and have dominion over the animals is replaced by a promise: God will put the fear of humans on all the animals. The reason for this alteration may not be obvious but may fairly well be intuited. Fear, or respect, was what Adam and Eve owed to God and what the animals owed them. But just as Adam and Eve abandoned their fear of God, so the animals gave up respecting humans. Such a state of affairs is anomia or lawlessness because humans were made to fear or revere God, and the animals were made to respect and be subordinate to humans—in other words, that was the law of their being in every case. However, once Satan entered the world and gained rights over it as suzerain, he brought lawlessness with him. It remains a mystery how it came to be, but since the Fall, animals do not respect humans as before, with the result that some of them would attack and maim humans and even devour them—a state of affairs alien to the spirit of Eden. So God now imposes on the animals, which lived in a state of disrespect of humans after the fall, a fear that will help to restore the human–animal balance of authority. So in this way, too, God is making a new earth, renewing conditions for Noah and his family so they can be somewhat as they were at the beginning. Of course, the renewal is imperfect because the world continues to be inhabited by sinful people. Only the second Adam will truly bring a new earth and a new humanity without sin. In that day, as Isaiah foretold, humans and animals will live together in complete harmony, with animals respecting humans and humans not fearing animals:

> The wolf will live with the lamb,
> the leopard will lie down with the goat,
> the calf and the lion and the yearling together,
> and a little child will lead them.
> The cow will feed with the bear,
> their young will lie down together,
> and the lion will eat straw like the ox.
> The infant will play near the hole of the cobra,
> and the young child put his hand into the viper's nest.
> They will neither harm nor destroy
> on all my holy mountain,
> for the earth will be full of the knowledge of the Lord
> as waters cover the sea. (Isa. 11:6–9)

The state of Edenic peace and proper reverence will occur because God will again be fully in the picture: All creatures will know his presence, and that presence will be the source of *shalom* or peace and wholeness. As we have indicated earlier, the Holy Spirit would be very much at work both sustaining all things in the new creation (as he does in the present creation) and maintaining them in a state of *shalom* (which is also a state of lawfulness and reverence to God); he does not do so extensively in the present creation.

Genesis 9 presents us with a renewal covenant, one that constitutes a renewed kingdom (earth) and a renewed vassal king and royalty (Noah and his family). As in the case of the Adamic covenant, the elements of the covenant form are to be found in the narrative itself and may be presented as follows:

Genesis 9:1–17		Second Millennium Covenant Structure
Title	9:1	"And *God* blessed"
Stipulations	9:1b	"Be fruitful and multiply, and fill the earth"
	9:4	"not eat flesh with its life, its blood"
	9:7	"be fruitful and multiply" = *INCLUSIO*
Blessings	9:1	"And God *blessed*"
	9:2	fear of man on all creatures
	9:3	all plants and animals for food
	9:11b	no second Flood
Curse	9:5–6	man's blood demanded from man and beast
Oath	9:9–11a	"I establish my covenant with you and your seed."
Sign	9:12–17	Rainbow and explanation of its meaning

The one thing that appears to be lacking in this schema is a historical prologue (which recounts the historical background that preceded the covenant), typically a major part of second millennium ancient near eastern covenants. As we have remarked, the narrative, Genesis 6:9–8:22, supplies that background, as it gives us the relevant historical data regarding the relationship of the suzerain-to-be (Yahweh) and the vassal-to-be (Noah). As I have argued elsewhere, and as was universally the case in the ancient Near East, some sort of relationship existed between the suzerain and the vassal before they entered into a covenant and actually became, with respect to each other, suzerain and vassal. That is the whole point of historical prologues in the ancient treaties: They describe the prior relationship between the two as a matter of historical record, on the basis of which they may now enter into a covenant relationship.[21] As a result of God's gracious intervention in Noah's life, by which he constituted Noah a prophet and gave him torah that saved him and his family, God now has the historical credentials, as it were, to call Noah into a suzerain–vassal covenant. To report that prior history is the literary and legal function of the narrative, Genesis 6:9–8:22.

The Noahic covenant itself or, rather, the narrative that enshrines it has some interesting features that deserve further notice. One of these is God's repetition of his command to "be fruitful and multiply" (Gen. 9:1b, 7). This repetition forms an *inclusio* around the establishment of the fear of humans on all creatures (Gen. 9:2), the provision of all plants and animals for food (Gen. 9:3), the stipulation not to eat the flesh with its blood (Gen. 9:4), and the death mandate for all who shed human blood (Gen. 9:5–6). In other words, the *inclusio* brackets the essential blessing, stipulation, and curse material of the passage. Since these are the essential torah of the covenant, they may be said to stand for the whole covenant (on the principle of *pars pro toto*), and the *inclusio* around them thus emphasizes God's commitment to stand by this covenant, this torah, with the result that humans will indeed be able to "be fruitful and multiply." Repetition here is for emphasis (as often), and God further emphasizes the point by promising not to bring another Flood upon the earth (Gen. 9:11b).

Another matter that deserves attention is the death penalty God imposes on any who shed human blood:

a	b
Whoever sheds the blood	of the human,
b'	a'
by the human	shall his blood be shed;
c	d
for in the image of God	has God made the human
	(Gen. 9:6, author's translation)

---

21. Cf. Niehaus, "An Argument," 270; "Covenant: An Idea," 234–40; for the form criticism of Genesis 9:1–17 and for further discussion, cf. Niehaus, "Covenant and Narrative," 541–42.

This poetic assertion reinforces (with a chiastic statement) what God has said in the previous verse: He will surely demand an accounting from any human or animal that sheds human blood. The poetic restatement of God's intent makes it clear that the form of "accounting" he will demand is death, and those who wish to find a biblical ground for the death penalty in cases of murder in any society must begin here. This passage makes it clear that the death penalty for murder not only is a feature of the later Mosaic covenant, which may be said to have passed away (cf. Heb. 8:13), but comes before that covenant, and the Noahic covenant in which it comes is a Common Grace covenant under which all humans stand to this day, and will until the end of time.

EXCURSUS: DEATH PENALTY UNDER THE MOSAIC COVENANT

Because the Mosaic covenant continues the Noahic death penalty, and because the issue of capital punishment has been so prominent in the politics of statecraft, we branch off our main discussion at this point to give an outline of what the Mosaic covenant later has to say about capital punishment in a theocratic state. We do not engage such issues as theonomy directly but consider some implications that we may feel free to explore further in volume 2 of this work. We submit, then, that the Mosaic covenant reaffirms the Noahic death penalty and gives further grounds for capital punishment. What follows is a synopsis and is not exhaustive:

1. Mosaic Covenant reaffirms the death penalty of the Noahic covenant
    a. Leviticus 24:17: "If anyone takes the life of a human being [כל־נפש אדם], he must be put to death."
    b. Leviticus 24:21: "Whoever kills an animal must make restitution, but whoever kills a man [אדם] must be put to death."

2. Other grounds for the death penalty under the Mosaic
    covenant
    a. Approach to a holy place by undesignated people
        (1) Mount Sinai, Exodus 19:12: "Whoever touches
            the mountain shall surely be put to death."
        (2) The tabernacle—anyone except Moses,
            Aaron, and his descendants
            Numbers 1:51, 3:10.38, and so on
    b. Blasphemy
        (1) Leviticus 24:16
    c. Following other gods in any form
        (1) Leviticus 20:2: someone who gives his child
            to Molech
        (2) Deuteronomy 13:5: a prophet or dreamer
            who says to follow other gods
    d. Mediums or spiritists
        (1) Leviticus 20:27
    e. Breaking the Sabbath
        (1) Exodus 31:15, 32:5
    f. Dishonoring father or mother
        (1) Exodus 21:25: by attacking them
        (2) Exodus 21:17 (Lev. 20:9): by cursing them
        (3) Leviticus 20:11: by sleeping with one's
            father's wife
    g. Sexual sins
        (1) Exodus 22:19 (Lev. 20:16): with an animal
        (2) Leviticus 20:10 (Lev. 20:12): adultery
        (3) Leviticus 20:13: homosexuality
    h. Kidnapping
        (1) Exodus 21:16
    i. Manslaughter, for example
        Exodus 21:29:

        If a bull gores someone and is a habitual gorer,
            and the owner has not penned it up,
        "the bull must be stoned and
            the owner also must be put to death"

   3. Summary: Two categories of sins deserve the death penalty
     a. Against God
       (1) Approach to a holy place by undesignated people
       (2) Blasphemy
       (3) Following other gods in any form
       (4) Mediums or spiritists
       (5) Breaking the Sabbath
     b. Against people
       (1) Dishonoring father or mother
       (2) Sexual sins
       (3) Kidnapping
       (4) Murder/manslaughter

The brief synopsis in this list affords us opportunity to reflect on the death penalty in a theocratic state. In such an entity, sins against God entail the death penalty, much in the spirit of God's first warning to humans that disobeying his command regarding the fruit (which is tantamount to transgression against God, who gave the command) would lead to death. The concept is entirely appropriate: God is life and the source of life, and any transgression against him or opposition to him is opposition to life and the source of it—and the just consequence is death.[22]

When it comes to sins against others, all humans are made in God's image and so, again, harm done to them is some form of assault on God (cf. James 3:9, "With the tongue we praise our Lord and Father, and with it we curse human beings, who have been made in God's likeness"). God has set the death penalty for such assaults when they are severe enough.

Although the form of God's kingdom under the Mosaic covenant was a nation state, the kingdom of God on earth since Pentecost has the form of the church. Consequently, the same laws that

---

22. We add now the fact that false prophets under the Mosaic covenant also merit capital punishment because, if the people were to follow them, their disobedience would entail the covenant curses and the dismantling of the state. In a sense, the false prophet is one who counsels high treason against Israel's king. We engage these issues in more detail in volume 2.

governed ancient Israel cannot be insisted on in any land today. God gave laws to a theocratic state, but no theocratic state exists today. Any human attempt to make one would be vain because only God can determine the form of his kingdom.[23] On the other hand, Jeremiah 18 makes it clear that the more a nation conforms to God's standards, even as accessible only under Common Grace, the more that nation will be blessed; the opposite is also true (cf. Jer. 18:1–10). To bring our somewhat proleptic discussion back to the death penalty of the Noahic covenant alone, we simply note again that the same penalty was affirmed in the Mosaic covenant, thus continuing that ancient, pre-Abrahamic (and thus pre–Special Grace as articulated in covenant) standard.

Another item that deserves our attention is the rainbow and God's explanation of its meaning. He says, "I have set my rainbow in the clouds, and it will be the sign of the covenant between me and you and all living creatures of every kind" (Gen. 9:13). God's statement may indicate that, before the Flood, the earth was completely covered by a cloud canopy, which got rained out when God opened the "floodgates of the heavens" (cf. Gen. 8:2), so that the sun became visible from earth for the first time after the Flood rains ceased. Or, God may simply be saying that he now constitutes the rainbow, which was always visible on earth, as a sign of the Noahic covenant. It remains unclear and probably irresolvable which explanation is correct, but either way, it is clear that God now designates the rainbow as the sign of this covenant. The sign may be an allusion in the natural realm to God's heavenly glory presence, since we read in the theophanies of Ezekiel 1 and Revelation 4 that a rainbow surrounds the throne presence of God (cf. Ezek. 1:28, Rev. 4:3). If so, we understand more deeply the beauty of the statement in Psalm 29

23. In a similar vein, only God can renew a divinely initiated covenant, —for example, he renews the Sinai covenant with a later generation on the planes of Moab (Deuteronomy). Any human efforts to "renew" such a covenant can never rise above the level of human recommitments to the existing covenant. Cf. discussion later.

that "the Lord sits enthroned over the Flood; the Lord is enthroned as king forever" (Ps. 29:10): His session on his throne over the Flood would then have included the theophanic "rainbow" presence (both during the Flood and as it came to an end) reported in Ezekiel and Revelation. There may be a different, or additional, significance to the rainbow, however. As Mendenhall has reminded us, the Assyrians portrayed their chief god, Ashur, as one victorious in war, and at the end of battle, his bow hung suspended (i.e., he hung up his bow) as a sign that the war was over and that he had won it. It may be that this later concept harks back to the time when God, victorious in his war of judgment against his foes, designated a bow of light as the symbol of his victory and a promise that he would never again wage such a war.

Of course, God will again come to wage war against his foes, only it will not be with water but with fire. That is why Peter can draw such a clear parallel between the Flood and the Lord's eschatological return in judgment: "But they [scoffers] deliberately forget that long ago by God's word the heavens existed and the earth was formed out of water and by water. By these waters also the world of that time was deluged and destroyed. By the same word the present heavens and earth are reserved for fire, being kept for the day of judgment and destruction of ungodly men" (2 Pet. 3:5–7). He can affirm that the heavens and earth of long ago existed "by the word of God" because we read the same in Genesis 1. But he can further affirm that the present heavens and earth have been stored up for judgment by fire "by the same word" (τῷ αὐτῷ λόγῳ, 1 Pet. 3:7) because that "word" is God's covenantal word of creation, spoken by the Spirit through the preincarnate Son. Two factors lead to this conclusion. The first is the fact that ancient treaties were characterized as the "words" of the suzerain. The second is that all things were made through the Word. So the world was created through that preincarnate Word—as God spoke into being the heavens and the earth—by words that were Spirit (cf. John 6:63). By that same word of covenantal commitment, God will judge the present world and bring about a new heavens and earth through the incarnate, resurrected, and ascended Word: the second Adam.

THE NOAHIC COVENANT
AND ESCHATOLOGY

Peter's words open a door to eschatology. There is a phrase in Genesis 9 that already points in the same direction, and it has to do with the nature of God's covenant with Noah. When God declared that he was making a covenant with Noah, he included a promise that he would never again bring a Flood on the earth (Gen. 9:11). God subsequently clarified that his covenant was a עולם ברית, translated by many as "everlasting covenant" (cf. NIV, Gen. 9:16). This translation is unfortunate, however, as further consideration can show. The first thing to consider is the root meaning of the term translated "everlasting" (עולם), which comes from a root that means "hidden." The Hebrew words for *male* and *female virgin* come from the same root, the sense possibly being that, under the Mosaic covenant, for anyone who had never married, certain parts of the anatomy should have remained "hidden" from view (at least, from the view of a would-be partner). In any case, when applied to time, the meaning of the term is determined by its context. For instance, the same word is used in Isaiah 63:11: "Then his people recalled the days of old [עולם], the days of Moses and his people" (lit., "The days of old, Moses, his people," a simple case of double duty usage ["The days"] and asyndeton ["of Moses, his people"]). Now clearly, the days of Moses were not eternally remote from Isaiah and his contemporaries nor are they eternally remote even from us. The meaning of עולם, when applied to time, is consequently: so far removed from the speaker/writer that the period designated is "hidden" from view. The days of Moses were that remote for Isaiah and his contemporaries. If the period in question is *eternally* far removed, a translation can reflect the same, rendering עולם by such words as *eternal* or *everlasting*. In other words, if the Noahic covenant were to endure forever, it could truly be termed an *everlasting covenant*. However, we know that the Noahic covenant has to do with the present and ongoing heavens and earth and with people's stewardship of the present and ongoing world. One day, however, that world will come to an end. One day there will be a "new heavens and earth." When that day comes, the Noahic covenant will no longer be in effect, with, for example, its provision of the death penalty for murder, for in that day there will be no murder, and the present heavens and earth will have passed away.

Isaiah portrays those last days in a passage that scholars have called the "Isaiah Apocalypse," Isaiah 24.[24] The passage presents a scenario of divine judgment that is clearly both universal and final, and it concludes with God among his people in glory.[25] A key term at the outset of Isaiah's vision is the one we have already discussed in Genesis 9:16, the ברית עולם—*everlasting covenant*:

> The earth lies polluted
> Under its inhabitants;
> For they have transgressed the laws,
> Violated the statutes,
> Broken the *everlasting covenant* (ברית עולם). (NIV)

It is important to recognize at the outset the global, or cosmic, nature of this judgment. We read that the inhabitants of the earth have "transgressed the laws" and "violated the statutes"—terms used in covenantal contexts in the Old Testament. But what "laws" or "statutes" govern the people of the whole earth? Clearly, they are God's laws and statutes, since he is the one bringing judgment. And clearly the judgment is cosmic because we read that the Lord will punish the hosts of heaven in heaven (המרום, which can only mean "heaven" in context) and the kings of the earth on the earth (Isa. 24:21–22). The clue to the nature of the laws and statutes lies in the term ברית עולם, translated "everlasting covenant" but better rendered something like "long-lasting covenant" or "long-enduring covenant." That translation makes sense of the phrase in Genesis 9:16, since, as we have seen, the Noahic covenant will one day come to an end, although it certainly has been of long duration and will endure until the eschaton.

---

24. Cf. discussion in Niehaus, *God at Sinai*, 319–21.
25. The discussion that follows was composed in 2006 and summarizes what I had taught on the matter for two decades. I was delighted to find many of the same concepts set forth subsequently by Paul Williamson in his *Sealed with an Oath: Covenant in God's Unfolding Purpose* (2007).

That is also the preferred translation in Isaiah 24, since the cosmic judgment that Isaiah describes can only be visited on a world full of people who have all broken covenant with God. In other words, the ברית עולם, which Isaiah describes as "broken" by everyone on earth, is the Noahic covenant. That is the only covenant characterized by that phrase that includes everyone on earth as God's vassals.[26]

The Noahic covenant, moreover, is actually a renewal of the Adamic covenant, as we have noted, and the two covenants together form one legal package. The same is true of the covenant God made on Sinai and the renewal of it (i.e., Deuteronomy; cf. Deut. 29:1) that he made with Israel just before the Conquest. God made that renewal covenant with the children of the dead vassals (i.e., all the Israelites whose bodies fell in the desert) and also with the faithful survivors of that older generation—namely, Joshua and Caleb (and of course Moses, who wrote the book). So both God's original covenant with Israel through Moses (Exodus 20–Numbers) and the renewal of that covenant (Deuteronomy) together form the Mosaic covenant, and that is why, as scholars have noted, the laws of Deuteronomy enshrine further changes and nuancing of their counterparts in the earlier Sinai covenant.[27]

---

26. The same phrase also characterizes the Abrahamic covenant (Gen. 17:7.13.19), the Mosaic covenant (e.g., Exod. 31:16), the Davidic covenant (2 Sam. 23:5), and the New covenant (Isa. 55:3, Ezek. 37:26). We discuss these matters further in volume 2.

27. Cf. Niehaus, "An Argument," passim. I would only now note (as a refinement of some comments I made in that article) that I would no longer apply the term *renewal* to such covenant recommitment acts as those recorded in Joshua 24. I now think it more accurate to distinguish (as I have above) between a renewal of a divine–human covenant initiated by God (such as we have just mentioned in the case of the Mosaic covenant) and any human decisions to recommit or renew their commitment to such a covenant. To use marriage as an analogy, a man and a woman who are married may choose to walk down the aisle once again, later in life, and so "renew" their marriage. But when they do so, they are in fact *still married*. Their act is merely an expression on their part of a recommitment to their marriage covenant. By contrast, God chooses to renew certain covenants with *offspring* of the original vassals, offspring who have *not yet on their own account* formally chosen to be part of the covenant relationship (e.g., the generation with whom the Lord renews the Mosaic/Sinai covenant at Moab, as enshrined in Deuteronomy). In other words, there is only *one* renewal of the Mosaic covenant, and it was recorded on the plains of Moab. Any subsequent recommitments to the Mosaic covenant do not *renew* it—because it is *still in force*—but only express

The result of what we have understood is this: God will visit a cosmic judgment on the heavens and earth. He will do so because humanity has violated its creation mandates and thus broken the ברית עולם, or "durable covenant." The earth lies "polluted under its inhabitants" (Isa. 24:5). John later puts it this way: "The time has come . . . for destroying those who destroy the earth" (Rev. 11:18). The situation is as bad as, or worse than, the days of Noah—as we learn from the fact that they have broken the ברית עולם. Because of this, the earth suffers an unparalleled divine judgment: "The Lord will lay waste the earth, and make it desolate, and he will twist its surface and scatter its inhabitants" (Isa. 24:1). Fire will be a judgment instrument, as we read, "Therefore its inhabitants are burned up" (Isa. 24:6). The judgment also uses, by way of poetic allusion, terminology used in the Flood as an echo of that prior cosmic judgment: "The floodgates of the heavens are opened" (Isa. 24:18; for ארבות, "floodgates," cf. Gen. 7:11).

EXCURSUS: WHAT POLLUTES THE EARTH?

God's judgment will come upon the world's inhabitants because "The earth lies polluted / Under its inhabitants" (the Hebrew verb for *pollute* being חנף, Isa. 24:5). Isaiah's eschatological judgment portrayal has information behind it provided by the Mosaic covenant as to what may cause *pollution* of the earth or a land. A brief survey of those data can furnish us with the later OT commentary, as it were, on what violation of the Common Grace Noahic covenant may imply.

Pollution, as defined in the literature of the Mosaic covenant, may occur because of three major sins, the capital of which is murder. In Psalm 106:38, for example, we read the following:

_____

a recommitment to the *existing* covenant on the part of vassals who are under that covenant in any case.

> They shed innocent blood,
> the blood of their sons and daughters,
> whom they sacrificed to the idols of Canaan,
> and the land was *desecrated* (חָנֵף) by their blood.

Murder recalls the sin of Cain, a result of which was that the land would not yield its crops for him (Gen. 4:10–12).

Other things that pollute the land under the Mosaic covenant—as made clear by the covenant lawsuit prophets of that covenant—are sexual sins (e.g., Jer. 3:1–2) and idolatry (e.g., Jer. 3:9). If we consider that the three major categories of sin connected with pollution of the land/world are sexual sins, idolatry, and murder, we see that the eschatological indictment that "the earth lies polluted under its inhabitants" is foreshadowed and has indeed been earned by every society that has ever existed after the Fall. Our nation is, sadly, far from being an exception—and increasingly so.

Isaiah employs other terminology that alludes to the Adamic, or Creation covenant. We read, "The city of chaos is broken down" (Isa. 24:10). This city of chaos is probably the archetypal "City of Man," to borrow Augustine's term. The word translated "chaos" (תהו) is the same used in Genesis 1:2: "And the earth was formless [תהו] and empty." Jeremiah uses the same term to portray the sinful land of Judah under judgment:

> I looked at the earth,
> and it was formless and empty;
> and at the heavens,
> and their light was gone. (Jer. 4:23)

The phrase translated "formless and empty" (תהו ובהו) is the same phrase used at Genesis 1:2: "Now the earth was formless and empty." What is the significance of such terminology? Why do biblical authors use it to describe, on the one hand, a stage of the original creation

(Gen. 1:2) and, on the other, a sinful land under judgment (Jeremiah) and a sinful "city," or world system, under final judgment (Isaiah)?

The meaning of the phrase in question is nuanced by the different contexts in which it appears, but the fundamental sense of the phrase also contributes deeper meaning to any context in which it appears. We can be thankful that it first appears in Genesis 1:2. In that verse, we are given a brief but profoundly important picture of the preemergent chaos of the world. We use the word *chaos* in a completely neutral sense here, however. The word often, even typically, has negative connotations. However, primordial chaos was not negative. It was, rather, positive, or at least prepositive, or as one might say, precosmic. That is, the original state of the world, "formless and empty," was not a bad thing; rather, it was simply what it had to be as an early stage in the process of the world's formation—the formation that resulted in a world that God could pronounce "very good" (Gen. 1:31). We are told that the world was "formless and empty" as a way of informing us that the world was created by a *process*. At an early stage, that process looked *chaotic* or formless. Gradually, over an unknown time span, God brought forth *cosmos* (Greek, "order, beauty") out of chaos.

That context helps us understand the use of the phrase in other key passages. So when Isaiah writes of a "city of chaos" (תהו) that comes under divine judgment, we can understand the meaning of the phrase: A *city* or a systemically organized place (at the end, the world) that is chaotic at its core is "Babylon the Great" of Revelation 18:2. It may not be chaotic with regard to its own systematic or organized nature, but it is profoundly chaotic vis-à-vis God's torah or standards (or God's nature, since his standards articulate his nature). Jesus said that Satan comes "only to steal and kill and destroy" (John 10:10). That is, Satan embodies lawlessness (*anomia*). All that he does is out of order, chaotic. God, by his divine word or torah, created *cosmos*; Satan, by anomia, would uncreate it and bring everything back to a state of chaos (תהו). So although chaos, or a condition of being "formless [and empty]," was fine at the beginning (Gen. 1:2), it is not fine at a later stage of the world's development (e.g., Isa. 24:10). Chaos in the latter sense would not exist in the world were it not for the work of Satan, who reduces cosmos to chaos and who is lawless and chaotic in his own nature. That is why the term *formless*

(תהו) can be used in both Genesis 1:2 and Isaiah 24:10 with corresponding justice. Isaiah 24 informs us that God will come to destroy the world system of *tohu*—that is, his time will come "to destroy those who destroy the earth" (Rev. 11:18, NASB).

The same term can also be used for the consequences of God's judgment and with equal justice. When God brought the Flood, he returned the world to a preemergent state, a state of total inundation, as we have observed. For this reason alone, it seems fitting that a worldwide flood occurred, not simply a local flood or even a large local flood. Such theological considerations only support the tone and character of the statements made in the Genesis Flood account, which on any natural reading portray a world-covering Flood, as noted earlier. The Flood returned the world to the state it was in before God separated the land from the waters. That is, God returned the world to the condition described in Genesis 1:2, when everything was "formless and empty." So when God brings global judgment, that is the result. However, even when God declares a local judgment, it can be portrayed in the same way in an implicit allusion to the coming judgment. Jeremiah describes the land of Judah after God has brought his wrath on it:

> I looked at the earth,
> and it was formless and empty;
> and at the heavens,
> and their light was gone.
> I looked at the mountains,
> and they were quaking;
> all the hills were swaying.
> I looked, and there were no people;
> every bird in the sky had flown away.
> I looked, and the fruitful land was a desert;
> all its town lay in ruins
> before the Lord, before his fierce anger. (Jer. 4:23–26)

Jeremiah seems at first to be describing an eschatological and cosmic judgment, as the stock word pair "heavens and earth" (Jer. 4:23) might suggest. However, it soon becomes clear that he only intends to portray the condition of Judah, "the fruitful land," which has become a desert (מדבר, used elsewhere in connection with *tohu*, for example, "He found him [that is, Jacob] in a desert land / And in a howling waste of a wilderness" [בארץ מדבר ובתהו; Deut. 32:10]). Judah's deserted state is the result of the Lord's coming in judgment. His fierce anger has desolated the land. Jeremiah portrays the state of affairs in apocalyptic terms, but in doing so, he only does what other prophets also do. Every time the Lord breaks into history in judgment, it is a "Day of the Lord," and every "Day of the Lord" can be described with theophanic/eschatological phenomena and dread. So for instance, Amos warns the people of the northern kingdom not to want the Day of the Lord. They may imagine the Lord will come with a judgment in their favor, but it will be otherwise:

> Woe to you who long
> for the day of the Lord!
> Why do you long for the day of the Lord?
>
> Will not the day of the Lord be darkness, not light—
> pitch dark, without a ray of brightness? (Amos 5:18.20)

The darkness will be that which attends the Lord's stormy advent— like the darkness of the clouds that heralded the Flood and like the darkness that covered the land at Jesus's crucifixion (Matt. 27:45), which Peter subsequently connects with the prophecy of Joel:

> The sun will turn to darkness
> and the moon to blood
> before the coming of the great and glorious
> day of the Lord. (Acts 2:20; Joel 2:28–31)

Such darkness also echoes the primordial darkness, before God said, "Let there be light." In short, every Day of the Lord is a foreshadowing of that final and dreadful—and glorious—Day of the Lord, when the sun will turn dark, the moon will turn to blood, the heavenly bodies will be shaken, and the Son of Man will return on the clouds with great power and glory.

The concept of the Day of the Lord is thus a profoundly unifying concept for the Bible. By using the same phrase to characterize both historical and eschatological judgments, the biblical writers are telling us that all judgments are, at root, the same. They are all expressions of God's holiness in conflict with, and in defeat of, the forces of anomia, the forces that produce *tohu*—the forces that would ultimately undo cosmos and humanity, the vassals to whom God entrusted the stewardship of his creation. Moreover, since God is going to bring a new heavens and earth, the time will come when his judgment also results in *tohu*—that is, the complete uncreating of what he has created. Satan produces tohu by working anomia. God produces tohu by destroying the devil's work. When God comes in judgment, he undoes the object of judgment. If that object is the world, then God undoes or destroys the world. If that object is the land of Judah, as in Jeremiah 4, then God destroys that land, and its condition can poetically and appropriately be portrayed in eschatological terms—*tohu* and a *Day of the Lord*. That is why God's judgment on Judah can result in a condition in which the land is "formless and empty" (Jer. 4:23) and "a desert" (Jer. 4:26). God's judgment returns the land to a condition that evokes the primordial chaos, a chaos that was benign when it was part of the process of a pristine creation, but that has become poetically useful as a way of characterizing the result of God's judgment on sin.

The Isaiah Apocalypse not only presents a picture of God's eschatological judgment but also makes allusions to God's very first covenants with humans. The "City of *tohu*" (Isa. 24:10) alludes to the Creation covenant by using a term evocative of, and first appearing at, Genesis 1:2. The ברית עולם ("everlasting covenant," Isa. 24:5) alludes to the Re-Creation (Noahic) covenant by using a term evocative of, and first appearing at, Genesis 9:16. This is no accident. The specific terms evoke the two covenants that, together, form one legal package that governs all humans on earth. All people are vassals to

God under the terms of these covenants. That is why we call them Common Grace covenants. We now understand more clearly, on the basis of ancient near eastern analogies, that the Noahic covenant is a renewal of the Adamic covenant. Together they form one legal package or set of arrangements under which and to which all are accountable—and all flourish and suffer: We are fruitful and multiply, we rule and subdue the earth, but we also die. Moreover, we will pay the price for our mismanagement of the world, as Isaiah 24 (cf. Rev. 11:18) warns us.

The Isaiah Apocalypse has more to teach us, however, for in it we see how things will stand once God's judgment is complete. Here again, the correct translation is all-important. First, we read that God will bind his foes:

> They will be herded together
> like prisoners bound in a dungeon;
> they will be shut up in prison
> and be punished after many days. (Isa. 24:22)

The ones bound here are the "powers in the heavens above" and the "kings on the earth below" (Isa. 24:21), and the scene resembles what we see in Revelation 20 and may be the same—in which Satan is bound for a thousand years after his defeat and before the final judgment (Rev. 20:2–3).

After God has bound his foes, he appears in glory among his people. His appearance is portrayed in terms also echoed by John in Revelation:

> The moon will be abashed, the sun ashamed;
> the Lord Almighty will reign
> on Mount Zion and in Jerusalem,
> and before its [or, "his"] elders gloriously. (Isa. 24:23)

The language we find here about the sun and the moon also appears later in Isaiah. The breaking of the עולם ברית ("everlasting covenant") leads to a final punishment but also to a totally new state of affairs.

That is indicated in Isaiah 60:19ff., where we are told that the Lord will replace the sun and moon as light for his people, and in Isaiah 65:17ff. and 66:22, where we read God's promise of a new heaven and a new earth. Echoing those Isaiah passages and the Isaiah Apocalypse, John's Apocalypse makes it clear that these things belong together: "Then I saw a new heaven and a new earth: for the first heaven and the first earth had passed away, and the sea was no more. And I saw the holy city, new Jerusalem, coming down out of heaven from God . . . And the city has no need of sun or moon to shine upon it, for the glory of God is its light, and its lamp is the Lamb" (Rev. 21:1–2, 23). The consummation of the eschatological period is just this: The glory of God appears before and among his people. What John shows us in Revelation 21:23 is what Isaiah had already shown in Isaiah 24:23. The correct translation of Isaiah is critical at this point. Whereas some translate Isaiah 24:23 "for the Lord Almighty will reign on Mount Zion and in Jerusalem, and before its elders, gloriously" (NIV), a better translation is "for the Lord Almighty will reign on Mount Zion and in Jerusalem, and before *his* elders [will be] Glory" (author's translation; cf. NASB). The term here translated "Glory" (כבוד) is in fact a noun. It can be translated as an adverbial accusative, as the NIV and many other versions have done, but to do so misses a crucial point: Once God has done away with sin, he can again appear in his full glory before humans. That has not been possible since the Fall. Once humans were in a fallen condition, God had to deal with them via a mediator, and even then he had to limit the effulgence of his glory in theophany when he appeared to or among them. That was the case with all the prophets, even the covenant mediator prophets (Noah [presumably, although the Noahic material gives us no theophanic account of any kind], Abram, Moses, and David) after the Fall. The incarnation was the beginning of the end of this problem, when Jesus could say, "Anyone who has seen me has seen the Father" (John 14:9). But the true end of it will only come at the eschaton, as John (and Isaiah before him) has told us. That is why John can say "the Glory of the Lord" *is the illumination* of the heavenly city come to earth (Rev. 21:23). And that is why Isaiah 24:23 should be translated in a way that makes plain the same truth. The Lord will not simply reign "gloriously" before his elders at the end.

Now that sin has been done away with, the Lord will be able to appear in his unrestrained, unmitigated, unmediated glory before them— hence the translation, "before his elders [will be] Glory." He will no longer need to conceal himself in "cloud(s)" and "thick darkness" (paraphrasing Heb. חשׁך ענן וערפל, Deut. 4:11; cf. 5:18) in order to protect his people from his holy presence. In that day, we will be like him, because we will see him as he is and will shine like the sun (Matt. 13:43), reflecting his Glory.

CONCLUDING THOUGHTS

We have seen that the Noahic or Re-Creation covenant is, in fact, a renewal of the Adamic or Creation covenant. According to ancient usage, those two covenants form one legal package, an arrangement that now governs human life on earth. The Adamic covenant gave us a "heaven and earth" and a humanity to be fruitful and multiply and rule the earth. The Noahic covenant gave us a "new" world too, although only provisionally renewed, since, although God cleansed it of egregiously sinful people, the world remained, to use Paul's phrase, "in bondage to decay." The Noahic covenant also gave humans a fresh start, but however righteous Noah may have been, he was not without sin nor was his family. So we must await the return of the second Adam, the one without sin, in order to receive at his hands a truly new heavens and earth, just as, in an anticipatory way, we have received from him that creative Spirit who has already begun to make us into a new humanity—reforming us into his image and likeness.

All humans now live under that combination of the Adamic and Noahic arrangements. As we anticipate a new heavens and earth, we have also traced the outlines of a biblical eschatology that is rooted in those two covenants. The God who created the heavens and earth is also committed to creating a new heavens and earth once he has "destroyed those who destroy the earth." That same God is also committed to re-creating humanity as sinless vassals in that new world. Those who are redeemed and made into that new humanity will indeed reign with him (2 Tim. 2:12, Rev. 20:4.6) in that day when his glory fills all in all.

CHAPTER SEVEN

LIFE UNDER TWO COVENANTS

All humanity now live under two covenants: the Adamic and the Noahic (or the Creation and the Re-Creation) covenants. Theologians call these covenants Common Grace covenants because they administer God's grace to all humanity. They are distinguished from Special Grace or Special Revelation covenants that administer God's grace in a special way to chosen people. The *special way* has to do with redemption, or salvation. God's covenant with Abraham, for example, is a special arrangement with one individual, chosen from among his many contemporaries and with his offspring. One might say the same of the Noahic covenant, but in Abraham's case, God was not destroying all people except the covenant mediator and his family. Other humans continued to live and go about their business while the Lord was cutting his covenant with Abraham, but the vast majority of humanity in Abraham's day had no part in that Special Grace covenant. The same has been true of God's other Special Grace covenants—the Mosaic, the Davidic, and for us, the New covenant. It is clear, then, that there is a great difference between the Common Grace covenants and the Special Grace covenants. The Common Grace covenants apply to all people until the end of time, at which moment they will terminate. The

Special Grace covenants apply to chosen people and culminate in the New covenant, which endures until the end of time and beyond, into eternity.

Some covenant schemes regrettably do not recognize this crucial distinction (cf. the schema presented at the end of our Prolegomena). The classic formulation of covenant theology, for example, calls the Adamic covenant a "covenant of works" and groups all of the other covenants together and calls them a "covenant of grace."[1] Apart from the matter of works and grace discussed earlier, it is immediately obvious that this arrangement obscures the covenant and covenant renewal aspects of the Adamic and Noahic covenants, and also does not indicate the difference between the Common Grace nature of the Noahic covenant and the Special Grace nature of the subsequent covenants.[2] More recently, some scholars have seen all God's covenants as one, but can only accomplish their goal by blurring over the distinctions that make the covenants different.[3] Such an approach, although it has found favor recently in some quarters, is truly a form of idealism that can succeed only by abstracting a few things common to all covenants (e.g., that God has provided for his vassals in the past, that he requires certain things of them in the present, and that he promises to provide for them in the future) and declaring all the covenants to be one because they share those elements. Although a full discussion of the issues would require more space than is appropriate here, the failure of this approach is most easily illustrated when we consider the basic differences between the

---

1. For a modern advocate of this view, cf. Meredith G. Kline, *Kingdom Prologue*; for counterarguments, cf. Niehaus, "An Argument," 260–62.

2. For a variation on the classic arrangement, cf. John H. Walton, *Covenant: God's Purpose, God's Plan* (Grand Rapids: Zondervan, 1994), who does not recognize an Adamic covenant but does distinguish between the Common Grace Noahic covenant and the Special Grace covenants, which latter covenants he combines as one under the title "The Covenant," a sort of counterpart to the older "Covenant of Grace" (minus the Noahic covenant).

3. Cf. Dumbrell, *Covenant and Creation*; Scott J. Hafemann, *The God of Promise and the Life of Faith* (Wheaton: Crossway, 2001). Hafemann, my good former colleague, speaks of "one covenant relationship" but does not seem to recognize that, as there is no covenant relationship without a covenant, he is de facto speaking of one covenant that pervades the whole Bible.

Common Grace covenants and the Special Grace covenants.[4] The two sets of covenants are different in their provisions and in their promises. The Noahic covenant, for example, does not offer a way of eternal salvation for anyone—although all people live under it.[5]

The Adamic and the Noahic covenants together do, however, form one legal package, as we have seen. They thus conform to the pattern of ancient covenant renewals (with the Sinai covenant and its Moab covenant renewal constituting the premier example). It may be that all such arrangements hark back to this very thing: God set the pattern for all covenant renewals when he renewed his covenant with all human-ity through Noah, just as he set the pattern for all covenants by his original relationship with the created order and the first humans.[6] We know the ancients most prized what was most ancient. They thought those things that were oldest were most likely to be true because they were from days that were closer to the beginning of time. For example, the job of every pharaoh was to restore things "as at the beginning."[7] In any case, humanity now lives under those two covenants so that their combined provisions and stipulations apply to everyone.

THE SIN OF HAM

Although God judges the world by the Flood and gives humanity a new world to inhabit, it soon becomes clear that the "new earth" is still inhabited by the "old man," to use Paul's phrase (Eph. 4:22, Col. 3:9, KJV). Noah plants a vineyard and becomes drunk on its wine. However righteous the prophet may have been, his act does smack of inordinacy, and it quickly reminds us that we are reading about people in a fallen condition. His son, Ham, shows us the same truth, although in a different way.

---

4. I have outlined the problems with this approach as part of a fuller discussion of the issues: cf. Niehaus, "An Argument," 259–73.
5. We recall that, although God does save Noah and his family through the ordeal of the Flood, the Lord makes his covenant with Noah after the Flood has passed.
6. Not that people remembered the creation events in any detail, but that, by display-ing the covenantal nature of the relationship in Genesis 1:1–2:3, God has shown us that such elements as we find there naturally appear in all human power relationships because we are all made in the *imago Dei* (cf. chapter 1).
7. Cf. Niehaus, *ANETBT*, 171–72.

Ham's sin appears to have been mockery of his father or lack of respect for him. The text does not say so, but the narrative evidently contrasts the behavior of Shem and Japheth with that of Ham regarding their father's nakedness. Ham finds his father naked and tells his brothers—the phrase "tells on him" may best capture the idea. His brothers cover their father's nakedness and turn their faces away as they walk backward approaching him so as not to see his nakedness before they cover it (Gen. 9:23). The contrast implies, at the very least, a lack of reverence in Ham, juxtaposed with reverence in Shem and Japheth.

EXCURSUS: EXPOSURE OF NAKEDNESS UNDER THE MOSAIC COVENANT

As we did with the death penalty, we take a moment now to consider the Mosaic covenant's later and more nuanced legislation regarding the uncovering of human nakedness. The Mosaic covenant provides injunctions against uncovering nakedness in a variety of relations: of one's kin in general (Lev. 18:6), of one's father or mother (Lev. 18:7), of one's father's wife (Lev. 18:8), of one's sister (Lev. 18:9), of one's son's or daughter's daughter (Lev. 18:10), of one's father's or mother's sister (Lev. 18:13), of one's father's brother (Lev. 18:14), of one's daughter-in-law (Lev. 18:15), and so on, including even a woman not specifically kindred (cf. Lev. 18:16–19; Lev. 20:11–21). The later Special Grace covenant apparently addresses not the type of offense reported under the Common Grace covenant (the Noahic covenant) but the offense of *uncovering* a relative's nakedness.[8]

---

8. For the view that both the Noahic and the Mosaic data have to do with incest, cf. John Sietze Bergman and Scott Walker Hahn, "Noah's Nakedness and the Curse on Ham (Genesis 9:20–27)," http://www.godawa.com/chronicles_of_the_nephilim/Articles_By_Others/Bergsma-Noahs_Nakedness_And_Curse_On_Canaan.pdf.

The Mosaic covenant adds cases of a different sort from the Noahic event, much as it does regarding the death penalty. Interestingly, the exposure of nakedness and the death penalty for shedding human blood are combined subsequently in one of the later covenant lawsuit prophets of the Mosaic covenant, Habakkuk:

> Woe to him who gives drink to his neighbors,
>   pouring it from the wineskin till they are drunk,
> so that he can gaze on their naked bodies!
>   You will be filled with shame instead of glory.
> Now it is your turn! Drink and let your nakedness be exposed!
>   The cup from the LORD's right hand is coming
>   around to you,
> and disgrace will cover your glory.
>   The violence you have done to Lebanon will over-
>   whelm you,
> and your destruction of animals will terrify you.
>   For you have shed human blood;
> you have destroyed lands and cities and everyone in them.
>   (Hab. 2:15–17)

The prophet foretells judgment on Babylon (and implicitly on all who are like the pagan city/empire), and two important counts against it are that it made others drunk and gazed on their nakedness (vs. 15) and that it shed human blood (vs. 17), evocative of the Noahic context. The judgments on Babylon will be appropriately ironic: It will drink and have its nakedness exposed (vs. 16), and violence and death (implicitly) and destruction will come its way.[9]

Nakedness itself is an important matter. Before the Fall, nakedness was no problem: It was a natural part of a sinless human condition.

---

9. Another important count against Babylon is its "destruction of animals" (vs. 17). This places Babylon firmly in the company of "those who destroy the earth" (Rev. 11:18) and shows in advance the spirit of Satan who comes "to steal, kill and destroy" (John 10:10).

After the Fall, however, nakedness is a problem, first for Adam, who hid himself because he was naked and afraid, and now for Noah, whose nakedness offers scope for Ham's sin, but also subsequently for any human. Having one's nakedness exposed becomes a phrase for humiliation, in the context of divine judgment in the Old Testament, as we have seen in the example from Habakkuk.[10]

How can this be? The end of Genesis 2 and the beginning of Genesis 3 may offer us an answer. We are told that "the man and his wife were both naked, and they felt no shame" (Gen. 2:25). We are then told, "The serpent was more crafty than any of the wild animals the Lord God had made" (Gen. 3:1). It was noted that the words *naked* and *crafty* are homonyms in Hebrew (ערום). If we consider that the "craftiness" is that of the serpent, who is a sinful being, there seems to be an implicit link—or an allusion to a link—between the sinfulness of the serpent (after all, his craftiness makes him a good tempter) and the nakedness of the humans. Once humans are in a sinful condition, their nakedness is shameful to them. So the deceptiveness of sin—its craftiness—has brought the exposure of nakedness into sinful disrepute.

Because humans were made in God's image, they were meant to display his glory. To some degree they can do so even in a fallen world. So Paul can say that a man "is the image and glory of God" (though not without sin, Rom. 3:23) but also that a woman "is the glory of man" (1 Cor. 11:7). We examine this important passage in more detail later. For now, it is enough to recognize that being made in the *imago Dei* involves an imaging forth of the "Spirit of Glory and of God" (1 Pet. 4:14), which imaging is called glory. In a sinless condition, humans could display that glory image in their nakedness. In a fallen and sinful condition, however, the very nakedness of humans becomes a statement of their weakness and fallenness. Adam was aware of his weakened condition when he found that he was afraid to face God in his nakedness. Instead of simply manifesting the glory of God, his nakedness had become somehow inadequate or problematic. Not only could it not image forth God's glory without sin,

10. Cf. also the Lord's pronouncement on Babylon through Isaiah, "Your nakedness will be exposed and your shame uncovered. I will take vengeance; I will spare no one" (Isa. 47:3).

it could not face God's glory. So he felt he needed a covering before God. Adam's problem was and remains the human problem, but God ultimately provides the answer to it when he covers over our sin through his Son so that we may "put on" the Lord Jesus Christ and be clothed with his righteousness.[11]

THE CURSE OF CANAAN
AND THE SONS OF NOAH

When Noah discovers what Ham has done to him, he utters both a curse and a blessing:

> Cursed be Canaan!
> The lowest of slaves
> will he be to his brothers.
> Blessed be the Lord, the God of Shem!
> May Canaan be the slave of Shem.
> May God extend the territory of Japheth
> may Japheth live in the tents of Shem,
> and may Canaan be his slave. (Gen. 9:25–27)

It is important to note here that Noah does not explicitly curse Ham. Some interpreters, most notably the Mormons but not they alone, have construed the passage to mean that the Hamitic peoples—that is, the Africans (Gen. 10:6–7)—are accursed, and have understood their dark skin to be part of that cursed condition.[12] Quite apart from the very mixed history of African peoples, which included Egypt ("Mizraim," Gen. 10:6)—a nation that enslaved others rather than being a slave or a vassal itself—the interpretation fails at its very beginning. Noah's curse is not on Ham: It is on Ham's son Canaan, who did indeed become slave (or vassal) to both Shem and

---

11. Niehaus, *God at Sinai*, follows this theme through the Bible as it explores the biblical theophanies and the problem they present after the Fall en route to seeing how God addresses and begins to resolve the problem by the Incarnation.

12. Cf. Reed R. Simonsen, *If Ye Are Prepared: A Reference Manual for Missionaries* (Centerville: Randall, 1991), 243–66.

Japheth (Gen. 9:26–27). There is no way to know what curse may have befallen Ham; whatever it was, the text does not tell us. The fact that Noah curses Ham's son Canaan may seem unfair, but it can be understood, or partly understood, on the basis of a principle that appears often in the Bible and in the ancient Near East as well: the principle of household judgment. When a man sins, both he and his household are judged and punished for the sin. This was the case with Achan and his household (Joshua 7, where we must trust the justice of God that only the guilty were punished). It is also the case in Jesus's parable of the unforgiving servant, whose master intended to sell him and his family into slavery to pay the servant's debt (Matt. 18:25). Other ancient cultures display the same ethos. The Egyptians, Assyrians, Babylonians, and Hittites all wrought vengeance on covenant breaking vassals by punishing both the ruler and his household with either death or enslavement.[13] As I have argued elsewhere, household punishment of covenant breakers may go back to the first of that type, Adam. God judged Adam and in him all his household—namely, the human race—to frustration and death. But God also provided a second Adam so that through faith we might become members of his household and be saved.[14]

In any case, Noah's curse on Canaan may be of this type— namely, a curse on all of Ham's household for what Ham has done.

Not only does Noah curse, however; he also blesses. His first blessing regards Shem but directly blesses God: "Blessed be the Lord, the God of Shem" (Gen. 9:26). The true blessing for Shem consists of the fact that his name alone is linked with that of the Lord God: the Lord is "the God of Shem." Noah's statement links God to Shem in a covenantal statement because the god of anyone in the ancient world was that person's lord or suzerain, and the person was, in effect, the god's vassal. Moreover, Noah uses the name "Lord" in this connection, and that name (יהוה, "Yahweh") tends to be used when

---

13. Cf. Jeffrey J. Niehaus, "The Covenantal Household: A Study of the Destruction and Salvation of Households in the Bible and the Ancient Near East," in *Creator, Redeemer, Consummator: A Festschrift for Meredith G. Kline*, ed. Howard Griffith and John R. Muether (Greenville: Reformed Academic Press, 2000), 51–63; cf. further, Niehaus, "The Covenantal Household: Destruction and Salvation," in *ANETBT*, 139–65.

14. Niehaus, *ANETBT*, 164–65.

God is the subject in a Special Grace covenant with his people, especially in the Pentateuch (as Cassuto has argued).[15] Therefore, Noah's blessing implies some sort of ongoing and future covenantal relationship between the Lord God and Shem's household. In reality, there will be more than one covenant involved: the Abrahamic, the Mosaic, the Davidic, and ultimately, the New covenant. So Noah's blessing does not create any covenants, but in retrospect, we can see that it implies them.[16]

Noah's second blessing is on Japheth: "May God extend the territory of Japheth" (Gen. 9:27). Noah does not use that Special Grace covenantal name of God, "the Lord" ("Yahweh"), and so he implies a Common Grace relationship between God and Japheth. However, God will "extend the territory" of Japheth—that is, he will grant offspring and expansion to Japheth's household—which will indeed become powerful and include the great maritime powers of the Mediterranean, and ultimately Rome, which would one day be able to call that sea *mare nostrum*, "our sea" (cf. Gen. 10:5).[17] The blessing is only a Common Grace blessing, however: God will bless Japheth's household with expansion, with *imperium*, just as he would bless and give land to the households of Esau (namely, Seir; Deut. 2:5) and Lot (namely, Moab, and also the land of the Ammonites; Deut. 2:9.19). But along with this Common Grace blessing, a greater blessing lies in store for the house of Japheth. Noah declares, "May Japheth live in the tents of Shem" (Gen. 9:27). This hope does not imply conquest nor does it entail mere hospitality; rather, as families dwelt in tents in the ancient Near East, so the blessing is that Japheth will join the family of Shem—that the two households will become one. This merger comes to pass when both are united by faith in the Lord God of Shem, so that—as Paul later says to people in the Roman Empire—because of what Christ has done, "You are no longer foreigners and aliens, but fellow citizens with God's people

15. Umberto Cassuto, *The Documentary Hypothesis* (Jerusalem: Magnes, June 1983).

16. Of course for God, outside time, all of those covenants were implicit, created, and in their various degrees fulfilled, from the standpoint of his eternal present.

17. It is of passing interest that under Mussolini Italian maps labeled the Mediterranean with that same ancient Roman name as a claim to recaptured Roman greatness.

and members of God's household" (Eph. 2:19). God in Christ "has
made the two one and has destroyed the barrier, the dividing wall of
hostility" (Eph. 2:14). The "tents of Shem" become the tents of the
Lord, as he not only has tabernacled among us (cf. John 1:14) but
also dwells within us (within our earthly tents; cf. 2 Pet. 1:13), making us one body, one household—the household of faith (Gal. 6:10).

GOD OF THE NATIONS

Noah's blessings imply the authority of God. He calls on God to
accomplish certain blessings in the earth, and the implicit assumption or understanding is that God can and will do so. When the
Bible tells us that "in the beginning God created the heavens and
the earth" (Gen. 1:1), it makes a statement that ancient near eastern people would have understood. As noted, the verse declares God
to be the great suzerain over all the earth because, as the ancients
understood, the creator god is also the ruler of all—both heaven and
earth—and the source of all authority. As such, he is also "judge of
all the earth," as Abraham could affirm (Gen. 18:25). Noah's curse on
Canaan implies the same, just as his blessings on Shem and Japheth
imply God's covenantal nature (Shem) as well as his authority to
grant increase to the nations (Japheth).

It is thus no accident or random juxtaposition that places the
so-called Table of Nations just after Noah's blessings and curse. The
stage is set for the expansion of humanity after the Flood (in accordance with God's command to Noah), and that expansion will be
into many nations, the many *goyyim* or *ethnoi*—people groups or
ethnic groups—who now populate the world. Noah's blessing on
Japheth calls for such an expansion ("May God extend the territory
of Japheth," Gen. 9:27), and the "account" (lit., "offspring/genera-
tions," תולדת) of Japheth (Gen. 10:1) shows us the start of the same.
It concludes with the statement, "From these the maritime peoples
spread out into their territories by their clans within their nations,
each with its own language" (Gen. 10:4), and this latter information
anticipates the Tower of Babel event in Genesis 11.

We will not explore the "Table of Nations" in detail here. Scholarship has sufficiently indicated the schematic nature of it. One point

of particular interest is the extended mention of Nimrod, who "grew to be a mighty warrior on the earth" (Gen. 10:8) and also "was a mighty hunter before the Lord" (Gen. 10:9). The combination of these attributes, like the juxtaposition of Noah's blessings and curse and the Table of Nations, is no accident. Later in history, we find pagan emperors, such as the pharaohs and suzerains of Assyria, boasting of their prowess as both warriors and hunters. Moreover, we read that Nimrod built several cities, including Nineveh (Gen. 10:11–12), and here again we find a type of royal activity on which later pharaohs and emperors prided themselves. In other words, we find in Nimrod the very type of the ancient near eastern emperor: a man who is mighty in battle, skilled in the hunt, a builder of cities, and a ruler of nations. The impression (or the hoped for impression) is that he is all that a man should be—virtually a god—and of course many ancient rulers claimed divine or semidivine status. Perhaps one term applied to him epitomizes his nature: He was a *warrior*. The term (גבור) indicates someone of not only exceptional training and preparedness for war but also exceptional physique—certainly an asset on the field of battle, ancient or modern. So, for example, Saul warns the zealous stripling, David, that Goliath has been "a warrior (גבור) from his youth" (1 Sam. 17:33). If Nimrod was a type of such later warrior–hunter emperors—those who would rule the nations—that may be the reason so much space is devoted to him in the Table of Nations, since he alone stands out as an individual in that otherwise summary genealogical schema.

THE TOWER OF BABEL

The Tower of Babel account fires the imagination as much, perhaps, as any narrative in the Primordial History. Certainly, it agitated the minds of earlier critical scholars to such a pitch that Delitzsch felt motivated to devote a whole book to the topic, *Babel and Bible* (German, *Babel und Bibel*). His book contained two long lectures presented before the German Kaiser at the Prussian Academy of Sciences, in which Delitzsch asserted (with some demonstration) the superiority of Babylon and its culture to the people and culture of Israel. I have discussed his arguments and suggested their shortcomings elsewhere, including some account of the anti-Semitism that laces his and other critical German scholarship in its heyday, and will not review such matters here.[18] The account presents us with a scenario that may be evocative of Babylon, but like the Nimrod account, it offers something archetypal. In the Babel of Genesis 11, we see the essential spirit of Babylon with its human ambitions, its pretensions to an exalted and perhaps even divine status, and its ultimate futility and dissolution at the hands of a just and holy God. It is the apt type of that eschatological "City of *tohu*" (Isa. 24:10) or "Babylon the Great" (Rev. 18:2) that will embody the world system of politics and culture unalterably opposed to "the Lord and his Messiah" (or "Anointed One," Ps. 2:2).

Babel is a hub of human pretension, and its pretension is rooted in the insecurity of its sinful condition. Sin cuts us off from God and renders us profoundly insecure. One natural response to insecurity is self-assertion, and that is the response of the builders of the tower. They plan to bake brick and use it instead of stone for building material—a situation typical of Mesopotamia, such that Assyrian and Babylonian royal inscriptions boast about how the emperors had bricks made in order to build palaces, temples, or ziqqurats. With those materials in hand, they say, "Come, let us build ourselves a city, with a tower that reaches to the heavens, so that we may make a name for ourselves and not be scattered over the face of the whole earth" (Gen. 11:4). We have noted before, in the case of Cain, how insecurity has led to the construction of a city, with all the watchfulness and defensive posture that the very word implies. Now in addition to that, the people of Babel want to build a tower. The word for *tower* in Hebrew comes from a root that means "to be great" (גדל; cf. מגדל, "tower"). The word first appears here and in a context that tells us that the goal of the tower's construction is not only to "reach to the heavens," with all the divine pretension that implies, but also to palliate human insecurity "so that we may make a name for ourselves and not be scattered over the face of the whole earth" (Gen. 11:4). The people of Babel seek security in fame and in ethnic unity. Fame can make them secure because, when would-be foes see the

---

18. See Niehaus, *ANETBT*, 21–30.

magnificence of their accomplishment, they might well hesitate to attack them, reasoning that they could not overthrow so mighty a people. And ethnic cohesion can contribute to the same end, making the people group a cohesive and thus more potent force. It is no incidental consideration that Heinrich Himmler, head of the Nazi SS and an avid racial purist, entertained for Germany the ambition of rapidly producing a population of two hundred million blonde, physically excellent citizens for global conquest and domination.

The irony, of course, is that God will bring upon them the very thing they fear. Their goal is to avoid being scattered over the face of the whole earth (עַל כָּל פְּנֵי הָאָרֶץ; Gen. 11:4), but God's judgment on them brings about exactly that result: "From there the Lord scattered them over the face of the whole earth" (identical phrasing: עַל כָּל פְּנֵי הָאָרֶץ; Gen. 11:9). God's judgment on them anticipates his eschatological judgment because it is the dissolution of a pretentious city and the dismantling of the symbols of its pretension. In Genesis 11, God prevents the construction of the symbolic tower; in Isaiah's later vision, which is both historical and eschatological,

> The Lord Almighty has a day in store
> for all the proud and lofty,
> for all that is exalted
> (and they will be humbled),
> for every lofty tower
> and every fortified wall
> for every trading ship
> and every stately vessel.
> The arrogance of man will be brought low
> and the pride of men humbled;
> for the Lord alone will be exalted in that day
> and the idols will totally disappear. (Isa. 2:12–17)

God judges the human enterprise—or what we might call the human project—in the Tower of Babel event, and that judgment anticipates his eschatological judgment on Babylon the Great, the global whore of culture including commerce, politics, and false religion that epitomizes the traffic with the East and the idolatry that we see judged in Isaiah 2. In that Day of the Lord, he alone will be exalted, and his everlasting kingdom, which Daniel 2 portrays so eloquently, will be established forever.

THE TABLE OF THE NATIONS: FINAL REFLECTIONS

There are two large areas of theological concern implied by the Table of the Nations. One is the divine source of all human authority in nation states. The other is the question of divine oversight of those nations that he blesses and empowers. The answer to the first question has clearer biblical data to its name than does the second, although both questions raise issues that may not be resolvable to everyone's satisfaction.

THE DIVINE SOURCE OF HUMAN AUTHORITY

The Bible makes it clear that all authority derives from God. As we should expect, the New Testament has the final say in this matter, as in others, since it is the final written revelation of God. The Old Testament is not, however, devoid of statements on this issue, and it also points in the same direction.[19] When the Lord tells Elijah to anoint Hazael as king over Damascus (1 Kings 19:15), he makes it clear that royal authority comes from God—in this case, through his prophet. When God speaks predictively of Cyrus through Isaiah, he makes it clear that God has been the source of Cyrus's authority and success:

> This is what the Lord says to his anointed,
> to Cyrus, whose right hand I take hold of
> to subdue nations before him
> and to strip kings of their armor,
> to open doors before him
> so that gates will not be shut:

---

19. The discussion that occupies us now reprises briefly (in a different context and with somewhat different application) the earlier and more detailed observations of chapter 4.

I will go before you
and will level the mountains;
I will break down the gates of bronze
and cut through bars of iron.
I will give you the treasures of darkness,
riches stored in secret places,
so that you may know that I am the Lord,
the God of Israel, who summons you by name. (Isa. 45:1–3)

True, God gives Cyrus all this conquest, wealth, and authority "for the sake of Jacob my servant, of Israel, my chosen" (Isa. 45:4), but this is just one specimen of the larger principle: God manages the nations for the sake of his people. Sometimes that management involves the use of a pagan nation for judgment on his people (the fulfillment of covenantal curse), as in the case of Assyria in Isaiah 10. Sometimes it involves blessing, as here, where God anoints Cyrus to release his people and let them return to their homeland from Babylonian exile. The term translated "anointed" (Isa. 45:1, NIV) is the Hebrew מְשִׁיחַ—that is, *messiah*. The term means "anointed one," but it is important to understand with what God anoints. Elijah was to anoint Hazael with oil, just as Samuel anointed Saul and David (the root verb מָשַׁח is used in each case). Samuel's anointings make it clear that the oil bestowed was symbolic of the Holy Spirit, who in fact descended on both Saul and David after their anointings. Jesus, who was the "anointed One," or Messiah par excellence, saw the Holy Spirit descend upon him in an avian fashion and received the Spirit without limit (John 3:34). The church since Pentecost also partakes of the Spirit's anointing. So when God refers to Cyrus as his anointed, he is saying that Cyrus was empowered by the Holy Spirit to accomplish all that he did. The same was true earlier of Hazael. These considerations suggest that authority among humans can involve the work of the Holy Spirit. Such is arguably the case when it comes to such royal positions as we have noted, involving kings who were a part of God's purposes with respect to the future of his covenant people and who were called *anointed*. Evidence regarding the role of the Holy Spirit in empowering rulers in general is not apparent, but it is also not apparent that such is not the case.

It is nevertheless clear from both testaments that God is the source of all governmental authority. Daniel declares this truth after his interpretation of Nebuchadnezzar's first dream: "Praise be to the name of God for ever and ever; wisdom and power are his. He changes times and seasons; he sets up kings and deposes them" (Dan. 2:20–21). Nebuchadnezzar is forced by God's humiliation of him to acknowledge a similar truth when he says about God, "He does as he pleases with the powers of heaven and the peoples of the earth. No one can hold back his hand or say to him: 'What have you done?'" (Dan. 4:35). God does what he wants with "the peoples of the earth," a truth uttered by a pagan king after duress but true nonetheless. So when we read of the growth and implicit prosperity and power of the nations in Genesis 10, we are reading of events that God has made possible. We are also reading of governments whose authority derives implicitly from him. Paul makes this point as clear as one could wish in his commentary on Roman authority: "Everyone must submit to the governing authorities, for there is no authority except that which God has established. The authorities that exist have been established by God. Consequently, he who rebels against the authority is rebelling against what God has instituted, and those who do so will bring judgment upon themselves" (Rom. 13:1–2). Paul's phraseology indicates that the principle he articulates extends beyond the Roman rule: "There is no authority except that which God has instituted." Either it is hyperbole or it is simply true. As it stands, it is consistent with other biblical statements we have observed. It follows that even the authority of Satan, the "god of this world," is only his by God's sufferance—just like the power he exercised over Job's worldly welfare. Likewise, the authority that rulers anywhere possess is only theirs because it has come from God, and they will be answerable to God for how they use that authority just as Assyria and Babylon were. Consequently, it is also true that Satan's temptation of Jesus was *at best* half truth and half lie when he said of the kingdoms of this world, "I will give you all their authority and splendor, for it has been given to me, and I can give it to anyone I want to" (Luke 4:6). Satan is indeed the "god of this world," and in that sense, the kingdoms of the world are under his suzerainty, or "have been given" to him. But the Bible also makes it clear that the rule of earthly kingdoms—their "authority and splendor"—are *God's to give* just as he gave so much to Cyrus, even though he ultimately says of Cyrus, "You do not know me" (Isa. 45:4).[20] So Daniel tells Nebuchadnezzar, "The Most High is sovereign over all kingdoms on earth and gives them to anyone he wishes" (Dan. 4:14, 22 [Eng. 4:17, 25]).

GOD'S OVERSIGHT OF THE NATIONS

God is, as Abraham says, the "judge of all the earth" (Gen. 18:25), and we will explore the significance of that statement later. Suffice it to say now that being a *judge* in the ancient world could have connotations of both rule and juridical sentencing. The term is especially important in connection with theodicy—that is, the doctrine of God's judgments, for God has judged and still does judge the nations of the world. For now, however, we consider God's oversight, or his government of the nations, for God not only judges the nations but also watches over them. And although he is omnipresent and omniscient, he is pleased to use subordinate beings in the exercise of his oversight and authority. The same is true of his judgments, as we know from passages in which angels are involved in their execution (e.g., Daniel 4, Revelation 6ff.). But biblical evidence suggests that God also uses angels to watch over the nations.

One verse appears to speak directly to this issue: "When the Most High gave the nations their inheritance, when he divided all mankind, he set up boundaries for the peoples according to the number of the sons of Israel" (Deut. 32:8). It is not at first apparent what this verse has to do with angelic oversight of the nations, but the Dead Sea Scrolls and the Greek Old Testament read not "the sons of Israel" but "the angels of God," and scholarly consensus has favored this reading.[21] If it is correct, the poetry establishes some correlation between the number of the "angels of God" and the "boundaries for

---

20. The NIV translates this as "though you do not acknowledge me," an inferior choice in this case, as sometimes elsewhere (cf. Hos. 6:3).
21. Cf. Garrett, *Angels and the New Spirituality*, 223.

the peoples." Though it seems a given that the "angels of God" are holy angels, our text (Deut. 32:8) does not allow us to say more about what these angels do; however, we know from Daniel 4 that the angels sent to execute judgment on Nebuchadnezzar are called "wakeful" or "watchful ones" (עירין, Dan. 4:14 [Eng. 4:17]; in the singular עיר, Dan. 4:10, 20 [Eng. 4:13, 23]). The name in context may suggest some sort of guardian function, perhaps also some sort of oversight function or witnessing function that the angels fulfill for God. That is, they may not only watch over nations but also communicate with God regarding any doings they are responsible to witness and perhaps even act on. Although such may be the case, however, one cannot insist on it because of the scantiness of evidence.

If such a portrayal commends itself, one could see here the origin of pagan, polytheistic accounts of divine government in which one god is supreme over the others, but the others have their subordinate roles in the government and oversight of human life in nation states on earth. The basic scheme may be set forth as follows, comparing the hierarchical divine structure of the Bible, Mesopotamia, Canaan, and the Greco-Roman cultures:

Bible	Mesopotamia	Canaan	Greece/Rome
Father	Anu	El	Chronos/Saturn
Son	Enlil	Baal	Zeus/Jupiter
angels	divine council	divine council	divine council
humans	humans	humans	humans

It is of passing interest in this schema that in all of the cultures there is a chief god, a father figure, with whom all authority resides and from whom all authority derives: the Father, Anu, El, and Chronos/Saturn, respectively. But there is also another god who actually "gets things done," and he is the storm god: Zeus/Jupiter (the Latin spelling), Baal, Enlil, and in the Bible, the Son, who is of course not another god but who is of the Godhead, and who will come at the end on the clouds with great power and glory. He is the true counterpart and source of such pagan distortions as "Baal, rider of the clouds," and "Zeus, cloud-gatherer."

The object of our interest at the moment is the *divine council*, or to use the terminology of Deuteronomy 32:8 (LXX), the "angels of God." Those angels seem to have oversight of the nations, and the boundaries of those nations correlate in some way to the number of the "angels of God." Their guardian function may parallel, in the realm of Common Grace, the guardian role of angels over churches in the realm of Special Grace, which seems to be the case in the letters to the churches in Revelation (cf. Rev. 1:20; 2:1, 8, 12, 18; 3:17, 14). A further parallel may exist to guardian angels for Eden (the guardian cherubim, Gen. 3:24), for the tabernacle and temple in the Old Testament (Exod. 26:1, cherubim woven into the tabernacle curtains; 1 Kings 6:29, 32, cherubim portrayed on the inner walls of the temple), and for believers in the New Testament who are temples of the Holy Spirit (cf. perhaps Matt. 18:10, Heb. 1:14).[22] If individual believers do have guardian angels, and if those angels are cherubim, as they were in the Old Testament, how formidable, then, those guardian angels must be!

TERRITORIAL SPIRITS

If God has appointed angels as watchers over the nations, and there are positive biblical data that point in that direction, there are also biblical data that suggest the enemy has his counterparts to God's appointments—much as, perhaps, the party out of power in England has or forms a shadow government.[23] The data come primarily from Daniel 10, which is the one place in the Bible that speaks clearly of anything like an evil spirit over a nation or kingdom.

Daniel 10 reports an angelic visit to Daniel after he had prayed and fasted for three weeks (Dan. 10:2–3). The angel is not named, but he tells Daniel that for twenty-one days he had been prevented from

---

22. The evidence, of course, is spotty and inconclusive, and the suggestions we have made are only inferences. Still, this is what the Bible tells or implies about God's oversight of nations and his guardianship of his temple in its historically reported forms.

23. A key difference being, of course, that the "shadow government" among men cannot actually govern the nation, whereas the enemy's spiritual rulers do indeed appear to have influence over nations.

reaching him.[24] The one who prevented him was "the prince of the Persian kingdom" (Dan. 10:13), whom he also calls "the king of Persia" (Dan. 10:13). Now it is clear that the one who prevented God's angel from completing his errand cannot have been any flesh and blood prince or king of Persia. Daniel's visitant is described with the splendor of a theophany, with a face like lightning, and eyes like flaming torches (Dan. 10:5–6), and the effect of his advent even on those who cannot see him is to frighten them away (Dan. 10:7). No human prince or king of Persia, however mighty, could have prevented such an angelic messenger from fulfilling his appointed task. Moreover, the angel tells Daniel that Michael came to assist him against the "king of Persia" so that he was able to continue on his journey to Daniel, and he refers to Michael as "one of the chief princes" (Dan. 10:13). This statement makes it clear that the term *prince* is being used to designate an angelic power in this context. Consequently, the "prince of Persia" seems to be an angelic power over Persia: an angel with authority to rule over Persia, since he is also called the "king of Persia." Here alone in the Bible we have a clear designation of an angelic power as a ruler (or principality) over an earthly kingdom. But what sort of power is this? It cannot be a holy angel or power, because it resisted the angel God sent to Daniel. God's kingdom is not divided against itself; one holy angel does not resist another. Those angels are without sin, which means they are all in step with God's Spirit and intentions at all times. Therefore, the angel who resists Daniel's messenger must be an evil or fallen angel. But how can an evil or fallen angel be the prince or king of Persia?

Before we attempt to answer that question, we reaffirm what the text states: There was a supernatural entity that resisted God's angel and was called the prince and king of Persia and had the authority and rule that such titles connote. This is the clearest designation anywhere in the Bible of what is popularly termed a *territorial spirit*— that is, an evil spirit with sway or influence over a given territory on earth. The concept may be unattractive to some, but be that as

---

24. Frank E. Peretti, in his novel *This Present Darkness* (Wheaton: Crossway, 2003), gives the angel the name "Tal." Since Mr. Peretti does not claim divine inspiration for this datum, we attribute it to the admirable freedom enjoyed by a creative writer.

it may, the present case seems to present rather clearly the existence of supernatural, *territorial* entities. If there were (and presumably are) such beings, how did they gain their positions of authority? We recall that Satan is the god of this world. That means he is suzerain over the world, and as such, he has a kingdom. Jesus tells us that the devil has his angels. If they are his, they are under his authority. Now God is also a king, the suzerain over all. He has angels under him who do his bidding, and the existence of the term *archangel* (1 Thess. 4:16, Jude 1:9) tells us that there is a hierarchy of authority among angels in God's kingdom under God. The Bible does not tell us much about that hierarchy, and although Christian writers in the postbiblical era—and especially in the Middle Ages—lavished speculation on the topic, we have no real knowledge of the authority structure of God's kingdom except that he rules it and that he has archangels and angels who do his bidding. Even these limited data, however, help us in our quest. They tell us that human kingdoms or governments operate on a principle of hierarchy or authority structure that has some heavenly analogue, however dimly we may perceive it. So Paul can use the same terms of both human and divine governmental positions.[25] And indeed, God is a God of authority, who gives authority to those under him in varying degrees according to his wisdom. Humans who are made in God's image naturally reflect this quality of God when they develop their own authority structures in governments and institutions.

What is true of humans is also true of Satan and his kingdom, because angels, like humans, partake of the *imago Dei*, and because God is the ultimate source of imagination and ideas (cf. chapter 4). Satan, too, would develop authority structures for his own purposes and for the administration of his own kingdom. C. S. Lewis displayed (his usual) remarkable insight into this matter when he portrayed the kingdom of darkness as a bureaucracy.[26] The evidence in Daniel 10 bears directly on this question, since it makes it

---

25. For example, "authorities" (Gk. ἐξουσίαι, earthly, Rom. 13:1; heavenly, Eph. 3:10); "rulers/ powers" (Gk. ἀρχαί, earthly [apparently], Eph. 6:12; heavenly, Col. 2:15; ambiguously, Rom. 8:38, Col. 1:16); and "thrones" (Gk. θρόνοι, ambiguously, Col. 1:16).

26. C. S. Lewis, *The Screwtape Letters* (London: Collins, 1942), passim.

very clear that evil angels have sway over human nations. The point is driven home further by the angel's remark that "when I go, the prince of Greece will come" (Dan. 10:20). What this means on the ground is that Alexander the Great will sweep through the Near East, conquering Persia en route to India, as he did.

We are now in a position to propose the following: Satan has his princes, who hold sway—in ways allowed but also limited by God—over human kingdoms. Satan mimics God, who has already positioned angels over kingdoms, as we infer from the fact that the number of angels correlates somehow with the boundaries or limits of the nations (Deut. 32:8). If the behavior of angels with regard to nations is like their behavior with regard to believers or churches, we can suggest that it is benign, protective, and minimally intrusive, although God may use them for judgment at any time, as he did with David (2 Sam. 24:16–17; 1 Chron. 21:12.15–16) and as he will do in the horrific judgments of Revelation.[27] But Satan has also established his own princes or kings over nations, and if their behavior is like the behavior of fallen angels or demons toward people, then we may suggest that it is far from benign, is not protective but rather offensive, and is far from being minimally intrusive. Further, just as demons can create a spiritual climate of temptation and tempt people into sin as did the serpent at the beginning, and just as they can invade those who sin and can trouble their lives, so territorial spirits and those spirits that function under their authority may create climates of temptation in cultures and nations and corrupt the life of any people. Such has always been the case with pagan cultures, and their very religions are demonically inspired and lead them astray. So Paul can warn that "the sacrifices of pagans are offered to demons, not to God" (1 Cor. 10:20). Human sin on the ground, as a response to temptation, further opens the door to such demonic involvement on the individual and cultural level.

Daniel's narrative reveals yet more about the authority structure of evil spirits and their relationship to pagan cultures when he is told that the prince of Greece will come after, or succeed, the prince

---

27. We reserve fuller discussion of such matters for volume 2 of this work, which deals with the Special Grace covenants and life under them.

of Persia. This means Alexander will come, conquer, and bring with him Hellenistic culture and its practices and gods, all of which are overseen by the "prince of Greece." When the invaders come, they bring their culture, their religion, and their demons with them. The pagans had a darkened understanding of this process, and by means of it they explained success and defeat in war. They believed that, when two kingdoms or armies fought, it was not only the soldiers on the ground who engaged in combat; their gods in heaven above also waged war—gods against gods, gods against men.[28] Egyptian and Assyrian accounts amply illustrate this theology, and we find it in Homer as well. We can diagram the concept as follows:

	Persian Kingdom		Greek Kingdom
In heaven	Persian gods	contra	Greek gods
On earth	Persian army	contra	Greek army

We use the Persians and Greeks for convenience since they are the ones mentioned in Daniel 10. The pagans thought that the kingdom or army who lost the war did so for one of two reasons: Either the enemy's gods were stronger, or their own gods had abandoned them and thus left their army without divine support in the war. The angel in Daniel 10:20 gives us the true picture when he declares that, at some unspecified time after he has returned to fight the prince of Persia, the prince of Greece will come. In God's sovereign allocation of authority, the prince of Persia will now be occupied with two heavenly opponents, Michael and the unnamed angel who visited Daniel. Perhaps that conflict is a judgment on the prince of Persia for opposing God's messenger in the first place; perhaps that conflict results in the banishment of the prince of Persia to some place unknown to us. Whatever the case, he will be replaced in the heavens over the Persian empire at some future date by the prince of Greece when Alexander marches victoriously through the Near East. The Persians would interpret his victory to mean that the Greek gods were more powerful than their gods, or they might think that their gods had abandoned them, which might be closer to the truth.

---

28. Cf. Niehaus, *ANETBT*, 116–37.

CONCLUSION

The fact that God is the God of the nations is implicit in the statement that he created the heavens and the earth. That truth lays the foundation for all theodicy because all nations and peoples are, as entities created or empowered by God, accountable to him whether they know him or not. Such is the state of things under Common Grace. But God is not content to let things remain in that condition. He also initiates a series of Special Grace covenants that work together, building one on the other, to achieve the ultimate goals of a new heavens and earth and a new humanity to inhabit them, where they will be coheirs and corulers with the second Adam. The Abrahamic covenant is the first of those Special Grace covenants. It is unique among them, not only because it is the first, but also because it prefigures and anticipates all the others.

APPENDIX A
GOD'S IMAGINATION
AND CREATIVITY[1]

We turn now to a short discussion of what S. T. Coleridge termed the *primary imagination* and the *secondary imagination*—a discussion that I hope will be ancillary to our comments in the Prolegomena on God as Creator, especially as Coleridge's thought was grounded in the revelation of the divine name in Exodus 3:14. Unfortunately, the philosopher–poet did not elaborate much on the terms beyond a brief account of them that he gave at the end of the thirteenth chapter of his *Biographia Literaria*. He wrote enough, however, to open the discussion and imply a direction for it, and we venture to take up the thread where he left it. I, moreover, address this matter on the basis of my own experience as a poet—experience that, after all, motivated me to consider attempting such a work as *God the Poet*.

Coleridge defined the *primary imagination* as "the living power and prime agent of all human perception, and as a repetition in the finite mind of the eternal act of creation in the infinite I AM."[2] By

---

1. What follows is an adaptation of observations made in the first chapter of Niehaus, *God the Poet*.
2. S. T. Coleridge, *Biographia Literaria*, vol. I, ed. J. Shaw Cross (Oxford: Oxford University Press, 1967), 202.

"the eternal act of creation," Coleridge meant first the role of imagination in enabling the subject to see itself as an object in an ongoing
process of self-creation, in the case of God, so that God *is* because
of himself ("I AM *because* I AM"—what the theologians call God's
aseity, his self-existence).[3] If we ignore the Masoretic vocalization
and read the verbs differently (e.g., "I cause to be what I will be"), the
idea of God's aseity is even more clearly what the divine self-naming
is about. One could also translate the phrase "I will create what I will
create," a statement of God's apparently ongoing "creation"—that is
re-creation—of the created order to which Hebrews 1:3 also points.
Finally, all three translations, "I am (will be) that/because I am (will
be)," "I will create what I will be," and "I will create what I will create," are possible and could occur to a reader of the prevocalized text,
and it may be a glimpse of God's wittiness that what he said to Moses
could subsequently be handed down in an originally unvocalized
text that implies all three things, all three of which are true.

What he says also implies essentially what we read in Hebrews
1:3: "The Son is the radiance of God's glory and the exact representation of his being, sustaining all things by his powerful word." That is,
God sustains all things by constantly "creating" them or re-creating
them—maintaining them in a created status (from nanosecond to
nanosecond, so to speak)—as suggested by the passages noted earlier (Isa. 42:5, Job 34:14). Coleridge's statement therefore assigns the
primary imagination a twofold role: to enable perception that agrees
with the Creator's ongoing sustaining of creation in a created status
and also, thereby, to lay the foundation for creativity that employs
perceived data as a shared, sustained, and ordered frame of reference in which and on the basis of which the secondary imagination
will create whatever it will create. However, although this agency in
a human being is enabled somehow by the Holy Spirit, the primary
imagination does not create ex nihilo as God did, but it is in perfect
harmony with God's ongoing support (or creation) of all things and
gives us a faithful and organized perception of them.

As the primary imagination enables perception in all people, it is
also essentially what underlies a poet's ability as a creator. As it works

3. Ibid., 202.

within a poet, it lays a foundation for poetry, and the poetic beauty and truth produced are in harmony with that foundation. This sort of poetic production is what one could justly call *inspired*—to the extent that the poet can allow its ideas to flow without obstruction in the act of composition.

APPENDIX B
KLINE ON TIME

MEREDITH KLINE ON THE DAYS OF GENESIS 1:1–2:3

Space and time, the cosmological coordinates, are correlative. Interlocking of the two is pronounced in God's seventh day rest, a temporal concept that connotes the spatial reality of the holy site of God's enthronement. Also indicative of their correlation is the giving of the temporal names "day" and "night" to the spatial phenomena of light and darkness (Gen. 1:5). It is inevitable then that the two-register structuring of the spatial dimension will also be found in the temporal dimension, and with it the archetype-replica relationship between the two registers. We have seen that by reason of this replication relationship earthly things are a rich source of metaphor for the realities of the invisible heaven. God is portrayed as hovering like an eagle over its nest and as resting like a man after his work is done (cf. Exod. 31:17); upper register space is designated "heaven" after the upper level of visible space; etc. We naturally expect then that in the case of time, as of space, the upper register will draw upon the lower register for its figurative depiction. Therefore, when we find that God's upper level activity of issuing creative fiats from his heavenly throne is pictured as transpiring in a week of earthly days, we readily recognize that, in keeping with the pervasive contextual pattern, this is a literary figure, an earthly, lower register time metaphor for an upper register, heavenly reality.[1]

---

1. Kline, "Space and Time," 9.

Meredith Kline, in an article already referenced, has made an attractive argument for heavenly–earthly correspondences as regards not only physical things on earth, such as the *imago Dei* and the tabernacle, but also the time component of the space–time continuum. Because we find his arguments attractive but also sometimes questionable, we engage his thought at some length in this appendix. We note that Kline speaks in terms of an *upper register* (heaven) and a *lower register* (the physical creation).

Kline argues that the six days of creation in Genesis 1 are not literal days but rather a structuring device, a view with which we agree:

> Under consideration here is the series of six numbered days and the accompanying evening-morning refrain. This refrain is not to be connected with the solar time phenomena of days one and four, for it is not confined to those two contexts but is included in all six day-sections and in every case is immediately conjoined to the numbered day. The imagery of the evening and morning is simply a detail in the creation-week picture. This refrain thus functions as part of the formularized framework of the account.[2]

It does seem that he tosses off the "evening and morning" refrain a little too lightly, but then again, he seems to account for their mention somewhat differently in the quote that follows.

Kline does not, apparently, think of the six days only as "part of the formularized framework of the account." He also seems to say they refer to supernal archetypes:

> The question whether the references to the six days (with their evenings and mornings) describe lower register time phenomena *or whether they belong to the upper register* is answered *in favor of the latter* by the interlocking of the six days on both sides with upper register temporal features. Certainly the six days are part of the same strand as the seventh day, and the "beginning," as suggested above, is to be taken as the threshold of the creation week. Psalm 104 reflects this by similarly bracketing its treatment of the works of the six creation days

---

2. Ibid., 13.

(vv. 5–26 or 30) with upper register scenes of God in heaven, before (vv. 1–4) and after (vv. 27 or 31–35).[3]

If we grant the comparison with Psalm 104 (which I do believe just barely works), we have a statement outside Genesis 1 that adds some force to Kline's way of seeing the six days. Be that as it may, the point at issue is the existence of supernal days—that is, days in heaven—which Kline apparently affirms by deciding that "the references to the six days . . . belong to the upper register." The only way I can see to understand this is that, in Kline's view, heaven has days. Again he says, "The six evening-morning days then do not mark the passage of time in the lower register sphere. They are not identifiable in terms of solar days, but relate to the history of creation at the upper register of the cosmos."[4] Likewise, he says regarding Genesis 1:1, "'In the beginning' is a time coordinate of invisible space. Entry into the six days that it is, 'the beginning' serves to identify them as also belonging to the invisible cosmological register."[5] For Kline, then, the six days of creation are supernal days, marked off in the narrative by refrains ("and there was evening, and there was morning, the Nth day") that also mark them as structuring devices for the body of the creation account.

Kline's view of the seventh day (the Sabbath) is consistent with this heavenly day view, as his comment related to Exodus 20:11 shows: "Like man's nature as image of God, man's walk in imitation of God's sabbatical way is not a matter of one-to-one equivalence but of analogy, of similarity with a difference. Like all the other lower register replicas, the sabbatical week of the ordinance is a likeness of its original, not exactly the same; it is an earthly metaphor for the heavenly archetype."[6] And again, on the topic of the seventh day:

---

3. Ibid.; emphasis added. By "the interlocking of the six days on both sides with upper register temporal features," Kline means the mention of God's creation of heaven in Genesis 1:1 and his Sabbath rest in Genesis 2:2 were both understood as having to do with a place outside the physical order—that is, heaven or the "upper register."

4. He adds, "The creation 'week is to be understood figuratively, not literally' that is the conclusion demanded by the biblical evidence," 13.

5. Ibid., 9.

6. Ibid., 14.

God is present at the beginning of creation; he is "the beginning." He is also "the end," for he appears at the completion of creation as the Sabbath Lord. The seventh day has to do altogether with God, with the upper register. The divine rest which characterizes the seventh day is the reign of the finisher of creation, enthroned in the invisible heavens in the midst of the angels. It is precisely the (temporary) exclusion of man from this heavenly Sabbath of God that gives rise to the two-register cosmological order. At the Consummation, God's people will enter his royal rest, the seventh day of creation (Heb. 4:4, 9, 10), but until then that seventh creation day does not belong to the lower register world of human solar-day experience. It is heaven time, not earth time, not time measured by astronomical signs.[7]

The concept of the seventh day, on which God rested, as an *eternal* Sabbath that redeemed humans look forward to entering (as Heb. 4:4.9–10 has been interpreted) is no new idea. It is, however, not clear that the "Sabbath rest" of Hebrews 4:9 is a one-day—even one eternal day—affair. To consider an analogy, we find Paul saying, "One person considers one day more sacred than another; another considers every day alike" (i.e., for someone, all days might be considered set apart, or Sabbaths, all in that regard "alike"; Rom. 14:5). In other words, God may *on that seventh day* have entered an eternal *rest*, but that does not mean his eternal rest was *one day long*. An eternal Sabbath could be an eternal rest from the *work of creating* but a rest that *lasts many heavenly days*—an infinite number, in fact.[8] We note that the word *Sabbath* does not mean "a day" but, rather, "rest" (from the verb שבת, "to rest," not "to rest for one day"). Moreover, although the phrase "day of the Sabbath" or "Sabbath day" ordained for humans (Exod. 20:8) may at first glance seem to support the idea of a heavenly

---

7. Ibid., 12–13.

8. Kline questions, "If the seventh day were not an unending Sabbath-rest for God but a literal day, would the next day be another work day, introducing another week of work and rest for him, to be followed by an indefinite repetition of this pattern? Are we to replace the Sabbath-Consummation doctrine of biblical eschatology with a mythological concept of cyclic time?" (ibid., 13). But this challenge to a literal day interpretation of the seventh day, fitting though it may seem, misses the point that the seventh day was a day of rest from God's *creative* work. It does not necessarily imply God's rest from work of any kind, and it need not be one eternal day.

Sabbath day that is ongoing (as a symbol, with its reference to Gen. 2:2, of that eternal Sabbath we are to enter), it in fact does the contrary. People work for six days and then are to rest on the seventh (the Sabbath). Likewise, God did his work of creating (Gen. 2:2) for six "days" and rested on the seventh, his Sabbath. That was the "day" on which he chose to cease *creating*. But as Jesus says, God *is working to this day* (John 5:17)—not work of creating but work of sustaining the cosmos, as well as whatever Special Grace works he does. Likewise we, when entering that heavenly Sabbath, will enter a supernal time of cessation from our earthly works. That Sabbath marks the end of *those* works, but it does not mean that other, supernal works might not await us or that those heavenly works might not be accomplished during an endless span of *heavenly days*—different, heavenly works following the one heavenly Sabbath "day" that marked our leaving our earthly works behind forever.

All this leaves unanswered what the source of Kline's concept of supernal days might be. Apart from his own brilliant (but perhaps not always rightly guided) imagination, we may be hard put to find a source within the Bible (apart from, perhaps, the figurative statement of Ps. 90:4, "A thousand years in your sight are like a day that has just gone by, or like a watch in the night"). In any case, the idea that cosmic time ought somehow to be modeled on supernal time, just as cosmic features are modeled on supernal ones (or, at a minimum, on ideas in the mind of the Creator), would be consistent and is attractive. The idea seems to appear even in hymns (e.g., "When we've been there ten thousand years"), and Milton portrayed heavenly days quite boldly:

> There is a Cave
> Within the Mount of God, fast by his Throne,
> Where light and darkness in perpetual round
> Lodge and dislodge by turns, which makes through Heav'n
> Grateful vicissitude, like Day and Night;
> Light issues forth, and at the other dore
> Obsequious darkness enters, till her houre
> To veile the Heav'n, though darkness there might well
> Seem twilight here; and now went forth the Morn

Such as in highest Heav'n, arrayd in Gold
Empyreal, from before her vanisht Night,
Shot through with orient Beams. (*Paradise Lost*, Book VI,
    lines 4–15)[9]

So to borrow Goethe's phrase, between human *Dichtung* and biblical *Wahrheit*, we hope we have at least caught some, even poetically
beautiful, glimpses of a truth.[10]

---

9. John Milton, *Paradise Lost*, ed. Merrit Y. Hughes (New York: Odyssey Press, 1935), 181–82; cf. Niehaus, *God the Poet*, 101–2.

10. Cf. Johann Wolfgang von Goethe, *Dichtung und Wahrheit* (Frankfurt am Main, Germany: Insel Verlag, 1965).

APPENDIX C
BETWEEN GENESIS 1:27B
AND GENESIS 2:27C

After a general discussion of the Genesis 1 account and the Genesis 2 account, we consider a brief overview of the data they provide about God's creation of the man and woman and his relationship with them. A synopsis of the relevant verses can enhance our appreciation of their covenantal elements. The following display presents the data in an ordered sequence (with references to Gen. 1:27 in bold type):

BETWEEN GENESIS 1:27B AND GENESIS 1:27C: COVENANTAL CREATION DATA

1:27b	In the image of God he created him
2:7	Yahweh God creates man
2:8–14	Eden described (trees, rivers)
2:15	Yahweh God puts man in garden to work it and take care of it
2:16	Command—eat any fruit
2:17	But not the fruit of the tree of the knowledge of good and evil
2:18	Yahweh God's plan to make a helper suitable
2:19–20	Man names the animals
2:21–22a	Yahweh God forms the woman

1:27c	Male and female he created them
2:22b	Yahweh God brings the woman to the man
2:23	Adam's reaction—Adam names the woman
2:24	They are one flesh
2:25	They are naked but not ashamed

The data in the table make it clear that before God made both male and female (**Gen. 1:27c**), he was in a relationship with the male that entailed the following:

1. Placement in Eden with purposes: to work it and care for it
2. Commands both positive and negative (regarding the trees and their fruit)
3. Presentation of the animals to Adam to see what he would name them

These data indicate that, before the completion of God's covenantal creation work, he had done the following:

1. Blessed the man by bringing him to a good place and giving him authority to work and care for that place and to name the animals
2. Instructed the man regarding his provision—hence, further blessing
3. Warned the man regarding a certain fruit with a stated curse as the result of disobedience

The blessings, instructions, and warnings also constitute what is later called *torah*.

These data make the following observations reasonable:

Once they came into being, the man and woman began to be aware of the happy surroundings into which God had placed them. That is to say, they became aware of the good he had done for them in the past. They knew God, who spoke to them, as a benefactor. However, God would soon tell them other things that would further qualify their relationship to him. He would, explicitly, bless them. He would command them to rule and subdue. He would give them the fruit of the Garden to eat. He would command them not to eat the fruit of one tree in particular. So their relationship moved from being a simple relationship between the Creator and the creature, to a more nuanced relationship between a ruler and those whom he blessed and empowered for rule, and to whom he gave provisions (further blessings), commands, and a warning (curse). Laconic as the passages are, the creation data of Genesis 1 and 2 thus give us information regarding a development of relations between God and the man and woman. The establishment, after the creation of the man and woman, of God's blessings, commands, and curse define that relationship in a way that it had not been defined before.[1]

The aforementioned data and observations highlight and illustrate the covenantal nature of the relationship that unfolds in Genesis 2 and introduce some of the particulars of that relationship.[2] We note that, although God gave Adam blessings, commands, and a curse warning before the creation of woman, it was only after her creation that "God's blessings, commands, and curse" defined *their* relationship to God "in a way that it had not been defined before."

---

1. Niehaus, "Covenant: An Idea," 234.
2. They also show the harmony of the two "accounts," both of which complement each other.

APPENDIX D
THE TERM "GLORY" IN THE GOSPELS

The following survey indicates that the term *glory* (Gk. δόξα) is used in the Gospels primarily in four ways: to refer to the Father's or the Son's eschatological or heavenly glory, to refer to the theophanic glory on earth, to refer rhetorically to human glory (akin to repute) given or sought by men, and to refer to the manifestation of God's glory in works of the Spirit done by Jesus. The following list is not exhaustive but illustrative/indicative.

I. Eschatological/heavenly glory
   A. Matthew
      1. 16:27
         "For the Son of Man is going to come in his Father's glory with his angels, and then he will reward each person according to what they have done."
      2. 24:30
         "Then will appear the sign of the Son of Man in heaven. And then all the peoples of the earth will mourn when they see the Son of Man coming on the clouds of heaven, with power and great glory."

3. 25:31

"When the Son of Man comes in his glory, and all the angels with him, he will sit on his glorious throne."

B. Mark

1. 8:38

"If anyone is ashamed of me and my words in this adulterous and sinful generation, the Son of Man will be ashamed of them when he comes in his Father's glory with the holy angels."

2. 10:37

"They replied, 'Let one of us sit at your right and the other at your left in your glory.'"

3. 13:26

"At that time people will see the Son of Man coming in clouds with great power and glory."

C. Luke

1. 9:26

"Whoever is ashamed of me and my words, the Son of Man will be ashamed of them when he comes in his glory and in the glory of the Father and of the holy angels."

2. 21:27

"At that time they will see the Son of Man coming in a cloud with power and great glory."

3. 24:26

"Did not the Messiah have to suffer these things and then enter his glory?"

D. John

1. 17:5

"And now, Father, glorify me in your presence with the glory I had with you before the world began."

2. 17:24

"Father, I want those you have given me to be with me where I am, and to see my glory, the glory you have given me because you loved me before the creation of the world."

II. Theophanic glory (or glory of God) on earth
   A. Luke
      1. 2:9
         "An angel of the Lord appeared to them, and the glory of the Lord shone around them, and they were terrified."
      2. 2:30–32

         For my eyes have seen your salvation,
         which you have prepared in the sight of all
              nations:
         a light for revelation to the Gentiles,
         and the glory of your people Israel.

      3. 9:32
         "Peter and his companions were very sleepy, but when they became fully awake, they saw his glory and the two men standing with him."
III. Glory associated with miracles/ministry
   A. John
      1. 1:14
         "The Word became flesh and made his dwelling among us. We have seen his glory, the glory of the one and only Son, who came from the Father, full of grace and truth."
      2. 2:11
         "What Jesus did here in Cana of Galilee was the first of the signs through which he revealed his glory; and his disciples believed in him."
      3. 11:40
         "Then Jesus said, 'Did I not tell you that if you believe, you will see the glory of God?'"
      4. 12:41
         "Isaiah said this because he saw Jesus's glory and spoke about him."
      5. 17:22
         "I have given them the glory that you gave me, that they may be one as we are one."

IV. Rhetorical

    A. John

        1. 5:44

           "How can you believe since you accept glory from one another but do not seek the glory that comes from the only God?"

        2. 8:54

           "Jesus replied, 'If I glorify myself, my glory means nothing. My Father, whom you claim as your God, is the one who glorifies me.'"

        3. 11:4

           "When he heard this, Jesus said, 'This sickness will not end in death. No, it is for God's glory so that God's Son may be glorified through it.'"

Our concern in producing this brief survey is to make it clear in the context of overall NT usage that the New Testament associates God's glory with works of the Holy Spirit. When Jesus does a miracle, it is accounted for as a manifestation of his glory, which is God's glory at work through him (cf. John 2:11, 11:40; with reference to the Spirit, cf. Mark 3:23–30). This is consistent with the doctrine that, for example, the gifts of healing and of doing miracles are gifts of the Spirit (1 Cor. 12:9–11). The implicit NT association of glory and the Spirit is also consistent with what we have said of the identity of the *glory* in Ezekiel 1:28 and the bearing of those remarks on our understanding of the *imago Dei* (cf. chapter 1).

BIBLIOGRAPHY

Aalders, G. C. *Genesis I, II.* 5th ed. Korte verklaring der Heilige Schrift. Kampen: Kok, 1974.

Aberbach, M., and B. Grossfeld. *Targum Onkelos to Genesis.* New York: KTAV, 1982.

Abir, S. "Denn im Bilde Gottes machen (Gen. 9:6 P)." *TGI* 72 (1982): 79–88.

Abou-Assaf, A., P. Bordreuil, and A. R. Millard. *La Statue de Tell Fekherye et son inscription bilingue assyro-araméenne.* Paris: Études Assyriologiques, Cahier 7, 1982.

Abramsky, S. "Nimrod and the Land of Nimrod." (Heb.) *BMik* 25 (1980/81): 237–55, 321–40.

Ahuviah, A. "In the Image of God He Created Him." (Heb.) *BMik* 30 (1984/85): 361–91.

Albertz, R. "Die Kulturarbeit im Atramhasis im Vergleich zur biblischen Urgeschichte." In *Werden und Wirken des Alten Testaments: FS für C. Westermann.* Edited by R. Albertz, 38–57. Göttingen: Vandenhoeck & Ruprecht, 1979.

Albright, W. F. "The Babylonian Matter in Gen 1–11." *JBL* 58 (1939): 91–103.

Alexander, P. S. "The Targumim and Early Exegesis of 'Sons of God' in Gen 6." *JJS* 23 (1972): 60–71.

Alexander, T. D. "From Adam to Judah: The Significance of the Family Tree in Genesis." *EvQ* 61 (1989): 5–19.

———. *From Eden to the New Jerusalem: An Introduction to Biblical Theology*. Grand Rapids: Kregel, 2008.

———. *From Paradise to the Promised Land: An Introduction to the Main Themes of the Pentateuch*. Grand Rapids: Baker, 1997.

Alonso-Schökel, L. "Sapiential and Covenant Themes in Gen 2–3." *TD* 13 (1965): 3–10.

Alster, B. "An Aspect of 'Enmerkar and the Lord of Aratta.'" *RA* 67 (1973): 101–9.

———. "Enki and Ninhursag." *UF* 10 (1978): 15–27.

Alter, Robert. *The Art of Biblical Narrative*. New York: Basic Books, 1981.

Anderson, B. W. "Creation and the Noahic Covenant." In *Cry of the Environment: Rebuilding the Christian Creation Tradition*. Edited by P. N. Joranson and K. Butigan, 45–61. Santa Fe: Bear & Co., 1984.

———. *Creation in the OT*. Philadelphia: Fortress, 1984.

———. "From Analysis to Synthesis: The Interpretation of Gen 1–11." *JBL* 97 (1978): 23–39.

———. "A Stylistic Study of the Priestly Creation Story." In *Canon and Authority*. Edited by G. W. Coats and B. W. Long, 148–62. Philadelphia: Fortress, 1977.

———. *Understanding the Old Testament*. 3rd ed. Englewood Cliffs: Prentice Hall, 1975.

———. "Unity and Diversity in God's Creation: A Study of the Babel Story." *CurTM* 5 (1978): 69–81.

Anderson, F. I. *The Hebrew Verbless Clause in the Pentateuch*. Nashville: Abingdon, 1970.

Andreasen, N. E. "Adam and Adapa: Two Anthropological Characters." *AUSS* 19 (1981): 179–94.

———. *The Old Testament Sabbath*. Missoula: Scholars Press, 1972.

———. "The Word 'Earth' in Gen 1:1." *Origins* 8 (1981): 13–19.

Angerstorfer, A. "Hebräisch *dmwt* und aramäisch *dmx*(t): Ein Sprachproblem der Imago-Die-Lehre." *BN* 24 (1984): 30–43.

Archer, Gleason. *A Survey of Old Testament Introduction*. Chicago: Moody, 1964.

Archi, A. "The Epigraphic Evidence from Ebla and the Old Testament." *Bib* 60 (1979): 556–66.

Arnold, B. T. *Genesis*. Cambridge: Cambridge University Press, 2009.

Ashbel, D. "The Four Rivers Leaving Eden." (Heb.) *BMik* 15 (1969/70): 100–104.

Astour, N. C. "Sabtah and Sabteca: Ethiopian Pharaoh Names in Genesis 10." *JBL* 84 (1965): 422–25.

Attridge, H. W., and R. A. Oden. *Philo of Byblos: The Phoenician History.* CBQMS 9. Washington, DC: Catholic Biblical Association of America, 1981.

Auffret, P. *La sagesse a bâti sa maison.* OBO 49. Fribourg: Editions Universitaires, 1982, 23–68.

Augustine. *The City of God.* New York: Random House, 1950.

Auzou, G. *Au commencement Dieu créa la monde.* Paris: Editions du Cerf, 1973.

Bailey, J. A. "Initiation and the Primal Woman in Gilgamesh and Gen 2–3." *JBL* 89 (1970): 137–50.

Baker, Charles F. *A Dispensational Theology.* Grand Rapids: Grace Bible College, 1971.

Baker, D. L. *Two Testaments, One Bible: The Theological Relationship between the Old and New Testaments.* 3rd ed. Downers Grove, IL: InterVarsity Press, 2010.

Baker, J. Wayne. *Heinrich Bullinger and the Covenant: The Other Reformed Tradition.* Athens: Ohio University Press, 1980.

———. "The Myth of Man's 'Fall'—A Reappraisal." *ExpTim* 92 (1981): 235–37.

Baltzer, K. *The Covenant Formulary in Old Testament, Jewish, and Early Christian Writings.* Philadelphia: Fortress, 1971.

Banon, D. "Babel ou l'idolâtrie embusquée." *BCPE* 32 (1980): 5–30.

Barbour, R. S. "Creation, Wisdom, and Christ." In *Creation, Christ, and Culture: Studies in Honour of T. F. Torrance.* Edited by W. A. McKinney, 22–42. Edinburgh: Clark, 1976.

Bar-Efrat, S. *Narrative Art in the Bible.* Translated by Dorothea Shefer-Vanson. Worcestor: Sheffield, 1989.

Barnard, A. N. "Was Noah a Righteous Man?" *Theology* 84 (1971): 311–14.

Barnouin, M. "Recherches numériques sur la généalorie de Gen 5." *RB* 77 (1970): 347–65.

Barr, J. "Biblical Theology." In *IDBSup.* Edited by K. Crim, 104–6. Nashville: Abingdon, 1976.

————. "The Image of God in the Book of Genesis—A Study of Terminology." *Bulletin of the John Rylands Library* 51 (1968–69): 11–26.

————. "Reflections on the Covenant with Noah." In *Covenant as Context: Essays in Honour of E. W. Nicholson.* Edited by A. D. H. Mayes and R. B. Salters, 11–22. Oxford: Oxford University Press, 2003.

————. "Some Semantic Notes on Covenant." In *Beiträge zur Alttestamentlichen Theologie: Festschrift Für Walther Zimmerli Zum 70. Geburstag.* Edited by H. Donner, R. Hanhart, and R. Smend, 23–38. Göttingen: Vandenhoeck & Ruprecht, 1977.

Barré, L. M. "The Poetic Structure of Gen 9:5." *ZAW* 96 (1984): 101–4.

Bartelmus, R. *Heroentum in Israel und seiner Umwelt.* ATANT 65. Zurich: Theologischer Verlag, 1979.

Barthélemy, D. *God and His Image: An Outline of Biblical Theology.* New York: Sheed and Ward, 1966.

————. "'Pour un homme', 'pour l'homme' ou 'Pour adam'?" In *De la Tôrah au Messie: Études offertes à H. Cazelles.* Edited by M. Carrez, J. Doré, and P. Grelot, 47–53. Paris: Desclee, 1981.

Bartholomew, C. G. "Covenant and Creation: Covenant Overload or Covenant Deconstruction." *CTJ* 30 (1995): 11–33.

————. "The Theology of Place in Genesis 1–3." In *Reading the Law: Studies in Honour of Gordon J. Wenham.* Edited by J. G. McConville and Karl Möller, 173–95. Library of Hebrew Bible/*OTS* 461. New York: T & T Clark, 2007.

Bartholomew, C. G., et al. *Canon and Biblical Interpretation.* Scripture and Hermeneutics Series 7. Grand Rapids: Zondervan, 2006.

Barton, J. "Covenant in Old Testament Theology." In *Covenant as Context: Essays in Honour of E. W. Nicholson.* Edited by A. D. H. Mayes and R. B. Salters, 23–38. Oxford: Oxford University Press, 2003.

Bassett, F. W. "Noah's Nakedness and the Curse of Canaan: A Case of Incest?" *VT* 21 (1971): 232–37.

Bassler, J. M. "Cain and Abel in the Palestinian Targums: A Brief Note on an Old Controversy." *JSJ* 17 (1986): 56–64.

Bastomsky, S. J. "Noah, Italy and the Sea-Peoples." *JQR* 67 (1976–77): 146–53.

Bateman, H. W., IV, ed. *Three Central Issues in Contemporary Dispensationalism: A Comparison of Traditional and Progressive Views.* Grand Rapids: Kregel, 1999.

Bauer, B. "Der priesterliche Schöpfungshymnus in Gen 1." *TZ* 20 (1964): 1–9.

Baumgarten, J. M. "Some Problems of the Jubilees Calendar in Current Research." *VT* 32 (1982): 485–89.

Bavinck, H. "Common Grace." Translated by R. Van Leeuwen. *CTJ* 24, no. 1 (1989): 35–65.

———. *Reformed Dogmatics.* Edited by John Bolt. Translated by John Vriend. Grand Rapids: Baker, 2006.

Beale, G. K. *The Temple and the Church's Mission.* Downers Grove, IL: InterVarsity Press, 2004.

Beale, G. K., and D. A. Carson, eds. *Commentary on the New Testament Use of the Old Testament.* Grand Rapids: Baker, 2007.

Beattie, D. R. G. "'Peshat' and 'Derash' in the Garden of Eden." *IrBS* 7 (1985): 62–75.

———. "What Is Genesis 2–3 About?" *ExpTim* 92 (1980/81): 8–10.

Beauchamp, P. *Création et séparation.* Paris: Desclée, 1969.

———. "Propositions sur l'Alliance de l'Ancien Testament comme structure Centrale." *RSR* 28 (1970): 161–93.

Beckerleg, C. "The 'Image of God' in Eden: The Creation of Mankind in Genesis 2:5–3:24 in Light of the *mīs pî pīt pî* and *wpt-r* Rituals of Mesopotamia and Ancient Egypt." PhD diss., Harvard University, 2009.

———. "New Light on Genesis 1–3 and Man as the Image of God." Paper presented at the annual meeting of the Evangelical Theological Society, Providence, RI, November 19, 2008.

Beckwith, R. T. "The Unity and Diversity of God's Covenants." *TB* 38 (1987): 93–118.

Beeston, A. F. L. "One Flesh." *VT* 36 (1986): 115–17.

Beltz, W. "Religionsgeschichtliche Anmerkungen zu Gen 4." *ZAW* 86 (1974): 83–86.

Benno, J. *Das Erste Buch der Tora—Genesis.* Berlin: Schocken, 1934.

Ben-Uri, A. M. "Noah's Ark: An Example of Construction Language in the Law." (Heb.) *BMik* 17 (1971): 24–31.

Ben Yashar, M. "Sin Lies for the Firstborn." (Heb.) *BMik* 7 (1963): 116–19.

———. "Zu Gen 4:7." *ZAW* 94 (1982): 635–37.

Berger, P. R. "Ellasar, Tarshish und Jawan, Gen 14 und 10." *WO* 13 (1982): 50–78.

Bergman, John Sietze, and Scott Walker Hahn. "Noah's Nakedness and the Curse on Ham (Genesis 9:20–27)." http://www.god awa.com/chronicles_of_the_nephilim/Articles_By_Others/ Bergsma-Noahs_Nakedness_And_Curse_On_Canaan.pdf.

Bergmeier, R. "Zur Septuagintaübersetzung von Gen 3:16." *ZAW* 79 (1967): 77–79.

Berkhof, L. *Principles of Biblical Interpretation: Sacred Hermeneutics.* 2nd ed. Grand Rapids: Baker, 1952.

———. *Systematic Theology.* 1941. Reprint, Grand Rapids: Eerdmans, 1982.

Bernard, A. N. "Was Noah a Righteous Man? Studies in Texts: Genesis 6, 8." *Theology* 74 (1971): 311–14.

Bettenzoli, G. "La tradizione del šabbāt." *Hen* 4 (1982): 265–93.

Beyer, K. "Althebräische Syntax in Prosa und Poesie." In *Tradition und Glaube, K. G. Kuhn FS.* Edited by G. Jeremias, H. W. Kuhn, and H. Stegemann, 76–96. Göttingen: Vandenhoeck & Ruprecht, 1971.

Bič, M. "The Theology of the Biblical Creation Epic." *SEÅ* 28/29 (1963/64): 9–38.

Bing, J. D. "Adapa and Immortality." *UF* 16 (1984): 53–56.

Bird, C. L. "Typological Interpretation *within* the Old Testament: Melchizedekian Typology." *Concordia Journal* 26 (2000): 36–52.

Bird, M. F. "Biblical Theology: An Endangered Species in Need of Defense." Blog. http://euange-lizomai.blogspot.com/2008/01/ biblical-theology-engangered-species-in.html.

Bird, P. A. "Male and Female He Created Them." *HTR* 74 (1981): 129–59.

Blaising, Craig A., and Darrell B. Bock. *Progressive Dispensationalism.* Wheaton: Victor Books, 1993.

Blake, William. "There Is No Natural Religion." In *The Poetry and Prose of William Blake.* Edited by David V. Erdman, 1. New York: Doubleday, 1965.

Blenkinsopp, J. "The Structure of P." *CBQ* 38 (1976): 275–92.

Blocher, H. *In the Beginning: The Opening Chapters of Genesis.* Translated by David G. Preston. Downers Grove, IL: InterVarsity Press, 1984.

———. *Original Sin: Illuminating the Riddle.* NSBT 5. Downers Grove, IL: InterVarsity Press, 2001.

Blythin, I. "A Note on Gen 1:2." *VT* 12 (1962): 120–21.

Bock, Darrell L. "Covenants in Progressive Dispensationalism." In *Three Central Issues in Contemporary Dispensationalism: A Comparison of Traditional and Progressive Views.* Edited by Herbert W. Bateman IV, 169–203. Grand Rapids: Kregel, 1999.

Boda, Mark J., and Jamie Novotny, eds. *From the Foundations to the Crenellations: Essays on Temple Building in the Ancient Near East and Hebrew Bible.* AOAT, Band 366. Münster: Ugarit–Verlag, 2010.

de Boer, P. A. H. "Quelques remarques sur l'arc dans la nuée." *Questions disputées d'Ancien Testament.* Edited by C. Brekelmans, 105–14. BETL 33. Leuven: Leuven University Press, 1974.

———. "The Son of God in the Old Testament." *Old Testament Studies* 18 (1973): 188–207.

Boice, James Montgomery. *Genesis 1:1–11:32.* Vol. 1 of *Genesis.* Grand Rapids: Zondervan, 1982.

Bonhoeffer, D. *Creation and Fall.* Translated by J. C. Fletcher. London: SCM, 1959.

Boomershine, T. E. "The Structure of Narrative Rhetoric in Gen 2–3." *Semeia* 18 (1980): 113–29.

Borgen, Peder. "God's Agent in the Fourth Gospel." In *Religions in Antiquity: Essays in Memory of Erwin Ramsdell Goodenough.* Edited by Jacob Neusner, 138–43. Leiden: Brill, 1968.

Borger, R. "Die Beschwörungsserie *Bît Mēseri* und die Himmelfahrt Henochs." *JNES* 33 (1974): 183–96.

———. "Gen 4:1." *VT* 9 (1959): 85–86.

Bradshaw, Jeffrey M., and Ronan James Head. *The Investiture Panel at Mari and Rituals of Divine Kingship in the Ancient Near*

East. Unpublished manuscript, October 24, 2013, 1–90. http://templethemes.net/publications/131024-The Investiture Panel at Mari-long.pdf.

Bravmann, M. M. "Concerning the Phrase 'And Shall Cleave unto His Wife.'" *Muséon* 85 (1972): 269–74.

———. "The Original Meaning of '. . . A Man Leaves His Father and Mother' (Gen 2:24)." *Muséon* 88 (1975): 449–53.

Bright, John. *Covenant and Promise: The Prophetic Understanding of the Future in Pre-Exilic Israel.* Philadelphia: Westminster, 1976.

Brinktrine, J. "Gen 2:4a: Überschrift oder Unterschrift?" *BZ* 9 (1965): 277.

Brodie, T. L. *Genesis as Dialogue: A Literary, Historical, and Theological Commentary.* Oxford: Oxford University Press, 2001.

Brown, Francis, S. R. Driver, and C. A. Briggs. *A Hebrew and English Lexicon of the Old Testament.* 1907. Reprint, Oxford: Clarendon, 1953.

Brown, Raymond E. *The Sensus Plenior of Sacred Scripture.* Baltimore: St. Mary's University, 1955.

Bruggemann, W. "The Covenanted Family: A Zone for Humanness." *Journal of Current Social Issues* 14 (1977): 18–23.

———. *The Covenanted Self: Explorations in Law and Covenant.* Minneapolis: Fortress, 1999.

———. "David and His Theologian." *CBQ* 30 (1968): 156–81.

———. "From Dust to Kingship." *ZAW* 84 (1972): 1–18.

———. *Genesis.* Interpretation Commentary. Atlanta: John Knox, 1982.

———. "The Kerygma of the Priestly Writers." *ZAW* 84 (1972): 397–414.

———. "Kingship and Chaos. (A Study in Tenth Century Theology)." *CBQ* 33 (1971): 317–32.

———. "Of the Same Flesh and Bone (Gen 2:23a)." *CBQ* 32 (1970): 532–42.

Byran, D. T. "A Reevaluation of Gen 4 and 5 in Light of Recent Studies in Genealogical Fluidity." *ZAW* 99, no. 2 (2009): 180–88.

Buccellati, G. "Adapa, Genesis and the Notion of Faith." *UF* 5 (1973): 61–66.

Buchanan, George W. *The Consequences of the Covenant.* Leiden: Brill, 1970.

Bullock, Alan. *Hitler: A Study in Tyranny.* Old Saybrook: Konecky and Konecky, 1962.

Burns, D. E. "Dream Form in Gen 2:4b–3:24: Asleep in the Garden." *JSOT* 37 (1987): 3–14.

Burns, J. Potocil. "Augustine on the Origin and Progress of Evil." *Journal of Religious Ethics* 16 (1988): 9–27.

Byron, Lord. *Childe Harold's Pilgrimage and Other Romantic Poems.* Edited by Samuel C. Chew. New York: Odyssey, 1936.

Calvin, John. *The First Book of Moses Called Genesis.* London: Banner of Truth, 1965.

———. *Institutes of the Christian Religion.* 2 vols. Edited by John T. McNeil. Translated by Ford Lewis Battles. Philadelphia: Westminster, 1960.

Caquot, A. *In Principio: Interprétations des premiers versets de la Genèse.* Paris: Centre d'Études des Religions du Livre, 1973.

Carson, D. A. "Systematic Theology and Biblical Theology." In *New Dictionary of Biblical Theology.* Edited by T. D. Alexander, Brian S. Rosner, D. A. Carson, and Graeme Goldsworthy, 89–104. Downers Grove, IL: InterVarsity Press, 2000.

Carson, D. A., and John D. Woodbridge, eds. *Hermeneutics, Authority, and Canon.* Grand Rapids: Zondervan, 1986.

Cassuto, Umberto. *A Commentary on the Book of Genesis 1–11.* Translated by I. Abrahams. 1961. Reprint, Jerusalem: Magnes, 1964.

———. *The Documentary Hypothesis: Eight Lectures.* Translated by I. Abrahams. Jerusalem: Magnes, 1983.

———. "The Episode of the Sons of God and the Daughters of Man." In *Biblical and Oriental Studies I.* Edited by U. Cassuto, 17–28. Jerusalem: Magnes Press, 1973.

Castellino, G. "Gen 4:7." *VT* 10 (1960): 442–45.

———. "Les origines de la civilization selon les textes bibliques et les textes cunéiforms." In *Congress Volume, 1956. VTSup* 4, 116–37. Lieden: Brill, 1957.

Chafer, Lewis Sperry. *Systematic Theology.* Grand Rapids: Kregel, 1993.

Charbel, P. A. "Gen 2:18–20: Una polemica sottintesa dello Jahwista." *BeO* 22 (1980): 233–35.

Childs, B. S. *Introduction to the Old Testament as Scripture.* Philadelphia: Fortress, 1972.

———. *Old Testament Theology in a Canonical Context.* Philadelphia: Fortress, 1986.

———. "Theme in Genesis 1–11." *JSOTSup* 10 (1979).

Chiltern, David. *Paradise Restored: An Eschatology of Dominion.* Tyler: Reconstruction, 1985.

Chryssides, George D. "Evil and the Problem of God." *Religious Studies Review* 23, no. 4 (1987): 467–75.

Clark, R. Scott. "Theses on Covenant Theology." http://www.wscal.edu/clark/covthese.php.

Clark, W. M. "The Animal Series in the Primeval History." *VT* 18 (1968): 433–49.

———. "The Flood and the Structure of the Prepatriarchal History." *ZAW* 83 (1971): 184–211.

———. "A Legal Background to the Yahwist's Use of 'Good and Evil' in Genesis 2–3." *JBL* 88 (1969): 266–78.

———. "The Righteousness of Noah." *VT* 21 (1971): 261–80.

Clements, Ronald E. *Old Testament Theology: A Fresh Approach.* Greenwood: Attic, 1978.

Clines, David J. A. "The Etymology of the Hebrew ṣelem." *JNSL* 3 (1974): 19–25.

———. "The Image of God in Man." *TB* 19 (1968): 53–103.

———. "Noah's Flood: The Theology of the Flood Narrative." *Faith and Thought* 100 (1972–73): 128–42.

———. "The Significance of the 'Sons of God' Episode (Gen 6:1–4) in the Context of the 'Primeval History' (Gen 1–11)." *JSOT* 13 (1979): 33–46.

———. "Theme in Gen 1–11." *CBQ* 38 (1976): 483–507.

———. *The Theme of the Pentateuch.* 2nd ed. Sheffield: SAP, 1997.

———. "The Tree of Knowledge and the Law of Yahweh." *VT* 24 (1974): 8–14.

Coats, G. W. *Genesis with an Introduction to Narrative Literature.* Grand Rapids: Eerdmans, 1983.

———. "The God of Death: Power and Obedience in the Primeval History." *Int* 29 (1975): 227–39.

Cohen, H. H. *The Drunkenness of Noah*. Tuscaloosa: University of Alabama Press, 1974.

Cohen, S. "Enmerkar and the Lord of Aratta." PhD diss., University of Pennsylvania, 1973.

Cohn, R. L. "Narrative Structure and Canonical Perspective in Genesis." *JSOT* 25 (1983): 3–16.

Cole, Graham A. *He Who Gives Life: The Doctrine of the Holy Spirit*. Wheaton, IL: Crossway, 2007.

Coleridge, S. T. *Biographia Literaria*. Vols. 1 and 2. Edited by J. Shaw Cross. Oxford: University Press, 1967.

Collins, Jack. "A Syntactical Note (Genesis 3.15): Is the Woman's Seek Singular or Plural?" *TB* 48, no. 1 (1997): 142–44.

Combs, E. "The Political Teaching of Gen 1–11." In *Studia Biblica 1978*. Edited by E. A. Livingstone, 105–10. JSOTSS 11. Sheffield: JSOT Press, 1979.

Combs, E., and K. Post. "Historicity and Necessity: Death in Genesis and the *Chāndoyga Upanishad*." *SR* 9 (1980): 41–52.

Cook, F. C. *Genesis-Exodus*. Speaker's Bible. London: Murray, 1871.

Cook, J. "Gen 1 in the Septuagint as an Example of the Problem: Text and Tradition." *JNSL* 10 (1982): 25–36.

———. "The Old Testament Concept of the Image of God." In *Grace upon Grace: Essays in Honor of L. J. Kuyper*. Edited by J. I. Cook, 85–94. Grand Rapids: Eerdmans, 1975.

Cooke, G. "The Sons of (the) God(s)." *ZAW* 76 (1964): 22–47.

Copeland, E. C. "The Covenant: The Key to Understanding the Bible." In *The Book of Books: Essays on the Scripture in Honor of Johannes G. Vos*. Edited by J. H. White, 29–37. Phillipsburg, NJ: Presbyterian and Reformed, 1978.

Coppens, J. "La nudité des protoplastes." *ETL* 46 (1970): 380–83.

———. "Une nouvelle date pour le document yahviste?" *ETL* 42 (1966): 567–71.

Couffignal, R. "Guides pour l'Eden: Approches nouvelles de Gen 2:4–3." *RevThom* 80 (1980): 613–27.

———. "La Tour de Babel: Approches nouvelles de Gen 11:1–9." *RevThom* 83 (1983): 59–70.

———. *Le drame de l'Eden: le récit de la Genèse et sa fortune littéraire*. Toulouse, France: Université Toulouse-le Mirail, 1980.

Creager, H. L. "The Divine Image." In *A Light unto My Path: Old Testament Studies in Honor of J. M Myers*. Edited by H. N. Bream, R. D. Heim, and C. A. Moore, 103–18. Philadelphia: Temple University Press, 1974.

Cross, Frank Moore. *Canaanite Myth and Hebrew Epic*. Cambridge: Harvard University Press, 1973.

———. "Kinship and Covenant in Ancient Israel." In *From Epic to Canon: History and in Ancient Israel*, 3–21. Baltimore: Johns Hopkins University Press, 1998.

———. "The 'Olden Gods' in Ancient Near Eastern Creation Myths." In *Magnalia Dei: The Mighty Acts of God. Essays on the Bible and Archaeology in Memory of G. E. Wright*. Edited by F. M. Cross, W. E. Lemke, and P. D. Miller, 329–38. Garden City: Doubleday, 1976.

Crüsemann, F. "Die Eigenständigkeit der Urgeschichte." In *Die Botschaft und die Boten, H. W. Wolff FS*. Edited by J. Jeremias and L. Perlitt, 11–29. Neukirchen: Neukirchenner Verlag, 1981.

da Cruz, F. C. "God's Covenant with Man: Basis of Biblical Spirituality." *Indian Theological Studies* 16 (1979): 298–325.

Cryer, F. H. "The Interrelationships of Gen 5:32; 11:10–11 and the Chronology of the Flood." *Bib* 66 (1985): 241–61.

Culley, R. C. "Action Sequences in Gen 2–3." *Semeia* 18 (1980): 25–33.

Cullmann, Oscar. *Christ and Time*. Translated by Floyd V. Filson. Philadelphia: Westminster, 1950.

Dahl, N. A. "Christ, Creation, and the Church." In *The Background of the New Testament and Its Eschatology: In Honour of Charles Harold Dodd*. Edited by W. D. Davies and D. Daube, 422–43. Cambridge: Cambridge University Press, 1956.

Dahlberg, B. "On Recognizing the Unity of Genesis." *TD* 24 (1976): 360–67.

Dahood, M. "Northwest Semitic Notes on Genesis." *Bib* 55 (1974): 76–82.

Damrosch, D. *The Narrative Covenant*. San Francisco: Harper & Row, 1987.

Dantinne, E. "Création et séparation." *Le Muséon* 74 (1961): 441–51.

Davidsen, O. "The Mythical Foundation of History: A Religio-Semiotic Analysis of the Story of the Fall." *LingBib* 51 (1982): 23–36.

Davidson, A. B. *The Theology of the Old Testament.* Edinburgh: T & T Clark, 1952.

Davidson, R. M. *Genesis 1–11, 12–50.* Cambridge Bible Commentary. 1973. Reprint, Cambridge: Cambridge University Press, 1979.

———. *Typology in Scripture: A Study of Hermeneutical Tupos Structures.* Berrien Springs, MI: Andrews University, 1981.

Davies, G. "Covenant, Oath, and the Composition of the Pentateuch." In *Covenant as Context: Essays in Honour of E. W. Nicholson.* Edited by A. D. H. Mayes and R. B. Salters, 71–90. Oxford: Oxford University Press, 2003.

Davies, J. D. *Beginning Now: A Christian Exploration of the First Three Chapters of Genesis.* Philadelphia: Fortress, 1971.

Davies, P. R. "Sons of Cain." In *A Word in Season: Essays in Honour of W. McKane.* Edited by J. D. Martin and P. R. Davies, 35–56. JSOTSS 42. Sheffield: JSOT Press, 1986.

Davies, P. R., and D. M. Gunn. "Pentateuchal Patterns: An Examination of C. J. Labuschagne's Theory." *VT* 34 (1984): 399–406.

Day, J. *God's Conflict with the Genesis Creation Story.* Cambridge: Cambridge University Press, 1985.

Deegan, Dan L. "Barth's Theology of Creation." *SJT* 14 (1961): 119–35.

Delitzsch, Friedrich. *Babel und Bibel.* Leipzig: J. C. Hinrichs, 1902.

———. *A New Commentary on Genesis.* Vols. 1–2. Translated by S. Taylor. Edinburgh: Clark, 1888. Reprint, Klock, 1978.

Dell, J. "Covenant and Creation in Relationship." In *Covenant as Context: Essays in Honour of E. W. Nicholson.* Edited by A. D. H. Mayes and R. B. Salters, 111–33. Oxford: Oxford University Press, 2003.

Dempster, Stephen G. *Dominion and Dynasty: A Biblical Theology of the Hebrew Bible.* NSBT 15. Downers Grove, IL: InterVarsity Press, 2003.

Dennison, C. G. "Thoughts on the Covenant." In *Pressing Toward the Mark.* Edited by C. G. Dennison and R. C. Gamble, 7–21. Philadelphia: Committee from the Historian of the Orthodox Presbyterian Church, 1986.

Dequeker, L. "'Green Herbage and Trees Bearing Fruit' (Gen 1:28–30; 9:1–3): Vegetarianism or Predominance of Man over the Animals?" *Bijd* 38 (1977): 118–27.

———. "Noah and Israel: The Everlasting Divine Covenant with Mankind." In *Questions disputées d'Ancien Testament*. Edited by C. Brekelmans, 115–29. Louvain: University of Louvain Press, 1974.

Descartes, Rene. *Discourse on Method and Meditations on First Philosophy*. Indianapolis: Hackett, 2011.

Dexinger, F. *Sturz de Göttersöhne oder Engel vor der Sintflut?* Vienna: Herder, 1966.

Diebner, B., and H. Schult. "Das Problem der Todes trafe an Tier und Mensch in Gen 9:5–6." *DBAT* 6 (1974): 2–5.

Dietrich, W. "'Wo ist dein Bruder?' Zu Tradition und Intention von Gen 4." *Beiträge zur Alttestamentlichen Theologie: FS für W. Zimmerli*. Edited by H. Donner, R. Hanhart, and R. Smend, 94–111. Göttingen: Vandenhoeck & Ruprecht, 1977.

van Dijk, J. "Existe-t-il un'poème de la création' sumérien?" In *Kramer Anniversary Volume: Cuneiform Studies in Honor of S. N. Kramer*. Edited by B. L. Eichler, J. W. Heimerdinger, and A. W. Sjöberg, 125–33. AOAT 25. Neukirchen: Neukirchener Verlad, 1976.

———. "La 'confusion des langues': Note sur le lexique et sur la morphologie d'Enmerkar." *Or* 39 (1970): 302–10.

Dillmann, A. "Die Genesis." *Kurzgefasstes exegetisches Handbuch*. 6th ed. Leipzig: Hirzel, 1982.

Dion, P. E. "Image et resemblance en araméen ancient (Tell fakhariyah)." *ScEs* 34 (1982): 151–53.

———. "Ressemblance et Image de Dieu." In *Supplements aux Dictionnaire de la Bible*. Edited by H. Cazelles and A. Feuillet, 55: 356–403. Paris: Letouzey & Ané, 1985.

Dockx, S. *Le Récit du Paradis*. Paris: Duculot, 1981.

Dodds, Marcus. *The Book of Genesis*. Vol. 1, *The Expositor's Bible*. Edited by W. Robertson Nicoll. 1888. Reprint, Grand Rapids: Eerdmans, 1947.

Dohmen, C. "Die Statue von Tell Fecherije und die Gottebenbild-lichkeit des Menschen: Ein Beitrag zur Bilderterminologie." *BN* 22 (1983): 91–106.

Donner, H., u. W. Röllig. *Kanaanäische und Aramäische Inschriften.* Wiesbaden: Harrasowitz, 1971 (vol. 1); 1973 (vol. 2); 1976 (vol. 3).

Doukhan, J. B. *The Genesis Creation Story.* Berrien Springs, MI: Andrews University, 1978.

———. *The Literary Structure of the Genesis Creation Story.* PhD diss., Andrews University, 1978.

Drewermann, E. *Strukturen des Bösen I: Die jehwistische Urgeschichte in exegetischer Sicht.* 4th ed. Paderborn: Schöningh, 1982.

Drews, R. "The Babylonian Chronicles and Berossus." *Iraq* 37 (1975): 39–55.

Driver, S. R. *The Book of Genesis.* 3rd ed. Westminster Commentary. London: Methuen, 1916.

Dubarle, A. M. *Le Péché originel dans l'écriture.* LD 20. 2nd ed. Paris: du Cerf, 1967.

Duchesne-Guillemin, J. "Gen 1:2c, Ugarit et l'Egypte." *CRAIBL* (1982): 512–25.

Dumbrell, William J. *Covenant and Creation: A Theology of the Old Testament Covenants.* Grand Rapids: Baker, 1984.

———. "The Covenant with Noah." *Reformed Theological Review* 38 (1979): 1–7, 8.

———. "Creation, Covenant and Work." *Evangelical Review of Theology* 13 (1989): 137–56.

———. *The End in the Beginning: Revelation 21–22 and the Old Testament.* Homebush West, NSW, Australia: Lancer, 1985.

———. *The Search for Order: Biblical Eschatology in Focus.* Grand Rapids: Baker, 1994.

Dunn, James D. G. *The Christ and the Spirit: Collected Essays of James D. G. Dunn, i. Christology.* Grand Rapids: Eerdmans, 1998.

Dyrness, William. *Themes in Old Testament Theology.* Downers Grove, IL: InterVarsity Press, 1979.

Ebach, J. H. *Weltentstehung und Kulturentwicklung bei Philo von Byblos.* Stuttgart: Kohlhammer, 1979.

Edwards, B., *Let My People Go: A Call to End the Oppression of Women in the Church.* Charleston: Createspace, 2011.

Egerton, F. N. "The Longevity of the Patriarchs: A Topic in the History of Demography." *Journal of the History of Ideas* 27 (1966): 575–84.

Ehrlich, A. B. *Randglassen zur hebräischen Bibel, vol. 1.* Hildesheim: Olms, 1968.

Eichrodt, Walther. "In the Beginning." In *Israel's Prophetic Heritage: Essays in Honor of J. Muilenburg.* Edited by B. W. Anderson and W. Harrelson, 1–10. New York: Harper and Row, 1962.

———. *Theology of the Old Testament.* 2 vols. Translated by J. A. Baker. Old Testament Library. Philadelphia: Westminster, 1961/1967.

Eissfeldt, O. *The Old Testament: An Introduction.* Translated by Peter Ackroyd. New York: Harper & Row, 1965.

Ellington, J. "Man and Adam in Gen 1–5." *BT* 30 (1979): 201–5.

Emanueli, M. "The Sons of God Took Wives Whomever They Chose." (Heb.) *BMik* 20 (1974): 150–52.

Enslin, M. S. "Cain and Prometheus." *JBL* 86 (1966): 88–90.

Erickson, Millard. *Christian Theology.* 2nd ed. Grand Rapids: Baker, 1998.

Eslinger, L. "A Contextual Identification of the *bene ha'elohim* and *benoth ha'adam* in Gen 6:1–4." *JSOT* 13 (1979): 65–73.

Evans, G. R. *Augustine on Evil.* Cambridge: Cambridge University Press, 1982.

Feilschuss-Abir, A. S. "'Da warden eure Augen geöffnet und ihr werdet sein wie Gott, wissend Gutes und Böses' (Gen 3:5)." *TGl* 74 (1984): 190–203.

Feinberg, J. S., ed. *Continuity and Discontinuity: Perspectives on the Relationship between the Old and the New Testaments.* Westchester, IL: Crossway, 1988.

Fensham, F. C. "The Covenant as Giving Expression to the Relationship between the Old and New Testament." *TB* 22 (1971): 82–94.

———. "Father and Son as Terminology for Treaty and Covenant." In *Near Eastern Studies in Honor of William Foxwell Albright.* Edited by H. Goedicke, 121–35. Baltimore: John Hopkins University Press, 1971.

Fenton, T. L. "Different Approaches of the Biblical Narrators to the Myth of Theomachy." In *Studies in Bible and the Ancient Near East Presented to S. E. Loewenstamm*. Edited by Y. Avishur and J. Blau, 337–81. Jerusalem: Rubinstein, 1977.

Ferguson, Sinclair B. *The Holy Spirit*. Downers Grove, IL: InterVarsity Press, 1996.

Fields, Weston W. *Unformed and Unfilled*. Grand Rapids: Baker, 1976.

Finkel, I. L. "Bilingual Chronicle Fragments." *JCS* 32 (1980): 65–80.

Finkelstein, J. J. "The Antediluvian Kings: A University of California Tablet." *JCS* 17 (1963): 39–51.

Fisher, E. "Gilgamesh and Genesis: The Flood Story in Context." *CBQ* 32 (1970): 392–403.

Fisher, I. R. "Creation at Ugarit and in the Old Testament." *VT* 15 (1965): 313–24.

———. "An Ugaritic Ritual and Gen 1:1–5." *Mission de Ras Shamra* 17. *Ugaritica* 6 (1969): 197–205.

Florovsky, G. *Creation and Redemption*. Belmont, MA: Nordland, 1976.

Fockner, Sven. "Reopening the Discussion: Another Contextual Look at the Sons of God." *JSOT* 32, no. 4 (2008): 435–56.

Foh, S. T. "What Is the Woman's Desire?" *WTJ* 37 (1974/75): 376–83.

Fohrer, G. *Theologische Grundstrukturen des Alten Testaments*. New York: Walter de Gruyter, 1972.

Fokkelmann, J. P. *Narrative Art in Genesis*. Assen: Van Gorcum, 1975.

Fossum, J. "Gen 1:26 and 2:7 in Judaism, Samaritanism and Gnosticism." *JSJ* 16 (1985): 202–39.

Fowler, Stuart. *The State in the Light of the Scriptures*. Potchefstroom, South Africa: Potchefstroom University Press, 1988.

Fox, M. V. "The Sign of the Covenant." *RB* 81 (1974): 557–96.

Fraade, S. D. *Enosh and His Generation*. SBLMS 30. Chico: Scholars Press, 1984.

Fraenkel, D. "Die Überlieferung der Genealogien Gen 5:3–28 und Gen 11:10–26 in den 'Antiquitates Iudaicae' des Flavius Josephus." In *De Septuaginta: Studies in Honour of J. W. Wevers*. Edited by A. Pietersma and C. Cox, 175–200. Mississauga: Benben Publications, 1984.

Fraine, J. de. *La Bible et l'origine de l'homme*. Bruges: Desclée, 1961.

Frame, John M. *The Doctrine of God*. Phillipsburg, NJ: P & R, 2002.

———. *The Doctrine of the Knowledge of God*. Phillipsburg, NJ: P & R, 1987.

———. *The Doctrine of the Word of God*. Phillipsburg, NJ: P & R, 2010.

Freedman, D. N. "Notes on Genesis." *ZAW* 64 (1952): 190–94.

Freedman, R. D. "The Dispatch of the Reconnaissance Birds in Gilgamesh XI." *JANESCU* 5 (1973): 123–29.

Frentz, A. "Der Turmbau." *VT* 19 (1969): 183–95.

Fretheim, T. E. *Creation, Fall and Flood*. Minneapolis: Augsburg, 1969.

Friedman, Richard Elliot. "The Hiding of the Face: An Essay on the Literary Unity of Biblical Narrative." In *Judaic Perspectives on Ancient Israel*. Edited by Jacob Neusner, Baruch A. Levine, and Ernest S. Frerichs, 207–22. Philadelphia: Fortress, 1987.

Friedman, T. "The Breath of God Hovered over the Water (Gen 1:2)." (Heb.) *BMik* 25 (1980): 309–12.

Fritz, V. "'Solange die Erde Steht'—Vom Sinn der jehwistischen Fluterzählung in Gen 6–8." *ZAW* 94 (1982): 599–614.

Frymer-Kensky, T. "The Atrhasis Epic and Its Significance for Our Understanding of Gen 1–9." *BA* 40 (1977): 147–55.

———. "What the Babylonian Flood Stories Can and Cannot Teach Us about the Genesis Flood." *BAR* 4, no. 4 (1974): 32–41.

Fuss, W. *Die sogenannte Paradieserzahlung*. Gütersloh: Gerd Mohn, 1968.

Gabriel, J. "Die Kainitengenealogie: Gen 4:17–24." *Bib* 40 (1959): 409–27.

Gaffin, Richard B., Jr., ed. *Redemption History and Biblical Interpretation: The Shorter Writings of Geerhardus Vos*. Phillipsburg, NJ: P & R, 2001.

Gage, Warren Austin. *The Gospel of Genesis: Studies in Protology and Eschatology*. Winona Lake, IN: Carpenter, 1984.

Galloway, A. D. "Creation and Covenant." In *Creation, Christ, and Culture*. Edited by R. McKinney, 108–18. Edinburgh: T & T Clark, 1976.

Gallus, T. *Die "Frau" in Gen 3:15*. Klagenfurt: Carinthia, 1979.

Garbini, G. "The Creation of Light in the First Chapter of Genesis." *PWCJS* 5 (1971): 1–4.

Garcia-Treto, F. O. "Covenant in Recent Old Testament Studies." *Austin Seminary Bulletin* 96 (1981): 10–19.

Garr, W. Randall. "'Image' and 'Likeness' in the Inscription from Tell Fakhariyeh." *IEJ* 50, nos. 3–4 (2003): 227–34.

———. *In His Own Image and Likeness: Humanity, Divinity, and Monotheism.* Culture and History of the Ancient Near East 15. Leiden: Brill, 2003.

Garrett, Duane. *Angels and the New Spirituality.* Nashville: B&H Books, 1995.

———. *Rethinking Genesis: The Sources and Authorship of the First Book of the Bible.* Grand Rapids: Baker, 1991.

Geisler, Norman L. *The Roots of Evil.* Grand Rapids: Zondervan, 1987.

Geisler, Norman L., and Kerby J. Anderson. *Origin Science: A Proposal for the Creation-Evolution Controversy.* Grand Rapids: Baker, 1987.

Gelb, I. J. "The Name of Babylon." *Journal of the Institute of Asian Studies* 1 (1955): 1–4.

Gentry, Peter J. "Kingdom through Covenant: Humanity as the Divine Image." *Southern Baptist Journal of Theology* 12, no. 1 (2008): 16–42.

Gerleman, G. "*Adam* und die alttestamentliche Anthropologie." In *Die Botschaft und die Boten.* Edited by J. Jeremias and L. Perlitt, 319–33. FS für H. W. Wolff. Neukirchen: Neukirchener Verlag, 1981.

Gese, H. "Die bewachte Lebensbaum und die Heroen: zwei mythologische Ergänzungen zur Urgeschichte der Quelle J." In *Wort und Geschichte: FS für K. Elliger.* Edited by H. P. Rüger. AOAT 18, 77–85. Kevelaer: Butzon and Bercker, 1973.

Gevaryahu, H. M. Y. "The Punishment of Cain and the City Which He Built." (Heb.) *BMik* 13 (1967): 27–36.

Gevirtz, Stanley. *Patterns in the Early Poetry of Israel.* Chicago: University of Chicago Press, 1963.

Gibson, J. C. L. *Genesis I, II.* Edinburgh: St. Andrew Press, 1981, 1982.

Gilbert, M. "Soyez féconds et multiplies (Gen 1:28)." *NRT* 96 (1974): 729–42.

———. "Une seule chair (Gen 2:24)." *NRT* 100 (1978): 66–89.

Gilchrist, Paul R. "Towards a Covenantal Definition of Torah." In *Interpretation and History*. Edited by R. Laird Harris, Sevee Hwaquck, and Robert J. Vannoy, 93–108. Singapore: Christian Life, 1956.

Gilkey, Langdon. *Maker of Heaven and Earth*. Garden City: Doubleday, 1959.

Gispen, W. H. "Exegeton over Gen 1–11." *GTT* 71 (1971): 129–36.

———. "Gen 2:10–14." In *Studia Biblica et Semitica: FS für T. C. Vriezen*, 115–24. Wageningen: Veenman, 1966.

———. *Genesis I–III*. Commentar op het Oude Testament. Kampen, Netherlands: Kok, 1974–83.

Goethe, Johann Wolfgang von. *Dichtung und Wahrheit*. Frankfurt am Main, Germany: Insel Verlag, 1965.

———. *Faust der Tragödie zweiter Teil*. Oxford: Basil Blackwell, 1943.

Goldenberg, David M. *The Curse of Ham: Race and Slavery in Early Judaism, Christianity, and Islam*. Princeton: Princeton University Press, 2003.

Golding, Peter. *Covenant Theology: The Key of Theology in Reformed Thought and Tradition*. Fearn, Ross-shire, UK: Mentor, 2004.

Goldingay, J. *Approaches to Old Testament Interpretation*. Downers Grove, IL: InterVarsity Press, 1981.

———. *Old Testament Theology: Volume One—Israel's Gospel*. Downers Grove, IL: InterVarsity Press, 2003.

Goldsworthy, Graeme. *According to Plan: The Unfolding Revelation of God in the Bible*. Downers Grove, IL: InterVarsity Press, 2002.

Golka, F. W. "Keine Gnade für Kain: Gen 4:1–16." *Werden und Wirken des Alten Testaments: FS für C. Westermann*. Edited by R. Albertz, 58–73. Göttingen: Vandenhoeck & Ruprecht, 1979.

Gonzales, Eliezer. "The Role of the Genesis Creation in the Writings of the Apostolic Fathers." *JATS* 23, no. 2 (2012): 3–29.

Goppelt, Leonhard. *Typos: The Typological Interpretation of the Old Testament in the New*. Translated by D. H. Madvig. Grand Rapids: Eerdmans, 1982.

Gordon, Cyrus. "Asymmetric Janus Parallelism." *EI* 16 (1982): 80–81.

———. "Building Up and Climax." In *Studies in Bible and the Ancient Near East Presented to S. E. Loewenstamm*. Edited by Y. Avishur and J. Blau, 29–34. Jerusalem: Rubinstein, 1978.

————. "Higher Critics and Forbidden Fruit." *CT* (1959): 3–6.

————. "The Seventh Day." *UF* 11 (1979): 299–301.

Görg, M. "Das Wort zur Schlange (Gen 3:14f): Gedanken zum sofenannten Protoevangelium." *BN* 19 (1982): 121–40.

————. "Ein architectonischer Fachausdruck in der Priesterschrift: zur Bedeutung von 'eden.'" *VT* 33 (1983): 334–38.

————. "Tohû wabohû—ein Deutugnsvorschlag." *ZAW* 92 (1980): 431–34.

————. "Wo lag das Paradies?" *BN* 2 (1977): 23–32.

————. "Zur Ikonographie des Chaos." *BN* 14 (1981): 18–19.

Granot, M. "For Dust Thou Art." (Heb.) *BMik* 17 (1971/72): 310–19.

Grant, A. M. "Adam and Ish: Man in the Old Testament." *AusBR* 25 (1977): 2–11.

Grant, J. A., and A. I. Wilson, eds. *The God of Covenant: Biblical, Theological and Contemporary Perspectives*. Leicester: Apollos, 2005.

Grau, J. *The Gentiles in Genesis: Israel and the Nations in the Primeval and Patriarchal Histories*. PhD diss., Southern Methodist University, 1980.

Graves, Robert, and Raphael Patai. *Hebrew Myths: The Book of Genesis*. Princeton: Princeton University Press, 1964.

Gray, J. *The Biblical Doctrine of the Reign of God*. Edinburgh: T & T Clark, 1979.

Green, W. H. "Primeval Chronology." *BSac* 47 (1890): 285–303.

Grelot, P. "Réflexions sur le problème du péché originel." *NRT* 89 (1967): 337–75, 449–84.

Grønbaek, J. H. "Baal's Battle with Yam—A Canaanite Creation Fight." *JSOT* 33 (1985): 27–44.

Groningen, Gerard van. "Genesis: Its Formation and Interpretation." In *Interpreting God's Word Today*. Edited by S. Kistemaker, 11–48. Grand Rapids: Baker, 1970.

————. "Interpretation of Genesis." *JETS* 13, no. 4 (1970): 199–218.

Groothuis, Rebecca Merrill. "The Bible and Gender Equality." Christians for Biblical Equality. http://www.cbeinternational.org.

Gross, H. "Der Universalismus des Heils: A. Nach der biblischen Urgeschichte Gen 1–11." *TTZ* 73 (1964): 145–53.

————. "Theologische Exegese von Gen 1–3." In *Mysterium Salutis II*. Edited by J. Feiner and M. Lohrere, 421–39. Einsiedeln: 1967.

Gross, W. "Bundeszeichen und Bundesschluss in der Priesterschrift." *TTZ* 87 (1978): 98–115.

———. "Die Gottebenbildlichkeit des Menschen im Kontext der Priesterschrift." *TQ* 161 (1981): 244–64.

———. "Syntaktische Erscheinungen am Anfang althebräischer Erzählungen: Hintergrund und Vordergrund." *VTSup* 32 (1981): 131–45.

GrossFeld, B. "Targum Onkelos and Rabbinic Interpretation to Gen 2:1, 2." *JJS* 24 (1973): 176–78.

Gruber, M. I. "The Tragedy of Cain and Abel: A Case of Depression." *JQR* 69 (1978): 89–97.

Grudem, Wayne, et al. *Biblical Foundations for Manhood and Womanhood*. Wheaton: Crossway, 2002.

Guest, T. H. "The Word 'Testament' in Hebrews 9." *ExpTim* 25 (1913–14): 379.

Guinan, M. D. *Covenant in the Old Testament*. Chicago: Franciscan Herald, 1975.

Gunkel, H. *Genesis*. Translated by M. E. Biddle. Macon, GA: Mercer University Press, 1997.

———. *Genesis übersetzt und erklärt*. Göttingen: Vandenhoeck & Ruprecht, 1901.

———. *The Legends of Genesis*. New York: Schocken, 1964.

Gunn, D. M. "Deutero-Isaiah and the Flood." *JBL* 94 (1975): 493–508.

Gunneweg, A. H. J. "Urgeschichte und Protevangelion." In *Sola Scriptura*, 83–95. Göttingen: Vandenhoeck & Ruprecht, 1983.

Gunton, Colin. *The Triune Creator: A Historical and Systematic Study*. Grand Rapids: Eerdmans, 1998.

Gurney, O. R., and S. N. Kramer. *Sumerian Literary Texts in the Ashmolean Museum*. Oxford: Clarendon Press, 1976.

Ha, J. *Genesis 15: A Theological Compendium of Pentateuchal History*. New York: Walter de Gruyter, 1989.

Haag, E. *Der Mensch am Anfang: Die alttestamentliche Paradiesvorstellung nach Gen 2–3*. Trier: Paulinus, 1970.

Haag, H. *Biblische Schöpfungslehre und kirchliche Erbsündenlehre*. SBS 10. Stuttgart, Germany: Katholisches Bibelwerk, 1966.

———. "Die Komposition der Sündenfall-Erzählung." *TQ* 146 (1966): 1–7.

Habel, N. C. "Ezekiel 28 and the Fall of the First Man." *CTM* 38 (1967): 516–24.

Hafemann, Scott J. *The God of Promise and the Life of Faith.* Wheaton: Crossway, 2001.

Hahn, S. W. "Covenant in the Old and New Testaments: Some Current Research (1994–2004)." *Catholic Biblical Review* 3 (2005): 263–92.

———. *Kinship by Covenant: A Canonical Approach to the Fulfillment of God's Saving Promises.* New Haven: Yale, 2009.

Hallo, W. W. "Antediluvian Cities." *JCS* 23 (1970): 57–67.

Hamilton, James M., Jr. *God's Indwelling Presence: The Holy Spirit in the Old and New Testament.* Nashville: B & H, 2006.

Hamilton, Victor P. *The Book of Genesis, 1–17.* NICOT. Grand Rapids: Eerdmans, 1990.

———. *Handbook on the Pentateuch.* Grand Rapids: Baker, 1982.

Hanson, P. "Rebellion in Heaven: Azazel and Euhemeristic Heroes in 1 Enoch 6–11." *JBL* 96 (1977): 195–233.

Haran, M. "The Berit 'Covenant': Its Nature and Ceremonial Background." In *Tehillah le-Moshe: Biblical and Judaic Studies in Honor of Moshe Greenberg.* Edited by M. Cogan, B. L. Eichler, and J. H. Tigay, 203–19. Winona Lake, IN: Eisenbrauns, 1997.

Harless, H. *How Firm a Foundation: The Dispensations in the Light of Divine Covenants.* New York: Peter Lang, 2004.

Harrelson, Walter. *Interpreting the Old Testament.* New York: Holt, Rinehart, and Winston, 1964.

———. "The Significance of Cosmology in the Ancient Near East." In *Translating and Understanding the Old Testament: Essays in Honor of H. G. May.* Edited by H. T. Frank and W. L. Reed, 237–52. Nashville: Abingdon Press, 1970.

Harris, R. Laird. "The Mist—The Canopy at the Rivers of Eden." *JETS* 11, no. 4 (1968): 177–79.

Harrison, R. K. *Introduction to the Old Testament.* Grand Rapids: Eerdmans, 1969.

Hartman, T. C. "Some Thoughts on the Sumerian King List and Gen 5 and 11B." *JBL* 91 (1972): 25–32.

Harvey, Anthony. "Christ as Agent." In *The Glory of Christ in the New Testament: Studies in Christology in Memory of George Bradford Caird*. Edited by L. D. Hurst and N. T. Wright, 239–50. Oxford: Clarendon, 1987.

Hasel, Gerhard F. "The Genealogies of Gen 5 and 11 and Their Alleged Babylonian Background." *AUSS* 16 (1978): 361–74.

———. "The Meaning of 'Let Us' in Gen 1:26." *AUSS* 13 (1975): 58–66.

———. "The Nature of Biblical Theology: Recent Trends and Issues." *AUSS* 32, no. 3 (1994): 211–14.

———. *Old Testament Theology: Basic Issues in the Current Debate*. 2nd ed. Grand Rapids: Eerdmans, 1991.

———. "The Polemic Nature of the Genesis Cosmology." *EvQ* 46 (1974): 81–102.

———. "Recent Translations of Gen. 1:1: A Critical Look." *BT* 22 (1971): 154–67.

———. "The Significance of the Cosmology in Gen 1 in relation to Ancient Near Eastern Parallels." *AUSS* 10 (1972): 1–20.

Hauser, A. J. "Genesis 2–3: The Theme of Intimacy and Alienation." In *Art and Meaning: Rhetoric in Biblical Literature*. Edited by D. J. A. Clines, D. M. Gunn, A. J. Hauser, 20–36. JSOTSS 19. Sheffield: JSOT Press, 1982.

———. "Linguistic and Thematic Links between Gen 4:1–16 and Gen 2–3." *JETS* 23 (1980): 297–305.

Hayward, A. *Creation and Evolution*. London: SPCK, 1985.

Hegermann, Harald. *Die Vorstellung vom Schöpfungsmittler im Hellenistischen Judentum und Urchristentum*. Edited by O. von Harnack and A. von Gebhardt. Texte und Untersuchungen zur Geschichte der altchristlichen Literatur 82. Berlin: Akademie, 1961.

Heidel, Alexander. *The Babylonian Genesis*. Chicago: University of Chicago Press, 1950.

———. *The Gilgamesh Epic and Old Testament Parallels*. 2nd ed. Chicago: University of Chicago Press, 1949.

Hendel, R. S. "'The Flame of the Whirling Sword': A Note on Gen 3:24." *JBL* 104 (1985): 671–74.

———. "Of Demigods and the Deluge: Toward an Interpretation of Genesis 6:1–4." *JBL* 106 (1987): 13–26.

Hengstenberg, E. W. *Christology of the Old Testament*. Vol. 1. Translated by T. Meyer. Edinburgh: Clark, 1858.

Henry, Thomas F. *Covenant and Kingdom, Or, a Right Relationship*. Unpublished thesis. St. Louis: Covenant Theological Seminary, 1989.

Hermant, D. "Ánalyse littéraire du premier récit de la création." *VT* 15 (1965): 437–51.

Herrmann, S. "Die Naturlehre des Schöpfungsberichtes." *TLZ* 86 (1961): 413–24.

Hershon, Paul Isaac. *A Rabbinical Commentary on Genesis*. London: Hodder and Stoughton, 1885.

Hess, Richard S. "Splitting the Adam: The Usage of 'ĀDĀM in Genesis I–V." In *Studies in the Pentateuch*. VTSup 41. Edited by J. A. Emerton, 1–15. Leiden: Brill, 1990.

Heyde, H. *Kain, der erste Jahwe-Verehrer*. Arbeiten zur Theologie 23. Stuttgart: Calwer Verlag, 1965.

Hidal, S. "The Land of Cush in the Old Testament." *SEÅ* 41–42 (1976–77): 97–106.

Hillers, Delbert R. *Covenant: The History of a Biblical Idea*. Baltimore: John Hopkins University Press, 1969.

———. "A Note on Some Treaty Terminology in the OT." *BASOR* 176 (1964): 46–47.

———. *Treaty Curses and the Old Testament Prophets*. Rome: Pontifical Biblical Institute, 1964.

Hirsch, Samson R. *The Pentateuch*. Translated by Isaac Levy. New York: Judaic, 1971.

Hodge, Charles. *Systematic Theology*. Grand Rapids: Eerdmans, 1982.

Hoekema, Anthony A. *The Bible and the Future*. Grand Rapids: Eerdmans, 1979.

———. *Created in God's Image*. Grand Rapids: Eerdmans, 1986.

Hoftijzer, J. "Some Remarks to the Tale of Noah and His Blessing." *OTS* 12 (1958): 22–27.

Holladay, William. *A Concise Hebrew and Aramaic Lexicon of the Old Testament*. Grand Rapids: Eerdmans, 1971.

Holwerda, D. "The Historicity of Genesis 1–3." *Reformed Journal* 17, no. 8 (1967): 11–15.

Hooker, M. D. *From Adam to Christ: Essays on Paul.* New York: Cambridge University Press, 1990.

Horowitz, M. C. "The Image of God in Man—Is Woman Included?" *HTR* 72 (1979): 175–206.

Horton, Michael S. *Covenant and Eschatology: The Divine Drama.* Louisville: Westminster John Knox, 2002.

———. *God of Promise: Introducing Covenant Theology.* Grand Rapids: Baker, 2006.

House, Paul R. *Old Testament Theology.* Downers Grove, IL: InterVarsity Press, 1998.

Houston, W. J. "'And Let Them Have Dominion . . .': Biblical Views of Man in Relation to the Environmental Crisis." In *Studies Biblica 1978.* Edited by E. A. Livingstone, 161–84. JSOTSS 11. Sheffield: JSOT Press, 1978.

Houtman, C. "Het verboden huwelijk: Gen 6:1–4 in haar context." *GTT* 76 (1976): 65–75.

Huegel, F. J. *That Old Serpent the Devil.* Grand Rapids: Zondervan, 1954.

Hugenberger, Gordon P. *Marriage as a Covenant: A Study of Biblical Law and Ethics Governing Marriage, Developed from the Perspective of Malachi.* Leiden: Brill, 1994.

Humbert, P. "Encore le premier mot de la bible." *ZAW* 76 (1964): 121–31.

———. *Études sur le récit du paradis et de la chute dans la Genèse.* Neuchâtel: Université, 1940.

Hutter, M. "Adam als Gärtner und König (Gen. 2:8, 15)." *BZ* 30 (1985): 258–62.

Hyer, C. *The Meaning of Creation.* Atlanta: John Knox, 1984.

Ishida, T. "The Structure and Historical Implications of the Lists of the Pre-Israelite Nations." *Bib* 60 (1979): 461–90.

Jacob, B. *Das erste Buch der Tora.* 1934. Reprint, New York: Ktav, 1974.

———. *The First Book of the Bible, Genesis.* New York: KTAV, 1974.

Jacob, Edmund. *The Theology of the Old Testament.* Translated by Arthur W. Heathcote and Philip Alcock. New York: Harper Brother, 1958.

Jacobsen, Anders-Christian. "The Importance of Genesis 1–3 in the Theology of Irenaeus." *Zeitschrift für Antikes Christentum* 8 (2004): 299–316.

Jacobsen, T. "The Eridu Genesis." *JBL* 100 (1981): 513–29.

Jansma, T. "Some Remarks on the Syro-Hexaplaric Reading of Gen 1:2." *VT* 20 (1970): 16–24.

Jaroš, K. "Die Motive der heiligen Bäume und der Schlange in Gen 2–3." *ZAW* 92 (1980): 204–15.

Jathanna, C. "The Covenant and Covenant Making in the Pentateuch." *BTF* 3 (1969–71): 27–54.

Jennings, Frederick C. *Satan, His Person, Work and Destiny.* Glasgow: Pickering & Inglish, n.d.

Jobling, D. "And Have Dominion . . . : The Interpretation of Gen 1:28 in Philo Judaeus." *JSJ* 8 (1977): 50–82.

———. "Myth and Its Limits in Gen 2:4b–3:24." In *The Sense of Biblical Narrative: Structural Analyses in the Hebrew Bible II.* JSOTSS 39, 17–43. Sheffield: JSOT Press, 1986.

———. "The Myth Semantics of Gen 2:4b–3:24." *Semeia* 18 (1980): 41–49.

Jocz, Jakob. *The Covenant: A Theology of Human Destiny.* Grand Rapids: Eerdmans, 1968.

Joez, Jacob. *The Covenant.* Grand Rapids: Eerdmans, 1968.

Johag, I. "TOB. Terminus technicus in Vertragund Bündnisformularen des Alten Orients und des Alten Testaments." In *Bausteine biblischer Theologie.* Edited by H.-J. Fabry, 3–23. Cologne-Bonn: Bonner Biblische Beiträge, 1977.

Johnson, Elliott E. "Covenants in Traditional Dispensationalism." In *Three Central Issues in Contemporary Dispensationalism: A Comparison of Traditional and Progressive Views.* Edited by Herbert W. Bateman IV, 121–68. Grand Rapids: Kregel, 1999.

Johnson, M. D. *The Purpose of Biblical Genealogies.* New York: Cambridge University Press, 1969.

Johnson, S. L. *The Old Testament in the New.* Grand Rapids: Zondervan, 1980.

Joines, K. R. "The Serpent in Gen 3." *ZAW* 87 (1975): 1–11.

Jongeling, B. "Some Remarks on the Beginning of Gen 1:2." *Folia Orientalia* 21 (1980): 27–32.

Jónsson, Gunnlauger A. *The Image of God: Genesis 1:26–28 in a Century of Old Testament Research.* Coniectanea Biblica: Old Testament Series 26. Lund, Sweden: Almqvist & Wiksell, 1988.

Junker, H. *Das Buch Genesis.* Echter Bibel. 4th ed. Wurzburg: Echter Verlag, 1965.

———. "In Principio Creavit Deus Coelum et Terram." *Bib* 45 (1964): 477–90.

Kaiser, O. *Introduction to the Old Testament.* Minneapolis: Augsburg, 1975.

Kaiser, Walter C., Jr. *The Messiah in the Old Testament.* Grand Rapids: Zondervan, 1995.

———. *Toward an Old Testament Theology.* Grand Rapids: Zondervan, 1978.

Kaiser, Walter C., and Moisés Silva. *Introduction to Biblical Hermeneutics: The Search for Meaning.* 2nd ed. Grand Rapids: Zondervan, 2007.

Kalluveettil, P. "Covenant and Community: Insights into the Relational Aspect of Covenant." *Jeevadhara* 11 (1981): 94–104.

———. *Declaration and Covenant.* Rome: Biblical Institute Press, 1982.

Kaminski, C. M. *From Noah to Israel: Realization of the Primeval Blessing after the Flood.* London: T & T Clark, 2004.

Kapelrud, A. S. "Baal, Schöpfung und Chaos." *UF* 11 (1979): 407–12.

———. "Creation in the Ras Shamra Texts." *ST* 34 (1980): 1–11.

———. "Die Theologie der Schöpfung im Alten Testament." *ZAW* 91 (1979): 159–70.

———. "The Mythological Features in Genesis 1 and the Author's Intentions." *VT* 24 (1974): 178–86.

Karlberg, Mark. "Covenant and Common Grace." *WTJ* 50 (1988).

Keel, O. *Vögel als Boten.* OBO 14. Freiburg: University of Freiburg Press, 1977.

Keil, C. F., and F. Delitzsch. *Commentary on the Old Testament: The Pentateuch.* Vol. 1. Peabody, MA: Hendrickson, 2011.

Kelly, John. *The Divine Covenants: Their Nature and Design.* London: Reed and Pardon, 1861.

Kessler, M. "Rhetorical Criticism of Gen 7." In *Rhetorical Criticism: Essays in Honor of J. Muilenburg.* Edited by J. J. Jackson and M. Kessler, 1–17. Pittsburg: Pickwick Press, 1974.

Kidner, Derek. *Genesis: An Introduction and Commentary*. Tyndale OT Commentary. London: Tyndale, 1967.

Kikawada, I. M. "The Double Creation of Mankind in 'Enki and Ninmah,' 'Atrahasis I, 1–351' and 'Gen 1–2.'" *Iraq* 45 (1983): 43–45.

———. "The Irrigation of the Garden of Eden." In *Actes du 29e Congrès international des Orientalistes Études Hébraiques*, 29–33. Paris: L 'Asiathèque, 1975.

———. "The Shape of Genesis 11:1–9." In *Rhetorical Criticism: Essays in Honor of J. Muilenburg*. Edited by J. J. Jackson and M. Kessler, 18–32. Pittsburgh: Pickwick Press, 1974.

———. "Two Notes on Eve." *JBL* 91 (1972): 33–37.

Kilian, R. "Gen 1:2 und die Urgötter von Hermopolis." *VT* 16 (1966): 420–38.

Killmer, A. D. "The Mesopotamian Concept of Overpopulation and Its Solution as Reflected in Mythology." *Or* 41 (1972): 160–77.

King-Farlow, J., and D. W. Hunt. "Perspectives on the Fall of Man." *SJT* 35 (1982): 193–204.

Kitchen, Kenneth A. *Ancient Orient and Old Testament*. Downers Grove, IL: InterVarsity Press, 1966.

———. *The Bible in Its World: The Bible and Archaeology Today*. Downers Grove, IL: InterVarsity Press, 1978.

———. "Egypt, Ugarit, Qatna, and Covenant." *UF* 11 (1979): 453–64.

———. *On the Reliability of the Old Testament*. Grand Rapids: Eerdmans, 2003.

Klemm, P. "Kain und die Kainiten." *ZTK* 78 (1981): 391–408.

Klien, R. W. "Archaic Chronologies and the Tetual History of the Old Testament." *HTR* 67 (1974): 255–63.

Kline, Meredith G. "Because It Had Not Rained." *WTJ* 20 (1958): 146–57.

———. *By Oath Consigned: A Reinterpretation of the Covenant Signs of Baptism Circumcision*. Grand Rapids: Eerdmans, 1968.

———. "Creation in the Image of the Glory-Spirit." *WTJ* 39 (1977): 250–72.

———. "Divine Kingship and Gen 6: 1–4." *WTJ* 24 (1963): 187–204.

———. *God Heaven and Har Magedon*. Eugene: Wipf & Stock, 2006.

———. *Images of the Spirit*. 1980. Reprint, Eugene: Wipf & Stock, 1999.

————. *Kingdom Prologue.* Overland Park: Two Age Press, 2000.

————. "Space and Time in the Genesis Cosmogony." *Perspectives on Science and Christian Faith* 48 (1996): 1–22.

————. *The Structure of Biblical Authority.* Grand Rapids: Eerdmans, 1975.

————. *Treaty of the Great King.* Grand Rapids: Eerdmans, 1963.

Kloos, C. J. L. "The Flood on Speaking Terms with God." *ZAW* 94 (1982): 639–42.

Knight, Douglas. "Cosmogony and Order in the Hebrew Tradition." In *Cosmology and Ethical Order.* Edited by Robin W. Lovin and Frank E. Reynolds, 133–57. Chicago: University of Chicago Press, 1985.

Knight, G. A. F. *Theology in Pictures: A Commentary on Gen 1–11.* Edinburgh: Handsel Press, 1981.

Kohler, Ludwig. *Theologie des Alten Testament.* Tübingen: Mohr, 1966.

König, E. *Die Genesis eingeleitet, übersetzt erklärt.* Gütersloh: Bertelsman, 1919.

Koole, J. L. "De Stamvader (Gen 1–3)." *Schrift en uitleg: Studies aangeboden aan W. H. Gispen,* 79–94. Kampen: Kok, 1970.

————. "Het Litterair Genre van Genesis 1–3." *GTT* 63 (1963): 81–122.

Koroçec, V. *Hethitische Staatsverträge.* Leipzig: Weicher, 1931.

Köster, H. M. *Urstand, Fall und Erbsunde in der katholischen Theologie unseres Jarhrhunderts.* Regensburg: Friedrich Pustet, 1981.

Kramer, S. N. "The 'Babel of Tongues': A Sumerian Version." *JAOS* 88 (1968): 108–11.

————. "Enki and His Inferiority Complex." *Or* 39 (1970): 103–10.

————. "'The Sumerian Deluge Myth' Reviewed and Revised." *AnSt* 33 (1983): 115–21.

Krinetzki, G. "Prahlerei und Sieg im alten Israel (Gen 4:23ff etc)." *BZ* 20 (1976): 45–58.

Kruse, H. "Vorstufen der Erbschuldlehre." *MTZ* 20 (1969): 288–314.

Kselman, J. S. "A Note on Gen 7:11." *CBQ* 35 (1973): 491–93.

————. "The Recovery of Poetic Fragments from the Pentateuchal Priestly Source." *JBL* 97 (1978): 161–73.

Kuiper, Herman. *Calvin on Common Grace*. Grand Rapids: Smitter, 1928.

Kulikovaky, Andrew S. *Creation, Fall, Restoration: A Biblical Theology of Creation*. Fearn, Ross-shire, UK: Mentor, 2009.

Kümmel, H. M. "Bemerkungen zu den altorientalischen Berichten von Menschenschöpfung." *WO* 7 (1973–74): 25–38.

Kurtz, J. H. *Die Söhne Gottes in 1 Mos 6:1–4 und die sündigenden Engel*. Mitan: Neumann's Verlag, 1858.

Kutsch, E. "Die Paradieserzählung Gen 2–3 und ihr Verfasser." In *Studien zum Pentateuch: FS für W. Kornfeld*. Edited by G. Braulik, 9–24. Vienna: Herder, 1977.

Labuschagne, C. J. "Additional Remarks on the Pattern of the Divine Speech Formulas in the Pentateuch." *VT* 34 (1984): 91–95.

———. "The Literary and Theological Function of Divine Speech in the Pentateuch." In *Congress Volume, 1983*. VTSup 36. Edited by J. A. Emerton, 154–73. Leiden: Brill, 1985.

———. "The Pattern of the Divine Speech Formulas in the Pentateuch." *VT* 32 (1982): 268–96.

———. "Pentateuchal Patterns: A Reply to P. R. Davies and D. M. Gunn." *VT* 34 (1984): 407–13.

Ladd, G. E. "Biblical Theology, History of," and "Biblical Theology, Nature of." In *International Standard Bible Encyclopedia*. Rev. ed. 4 vols. Vol. 1, 498–509. Grand Rapids: Eerdmans, 1979.

Lafont, G. *God, Time, and Being*. Petersham, MA: St. Bede's, 1992.

Lagrange, M.-J. "La Paternité de Dieu dans l'Ancien Testament." *RB* 5 (1908): 482–83.

Lamberg-Karlovsky, C. C. "Dilmun: Gateway to Immortality." *JNES* 41 (1982): 45–50.

Lambert, W. G. "New Evidence for the First Line of *Atrahasis*." *Or* 38 (1969): 533–38.

———. "A New Fragment from a List of Antediluvian Kings and Marduk's Chariot." In *Symbolae Biblicae et Mesopotamicae F. M. T. de L. Böhl dedicatae*. Edited by M. A. Beek, A. A. Kampman, D. Nijland, and J. Ryckmans, 271–80. Leiden: Brill, 1973.

———. "New Fragments of Babylonian Epics." *AfO* 27 (1980): 71–82.

————. "A New Look at the Babylonian Background of Genesis." *JTS* 16 (1965): 287–300.

Lambert, W. G., and A. R. Millard. *Atrahasis: The Babylonian Story of the Flood.* Oxford: Clarendon Press, 1969. Reprint, Winona Lake: Eisenbrauns, 1999.

Landes, G. M. "Creation Tradition in Prov 8:22–31 and Gen 1." In *A Light unto My Path: Old Testament Studies in Honor of J. M. Myers.* Edited by H. N. Bream, R. D. Heim, and C. A. Moore, 279–93. Philadelphia: Temple University Press, 1974.

Landy, F. "The Song of Songs and the Garden of Eden." *JBL* 98 (1979): 513–28.

Lane, Daniel C. "The Meaning and Use of the Old Testament Term for 'Covenant' (*bᵉrît*): With Some Implications for Dispensationalism and Covenant Theology." PhD diss., Trinity International University, 2000.

Lane, W. R. "The Initiation of Creation." *VT* 13 (1963): 63–73.

Lang, B. "Non-Semantic Deluge Stories and the Book of Genesis: A Bibliographical and Critical Survey." *Anthropos* 80 (1985): 605–16.

Langkammer, Hugolinus. "Der Ursprung des Glaubens an Christus den Schöpfungsmittler." *Liber Annuus (Annual of the Studium Biblicum Franciscanum)* 18 (1968): 55–93.

Larsson, E. *Christus als Vorbild.* Uppsala: Almqvist & Wiksells, 1962.

Larsson, G. "Chronological Parallels between the Creation and the Flood." *VT* 27 (1977): 490–92.

————. "The Documentary Hypothesis and the Chronological Structure of the OT." *ZAW* 97 (1985): 316–33.

LaSor, W. S. "Prophecy, Inspiration and *Sensus Plenior.*" *TB* 29 (1978): 49–60.

Laurin, R. B. "The Tower of Babel Revisited." In *Biblical and Near Eastern Studies: Essays in Honor of W. L. Lasor.* Edited by G. A. Tuttle, 142–45. Grand Rapids: Eerdmans, 1978.

Leibowitz, N. *Studies in Bereshit.* 4th ed. Jerusalem: World Zionist Organization, 1981.

Lella, A. A. di. "Gen 1:1–10: A Formal Introduction to P's Creation Account." In *Mélanges bibliques et orientaux en l'honneur de*

M. Delcor. Edited by A. Caquot, S. Légasse, and M. Tardieu, 127–37. AOAT 215. Kevelaer: Butzon and Bercker, 1985.

Lemche, N. P. "The Chronology in the Story of the Flood." *JSOT* 18 (1980): 52–62.

Letham, Robert. *The Holy Trinity: In Scripture, History, Theology, and Worship*. Phillipsburg, NJ: P & R, 2004.

Levenson, Jon D. *Creation and the Persistence of Evil: The Jewish Drama of Divine Omnipotence*. San Francisco: Harper & Row, 1988.

Lever, Jan. *Creation and Evolution*. Translated by Peter G. Berkhout. Grand Rapids: International, 1958.

Levin, S. "The More Savory Offering: A Key to the Problem of Gen 4:3–5." *JBL* 98 (1979): 85.

Levine, E. "The Syriac Version of Gen 4:1–16." *VT* 26 (1976): 70–78.

Lewis, C. S. *Perelandra*. New York: Macmillan, 1944.

———. *The Screwtape Letters*. London: Collins, 1942.

———. *That Hideous Strength*. New York: Macmillan, 1965.

Lewis, Jack P. "The Days of Creation: An Historical Survey of Interpretation." *JETS* 32, no. 4 (1989): 433–55.

———. *A Study of the Interpretation of Noah and the Flood in Jewish and Christian Literature*. Leiden: Brill, 1968.

L'Hour, J. "Yahweh Elohim." *RB* 81 (1974): 524–56.

Lincoln, A. T. *Paradise Now and Not Yet*. New York: Cambridge University Press, 1981.

Lipinski, É. "Ancient Types of Wisdom Literature in Biblical Narrative." In *Essays on the Bible and the Ancient World III: I. L. Seeligman Volume*. Edited by A. Rofé and Y. Zakovitch, 39–55. Jerusalem: Rubinstein's Publishing House, 1983.

———. "Études sur des textes 'messianiques' de l'A.T." *Sem* 20 (1970): 41–57.

———. "Garden of Abundance, Image of Lebanon." *ZAW* 85 (1973): 358–59.

———. "Nimrod et Aššur." *RB* 73 (1966): 77–93.

Liverani, M. "Un'ipotesi sul nome di Abramo." *Hen* 1 (1979): 9–18.

Livingston, David N. "Evangelicals and Evolution: Retrospect and Prospect." *Pro Rege* 19, no. 1 (1990): 12–23.

Loader, J. A. "Onqelos Gen 1 and the Structure of the Hebrew Text." *JSJ* 9 (1978): 198–204.

Loewenclau, I. von. "Gen 4:6–7—eine jehwistische Erweiterung." *Congress Volume, 1977. VTSup* 29. Edited by J. A. Emerton, 177–88. Leiden: Brill, 1978.

Loewenstamm, S. E. "Beloved Is Man in That He Was Created in the Image." In *Comparative Studies in Biblical and Ancient Oriental Literatures.* AOAT 204, 48–50. Kevelaer: Butzon and Bercker, 1980.

———. "Die Wasser der biblischen Sintflut: ihr Hereinbrechen und ihr Verschwinden." *VT* 34 (1984): 179–84.

———. "The Flood." *Comparative Studies in Biblical and Ancient Oriental Literatures.* AOAT 204, 93–121. Kevelaer: Butzon and Bercker, 1980.

———. "The Seven-Day-Unit in Ugaritic Epic Literature." *IEJ* 15 (1965): 122–33.

Lohfink, N. "The Concept of 'Covenant' in Biblical Theology." In *The God of Israel and the Nations: Studies in Isaiah and the Psalms.* Edited by N. Lohfink and E. Zenger, 11–31. Collegeville, MN: Liturgical Press, 2000.

———. "Die Priesterschrift und die Geschichte." *VTSup* 29 (1978): 189–225.

———. "Gen 2f als 'geschichtliche' Ätiologie." *Scholastik* 38 (1963): 321–34.

———. *Great Themes from the Old Testament.* Edinburgh: T & T Clark, 1982.

———. "Wie sollte man das Alte Testament auf die Erbsunde hin befragen?" In *Zum Problem der Erbsunde: Theologische und philosophische Versuche,* 9–52. Essen: Ludgerus Verlad, 1981.

Longacre, R. "The Discourse Structure of the Flood Narrative." *JAAR* 47 Supplement (1979): 89–133.

Longenecker, Richard. *Biblical Exegesis in the Apostolic Period.* Grand Rapids: Eerdmans, 1975.

Longman, Tremper, III. *Literary Approaches to Biblical Interpretation.* Grand Rapids: Zondervan, 1987.

Loretz, O. "Aspeckte der kanaanäischen Gottes-So[ö]hn[e]-Tradition im Alten Testament." *UF* 7 (1975): 586–89.

——. *Die Gottenbenbildlichkeit des Menschen*. Munich: Kösel-Verlag, 1967.

——. *Habiru-Hebräer: Eine sozio-linguistische Studie über die Herkunft des Gentiliziums*. BZAW 160, 183–94. Berlin: de Gruyter, 1984.

——. *Schöpfung und Mythos: Mensch und Welt nach den Anfangskapiteln der Genesis*. SBS 32. Sruttgart: KBW Verlad, 1969.

——. "Wortbericht-Vorlage und Tatbericht-Interpretation im Schöpfungsbericht Gen 1:1–2:4a." *UF* 7 (1975): 279–87.

Los, F. J. "The Table of Peoples of the Tenth Chapter of Genesis." *Mankind Quarterly* 7 (1967): 144–52.

Lubsczyk, H. "Elohim beim Jehwisten." *VTSup* 29 (1978): 226–53.

Luke, K. "The Genealogies in Gen 5." *IndTS* 18 (1981): 223–44.

——. "The Nations of the World." *BibBh* 8 (1982): 61–80.

Lundquist, J. M. "What Is a Temple? A Preliminary Typology." In *The Quest for the Kingdom of God*. Edited by H. B. Huffmon, F. A. Spina, and A. R. W. Green, 205–19. Winona Lake, IN: Eisenbrauns, 1983.

Luria, B. S. "The Curse of Noah and His Blessing." (Heb.) *BMik* 15 (1970): 298–306.

Luther, Martin. *Die Luther—Bibel von 1534 Vollständiger Nachdruck*. Köln: Taschen, 2002.

Luyster, R. "Wind and Water: Cosmogonic Symbolism in the Old Testament." *ZAW* 93 (1981): 1–10.

MacKenzie, Iain. *Irenaeus' Demonstration of the Apostolic Preaching: A Theological Commentary and Translation*. Aldershot: Ashgate, 2002.

Malamat, A. "King Lists of the Old Babylonian Period and Biblical Genealogies." *JAOS* 88 (1968): 163–73.

——. "Longevity: Biblical Concepts and Some Ancient Near Eastern Parallels." *AfO Beiheft* 19 (1982): 215–24.

——. "Tribal Societies: Biblical Genealogies and African Lineage Systems." *Archives européennes de Sociologie* 14 (1973): 126–36.

Mallowan, M. E. L. "Noah's Flood Reconsidered." *Iraq* 26 (1964): 62–82.

Mann, T. W. *The Book of the Torah: The Narrative Integrity of the Pentateuch*. Atlanta: John Knox, 1988.

Margalit, B. "The Ugaritic Creation Myth: Fact or Fiction." *UF* 13 (1981): 137–41.

———. "Weltbaum and Weltberg in Ugaritic Literature: Notes and Observations on RŠ 24.245." *ZAW* 86 (1974): 1–23.

Margulis, B. "A 'Weltbaum' in Ugaritic Literature?" *JBL* 90 (1971): 481–82.

Marrs, R. "The Sons of God." *ResQ* 23 (1980): 218–24.

Martens, Elmer A. *God's Design: A Focus on Old Testament Theology.* Grand Rapids: Baker, 1981.

Martin, R. A. "The Earliest Messianic Interpretation of Gen 3:15." *JBL* 84 (1965): 425–27.

Martin, W. J. *"Dischronologized Narrative" in the Old Testament.* *VTSup* 17, 179–86. Leiden: Brill, 1969.

Marzel, Y. "Light and Lights (Gen 1:2–19)." (Heb.) *BMik* 28 (1982/83): 156–61.

Mason, S. D. *"Eternal Covenant" in the Pentateuch: The Contours of an Elusive Phrase.* New York: T & T Clark, 2008.

Maston, T. B. *The Bible and Family Relations.* Nashville: Broadman, 1983.

Mathews, Kenneth A. *Genesis 1–11:26.* Nashville: Broadman & Holman, 1996.

Mawhinney, A. "God as Father: Two Popular Theories Reconsidered." *JETS* 31 (1988): 181–90.

Mayes, A. D. H. "The Nature of Sin and Its Origin in the Old Testament." *ITQ* 40 (1973): 250–63.

Mayes, A. D. H., and R. B. Salters, eds. *Covenant as Context: Essays in Honour of E. W. Nicholson.* Oxford: Oxford University Press, 2003.

Mazar, B. "The Historical Background of the Book of Genesis." In *The Early Biblical Period: Historical Studies.* Edited by S. Ahituv and B. A. Levine, 49–62. Jerusalem: Israel Exploration Society, 1986.

McCarthy, D. J. *"Berît* in Old Testament History and Theology." *Bib* 53 (1972): 110–21.

———. "Covenant 'Good' and an Egyptian Text." *BASOR* 245 (1982): 63–64.

———. "Covenant in the Old Testament: The Present State of Inquiry." *CBQ* 27 (1965): 217–40.

———. "Covenant-Relationships." In *Questions disputes d'Ancien Testament*. Edited by C. Berkelmans, 91–103. Leuven: Leuven University Press, 1974.

———. "Further Notes on the Symbolism of Blood and Sacrifice." *JBL* 92 (1973): 205–10.

———. *Old Testament Covenant: A Survey of Current Opinions*. Richmond: John Knox, 1972.

———. "Theology and Covenant in the Old Testament." *TBT* 42 (1969): 2904–8.

———. "Three Covenants in Genesis." *CBQ* 26 (1964): 179–89.

———. *Treaty and Covenant*. Rome: Pontifical Biblical Institute, 1963.

———. *Treaty and Covenant*. 2nd ed. Rome: Biblical Institute Press, 1978.

———. "Twenty-Five Years of Pentateuchal Study." In *The Biblical Heritage in Modern Catholic Scholarship*. Edited by J. J. Collins and J. D. Crossan, 34–57. Wilmington, DE: Michael Glazier, 1986.

McComiskey, T. E. *The Covenants of Promise: A Theology of the Old Testament Covenants*. Grand Rapids: Baker, 1985.

McDonough, Sean. *Christ as Creator*. Oxford: Oxford University Press, 2009.

McEvenue, S. *The Narrative Style of the Priestly Writer*. Rome: Biblical Institute Press, 1971.

McKenzie, J. L. "The Literary Characteristics of Gen 2–3." *TS* 15 (1954): 541–72.

———. *A Theology of the Old Testament*. Garden City, NJ: Doubleday, 1974.

McKenzie, S. L. *Covenant, Understanding Biblical Themes*. St. Louis: Chalice, 2000.

McKnight, Scot. "Covenant." In *The Dictionary for Theological Interpretation of the Bible*. Edited by Kevin VanHoozer, 141–43. Grand Rapids: Baker, 2005.

McNamara, M. *The New Testament and the Palestinian Targum to the Pentateuch*. AnBib 27, 217–22. Rome: Pontifical Biblical Institute, 1966.

Meir, Sternberg. *The Poetics of Biblical Narrative*. Bloomington: Indiana University Press, 1985.

Mellinkoff, R. *The Mark of Cain*. Berkeley: University of California Press, 1981.

Mendenhall, G. E. "Covenant Forms in Israelite Tradition." *BA* 17 (1954): 49–76.

———. *Law and Covenant in Israel and the Ancient Near East*. Pittsburgh: The Biblical Colloquium, 1955.

———. "The Shady Side of Wisdom: The Date and Purpose of Gen 3." In *A Light unto My Path: Old Testament Studies in Honor of J. M. Myers*. Edited by H. N. Bream, R. D. Heim, and C. A. Moore, 319–34. Philadelphia: Temple University Press, 1974.

———. "The Suzerainty Treaty Structure: Thirty Years Later." In *Religion and Law: Biblical-Judaic and Islamic Perspectives*. Edited by E. B. Firmage, B. Weiss, and J. Welch, 85–100. Winona Lake, IN: Eisenbrauns, 1990.

———. *The Tenth Generation: The Origins of the Biblical Tradition*. Baltimore: Johns Hopkins University Press, 1973.

Mendenhall, G. E., and G. A. Herion. "Covenant." In *AYBD*. Edited by D. N. Freedman, 1: 1179–1202. New York: Doubleday, 1992.

Merkley, P. *The Greek and Hebrew Origins of Our Idea of History*. Lewiston, NY: Edwin Mellen, 1987.

Merode, M. de. "'Une aide qui lui corresponde': L'exégèse du Gen 2:18–24 dans les ecrits de l'A.T., du judaisme et du NT." *RTL* 8 (1977): 329–52.

Merrill, Eugene H. "Covenant and the Kingdom: Genesis 1–3 as Foundation for Biblical Theology." *Criswell Theological Review* 1, no. 2 (1987): 295–308.

———. *Everlasting Dominion: A Theology of the Old Testament*. Nashville: B & H, 2006.

———. "A Theology of the Pentateuch." In *A Biblical Theology of the Old Testament*. Edited by Roy B. Zuck, 7–87. Chicago: Moody, 1991.

Mettinger, Tryggvie N. D. "Abbild Oder Urbild? Imagio Dei in Tranditionsgeschichtlicher Sicht." *Zeitschrift fur die Alttestamentische Wissenschaft* 86 (1974): 403–24.

Metzger, M. *Die Paradieserzählung: Die Geschichte ihrer Auslegung von J. Clericus bis W. M. L. de Wette.* Bonn: Bovier, 1959.

Meyers, C. L. "Gender Roles and Gen 3: 16 Revisited." In *The Word of the Lord Shall Go Forth: Essays in Honor of D. N. Freedman.* Edited by C. L. Meyers and M. O'Connor, 337–54. Winona Lake, IN: Eisenbrauns, 1983.

Michl, J. "Der Weibessame (Gen 3:15) in spätjüdischer und früh-christlicher Auffassung." *Bib* 33 (1952): 371–401, 476–505.

Mickelsen, A. Berkeley. *Interpreting the Bible.* Grand Rapids: Zonder-van, 1962.

Mikaelsson, L. "Sexual Polarity: An Aspect of the Ideological Struc-ture in the Paradise Narrative, Gen 2:4–3:24." *Temenos* 16 (1980): 84–91.

Milgrom, J. "Covenants: The Sinaitic and Patriarchal Covenants in the Holiness Code (Leviticus 17–27)." In *Sefer Moshe: The Moshe Wienfeld Jubilee Volume.* Edited by C. Cohen, A. Hurvitz, and S. M. Paul, 91–101. Winona Lake, IN: Eisenbrauns, 2004.

Millard, A. R. "The Etymology of Eden." *VT* 34 (1984): 103–6.

———. "A New Babylonian 'Genesis' Story." *TB* 18 (1967): 3–18.

Miller, J. M. "The Descendants of Cain: Notes on Gen 4." *ZAW* 86 (1974): 164–74.

———. "In the 'Image' and 'Likeness' of God." *JBL* 91 (1972): 289–304.

Miller, J. W. *Biblical Faith and Fathering.* New York: Paulist, 1989.

Miller, P. D. "Eridu, Dunnu and Babel: A Study in Comparative Mythology." *HAR* 9 (1985): 227–51.

———. *Genesis 1–11: Studies in Structure and Theme.* JSOTSS 8. Sheffield: JSOT Press, 1978.

Mitchell, C. W. *The Meaning of BRK "To Bless" in the Old Testament.* Atlanta: Scholars Press, 1987.

Moberly, R. W. L. *From Eden to Golgotha: Essays in Biblical Theology.* Atlanta: Scholars Press, 1992.

Möller, Hans. *Alttestamentliche Bibelkunde.* Berlin: Evangelische Ver-lagsanstalt, 1986.

Moltmann, J. *God in Creation.* San Francisco: HarperCollins, 1991.

Moo, Douglas J. "The Problem of Sensus Plenior." In *Hermeneutics, Authority, and Canon*. Edited by D. A. Carson and John D. Woodbridge, 179–211. Grand Rapids: Zondervan, 1986.

Moran, W. L. "Atrahasis: The Babylonian Story of the Flood." *Bib* 52 (1971): 51–61.

———. "The Creation of Man in Atrahasis 1:192–248." *BASOR* 200 (1970): 48–56.

Morawe, G. "Erwägungen zu Gen 7:11 und 8:2: Ein Beitrag zur Überlieferungsgeschichte des priesterlichen Flutberichtes." *Theologische Versuche* 3 (1971): 31–52.

Morris, Henry M. *The Genesis Record: A Scientific and Devotional Commentary on the Book of Beginnings*. Grand Rapids: Baker, 1976.

Moye, R. H. "In the Beginning: Myth and History in Genesis and Exodus." *JBL* 109 (1990): 577–98.

Muilenburg, J. "The Form and Structure of the Covenantal Formulations." *VT* 9 (1959): 347–65.

Müller, H. P. "Das Motiv für die Sintflut." *ZAW* 97 (1985): 295–316.

———. "Mythische Elemente in der jahwistischen Schopfungserzahlung." *ZTK* 69 (1971): 259–89.

Muller, Richard. *Past-Reformation Reformed Dogmatics: The Rise and Development of Reformed Orthodoxy, ca. 1520 to ca. 1725*. 4 vols. Grand Rapids: Baker, 2003.

Muraoka, T. "Hebrew Philological Notes." *AJBI* 5 (1979): 88–104.

Murray, John. "The Adamic Administration." In *Collected Writings of John Murray*. 4 vols. Vol. 2, 47–59. Edinburgh: Banner of Truth Trust, 1976.

———. "Common Grace." In *Collected Writings of John Murray*. 4 vols. Vol. 2, 93–119. Edinburgh: Banner of Truth, 1977.

———. "Covenant Theology." In *Collected Writings of John Murray*. 4 vols. Vol. 4, 216–40. Edinburgh: Banner of Truth, 1982.

Murray, R. *The Cosmic Covenant*. London: Sheed & Ward, 1992.

Murtonen, A. "The Use and Meaning of the Words *lebarek* and *berekhah* in the OT." *VT* 9 (1959): 158–77.

Mutius, H. G. von. "Gen 4:26, Philo von Byblos und die jüdische Haggada." *BN* 13 (1980): 46–48.

Naidoff, B. D. "A Man to Work the Soil: A New Interpretation of Gen 2–3." *JSOT* 5 (1978): 2–14.

Naor, M. "In the Beginning He Created—Of Creation?" (Heb.) *BMik* 16 (1971): 306–11.

———. "The Nephilim Were in the Earth." (Heb.) *BMik* 11 (1965): 26–33.

———. "Sons of Seth and Sons of Cain." (Heb.) *BMik* 18 (1972–73): 198–204.

Naylor, P. J. "The Language of Covenant: A Structural Analysis of the Semantic Field of ברית in Biblical Hebrew, with Particular Reference to the Book of Genesis." DPhil diss., Oxford University, 1980.

Neiman, D. "Gihon and Pishon: Mythological Antecedents of the Two Enigmatic Rivers in Eden." *PWCJS* 1 (1977): 321–28.

———. "The Two Genealogies of Jephet." In *Orient and Occident: Essays Presented to C. H. Gordon.* Edited by H. A. Hoffner, 119–26. AOAT 22. Kevelaer: Butzon and Berker, 1973.

Neiman, J., and W. Major. *In the Beginning: Creation Myths from Ancient Mesopotamia, Israel and Greece.* Chico: Scholars Press, 1982.

Neveu, L. *Avant Abraham (Gen 1–11).* Angers: Université Catholique de l'Ouest, 1984.

———. "Le paradis perdu: recherches sur la structure littéraire de Gen 2:4b–3:24." *Impacts* 4 (1982): 27–74.

Newman, A. "Gen 2:2: An Exercise in Interpretative Competence and Performance." *BT* 27 (1976): 101–4.

Nicholson, E. W. "Covenant in a Century of Study since Wellhausen." *OTS* 24 (1985): 54–69.

———. *God and His People: Covenant and Theology in the Old Testament.* Oxford: Clarendon Press, 1986.

Niditch, S. *Chaos to Cosmos: Studies in Biblical Patterns of Creation.* Chico: Scholars Press, 1985.

Niehaus, Jeffrey Jay. "Amos." In *The Minor Prophets: An Exegetical and Expository Commentary.* Edited by T. E. McComiskey, 1: 318–20. Grand Rapids: Baker, 1992.

———. *Ancient Near Eastern Themes in Biblical Theology.* Grand Rapids: Kregel, 2008.

———. "An Argument against Theologically Constructed Covenants." *JETS* 50, no. 2 (June 2007): 259–73.

———. "The Covenantal Household: A Study of the Destruction and Salvation of Households in the Bible and the Ancient Near East." In *Creator, Redeemer, Consummator: A Festschrift for Meredith G. Kline*. Edited by Howard Griffith and John R. Muether, 51–63. Muether: Reformed Academic Press, 2000.

———. "Covenant and Narrative, God and Time." *JETS* 53, no. 3 (2012): 556–59.

———. "Covenant: An Idea in the Mind of God." *JETS* 52, no. 2 (2009): 225–46.

———. *God at Sinai: Covenant and Theophany in the Bible and Ancient Near East*. Grand Rapids: Zondervan, 1995.

———. "God's Covenant with Abraham." *JETS* 56, no. 2 (2013): 249–71.

———. *God the Poet: Exploring the Origin and Nature of Poetry*. Wooster: Weaver, 2014.

———. "God with Us: The Theme of Divine Presence in Scripture." Paper presented at a conference held in honor of Dr. Gary Pratico at Gordon-Conwell Theological Seminary, October 17–18, 2013.

———. "In the Wind of the Storm: Another Look at Genesis iii 8." *VT* 44, no. 2 (April 1994): 263–67.

———. *Preludes: An Autobiography in Verse*. Eugene: Wipf and Stock, 2013.

———. "The Warrior and His God: The Covenant Foundation of History and Historiography." In *Faith, Tradition and History— Old Testament Historiography in Its Near Eastern Context*. Edited by A. R. Millard, J. K. Hoffmeier, and David W. Baker, 299–312. Winona Lake: Eisenbrauns, 1994.

Nielsen, E. "Creation and the Fall of Man." *HUCA* 43 (1972): 1–22.

———. "Sur la théologie de l'auteur de Gen 2–4." In *De la Tôrah au Messie: Études offertes à H. Cazelles*. Edited by M. Carrez, J. Dore, and P. Grelot, 55–63. Paris: Desclee, 1981.

Nitzan, B. "The Concept of the Covenant in Qumran Literature." In *Historical Perspectives: From the Hasmoneans to Bar Kokhba in*

Light of the Dead Sea Scrolls. Edited by D. Goodblatt, A. Pinnick, and D. R. Shwartz, 85–104. Leiden: Brill, 2001.

Noble, Paul. *The Canonical Approach: A Critical Reconstruction of the Hermeneutics of Brevard S. Childs.* Leiden: Brill, 1995.

North, Gray. *Dominion and Common Grace: The Biblical Basis of Progress.* Tyler: Institute for Christian Economics, 1987.

————. *The Dominion Covenant: Genesis.* Tyler: Institute for Christian Economics, 1982.

Noth, Martin. *The Deuteronomistic History.* 2nd ed. JSOT supplement. Sheffield: Sheffield Academic Press, 2002.

————. *A History of Pentateuchal Traditions.* Englewood Cliffs, NJ: Prentice-Hall, 1972.

Novak, M. "Man and Woman: He Made Them." *Communio* 8 (1981): 229–49.

Nwachukwu, M. S. C. *Creation-Covenant Scheme and Justification by Faith: A Canonical Study of the God-Human Drama in the Pentateuch and the Letter to the Romans.* Rome: Editrice Pontifica Universita Gregoriana, 2002.

Oberforcher, R. *Die Flutprologe als Kompositionsschlüssel der biblischen Urgeschichte.* ITS 8. Innsbruck: Tyrolia Verlag, 1981.

Ockinga, B. *Die Gottebenbildlichkeit im Alten Ägypten und im AT.* Wiesbaden: Harrassowitz, 1984.

Oded, B. "The Table of Nations (Genesis 10)—A Sociocultural Approach." *ZAW* 98 (1986): 14–31.

Oden, R. A. "Divine Aspirations in Atrahasis and in Gen 1–11." *ZAW* 93 (1981): 197–216.

————. "Transformations in Near Eastern Myths: Gen 1–11 and the Old Babylonian Epic of Atrahasis." *Rel* 11 (1981): 21–37.

Ohler, A. "Die biblische Deutung des Mythos: Zur Deutung von Gen 1–3." *TRev* 66 (1970): 177–84.

————. *Studying the Old Testament from Tradition to Canon.* Edinburgh: T & T Clark, 1985.

Olson, W. S. "Has Science Dated the Biblical Flood?" *Zygon* 2 (1967): 274–78.

Oppenheim, A. L. "On Royal Gardens in Mesopotamia." *JNES* 24 (1965): 238–333.

Orlinsky, H. M. "The Plain Meaning of Gen 1:1–3." *BA* 46 (1983): 207–9.

Orr, James. *God's Image in Man and Its Defacement in the Light of Modern Denials.* Grand Rapids: Eerdmans, 1948.

Osborne, Grant R. *The Hermeneutical Spiral: A Comprehensive Introduction to Biblical Interpretation.* 2nd ed. Downers Grove, IL: InterVarsity Press, 2006.

Oss, Douglas A. "Canon as Context: The Function of *Sensus Plenior* in Evangelical Hermeneutics." *GTJ* 9 (1988): 105–27.

Oswalt, J. N. "The Myth of the Dragon and Old Testament Faith." *EvQ* 49 (1977): 163–72.

Otto, E. "Der Mensch als Geschöpf und Bild Gottes in Ägypten." In *Probleme biblischer Theologie: FS für G. von Rad.* Edited by H. W. Wolff, 335–48. Munich: Kaiser Verlad, 1971.

Otzen, B., H. Gottlieb, and K. Jeppesen. *Myths in the Old Testament.* London: SCM Press, 1980.

Ovid. *Metamorphoses.* Translated by Rolfe Humphries. Bloomington: Indiana University Press, 1955.

Packer, J. I. *Concise Theology.* Wheaton, IL: Tyndale, 1993.

Padgett, Alan G. "What Is Biblical Equality?" *Priscilla Papers* 16, no. 3 (Summer 2002): 22–25.

Parker, D. "Original Sin: A Study in Evangelical Theory." *EvQ* 61, no. 1 (1989): 51–69.

Parunak, H. V. D. "Oral Typesetting: Some Uses of Biblical Structure." *Bib* 62 (1981): 22–34.

Pasinya, L. M. "Le cadre littéraire de Gen 1." *Bib* 57 (1976): 225–41.

Patai, R. *Family, Love, and the Bible.* London: MacGibbon & Kee, 1960.

Pate, M. *The Glory of Adam and the Afflictions of the Righteous.* Lewiston, NY: Edwin Mellen, 1993.

Patte, D., and J. F. Parker. "A Structural Exegesis of Gen 2 and 3." *Semeia* 18 (1980): 55–75.

Patten, D. W. "The Biblical Flood: A Geographical Perspective." *BSac* 128 (1971): 36–49.

Payne, D. F. "Approaches on Gen 1:2." *TGUOS* 23 (1969–70): 61–71.

Payne, J. B. "The B'RITH of Yahweh." In *New Perspectives on the Old Testament.* Edited by J. B. Payne, 240–64. Waco, TX: Word, 1970.

————. *Genesis 1 Reconsidered*. London: Tyndale, 1964.

————. *The Theology of the Older Testament*. Grand Rapids: Zondervan, 1962.

Pearce, E. K. V. "The Flood and Archaeology." *Faith and Thought* 101 (1974): 228–41.

————. *Who Was Adam?* Exeter: Paternoster, 1970.

Pedersen, J. *Der Eid bei den Semiten*. Strassburg: Karl J. Trüner, 1914.

————. *Israel: Its Life and Culture*. 4 vols. London: Oxford University Press, 1926.

Peretti, Frank E. *This Present Darkness*. Wheaton: Crossway, 2003.

Perlitt, L. *Bundestheologie im Alten Testament*. Neukirchen-Vluyn: Neukirchener Verlag, 1969.

Petersen, D. L. "Covenant and Ritual: A Traditio-Historical Perspective." *BibRes* 22 (1977): 7–18.

————. "Gen 6:1–4, Yahweh and the Organization of the Cosmos." *JSOT* 13 (1979): 47–64.

————. "The Yahwist on the Flood." *VT* 26 (1976): 438–46.

Petit, Francois. *The Problem of Evil*. Translated by C. Williams. New York: Hawthorn, 1959.

Pettinato, G. "Die Bestrafung des Menschengeschlechts durch die Sintflut." *Or* 37 (1968): 165–200.

Phillips, A. "Uncovering the Father's Skirt." *VT* 30 (1980): 38–43.

Picchioni, S. A. *Il Poemetto di Adapa*. Budapest: Eötvos Loránd Tudományegyetem, 1981.

Pink, Arthur W. *The Divine Covenants*. Grand Rapids: Baker, 1973.

Piper, John, et al. *Recovering Biblical Manhood and Womanhood*. Wheaton: Crossway, 2012.

Pollard, W. G. "Science and the Bible." *IDB sup*, 789–94.

Poole, M. W. *Creation or Evolution: A False Antithesis?* Oxford: Latimer House, 1987.

Porten, B., and U. Rappaport. "Poetic Structure in Gen 9:7." *VT* 21 (1971): 363–69.

Porter, Stanley, ed. *The Messiah in the Old and New Testaments*. Grand Rapids: Eerdmans, 2007.

Poythress, V. *The Shadow of Christ in the Law of Moses*. Brentwood, TN: Wolgemuth & Hyatt, 1991.

————. *Symphonic Theology: The Validity of Multiple Perspectives in Theology.* Grand Rapids: Zondervan, 1987.

Preston, David G. *In the Beginning.* Downers Grove, IL: InterVarsity Press, 1984.

Prewitt, T. J. "Kinship Structures and the Genesis Genealogies." *JNES* 40 (1981): 87–98.

Pritchard, J. B. *Ancient Near Eastern Texts Relating to the Old Testament.* Rev. ed. Princeton: Princeton University Press, 1955.

Procksch, O. *Die Genesis übersetzt und erklärt.* 2nd ed. Leipzig: Deicherische Verlags-buchhandlung, 1924.

Pun, Pattle. *Evolution, Nature and Scripture in Conflict.* Grand Rapids: Zondervan, 1982.

de Pury, A. "La Tour de Babel et la vocation d'Abraham." *ETR* 53 (1978): 80–97.

Qoler, Y. "Creation of Man." (Heb.) *BMik* 28 (1982/83): 223–29.

von Rad, Gerhard. *Genesis: A Commentary.* Rev. ed. Translated by John H. Marks. London: SCM Press, 1961.

————. *Old Testament Theology.* 2 vols. New York: Harper and Row, 1965.

Radmacher, Earl D., and Robert D. Preus, eds. *Hermeneutics, Inerrancy, and the Bible.* Grand Rapids: Zondervan, 1984.

Raikes, R. L. "The Physical Evidence for Noah's Flood." *Iraq* 28 (1966): 52–63.

Rainey, A. F. "Toponymic Problems (cont.)." *TA* 9 (1982): 132–36.

Ramoroson, L. "A propos de Gen 4:7." *Bib* 49 (1968): 233–37.

Rapaport, I. *The Babylonian Poem "Enuma Elish" and Genesis Chapter One.* Melbourne: Hawthorn Press, 1979.

Rashi. *Pentateuch with Rashi's Commentary.* Translated by M. Rosenbaum and A. M. Silbermann. New York: Hebrew Publishing Company.

Rattray, S. "Marriage Rules, Kinship Terms and Family Structure in the Bible." *SBL 1987 Seminar Papers.* Edited by K. H. Richards. Atlanta: Scholars Press, 1987.

Reiner, E. "The Etiological Myth of the 'Seven Sages.'" *Or* 30 (1961): 1–11.

Reiser, W. "Die Verwandschaftsformel in Gen 2:23." *TZ* 16 (1960): 1–4.

Rendsburg, G. A. *The Redaction of Genesis*. Winona Lake, IN: Eisenbrauns, 1986.

Rendtorff, R. *Canon and Theology: Overtures to an Old Testament Theology*. Minneapolis: Fortress, 1993.

———. *The Canonical Hebrew Bible: A Theology of the Old Testament*. Leiderdorp: Deo, 2005.

———. "Canonical Interpretation: A New Approach to Biblical Tests." *Pro Ecclecia* 3 (1994): 141–51.

———. "Covenant as Structuring Concept in Genesis and Exodus." *JBL* 108 (1989): 385–93.

———. *The Covenant Formula: An Exegetical and Theological Investigation*. Translated by M. Kohl. Edinburgh: T & T Clark, 1998.

———. "Gen 8:21 und die Urgeschichte des Jehwisten." *KD* 7 (1961): 69–78.

———. *The Old Testament: An Introduction*. Translated by J. Bowden. Philadelphia: Fortress, 1986.

Reventlow, H. G. "Theology (Biblical), History of." In *Anchor Bible Dictionary*. 6 vols. Edited by David Noel Freedman, 6: 483–505. New York: Doubleday, 1992.

Reymond, Robert L. *A New Systematic Theology of the Christian Faith*. Nashville: Thomas Nelson, 1998.

Rice, G. "The Curse That Never Was (Gen 9:18–27)." *JRT* 29 (1972): 5–27.

Richardson, Alan. *Genesis 1–11*. London: SCM, 1953.

Ricoeur, P. "Sur l'exégèse de Gen 1:1–2:4a." In *Exégèse et herméneutique*. Edited by R. Barthes, 67–84. Paris: de seuil, 1971.

Ridderbos, H. *Paul: An Outline of His Theology*. Translated by John Richard de Witt. Grand Rapids: Eerdmans, 1975.

Ridderbos, Nico H. "Gen 1:1 und 2." *OTS* 12 (1958): 214–60.

———. *Is There a Conflict between Genesis 1 and Natural Science?* Grand Rapids: Eerdman, 1957.

Riemann, P. A. "Am I My Brother's Keeper?" *Int* 24 (1970): 482–91.

Ringgren, H. "Remarks on the Methods of Comparative Mythology." In *Near Eastern Studies in Honor of William Foxwell Albright*. Edited by H. Goedicke, 401–11. Baltimore: Johns Hopkins Press, 1971.

Roberts, J. J. M. "Myth *versus* History: Relaying the Comparative Foundations." *CBQ* 38 (1976): 1–13.

Robertson, Jon M. *Christ as Mediator: A Study of the Theologies of Eusebius of Caesarea, Marcellus of Ancyra, and Athanasius of Alexandria.* Oxford: Oxford University Press, 2007.

Robertson, O. Palmer. *The Christ of the Covenants.* Grand Rapids: Baker, 1980.

———. "Genesis 15:6: New Covenant Expositions of an Old Testament Text." *WTJ* 42 (1979/80): 259–89.

Robinson, G. "The Idea of Rest in the OT and the Search for the Basic Character of Sabbath." *ZAW* 92 (1980): 32–42.

Robinson, R. B. "Literary Function of the Genealogies of Genesis." *CBQ* 48 (1986): 595–608.

Rodd, C. W. "The Family in the Old Testament." *Bib Trans* 18 (1967): 19–26.

Roger, Jack B., and Donald K. McKim. *The Authority and Interpretation of the Bible.* San Francisco: Harper & Row, 1979.

Röllig, W. "Der Turm zu Babel." In *Der babylonische Turm: Aufbruch ins Masslose.* Edited by A. Rosenberg, 35–46. Munich: Kösel Verlag, 1975.

Rordorf, B. "'Dominez la terre' (Gen 1:28): Essai sur les résonnances historiques de ce commandement biblique." *BCPE* 31 (1979): 5–37.

Rosenberg, J. W. "The Garden Story Forward and Backward: The Non-narrative Dimension of Gen 2–3." *Prooftexts* 1 (1981): 1–27.

Rosner, Brian. "Biblical Theology." In *New Dictionary of Biblical Theology.* Edited by T. D. Alexander, Brain S. Rosner, D. A. Carson, and Graeme Goldsworthy, 3–11. Downers Grove: InterVarsity Press, 2000.

Ross, A. P. *Creation and Blessing.* Grand Rapids: Baker, 1988.

———. "The Dispersion of the Nations in Gen 11:1–9." *BSac* 138 (1981): 119–38.

———. "Studies in the Book of Genesis. Part I: The Curse of Canaan." *BSac* 137 (1980): 223–40.

———. "The Table of Nation in Genesis 10—Its Content." *Bib Sac* 138 (1981): 22–34.

————. "The Table of Nation in Genesis 10—Its Structure." *Bib Sac* 137 (1980): 340–53.

Ross, Hugh. *Creation and Time: A Biblical and Scientific Perspective on the Creation-Date Controversy.* Colorado Springs: NavPress, 1994.

Roth, Y. "The Intentional Double-Meaning Talk in Biblical Prose." (Heb.) *Tarbiz* 41 (1972): 245–54.

Rouillard, H. "Les feintes questions dans la Bible." *VT* 34 (1984): 237–42.

Rüger, H. P. "On Some Versions of Gen 3:15, Ancient and Modern." *BT* 27 (1976): 105–10.

Ruiten, J. A. T. G. van. "The Covenant of Noah in Jubilees 6.1–38." In *The Concept of the Covenant in the Second Temple Period.* Edited by S. E. Porter and J. C. R. de Roo, 167–90. Leiden: Brill, 2003.

Ruppert, L. "Die Sündenfallerzahlung (Gen 3) in vorjahwistischer Tradition und Interpretation." *BZ* 15 (1971): 185–202.

————. "'Urgeschichte' oder 'Urgeschehen'? Zur Interpretation von Gen 1–11." *MTZ* 30 (1979): 19–32.

Russell, Jeffrey Burton. *The Devil: Perceptions of Evil from Antiquity to Primitive Christianity.* Ithaca: Cornell University Press, 1977.

————. *Satan: The Early Christian Tradition.* Ithaca: Cornell University Press, 1981.

Rüterswörden, U. "Kanaanäisch-städtische Mythologie im Werk des Jehwisten: Eine Notiz zu Gen 4." *BN* 1 (1976): 19–23.

Ryrie, Charles C. *Dispensationalism.* Rev. ed. Chicago: Moody, 2007.

Sabourin, L. *The Bible and Christ: The Unity of the Two Testaments.* Staten Island: Alba House, 1980.

Saebo, M. "Die hebräischen Nomina 'ed und 'ēd-Zwei sumerisch-akkadische Fremdwörter?" *ST* 24 (1970): 130–41.

Sailhammer, J. H. "Exegetical Notes: Gen 1:1–2:4a." *TJ* 5 (1984): 73–82.

————. *Introduction to Old Testament Theology: A Canonical Approach.* Grand Rapids: Zondervan, 1995.

————. *The Meaning of the Pentateuch: Revelation, Composition, and Interpretation.* Downers Grove, IL: InterVarsity Press, 2009.

————. *The Pentateuch as Narrative: A Biblical-Theological Commentary.* Grand Rapids: Zondervan, 1992.

Sandmel, S. "Gen 4:26b." *HUCA* 32 (1961): 19–29.

Sarna, N. M. *Understanding Genesis*. New York: Schocken Books, 1970.

Sasson, J. M. "*Rehōvōt 'îr*." *RB* 90 (1983): 94–96.

———. "The 'Tower of Babel' as a Clue to the Redactional Structuring of the Primeval History." In *The Bible World: Essays in Honor of C. H. Gordon*. Edited by G. Rendsburg, R. Adler, M. Arfa, and N. H. Winter, 211–19. New York: Ktav, 1980.

———. "*Wělō' yitbōšāšû* (Gen 2:25) and Its Implications." *Bib* 66 (1985): 418–21.

———. "Word Play in Gen 6:8–9." *CBQ* 37 (1975): 165–66.

Saucy, Robert L. *The Case for Progressive Dispensationalism*. Grand Rapids: Zondervan, 1993.

Savasta, C. "Alcune considerazioni sulla lista dei discendenti dei figli di Noè." *RivB* 17 (1969): 89–102, 337–63.

———. "L'Età dei Patriarchi Biblici in un recente Commento à Gen 1–11." *RivB* 19 (1971): 321–25.

Sawyer, John F. A. *From Moses to Patmos*. London: SPCK, 1977.

———. "The Meaning of 'In the Image of God' in Gen 1–11." *JTS* 25 (1974): 418–26.

Scalise, Charles J. "The 'Sensus Literalis': A Hermeneutical Key to Biblical Exegesis." *SJT* 42 (1989): 45–65.

Schäfer, P. "Zur Interpretation von Gen 1:1 in der rabbinischen Literatur." *JSJ* 2 (1971): 161–66.

Scharbert, J. "'Berît' im Pentateuch." In *De la Tôrah au Messie*. Edited by M. Carrez, J. Doré, and P. Grelot, 163–70. Paris: Desclee, 1981.

———. "Der Sinn der Toledot-Formel in der Priesterschrift." In *Wort-Gebot-Glaube: FS fur W. Eichrodt*. Edited by J. J. Stamm and E. Jenni, 45–56. ATANT 59. Zurich: Zwingli Verlad, 1970.

———. *Prolegomena eines Alttestamentlers zur Erbsündenlehre*. Freiburg: Herder, 1968.

———. "Quellen und Redaktion in Gen 2:4b–4:16." *BZ* 18 (1974): 45–64.

———. "Traditions-und Redaktionsgeschichte von Gen 6:1–4." *BZ* 11 (1967): 66–78.

Scheer, Tanja S. *Die Gottheit und ihr Bild, Zetemata 105*. Munich: Beck, 2000.

Scheffczyk, Leo. *Creation and Providence.* Translated by R. Strachan. New York: Herder and Herder, 1970.

Schildenberger, J. "Ist die Erzählung von sündenfall ein Gleichnis?" *Erbe und Auftrag* 49 (1973): 142–47.

Schlisske, W. *Gottessöhne and Gottessohn im Alten Testament.* BWANT 97. Stuttgart: Kohlhammer, 1973.

Schlosser, J. "Les Jours de Noé et de Lot." *RB* 80 (1973): 13–36.

Schmid, H. H. *Der sogenannte Jahwist.* Zürich: Theologischer Verlag, 1976.

———. "Die 'Mutter-Erde' in der Schöpfungsgeschichte der Priesterschrift." *Judaica* 22 (1966): 237–43.

Schmidt, Werner H. *Die Schopfungs-Geschichte.* Neukirchen-Vluyn: Neukirchener Verlag, 1967.

Schmitt, A. "Die Angaboen über Henoch: Gen 5:21–24 in der LXX." *Forschung zur Bibel* 1 (1972): 161–69.

———. "Entrückung-Aufnahme-Himmelfahrt: Untersuchung zu einem Vorstellungsbereich im AT." *Forschung zur Bibel* 10 (1973): 152–93.

———. "Zum Thema Entrückung im AT." *BZ* 26 (1982): 34–49.

Schmutzer, A. J. *Be Fruitful and Multiply: A Crux of Thematic Repetition in Genesis 1–11.* Eugene, OR: Wipt & Stock Publishing, 2009.

Schoonenberg, P. *Covenant and Creation.* London: Sheed & Ward, 1968.

Schreiner, J. "Gen 6:1–4 und die Problematik von Leben und Tod." In *De la Tôrah au Messie: Études offertes à H. Cazelles.* Edited by M. Carrex, J. Doré, and P. Grelot, 65–74. Paris: Desclée, 1981.

Schunck, K. D. "Henoch und die erste Stadt: eine textkritische Ueberlegung zu Gen 4:17." *Hen* 1 (1979): 161–65.

Scobie, C. H. H. "History of Biblical Theology." In *New Dictionary of Biblical Theology.* Edited by T. D. Alexander, Brian S. Rosner, D. A. Carson, and Graeme Goldsworthy, 11–20. Downers Grove, IL: InterVarsity Press, 2000.

Scroggs, R. *The Last Adam.* Philadelphia: Fortress, 1966.

Scullion, J. J. "New Thinking on Creation and Sin in Gen 1–11." *AusBR* 22 (1974): 1–11.

Seethaler, P.-A. "Kliener Diskussionsbeitrag zu Gen 3:1–5." *BZ* 23 (1979): 85–86.

Selman, Martin J. "The Kingdom of God in the Old Testament." *TB* 40 (1989): 161–83.

Seters, A. van. "God and Family: From Sociology to Covenant Theology." *Themelios* 5 (1980): 4–7.

Seybold, K. "Der Turmbau zu Babel: Zur Entstehung von Gen 11:1–9." *VT* 26 (1976): 453–79.

Shea, W. H. "Adam in Ancient Mesopotamian Traditions." *AUSS* 15 (1977): 27–41.

Siegwalt, G. "L'actualité de Gen 1." *RHPR* 59 (1979): 319–25.

Siker-Gieseler, J. S. "The Theology of the Sabbath in the OT: A Canonical Approach." *StudBT* 11 (1981): 5–20.

Simons, J. "The 'Table of Nations' (Gen 10): Its General Structure and Meaning." *OTS* 10 (1964): 155–84.

Simonsen, Reed R. *If Ye Are Prepared: A Reference Manual for Missionaries.* Centerville: Randall, 1991.

Sioni, Y. "Un Verset difficile à traduire." *AMIF* 21 (1972): 990–1004.

Sjöberg, A. W. "Eve and the Chameleon." In *In the Shelter of Elyon: Essays in Honor of G. W. Ahlström.* Edited by W. B. Barrick and J. R. Spencer, 217–25. JSOTSS 31. Sheffield: JSOT Press, 1984.

Ska, J. L. "'Je vais lui faire un allié qui soit son homologue' (Gen 2:18): A propos du terme *ezer–'aide.'" *Bib* 65 (1984): 233–38.

———. "Séparation des eaux de la terre ferme dans le récit sacerdotal." *NRT* 103 (1981): 512–32.

Skinner, J. *Genesis: A Critical and Exegetical Commentary.* New York: T & T Clark, 1910.

———. *Genesis: A Critical and Exegetical Commentary.* Rev. ed. Edinburgh: T & T Clark, 1930.

Smith, G. V. "Structure and Purpose in Genesis 1–11." *JETS* 20 (1977): 307–19.

Smith, M. H. "The Church and Covenant Theology." *JETS* 21 (1978): 47–65.

Smith, P. J. "A Semotactical Approach to the Meaning of Term *rûah êlōhîm* in Gen 1:1." *JNSL* 8 (1980): 99–104.

Smith, W. R. *Kinship and Marriage in Early Arabia.* Edinburgh: Adam and Charles Black, 1885.

————. *The Religion of the Semites*. Edinburgh: Adam and Charles Black, 1889.

Soden, W. von. "'Als die Götter (auch noch) Mensch waren.' Einige Grundgedanken des altbabylonischen Atramhasis-Mythhus." *Or* 38 (1969): 415–32.

————. "Der Mensch bescheidet sich nicht: Überlegungen zu Schöpfungserzahlungen in Babylonien und Israel." In *Symbolae biblicae et mesopotamicae: F. M. T. de Liagre Bohl dedicatae*. Edited by M. A. Beek, A. A. Kampman, C. Nijland, and J. Ryckmans, 349–58. Leiden: Brill, 1973.

————. "Die erste Tafel des altbabylonischen Atramhasis-Mythus: 'Haupttext' und Parallelversionen." *ZA* 68 (1978): 50–94.

————. "Etemenanki von Asarhaddon nach der Erzahlung vom Turmbau zu Babel und dem Erra-Mythos." *UF* 3 (1971): 253–63.

————. "Grundsätzliches zur Interpretation des babylonischen Atramhasis-Mythus." *Or* 39 (1970): 311–14.

————. "Konflikte und ihre Bewältigung in babylonische Schopfungsund Fluterzahlungen." *MDOG* 111 (1979): 1–33.

————. "Mottoverse zu Beginn babylonischer und antiker Epen, Mottosätze in der Bibil." *UF* 14 (1982): 235–39.

————. "Zum hebräischen Wörterbuch." *UF* 13 (1981): 157–64.

Soggin, J. A. *Introduction to the Old Testament*. 2nd ed. Philadelphia: Westminster, 1980.

————. *OT and Oriental Studies*. BibOr 29. Rome: Biblical Institute Press, 1975.

Sohn, S.-T. "'I Will Be Your God and You Will Be My People': The Origin and Background of the Covenant Formula." In *Ki Baruch Hu: Ancient Near Eastern, Biblical, and Judaic Studies in Honor of Baruch A. Levine*. Edited by R. Chazan, W. W. Hallo, and L. H. Schiffman, 355–72. Winona Lake, IN: Eisenbrauns, 1999.

Sorabji, Richard. *Time, Creation, and the Continuum*. London: Duckworth, 1983.

Southwell, P. J. M. "Gen 1 Is a Wisdom Story." *Studia Evangelica*. Texte und Untersuchungen Band 126, vol. 7 (1982): 467–82.

Speiser, E. A. "ED in the Story of Creation." In *Oriental and Biblical Studies: Collected Writings of E. A. Speiser*. Edited by

J. J. Finkelstein and M. Greenberg, 19–22. Philadelphia: University of Pennsylvania Press, 1967.

———. *Genesis.* AB, Vol. 1. New York: Doubleday, 1969.

———. *Oriental and Biblical Studies.* Edited by J. J. Finkelstein and M. Greenberg. Philadelphia: University of Pennsylvania, 1967.

———. "The Rivers of Paradise." In *Oriental and Biblical Studies Collected Writings of E. A. Speiser. Edited by J. J. Finkelstein and M. Greenberg,* 23–34. Philadelphia: University of Pennsylvania Press, 1967.

———. "In Search of Nimrod." *Oriental and Biblical Studies.* Edited by J. J. Finkelstein and M. Greenberg, 41–52. Philadelphia: University of Pennsylvania, 1967.

———. "Word Plays on the Creation Epic's Version of the Founding of Babylon." *Or* 25 (1955/56): 317–23.

Spencer, Aída Besançon. *Beyond the Curse: Women Called to Ministry.* Grand Rapids: Baker, 1989.

Spiser, E. A. *Genesis.* Garden City: Doubleday, 1964.

Spriggs, D. S. *Two Old Testament Theologies.* London: SCM, 1974.

Spurrell, G. J. *Notes on the Text of the Book of Genesis.* 2nd ed. Oxford: Clarendon Press, 1896.

Stachowiak, L. "Der Sinn der sogenannten Noachitischen Gebote (Gen 9:1–7)." *VTSup* 29. Leiden: Brill, 1978, 395–404.

Stadelmann, L. Il J. *The Hebrew Conception of the World: A Philological and Literary Study.* AnBib 39. Rome: Pontifical Biblical Institute, 1970.

Stagg, Evelyn, and Frank Stagg. *Woman in the World of Jesus.* Philadelphia: Westminster, 1978.

Stamm, J. J. "Zur Frage der Imago Dei im AT." In *Humanität und Glaube: Credenkschrift für K. Guggisberg.* Edited by U. Neuenschwander, 243–50. Bern: Haupt, 1973.

Steck, O. H. *Der Schöpfungsbericht der Preisterschrift.* Göttingen: Vandenhoeck & Ruprecht, 1975.

———. *Die Paradieserzählung.* BibS 60. Neukirchen: Neukirchener Verlag, 1970.

———. "Gen 12:1–3 und die Urgeschichte des Jehwisten." In *Probleme biblischer Theologie: G. von Rad FS.* Edited by H. W. Wolff, 525–54. Munich: Kaiser Verlag, 1971.

Steenberg, M. C. *Irenaeus on Creation: The Cosmic Christ and the Saga of Redemption*. Leiden: Brill, 2008.

Steinberg, N. "The Genealogical Framework of the Family Stories in Genesis." *Semeia* 46 (1989): 41–50.

Steinmetz, D. *From Father to Son: Kinship, Conflict, and Continuity in Genesis*. Louisville: Westminster/John Knox, 1991.

Steck, O. H. "Gen 12:1–3 und die Urgeschichte des Jehwisten." In *Probleme biblischer Theologie: FS für G. von Rad*. Edited by H. W. Wolff, 525–54. Munich: Kaiser Verlag, 1971.

Stek, John H. "Biblical Typology Yesterday and Today." *CTJ* 5 (1970): 133–62.

————. "Covenant Overload in Reformed Theology." *CTJ* 29 (1994): 12–41.

Stendebach, F. J. "צלם *ṣelem*." In *Theological Dictionary of the Old Testament*. 15 vols. Edited by G. Johannes Botterweck, Helmer Ringgren, and Heinz-Josef Fabry, 12: 386–96. Grand Rapids: Eerdmans, 2003.

Sterchi, David A. "Does Genesis 1 Provide a Chronological Sequence?" *JETS* 39, no. 4 (1996): 529–36.

Stitzinger, M. F. "Gen 1–3 and the Male/Female Role Relationship." *GTJ* 2 (1981): 23–44.

Stoebe, H. J. "Sündenbewusstsein und Glaubensuniversalismus, Gedanken zu Genesis 3." *TZ* 36 (1980): 197–207.

Stolz, F. "Die Bäume des Gottesgartens auf dem Libanon." *ZAW* 84 (1972): 141–56.

Streett, Daniel R. "As It Was in the Days of Noah: The Prophets' Typological Interpretation of Noah's Flood." *Criswell Theological Review* 5 (2007): 33–51.

Strong, A. H. *Outlines of Systematic Theology*. Valley Forge, PA: Judson, 1907.

Strus, A. "La poétique sonore des récits de la Genèse." *Bib* 60 (1979): 1–22.

Stuart, Douglas K. "Curse." In *Anchor Bible Dictionary*. 6 vols. Edited by Davide Noel Freedman, 1: 1218–19. New York: Doubleday, 1992.

————. *Exodus: An Exegetical and Theological Exposition of Holy Scripture*. Nashville: Holman, 2006.

————. *Studies in Early Hebrew Meter*. HSM 13. Missoula: Scholars Press, 1976.

Szabo, A. "Nunquam Retrorsum: zur Frage des Protoevangeliums: Gen 3:15." *Judaica* 35 (1979): 120–24.

Tengström, S. *Die Toledotformel und die literarische Struktur der priesterlichen Erweiterungsschicht im Pentateuch*. ConB 17. Lund: Gleerup, 1981.

Thompson, J. A. "Samaritan Evidence for 'All of Them in the Land of Shinar' (Gen 10:10)." *JBL* 90 (1971): 99–102.

Thompson, P. E. S. "The Yahwist Creation Story." *VT* 21 (1971): 197–208.

Thompson, T. L. *The Historicity of the Patriarchs*. BZAW 133. Berlin: de Gruyter, 1974.

Thundyril, P. *Covenant in Anglo-Saxon Thought*. Calcutta: Macmillan of India, 1972.

Tigay, J. H. *The Evolution of the Gilgamesh Epic*. Philadelphia: University of Pennsylvania Press, 1982.

————. "The Stylistic Criteria of Source Criticism in the Light of Ancient Near Eastern Literature." In *Essays on the Bible and the Ancient World: I. L. Seeligmann Vol. III*. Edited by A. Rofé and Y. Zakovitch, 67–91. Jerusalem: Rubinstein, 1983.

Til, Cornelius van. *Common Grace*. Philadelphia: Presbyterian and Reformed, 1947.

Til, Howard van. *The Fourth Day*. Grand Rapids: Eerdmans, 1987.

Tobin, T. H. *The Creation of Man: Philo and the History of Interpretation*. CBQMS 14. Washington: Catholic Biblical Association of America, 1983.

Toeg, A. "Gen 1 and the Sabbath." (Heb.) *BMik* 18 (1972): 288–96.

Tomasino, A. J. "History Repeats Itself: The 'Fall' and Noah's Drunkenness." *VT* 42 (1992): 128–30.

Torrance, Thomas F. *Calvin's Doctrine of Man*. Grand Rapids: Eerdmans, 1957.

Treier, Daniel J. "Typology." In *Dictionary for Theological Interpretation of the Bible*. Edited by Kevin J. Vanhoozer, 823–27. Grand Rapids: Baker, 2005.

Trible, P. *God and the Rhetoric of Sexuality*. Philadelphia: Fortress, 1978.

Trudinger, L. P. "'Not Yet Made' or 'Newly Made': A Note on Gen 2:5." *EvQ* 47 (1975): 67–69.

Tsevat, M. "Der Schlangentext von Ugarit." UF 11 (1979): 759–78.

———. "The Two Trees in the Garden of Eden." (Heb.) In *N. Glueck Memorial Volume*, 40–43. Jerusalem: Israel Exploration Society, 1975.

Tsukimoto, A. "'Der Mensch ist geworden wie unsereiner'– Untersuchungen zum zeitgeschichtlichen Hintergrund von Gen 3:22–24 und 6:1–4." *AJBI* 5 (1979): 3–44.

Tucker, G. M. "Covenant Forms and Contract Forms." *VT* 15 (1965): 487–503.

———. "The Creation and the Fall: A Reconsideration." *LTQ* 13 (1979): 113–24.

Turner, L. A. "The Rainbow as the Sign of the Covenant in Genesis ix 11–13." *VT* 43 (1993): 119–24.

Tur-Sinai, N. H. "Jhwh Elohim in der Paradies-Erzählung Gen 2:4b-3:24." *VT* 11 (1961): 94–99.

Ullendorff, E. "The Construction of Noah's Ark." In *Is Biblical Hebrew a Language? Studies in Semitic Languages and Civilizations*, 48–49. Wiesbaden: Harrassowitz, 1977.

Ultvedt, A. W. "Genesis 1 og dens litteraere kilder." *NorTT* 81 (1980): 37–54.

Unger, Merrill. "Rethinking the Genesis Creation Account." *BSac* 115 (1958): 27–35.

VanGemeren, W. A. "The Sons of God in Gen 6:1–4 (An Example of Evangelical Demythologization?)." *WTJ* 43 (1981): 320–48.

Vanhoozer, Kevin J. *First Theology: God, Scripture, and Hermeneutics*. Downers Grove, IL: InterVarsity Press, 2002.

Vattioni, F. "Recenti studi nell'alleanza nella Bibbia e nell, Antico Oriente." *AION* 17 (1967): 181–232.

Vaux, R. de. *The Bible and the Ancient Near East*. Garden City: Doubleday, 1971.

Vawter, B. *Genesis*. Garden City, NY: Double Day, 1977.

Veenker, R. A. "Gilgamesh and the Magic Plant." *BA* 44 (1981): 199–205.

Vermes, G. "The Targumic Versions of Gen 4:3–16." In *Post-Biblical Jewish Studies*. SJLA 8, 92–126. Leiden: Brill, 1975.

Vermeylen, J. "Le récit du paradis et la question des origins du pen-
tateuque." *Bijd* 41 (1980): 230–50.

Vogels, W. *God's Universal Covenant: A Biblical Study.* Rev. ed.
Ottawa: University of Ottawa Press, 1986.

———. "L'être humain appartient au sol: Gen 2:4b-3:24." *NRT* 105
(1983): 515–34.

Vos, Geerhardus. *Biblical Theology: Old and New Testaments.* Grand
Rapids: Eerdmans, 1948.

———. "The Doctrine of the Covenant in Reformed Theology."
In *Redemptive History and Biblical Interpretation: The Shorter
Writings of Geerhardus Vos.* Edited by Richard B. Gaffin Jr. Phil-
lipsburg, NJ: P & R, 1979.

———. *The Idea of Biblical Theology as a Science and a Theological
Discipline.* New York: A. D. F. Randolph, 1894.

Vriezen, Theo E. *An Outline of Old Testament Theology.* 2nd ed.
Translated by S. Neuijen. Oxford: Blackwell, 1970.

Wakeman, M. K. *God's Battle with the Monster: A Study in Biblical
Imagery.* Leiden: Brill, 1973.

Wallace, H. N. *The Eden Narrative.* HSM 32. Atlanta: Scholars, 1985.

Wallis, G. "Die Stadt in den Überlieferungen der Genesis." *ZAW* 78
(1966): 133–48.

Walsh, J. T. "Gen 2:4b–3:24: A Synchronic Approach." *JBL* 96 (1977):
161–77.

Waltke, B. K. "Cain and His Offering." *WTJ* 48 (1986): 363–72.

———. "The Creation Account in Gen 1:1–3." *BSac* 132 (1975): 25–
36, 136–44, 216–28, 327–42; *BSac* 133 (1976): 28–41.

———. "The First Seven Days." *CT* 32, no. 11 (1988): 42–46.

———. *Genesis: A Commentary.* Grand Rapids: Zondervan, 2001.

———. "The Phenomenon of Conditionality within Unconditional
Covenants." In *Israel's Apostasy and Restoration: Essays in Honor
of Roland K. Harrison.* Edited by A. Gildeadi, 123–40. Grand
Rapids: Baker, 1988.

Waltke, B. K., and Charles Yu. *An Old Testament Theology.* Grand
Rapids: Zondervan, 2007.

Walton, John H. "The Antediluvian Section of the Sumerian King
List and Gen 5." *BA* 44 (1981): 207–8.

———. *Covenant: God's Purpose, God's Plan.* Grand Rapids: Zondervan, 1994.

———. *Genesis.* Grand Rapids: Zondervan, 2001.

———. *Genesis One as Ancient Cosmology.* Winona Lake, IN: Eisenbrauns, 2011.

———. *The Lost World of Genesis One: Ancient Cosmology and the Origins Debate.* Downers Grove, IL: InterVarsity Press, 2009.

Wambacq, B. N. "Or tous deux étaient nus . . . (Gen 2:25)." In *Mélanges B. Rigaux.* Edited by A. Descamps and A. de Halleux, 547–56. Gembloux: Duculot, 1970.

Ward, R. S. *God and Adam: Reformed Theology and the Creation Covenant.* Melbourne: New Melbourne Press, 2003.

Warfield, B. B. *Biblical and Theological Studies.* Philadelphia: Presbyterian and Reformed, 1952.

———. "The Spirit of God in the Old Testament." In *Biblical Doctrines*, 121–28. New York: Oxford University Press, 1929. Reprint, Carlisle, PA: Banner of Truth, 1988.

Watson, P. "The Tree of Life." *ResQ* 23 (1980): 232–38.

Webster, John. "Principles of Systematic Theology." *International Journal of Systematic Theology* 11, no. 1 (2009): 56–71.

———. "Systematic Theology." In *The Oxford Handbook of Systematic Theology.* Edited by John Webster, Kathryn Tanner, and Iain Torrance, 1–18. Oxford: Oxford University Press, 2007.

Weeks, N. "The Hermeneutical Problem of Genesis 1–11." *Themelios* 4 (1978): 12–19.

Weimar, P. "Die Toledot-Formel in der priesterlichen Geschichtsdarstellung." *BZ* 18 (1974): 65–93.

Weinfeld, M. "ברית *běrît.*" In *Theological Dictionary of the Old Testament.* 15 vols. Edited by G. Johannes Botterweck, Helmer Ringgren, and Heinz-Josef Fabry, 2: 253–79. Grand Rapids: Eerdmans, 2003.

———. "Berît—Covenant Versus Obligation." *Bib* 56 (1975): 120–28.

———. "The Common Heritage of Covenantal Traditions in the Ancient World." In *I trattati nel mondo antico: forma, ideologia, funzione.* Edited by L. Canfora, M. Liverani, and C. Zaccagnini, 175–91. Rome: L'Erma di Bretschneider, 1990.

―――. "The Covenant of Grant in the Old Testament and in the Ancient Near East." *JAOS* 90 (1970): 184–203.

―――. "Covenant Terminology in the Ancient Near East and Its Influence on the West." *JAOS* 93 (1973): 190–99.

―――. "Gen 7:11; 8:1–2 against the Background of Ancient Near Eastern Tradition." *WO* 9 (1978): 242–48.

―――. "God the Creator in Genesis 1 and in the Prophecy of Second Isaiah." (Heb.) *Tarbiz* 37 (1967/68): 105–32.

―――. "Sabbath, Temple and the Enthronement of the Lord—The Problem of the Sitz im Leben of Genesis 1:1–2:3." In *Mélanges bibliques et orientaux en l'honneur de M. Henri Cazelles.* Edited by A. Caquot and M. Delcor, 501–12. AOAT 212. Kevelaer: Verlag Butzon und Bercker, 1981.

―――. *Sefer Bereshit.* Tel-Aviv: Gordon, 1975.

Welker, Michael. "Creation: Big Band or the Work of Seven Days." *Theology Today* 522 (1995): 183–84.

Wellhausen, J. *Prolegomena to the History of Ancient Israel.* Translated by J. S. Black and A. Menzies. Edinburgh: A. & C. Black, 1885. Reprint, New York: Meridian, 1957.

Wells, P. "Covenant, Humanity, and Scripture: Some Theological Reflections." *WTJ* 48 (1986): 17–45.

Wenham, Gordon J. "The Coherence of the Flood Narrative." *VT* 28 (1978): 336–48.

―――. *Exploring the Old Testament: A Guide to the Pentateuch.* Downers Grove, IL: InterVarsity Press, 2003.

―――. *Genesis 1–15.* WBC 1. Waco, TX: Word, 1987.

―――. "Sanctuary Symbolism in the Garden of Eden Story." In *I Studied Inscriptions from before the Flood: Ancient Near Eastern, Literacy, and Linguistic Approaches in Genesis 1–11.* Edited by Richard S. Hess and David Toshio Tsumura, 399–404. Sources for Biblical and Theological Study 4. Winona Lake, IN: Eisenbrauns, 1994.

Westermann, C. *Genesis 1–11, 12–36, 37–50.* Translated by J. J. Scullion. Minneapolis: Augsburg, 1984.

Whitcomb, John C., and Henry M. Morris. *The Genesis Flood.* Phillipsburg: Presbyterian and Reformed, 1961.

White, H. C. "Direct and Third Person Discourse in the Narrative of the 'Fall.'" *Semeia* 18 (1980): 92–106.

———. *Narrative and Discourse in the Book of Genesis.* New York: Cambridge University Press, 1991.

———. "Word Reception as the Matrix of the Structure of the Genesis Narrative." In *The Biblical Mosaic: Changing Perspectives.* Edited by R. Polzin and E. Rothman, 61–83. Philadelphia: Fortress, 1982.

Whybray, R. N. *The Making of the Pentateuch.* Sheffield: JSOT Press, 1987.

Wifall, W. "The Breath of His Nostrils: Gen 2:7b." *CBQ* 36 (1974): 237–40.

———. "Gen 3:15—A Protoevangeliums?" *CBQ* 36 (1974): 361–65.

———. "Gen 6:1–4—A Royal Davidic Myth?" *BTB* 5 (1976): 294–301.

———. "God's Accession Year According to P." *Bib* 62 (1981): 527–34.

Wildberger, H. "Das Abbild Gottes." *TZ* 21 (1965): 245–59.

Wilder-Smith, A. E. *Man's Origin, Man's Destiny.* Minneapolis: Bethany Fellowship, 1968.

Willi, T. "Der Ort von Gen 4:1–6 innerhalb der althebräischen Geschichtsschreibung." In *Essays on the Bible and the Ancient World III: I. L. Seeligman Volume.* Edited by A. Rofé and Y. Zakovitch, 99–113. Jerusalem: Rubinstein's Publishing, 1983.

Williams, A. J. "The Relationship of Gen 3:20 to the Serpent." *ZAW* 89 (1977): 357–74.

Williams, J. G. "Genesis 3." *Int* 35 (1981): 274–79.

Williams, Michael D. *Far as the Curse Is Found: The Covenant Story of Redemption.* Phillipsburg, NJ: P & R, 2005.

Williamson, Paul R. *Abraham, Israel and the Nations: The Patriarchal Promise and Its Covenantal Development in Genesis.* Sheffield: Sheffield Academic Press, 2000.

———. *Sealed with an Oath: Covenant in God's Unfolding Purpose.* NSBT 23. Downers Grove, IL: InterVarsity Press, 2007.

Wilson, Alistair I., and Jamie A. Grant. *The God of Covenant: Biblical, Theological, and Contemporary Perspectives.* Edited by Jamie A. Grant and Alistair I. Wilson. Leicester: Apollos, 2005.

Wilson, R. R. *Genealogy and History in the Biblical World.* New Haven: Yale University Press, 1977.

—. "The Old Testament Genealogies in Recent Research." *JBL* 94 (1975): 169–89.

Winnett, F. V. "The Arabian Genealogies in the Book of Genesis." In *Translating and Understanding the Old Testament: Essays in Honor of H. G. May.* Edited by H. T. Frank and W. L. Reed, 171–96. Nashville: Abingdon, 1970.

Wiseman, D. J. "Mesopotamian Gardens." *AnSt* 33 (1983): 137–44.

—. "Palace and Temple Gardens in the Ancient Near East." In *Monarchies and Socio-Religious Traditions in the Ancient Near East.* Edited by T. Mikasa, 37–43. Wiesbaden: Harrassowitz, 1948.

—, ed. *Peoples of the Old Testament Times. (POTT).* Oxford: Clarendon Press, 1973.

de Witt, D. S. "The Generations of Genesis." *EvQ* 48 (1976): 196–211.

—. "The Historical Background of Gen 11:1–9: Babel or Ur?" *JETS* 22 (1979): 15–26.

Wolff, H. W. *Anthropology of the Old Testament.* Translated by M. Kohl. Philadelphia: Fortress, 1974.

—. "Das Kerygma des Jahwisten." *EvT* 24 (1964): 73–98.

Wöller, U. "Zu Gen 4:7." *ZAW* 91 (1979): 436.

—. "Zu Gen 4:7." *ZAW* 96 (1984): 271–72.

—. "Zur Übersetzung von כי in Gen 8:21 und 9:6." *ZAW* 94 (1982): 637–38.

Woodbridge, John D. *Biblical Authority.* Grand Rapids: Zondervan, 1982.

Woudstra, Marten H. "Recent Translations of Gen 3:15." *CTJ* 6 (1971): 194–203.

—. "The Story of the Garden of Eden in Recent Study." *VR* 34 (1980): 22–31.

—. "The Toledoth of the Book of Genesis and Their Redemptive Historical Significance." *CTJ* 5 (1970): 184–89.

Wright, C. J. H. *Knowing Jesus through the Old Testament.* London: Marshall Pickering, 1992.

Wright, G. E. "The Lawsuit of God: A Form-Critical Study of Deuteronomy 32." In *Israel's Prophetic Heritage*. Edited by B. W. Anderson and W. Harrelson, 26–67. New York: Harper, 1962.

———. *The Old Testament and Theology*. New York: Harper and Row, 1969.

———. "Women and Masculine Theological Vocabulary in the Old Testament." In *Grace upon Grace: Essays in Honor of L. J. Kuyper*. Edited by J. I. Cook, 64–69. Grand Rapids: Eerdmans, 1975.

Wright, N. T. *What St. Paul Really Said*. Grand Rapids: Eerdmans, 1997.

Wyatt, N. "Interpreting the Creation and Fall Story in Gen 2–3." *ZAW* 93 (1981): 10–21.

———. "Killing and Cosmogony in Canaanite and Biblical Thought." *UF* 17 (1986): 375–81.

Yamauchi, E. M. "Meshech, Tubal and Company: A Review Article." *JETS* 19 (1976): 239–47.

Young, Edward J. "The Days of Genesis." *WTJ* 25 (1962/63): 1–34, 143–71.

———. *Genesis 3*. London: Banner of Truth, 1968.

———. "The Interpretation of Gen 1:2." *WTJ* 23 (1960/61): 151–78.

———. *An Introduction to the Old Testament*. Grand Rapids: Eerdmans, 1953.

———. *Studies in Genesis One*. Phillipsburg: Presbyterian and Reformed, 1979.

———. *The Study of Old Testament Theology Today*. Cambridge: Lutterworth Press, 2004.

Zachmann, L. "Beobachtungen zur Theologie in Gen 5." *ZAW* 88 (1976): 272–74.

Zaclad, J. "Création, péché originel et formalism." *RHPR* 51 (1971): 1–30.

Zadok, R. "The Origin of the Name Shinar." *ZA* 74 (1984): 240–44.

Zandt, A. B. van. "The Doctrine of the Covenants Considered as the Central Principle of Theology." *Presbyterian Review* 3 (1882): 28–39.

Zevit, Z. "A Phoenician Inscription and Biblical Covenant Theology." *IEJ* 27 (1977): 110–18.

Ziegenaus, A. "Als Mann und Frau erschuf er sie' (Gen 1:27): Zum sakramentalen Verständnis der geschlechtlichen Differenzierung des Menschen." *MTZ* 31 (1980): 210–22.

Zimmerli, W. "Der Mensch im Rahmen der Natur nach den Aussagen des ersten biblischen Schöpfungsberichtes." *ZTK* 59 (1979): 139–58.

————. *Old Testament Theology in Outline.* Atlanta: John Knox, 1978.

Zlotowitz, M., and N. Scherman. *Bereishis = Genesis: A New Translation with a Commentary Anthologized from Talmudic, Midrashic, and Rabbinic Sources.* 2 vols. New York: Mesorah, 1978.

Scripture Index

Genesis

1	10n20, 11n21, 42, 43, 44, 45, 46, 52, 57, 61, 67, 68, 83, 86, 91, 92, 93, 116n22, 129, 194, 209, 252, 253, 257, 259
1–2	5
1–3	8n14, 106
1:1	28, 43, 44, 45, 46, 49, 66, 66n2, 68, 91, 162, 232, 253, 253n3
1:1–1:2	40
1:1–1:27	61
1:1–2:3	7, 7n14, 37, 38, 38n5, 39, 40, 41, 43, 45, 46, 47, 50, 63, 64, 65, 81, 107, 199, 225n6, 251
1:2	8, 9, 21n30, 44, 45, 50, 195, 196, 214, 215, 216, 218
1:2–2:3	66
1:3	42
1:3–1:31	44
1:3–1:5	40
1:5	81, 82, 83, 251
1:6	42
1:6–1:8	40

1:7	42
1:8	81, 82, 83
1:9	42
1:9–1:13	40
1:10	81, 82, 83
1:11	42
1:14	42
1:14–1:19	40, 48
1:15	42
1:16	59
1:20	42
1:20–1:23	40
1:21–1:22	42
1:24	42
1:24–1:25	67
1:24–1:31	40
1:26	42, 53, 57, 58n16, 92, 92n25, 99, 142
1:26–1:27	52, 67, 80, 158
1:26–1:30	66, 68
1:27	42, 60, 61, 62, 257, 258
1:28	22, 41, 42, 49, 49n11, 57, 62, 77, 91, 114, 115, 117, 129, 192
1:28–1:29	7, 63, 201

Numbers

1:51   206
1:53   77
3:10   206
3:25   77
3:38   206
4:26   77
4:28   77
4:31   77
4:33   77
6:24–6:26   135
7   39
7:1–7:11   40
7:1–7:88   40
7:12–7:17   40
7:12–7:88   66
7:18–7:23   40
7:24–7:29   40
7:30–7:35   40
7:36–7:41   40
7:42–7:47   40
7:48–7:53   40
7:54–7:59   40
7:60–7:65   40
7:66–7:71   40
7:72–7:77   40
7:78–7:83   40
7:84–7:88   40
11:17   70
11:25   70
11:26   70
11:29   70
13   175
13:32–13:33   175
24:2   70

Deuteronomy

1:28   175
2   231
2:5   231
4:1   48
4:11   106, 221
4:21   48
5:18   221
8:3   96
13:5   206
17   33
18:16–18:17   106
21:22–21:23   76, 103
25:5–25:6   172
28   116, 119, 120, 121
28:15   120
28:16   120
28:20   116
28:29   116
28:30   116
29:1   5, 212
32   106, 107n13, 118
32:8   239, 240, 241, 244
32:10   217
32:16   143
32:16–32:17   171
32:20   135
32:39   27n39
33:7   81n17
33:26   81n17
33:29   81n17

Joshua

7   109, 230
7:13–7:18   109
7:19   109

44:6   27
45:1   237
45:1–45:3   237
45:1–45:7   145
45:3   145n15
45:4   237, 239
47:3   228n9
48:12   27
55:3   212n26
57:15   27, 27n40
60:19   220
61:1–61:2   146
63:11   210
65:15   82
65:17   110, 220
66:22   110, 220

Jeremiah

3:1–3:2   214
3:9   214
4   218
4:23   214, 216, 218
4:23–4:26   216
4:26   218
18   208
18:1–18:10   208
33:20   47
33:21   47, 48
33:22   48
33:25   47
33:26   47, 48

Lamentations

2:1   198n19

Ezekiel

1   55, 57, 208
1:4–1:9   92
1:26   58
1:26–1:28   56, 57
1:28   31, 58, 58n16, 59, 208, 264
2:2   71
2:3–2:10   71
3:24–3:27   71
10:1   92
11:5   70
11:19   73
12:14   81n18
16   192
26:27   73
28:12–28:16   21
28:13   103n8
28:13–28:14   167
28:17   131
28:17–28:19   21
32   90
32:17–32:32   39
32:22–32:23   90
32:24   90
32:24–32:25   90
32:25   90
32:26–32:27   90
32:29   90
32:30   90
32:31–32:32   90
36:26   73
36:27   73, 174
37:14   73
37:26   212n26
47   74

23:12   118
23:35   127
24:30   261
24:31–24:32   194
24:36–24:41   193
25:31   262
26   6
26:39   103
26:64   194
27   5
27–28   6
27:45   217
28:19   91
28:20   137

Mark

3:23–3:30   264
8:38   262
10:37   262
13:26   262

Luke

1:17   72n10
1:18   132
1:34   132
2:9   263
2:30–2:32   263
2:52   178
3:37   53
3:38   21, 178
4:5–4:7   150
4:6   238
4:18–4:19   146
9:26   262
9:32   263
10:18   108n15

11:13   52
15:31   79, 122
17:26–17:27   193
18:8   18n27, 181, 195
21:27   262
24:26   262

John

1:1   50
1:1–1:2   10
1:10–1:11   144
1:12–1:13   147, 177
1:14   232, 263
1:30   14
2:11   263, 264
2:19–2:21   74
3:5   147, 196
3:7   196
3:34   74, 237
4:24   56
5:17   255
5:19   16, 19, 179
5:22   21
5:44   264
6:63   10, 11n22, 24, 25, 51, 92, 200, 209
7:38   74
7:38–7:39   174
7:39   74
8:44   96, 131
8:54   264
8:58   27n39
10   127
10:10   215, 227n8
11:4   264
11:40   263, 264

SUBJECT INDEX